ACCOUNTING PRINCIPLES

FIFTH CANADIAN EDITION

→ Jerry J. Weygandt *Ph.D., C.P.A.*
University of Wisconsin—Madison

→ Donald E. Kieso *Ph.D., C.P.A.*
Northern Illinois University

→ Paul D. Kimmel *Ph.D., C.P.A.*
University of Wisconsin—Milwaukee

→ Barbara Trenholm *M.B.A., F.C.A.*
University of New Brunswick—Fredericton

→ Valerie A. Kinnear *M.Sc. (Bus. Admin.), C.A.*
Mount Royal University

In collaboration with
Joan Barlow, Mount Royal University
Brad Witt, Humber Institute of Technology & Advanced Learning

WILEY
John Wiley & Sons Canada, Ltd.

To our students—past, present, and future

Library and Archives Canada Cataloguing in Publication

Accounting principles / Jerry J. Weygandt ... [et al.]. --

5th Canadian ed.

ISBN 978-0-470-16079-4 (pt. 1).--ISBN 978-0-470-67841-1 (pt. 2)

1. Accounting--Textbooks. I. Weygandt, Jerry J

HF5636.A33 2009a 657'.044 C2009-903891-9

Production Credits

Acquisitions Editor: Zoë Craig
Vice President & Publisher: Veronica Visentin
Vice President, Publishing Services: Karen Bryan
Creative Director, Publishing Services: Ian Koo
Director, Market Development: Carolyn Wells
Marketing Manager: Aida Krneta
Editorial Manager: Karen Staudinger
Developmental Editor: Daleara Jamasji Hirjikaka
Media Editor: Channade Fenandoe
Editorial Assistant: Laura Hwee
Design & Typesetting: OrangeSprocket Communications
Cover Design: Natalia Burobina
Printing & Binding: Quad/Graphics

Printed and bound in the United States
2 3 4 5 QG 14 13 12 11

WILEY

John Wiley & Sons Canada, Ltd.
6045 Freemont Blvd.
Mississauga, Ontario L5R 4J3
Visit our website at: www.wiley.ca

BRIEF CONTENTS

Part One

Part Two

Part Three

Part Four

CONTENTS – PART TWO

CHAPTER 8
ACCOUNTING FOR RECEIVABLES

bell aliant.ca

THE NAVIGATOR

- [ ] Understand *Concepts for Review*
- [ ] Read *Feature Story*
- [ ] Scan *Study Objectives*
- [ ] Read *Chapter Preview*
- [ ] Read text and answer *Before You Go On*
- [ ] Work *Demonstration Problem*
- [ ] Review *Summary of Study Objectives*
- [ ] Answer *Self-Study Questions*
- [ ] Complete assignments

CONCEPTS FOR REVIEW:

Before studying this chapter, you should understand or, if necessary, review:

a. How to record revenue. (Ch. 3, pp. 119–121 and Ch. 5, pp. 247–248)

b. Why adjusting entries are made. (Ch. 3, pp. 122–123)

c. How to calculate interest. (Ch.3, pp. 130–131)

Communications Company Makes an Effort to Collect from Incommunicado Clients

Bell Aliant is the product of the 1999 merger of four Atlantic telephone service providers: New Brunswick Telephone, Maritime Tel, Island Tel, and Newfoundland Tel. The history of these four companies goes back 100 years in providing telephone service to Atlantic Canadians. In 2009, the company expanded westward with the purchase of Bell Canada's rural telephone lines in Ontario and Quebec; at the same time, it sold Bell its wireless business. Today, Bell Aliant is predominantly a land-line provider with approximately 3 million access lines across six provinces serving 5.3 million customers. With a staff of approximately 9,000, the company earns $3.2 billion a year under the brands Bell Aliant in Atlantic Canada and Bell in Ontario and Quebec, as well as Télébec, Northern Tel, and Kenora Municipal Telephone Services.

Bell Aliant's main sources of revenue are fees for local and long-distance phone services and high-speed and dial-up Internet services. In most areas, the company's services are bundled with wireless services from Bell Mobility. It also receives revenue from equipment rentals and some information technology products and services provided to large enterprises.

"Our total receivables balance is around $450 million at any one month end," says Eleanor Marshall, Vice-President and Treasurer at Bell Aliant. On the balance sheet, this amount would be netted with amounts of accounts receivable the company has sold as part of its securitization program.

Bell Aliant's billing terms are regulated by the Canadian Radio-television and Telecommunications Commission (CRTC). The company bills monthly for services in arrears, and payments are due within 30 days of the billing date. This results in receivables being about 43 to 45 days outstanding, Marshall explains.

"The vast majority of our consumer customers pay on or slightly before the due date," she says. "We have very few accounts outstanding beyond 30 days." In contrast, businesses take longer to pay, usually 50 to 60 days.

The company allows a three-day grace period beyond a bill's due date, after which late-payment charges will begin to accrue. "The amount of those late-payment charges is also dictated by the CRTC," Marshall explains. "Ours is now approximately one percent per month." Bell Aliant classifies customers as low risk, high risk, or unknown, and this classification will determine how large and how far in arrears the company will allow the bill to get before taking action. It will send a reminder letter to these late customers with a new due date.

If the bill does not get paid, Bell Aliant will start making calls and perhaps negotiate new payment terms. If there is still no payment, the company will suspend the account for 21 days, then reconnect for one day, and contact the client again. If the bill still isn't paid, it will permanently disconnect the customer. The company then sends two notices to the client, and finally the bill goes to a collection agency.

"We establish provisions for bad debts long before it gets to this point," Marshall adds. Receivables are assigned aging categories and certain percentages, which are based on experience, apply to each to estimate the amount of bad debt. The company recognizes bad debt expense, which is typically about 1% of revenue, each month.

The Navigator

STUDY OBJECTIVES:

After studying this chapter, you should be able to:

1. Record accounts receivable transactions.
2. Calculate the net realizable value of accounts receivable and account for bad debts.
3. Account for notes receivable.
4. Demonstrate the presentation, analysis, and management of receivables.

The Navigator

PREVIEW OF CHAPTER 8

As indicated in our feature story, management of receivables is important for any company that sells on credit, as Bell Aliant does. In this chapter, we will first review the journal entries that companies make when goods and services are sold on account and when cash is collected from those sales. Next, we will learn how companies estimate, record, and then, in some cases, collect their uncollectible accounts. We will also learn about notes receivable, and the statement presentation and management of receivables.

The chapter is organized as follows:

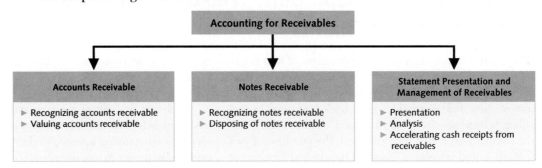

Accounting for Receivables

- **Accounts Receivable**
  - Recognizing accounts receivable
  - Valuing accounts receivable
- **Notes Receivable**
  - Recognizing notes receivable
  - Disposing of notes receivable
- **Statement Presentation and Management of Receivables**
  - Presentation
  - Analysis
  - Accelerating cash receipts from receivables

Accounts Receivable

The term "receivables" refers to amounts due from individuals and other companies. They are claims that are expected to be collected in cash. The two most common types of receivables are accounts receivable and notes receivable.

Accounts receivable are amounts owed by customers on account. They result from the sale of goods and services. These receivables are generally expected to be collected within 30 days or so, and are classified as current assets. **Notes receivable** are claims for which formal instruments of credit are issued as proof of the debt. A note normally requires the debtor to pay interest and extends for longer than the company's normal credit terms. Accounts and notes receivable that result from sale transactions are often called **trade receivables**. In this section, we will learn about accounts receivable. Notes receivable will be covered later in the chapter.

Accounts receivable are usually the most significant type of claim held by a company. Two important accounting issues—recognizing accounts receivable and valuing accounts receivable—will be discussed in this section. A third issue—accelerating cash receipts from receivables—is discussed later in the chapter.

Recognizing Accounts Receivable

STUDY OBJECTIVE 1

Record accounts receivable transactions.

Recognizing accounts receivable is relatively straightforward. For a service company, a receivable is recorded when the service is provided on account. For a merchandising company, a receivable is recorded at the point of sale of merchandise on account. Recall that in Chapter 5 we also saw how accounts receivable are reduced by sales returns and allowances and sales discounts.

To review, assume that Adorable Junior Garment sells merchandise on account to Zellers on July 1 for $1,000 with payment terms of 2/10, n/30. On July 4, Zellers returns merchandise worth $100 to Adorable Junior Garment. On July 10, Adorable Junior Garment receives payment from Zellers for the balance due. Assume Adorable Junior Garment uses a periodic inventory system. The journal entries to record these transactions on the books of Adorable Junior Garment are as follows:

Jan. 1	Accounts Receivable—Zellers	1,000	
	Sales		1,000
	To record sale of merchandise on account.		
4	Sales Returns and Allowances	100	
	Accounts Receivable—Zellers		100
	To record merchandise returned.		
10	Cash [($1,000 – $100) × 98%]	882	
	Sales Discounts [($1,000 – $100) × 2%]	18	
	Accounts Receivable—Zellers ($1,000 - $100)		900
	To record collection of accounts receivable.		

A	=	L	+	OE
+1,000				+1,000

Cash flows: no effect

A	=	L	+	OE
−100				−100

Cash flows: no effect

A	=	L	+	OE
+882 −900				−18

↑ Cash flows: +882

If Adorable Junior Garment used a perpetual inventory system, a second journal entry to record the cost of the goods sold (and the cost of the goods returned) would be required for the July 1 and July 4 transactions.

Subsidiary Accounts Receivable Ledger

Adorable Junior Garment does not have only Zellers as a customer. It has hundreds of customers. If it recorded the accounts receivable for each of these customers in only one general ledger account, as we did above in Accounts Receivable, it would be hard to determine the balance owed by a specific customer, such as Zellers, at a specific point in time.

Instead, most companies that sell on account use a subsidiary ledger to keep track of individual customer accounts. As we learned in Chapter 5, a subsidiary ledger gives supporting detail to the general ledger. Illustration 8-1 shows an accounts receivable control account and subsidiary ledger, using assumed data.

Illustration 8-1

Accounts receivable general ledger control account and subsidiary ledger

GENERAL LEDGER

Accounts Receivable is a control account.

Accounts Receivable — No. 112

Date	Explanation	Ref.	Debit	Credit	Balance
2010					
July 4				100	(100)
31			10,000		9,900
31				5,900	4,000

ACCOUNTS RECEIVABLE SUBSIDIARY LEDGER

The subsidiary ledger is separate from the general ledger.

Kids Online — No. 112-203

Date	Explanation	Ref.	Debit	Credit	Balance
2010					
July 11	Invoice 1310		6,000		6,000
19	Payment			4,000	2,000

Snazzy Kids Co. — No. 112-413

Date	Explanation	Ref.	Debit	Credit	Balance
2010					
July 12	Invoice 1318		3,000		3,000
21	Payment			1,000	2,000

Zellers Inc. — No. 112-581

Date	Explanation	Ref.	Debit	Credit	Balance
2010					
July 1	Invoice 1215		1,000		1,000
4	Credit Memo 1222			100	900
10	Payment			900	0

Each entry that affects accounts receivable is basically posted twice: once to the subsidiary ledger and once to the general ledger. Normally entries to the subsidiary ledger are posted daily, while entries to the general ledger are summarized and posted monthly. For example, the $1,000 sale to Zellers was posted to Zellers' account in the subsidiary ledger on July 1. It was also summarized with other sales entries (Kids Online $6,000 + Snazzy Kids $3,000 + Zellers $1,000 = $10,000) in a special sales journal and posted to the accounts receivable control account in the general ledger at the end of the month, on July 31.

Collections on account (Kids Online $4,000 + Snazzy Kids $1,000 + Zellers $900 = $5,900) were also posted individually to the subsidiary ledger accounts and summarized and posted in total to the general ledger account. Non-recurring entries, such as the sales return of $100, are posted to both the subsidiary and general ledgers individually.

Note that the balance of $4,000 in the control account agrees with the total of the balances in the individual accounts receivable accounts in the subsidiary ledger (Kids Online $2,000 + Snazzy Kids $2,000 + Zellers $0). There is more information about how subsidiary ledgers work in Appendix C at the end of this textbook.

Interest Revenue

At the end of each month, the company can use the subsidiary ledger to easily determine the transactions that occurred in each customer's account during the month and then send the customer a statement of transactions for the month. If the customer does not pay in full within a specified period (usually 30 days), most retailers add an interest (financing) charge to the balance due.

When financing charges are added, the seller recognizes interest revenue. If Kids Online still owes $2,000 at the end of the next month, August 31, and Adorable Junior Garment charges 18% on the balance due, the entry that Adorable Junior Garment will make to record interest revenue of $30 ($2,000 × 18% × $^1/_{12}$) is as follows:

A	=	L	+	OE
+30				+30

Cash flows: no effect

Aug. 31	Accounts Receivable—Kids Online	30	
	Interest Revenue		30
	To record interest on amount due.		

Bell Aliant in our feature story allows a three-day grace period beyond a bill's due date, after which it starts charging for late payments. The amount the company can charge—currently approximately 1% per month—is dictated by the CRTC. As discussed in Chapter 5, interest revenue is included in other revenues in the non-operating section of the income statement.

Nonbank Credit Card Sales

In Chapter 7, we learned that debit and bank credit card sales are cash sales. Sales on credit cards that are not directly associated with a bank are reported as credit sales, not cash sales. Nonbank credit card sales result in an account receivable until the credit card company pays the amount owing to the seller.

To illustrate, assume that Kerr Music accepts a nonbank credit card on October 24 for a $500 bill. The entry for the sale by Kerr Music (assuming a 4% service fee) is:

A	=	L	+	OE
+480				−20
				+500

Cash flows: no effect

Oct. 24	Accounts Receivable—Credit Card Company	480	
	Credit Card Expense ($500 × 4%)	20	
	Sales		500
	To record nonbank credit card sale.		

When Cash is received from the credit card company, Kerr Music will record this entry:

A	=	L	+	OE
+480				
−480				

↑ Cash flows: +480

Nov. 7	Cash	480	
	Accounts Receivable—Credit Card Company		480
	To record nonbank credit card sale.		

Advances in technology have created a rapidly changing credit card environment. Transactions and payments can be processed much more quickly, and often electronically, which reduces the time to collect cash from the credit card company. As collection time becomes shorter, credit card transactions are becoming more like cash transactions to the business.

How does a business know if it should debit Cash or Accounts Receivable when it processes a credit card transaction? Basically, it should consider how long it takes to collect the cash. If it takes longer than a few days to process the transaction and collect the cash, it should be treated as a credit sale, as shown above.

Companies that issue their own credit cards, such as Canadian Tire, always record sales paid by their cards as credit sales. When the credit card transaction results in an account receivable from the customer—as opposed to from the credit card company, as shown above—the accounting treatment is the same as we have previously seen for accounts receivable.

As discussed in Chapter 7, credit card expenses, along with debit card expenses, are reported as operating expenses in the income statement.

ACCOUNTING IN ACTION: ALL ABOUT YOU INSIGHT

Interest rates on bank credit cards can vary depending on the card's various features, however, the interest rates on regular Canadian bank credit cards range from 18.5% to 19.9%. Nonbank cards can charge significantly higher interest rates, such as retailer HBC's interest rate of 28.8%. At the same time, the Bank of Canada's prime lending interest rate was .25% and most of the Canadian banks' prime lending rate was 2.25%. The prime lending rate changes depending on the supply and demand for money. Credit card interest rates, on the other hand, hardly budge at all. Why are credit card rates so much higher than other interest rates?

The higher rate is due to the risk involved. A bank loan, such as a mortgage, is a secured loan because the loan is backed by a tangible asset: a house. Using a credit card is essentially taking out an unsecured loan because nothing physical is used as security for the lender. In addition, credit cards are much more susceptible to fraud, and thus require a consistently high interest rate.

Should you use credit cards or not?

BEFORE YOU GO ON . . .

Review It

1. The stores that form the Forzani Group do not have their own company credit cards. Customers use cash, debit cards, or bank credit cards to pay for merchandise. Why, then, does the company report accounts receivable on its balance sheet? (See Note 2(h) on Revenue Recognition.) The answer to this question is at the end of the chapter.
2. What are the similarities and differences between a general ledger and a subsidiary ledger?
3. How is interest revenue calculated and recorded on late accounts receivable?
4. What are the differences between bank credit cards and nonbank credit cards?

Do It

Information for Kinholm Company follows for its first month of operations:

Credit Sales			Cash Collections		
Jan. 5	Sych Co.	$12,000	Jan.16	Sych Co.	$9,000
9	Downey Inc.	5,000	22	Downey Inc.	3,500
13	Pawlak Co.	6,000	28	Pawlak Co.	6,000

Calculate (a) the balances that appear in the accounts receivable subsidiary ledger for each customer, and (b) the accounts receivable balance that appears in the general ledger at the end of January.

Action Plan

- Use T accounts as a simple method of calculating account balances.
- Create separate accounts for each customer and post their transactions to their accounts.
- Create one account for the Accounts Receivable control account.
- Post the total credit sales and the total cash collections to the general ledger.

Solution

ACCOUNTS RECEIVABLE SUBSIDIARY LEDGER

Sych Co.			
Jan. 5	12,000	Jan. 16	9,000
Bal.	3,000		
Downey Inc.			
Jan. 9	5,000	Jan. 22	3,500
Bal.	1,500		
Pawlak Co.			
Jan. 13	6,000	Jan. 28	6,000
Bal.	0		

GENERAL LEDGER

Accounts Receivable			
Jan. 31	23,000[a]	Jan. 31	18,500[b]
Bal.	4,500		

[a] \$12,000 + \$5,000 + \$6,000 = \$23,000

[b] \$9,000 + \$3,500 + \$6,000 = \$18,500

The Navigator

Related exercise material: BE8–1, BE8–2, BE8–3, BE8–4, E8–1, and E8–2.

Valuing Accounts Receivable

STUDY OBJECTIVE 2

Calculate the net realizable value of accounts receivable and account for bad debts.

After receivables are recorded in the accounts, the next question is how these receivables should be reported on the balance sheet. Receivables are assets, but determining the amount to report as an asset is sometimes difficult because some receivables will become uncollectible. A receivable can only be reported as an asset if it will give a future benefit. This means that only collectible receivables can be reported as assets in the financial statements. This collectible amount is called the receivables' **net realizable value**.

In order to minimize the risk of uncollectible accounts, companies assess the credit worthiness of potential credit customers. But even if a customer satisfies the company's credit requirements before the credit sale was approved, inevitably, some accounts receivable still become uncollectible. For example, a usually reliable customer may suddenly not be able to pay because of an unexpected decrease in its revenues or because it is faced with unexpected bills.

Why do companies still decide to sell goods or services on credit if there is always a risk of not collecting the receivable? Because they are expecting that the increase in revenues and profit from selling on credit will be greater than any uncollectible accounts or credit losses. Such losses are considered a normal and necessary risk of doing business on a credit basis.

Alternative terminology Bad debts expense is also sometimes called *uncollectible account expense.*

When receivables are written down to their net realizable value because of expected credit losses, owner's equity must also be reduced. This is done by recording an expense, known as **bad debts expense**, for the credit losses. The key issue in valuing accounts receivable is when to record these credit losses. If the company waits until it knows for sure that the specific account will not be collected, it could end up recording the bad debts expense in a different period than when the revenue is recorded.

Consider the following example. Assume that in 2010, Quick Buck Computer Company decides it could increase its revenues by offering computers to students without requiring any money down and with no credit approval process. On campuses across the country, it sells 100,000 computers with a selling price of \$700 each. This increases Quick Buck's receivables and revenues by \$70 million. The promotion is a huge success! The 2010 balance sheet and income statement look great. Unfortunately, in 2011, nearly 40% of the student customers default on their accounts. This makes the 2011 balance sheet and income statement look terrible. Illustration 8-2 shows that the promotion in 2010 was not such a great success after all.

WILEY PLUS

Tutorials: Bad Debts

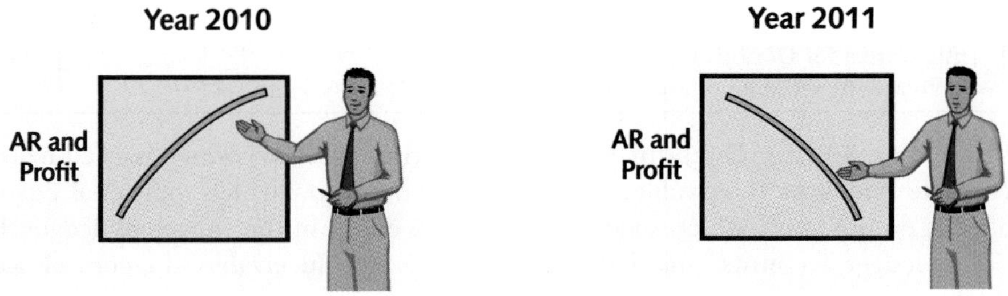

Huge sales promotion. Accounts receivable increase dramatically. Profit increases dramatically.

Customers default on amounts owed. Accounts receivable drop dramatically. Bad debts expense increases and profit decreases dramatically.

Illustration 8-2
Effects of mismatching bad debts

If credit losses are not recorded until they occur, the accounts receivable in the balance sheet are not reported at the amount that is actually expected to be received. Quick Buck Computer's receivables were overstated at the end of 2010, which misrepresented the amount that should have been reported as an asset.

In addition, bad debts expense will not be matched to sales revenues in the income statement. Recall from Chapter 3 that expenses that are directly related to revenue must be recorded in the same period as the sales they helped generate. Consequently, Quick Buck Computer Company's profit was overstated in 2010 and understated in 2011 because it did not match the bad debts expense with sales revenue.

To avoid overstating assets and profit, we cannot wait until we know exactly which receivables are uncollectible. Instead, in the accounting period where the sales occur, we must estimate the uncollectible accounts receivable. Because we do not know which specific accounts receivable will need to be written off, we use what is known as the allowance method.

The **allowance method** of accounting for bad debts estimates uncollectible accounts at the end of each accounting period. This ensures that receivables are reduced to their net realizable value on the balance sheet. It also gives better matching of expenses with revenues on the income statement because credit losses that are expected to happen from sales or service revenue in that accounting period are recorded in the same accounting period as when the revenue was earned.

The allowance method is required for financial reporting purposes when uncollectible accounts are material (significant) in amount. The allowance method has three essential features:

1. Recording estimated uncollectibles: The amount of uncollectible accounts receivable is estimated at the end of the accounting period. This estimate is treated as bad debts expense and is matched against revenues in the accounting period where the revenues are recorded.
2. Writing off uncollectible accounts: Actual uncollectibles are written off when the specific account is determined to be uncollectible.
3. Recovery of an uncollectible account: If an account that was previously written off is later collected, the original write off is reversed and the collection is recorded.

We will see that neither the write off nor the later recovery affect the income statement.

1. Recording Estimated Uncollectibles

To illustrate the allowance method, assume that Adorable Junior Garment has net credit sales of $1.2 million in 2010. Of this amount, $200,000 remains uncollected at December 31. The credit manager estimates (using techniques we will discuss in the next section) that $24,000 of these receivables will be uncollectible. The adjusting entry to record the estimated uncollectible accounts is:

A	=	L	+	OE
−24,000				−24,000

Cash flows: no effect

Dec. 31	Bad Debts Expense	24,000	
	Allowance for Doubtful Accounts		24,000
	To record estimate of uncollectible accounts.		

Note that Allowance for Doubtful Accounts—a contra asset account—is used instead of a direct credit to Accounts Receivable. Because we do not know which individual customers will not pay, we do not know which specific accounts to credit in the subsidiary ledger. Recall that subsidiary ledger accounts must balance with Accounts Receivable, the control account. This would not happen if the control account was credited and the subsidiary ledger accounts were not.

Assume that Adorable Junior Garment has an unadjusted balance of $1,000 in Allowance for Doubtful Accounts. After recording the estimate of its uncollectibles, the ending balance in the Allowance for Doubtful Accounts is $25,000 ($1,000 + $24,000). This is the amount of receivables that is expected to become uncollectible in the future.

The Allowance for Doubtful Accounts is deducted from Accounts Receivable to calculate the net realizable value of the accounts receivable, as presented by the formula shown in Illustration 8-3.

Illustration 8-3

Formula for calculating net realizable value

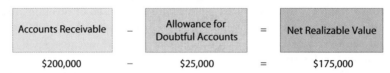

Accounts Receivable	−	Allowance for Doubtful Accounts	=	Net Realizable Value
$200,000	−	$25,000	=	$175,000

In the current assets section of the balance sheet, Accounts Receivable, the Allowance for Doubtful Accounts, and the net realizable value are reported as follows (using assumed data for the other current asset accounts):

ADORABLE JUNIOR GARMENT
Balance Sheet (partial)
December 31, 2010

Current assets		
Cash		$ 14,800
Accounts receivable	$200,000	
Less: Allowance for doubtful accounts	25,000	175,000
Merchandise inventory		310,000
Prepaid expenses		25,000
Total current assets		$524,800

Notice that the net realizable value of the accounts receivable—$175,000—is the amount added to cash, merchandise inventory, and prepaid expenses to calculate total current assets, not the total accounts receivable.

Approaches Used in Estimating the Allowance. To simplify the Adorable Junior Garment example, the amount of the expected bad debts expense in the journal entry above ($24,000) was given. But how was this estimate calculated? There are two approaches that most companies use to determine this amount: (1) percentage of receivables, and (2) percentage of sales.

Percentage of Receivables Approach. Under the **percentage of receivables approach**, management uses experience to estimate the percentage of receivables that will become uncollectible accounts. The easiest way to do this is to multiply the total amount of accounts receivable by a percentage based on an overall estimate of the total uncollectible accounts. However, the more common practice is to estimate uncollectible accounts using different percentages depending on how long the accounts receivable have been outstanding. This is more sensitive to the actual status of the accounts receivable. The longer a receivable is past due or outstanding, the less likely it is to be collected. Bell Aliant in our feature story uses this approach.

A schedule must be prepared, called an **aging schedule**, that shows the age of each account receivable. After the age of each account receivable is determined, the loss from uncollectible accounts is estimated. This is done by applying percentages, based on experience, to the totals in each category. The estimated percentage of uncollectible accounts increases as the number of days outstanding increases. Bell Aliant, in our feature story, follows this process. An aging schedule for Adorable Junior Garment is shown in Illustration 8-4.

Illustration 8-4
Aging schedule

		Number of Days Outstanding				
Customer	Total	0–30	31–60	61–90	91–120	Over 120
Bansal Garments	$ 6,000		$ 3,000	$ 3,000		
Bortz Clothing	3,000	$ 3,000				
Kids Online	4,500				$ 2,000	$ 2,500
Snazzy Kids Co.	17,000	2,000	5,000	5,000	5,000	
Tykes n' Tots	26,500	10,000	10,000	6,000	500	
Zellers	42,000	32,000	10,000			
Walmart	61,000	48,000	12,000	1,000		
Others	40,000	5,000	10,000	10,000	5,000	10,000
	$200,000	$100,000	$50,000	$25,000	$12,500	$12,500
Estimated percentage uncollectible		5%	10%	20%	30%	50%
Estimated uncollectible accounts	$ 25,000	$ 5,000	$ 5,000	$ 5,000	$ 3,750	$ 6,250

The $25,000 total for estimated uncollectible accounts is the amount of existing receivables that are expected to become uncollectible in the future. This amount represents the required balance in Allowance for Doubtful Accounts at the balance sheet date. The amount of the bad debts expense adjusting entry is the difference between the required balance and the existing balance in the allowance account.

Helpful hint Because the balance sheet is emphasized in the percentage of receivables approach, the existing balance in the allowance account must be considered when calculating the bad debts expenses in the adjusting entry.

Recall that we assumed the trial balance shows a credit balance of $1,000 in the Allowance for Doubtful Accounts. Therefore, an adjusting entry for $24,000 ($25,000 – $1,000) is necessary, as follows:

Dec. 31	Bad Debts Expense	24,000	
	Allowance for Doubtful Accounts		24,000
	To record estimate of uncollectible accounts.		

A	=	L	+	OE
−24,000				−24,000

Cash flows: no effect

After the adjusting entry is posted, the balance in the Allowance for Doubtful Accounts should be equal to the estimated uncollectible accounts calculated in Illustration 8-4. This is shown in Adorable Junior Garment's accounts:

Bad Debts Expense		Allowance for Doubtful Accounts	
Dec. 31 Adj. 24,000			Dec. 31 Bal. 1,000
			31 Adj. 24,000
			Dec. 31 Bal. 25,000

Occasionally, the allowance account will have a debit balance before recording the adjusting entry. This happens when write offs in the year are higher than the previous estimates for bad debts (we will discuss write offs in the next section). If there is a debit balance, prior to recording the adjusting entry, the debit balance is added to the required balance when the adjusting entry is made. For example, if there had been a $500 debit balance in the Adorable Junior Garment allowance account before adjustment, the adjusting entry would have been for $25,500 ($25,000 + $500) to arrive at a credit balance in the allowance account of $25,000.

Because a balance sheet account (Accounts Receivable) is used to calculate the required balance in another balance sheet account (Allowance for Doubtful Accounts), the percentage of receivables approach is also often called the **balance sheet approach**. The percentage of receivables approach is an excellent method of estimating the net realizable value of the accounts receivable.

Percentage of Sales Approach The **percentage of sales approach** calculates bad debts expense as a percentage of net credit sales. Management determines the percentage based on experience and the company's credit policy.

To illustrate, assume that Adorable Junior Garment concludes that 2% of net credit sales will become uncollectible. Recall that net credit sales for the calendar year 2010 are $1.2 million. The estimated bad debts expense is $24,000 (2% × $1,200,000). The adjusting entry is:

A	=	L	+	OE
−24,000				−24,000

Cash flows: no effect

Dec. 31	Bad Debts Expense	24,000	
	Allowance for Doubtful Accounts		24,000
	To record estimate of bad debts expense.		

Recall that Allowance for Doubtful Accounts had a credit balance of $1,000 before the adjustment. After the adjusting entry is posted, the accounts will show the following:

Bad Debts Expense		Allowance for Doubtful Accounts	
Dec. 31 Adj. 24,000			Dec. 31 Bal. 1,000
			31 Adj. 24,000
			Dec. 31 Bal. 25,000

Helpful hint Because the income statement is emphasized in the percentage of sales approach, the balance in the allowance account is not involved in calculating the bad debts expense in the adjusting entry.

When calculating the amount in the adjusting entry ($24,000), the existing balance in Allowance for Doubtful Accounts is ignored. This approach to estimating uncollectibles results in an excellent matching of expenses with revenues because the bad debts expense is related to the sales recorded in the same period. Because an income statement account (Sales) is used to calculate another income statement account (Bad Debts Expense), and because any balance in the balance sheet account (Allowance for Doubtful Accounts) is ignored, this approach is often called the **income statement approach**. Illustration 8-5 compares the balance sheet approach with the income statement approach.

Illustration 8-5

Comparison of approaches for estimating uncollectibles

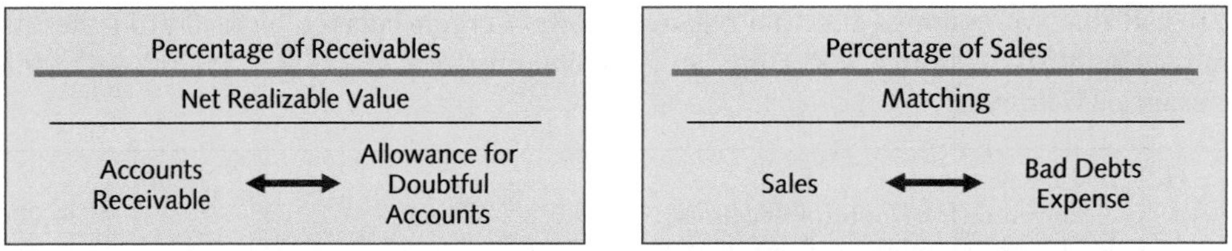

Balance Sheet Approach **Income Statement Approach**

Both the percentage of receivables and the percentage of sales approaches are generally accepted. The choice is a management decision. The percentage of sales approach is quick and easy to use and it is aimed at achieving the most accurate matching of expenses to revenues. On the other hand, the percentage of receivables approach is focused on presenting the correct net realizable value of accounts receivable in the balance sheet. As accounting standards increasingly emphasize the balance sheet, it has been argued that the percentage of receivables approach is the most appropriate method to use. While most companies prefer using the percentage of receivables approach, the percentage of sales method is still allowed.

Under both approaches, it is necessary to review the company's experience with credit losses. You should also note that, unlike in our example with Adorable Junior Garment, the two approaches normally result in different amounts in the adjusting entry.

2. Writing Off Uncollectible Accounts

Companies use various methods for collecting past-due accounts, including letters, calls, and legal actions. Bell Aliant, in our feature story, classifies customers by risk levels, which it uses to determine how large and how far in arrears it will allow the bill to get before taking action. Bell Aliant follows up on late accounts with letters and calls, and will cut back or suspend service if the customer does not negotiate new payment terms. If there is still no payment from the customer, service is permanently cut off. The final step involves sending the account to a collection agency.

When all the ways of collecting a past-due account have been tried and collection appears impossible, the account should be written off. To prevent premature write offs, each write off should be approved in writing by management. To keep good internal control, the authorization to write off accounts should not be given to someone who also has responsibilities related to cash or receivables.

To illustrate a receivables write off, assume that the vice-president of finance of Adorable Junior Garment authorizes the write off of a $4,500 balance owed by a delinquent customer, Kids Online, on March 1, 2011. The entry to record the write off is as follows:

Mar. 1	Allowance for Doubtful Accounts	4,500	
	Accounts Receivable—Kids Online		4,500
	Write off of uncollectible account.		

A	=	L	+	OE
+4,500				
−4,500				

Cash flows: no effect

Bad Debts Expense is not increased (debited) when the write off occurs. Under the allowance method, every account write off is debited to the allowance account rather than to Bad Debts Expense. A debit to Bad Debts Expense would be incorrect because the expense was already recognized when the adjusting entry was made for estimated bad debts last year.

Instead, the entry to record the write off of an uncollectible account reduces both Accounts Receivable and Allowance for Doubtful Accounts. After posting, using an assumed balance of $230,000 in Accounts Receivable on February 28, 2011, the general ledger accounts will appear as follows:

Accounts Receivable		Allowance for Doubtful Accounts	
Feb. 28 Bal. 230,000	Mar. 1 4,500	Mar. 1 4,500	Jan. 1 Bal. 25,000
Mar. 1 Bal. 225,500			Mar. 1 Bal. 20,500

A write off affects only balance sheet accounts. The write off of the account reduces both Accounts Receivable and Allowance for Doubtful Accounts. Net realizable value in the balance sheet remains the same, as shown below:

	Before Write Off	After Write Off
Accounts receivable	$230,000	$225,500
Less: Allowance for doubtful accounts	25,000	20,500
Net realizable value	$205,000	$205,000

As mentioned earlier, the allowance account can sometimes end up in a debit balance position after the write off of an uncollectible account. This can happen if the write offs in the period are more than the opening balance. It means the actual credit losses were greater than the estimated credit losses. The balance in Allowance for Doubtful Accounts will be corrected when the adjusting entry for estimated uncollectible accounts is made at the end of the period.

3. Recovery of an Uncollectible Account

Occasionally, a company collects cash from a customer after its account has been written off. Two entries are required to record the recovery of a bad debt: (1) the entry previously made when the account was written off is reversed to restore the customer's account; and (2) the collection is recorded in the usual way.

To illustrate, assume that on July 1, 2011, Kids Online pays the $4,500 amount that had been written off on March 1. The entries are as follows:

	(1)		
July 1	Accounts Receivable—Kids Online	4,500	
	Allowance for Doubtful Accounts		4,500
	To reverse write off of Kids Online account.		
	(2)		
July 1	Cash	4,500	
	Accounts Receivable—Kids Online		4,500
	To record collection from Kids Online.		

A	=	L	+	OE
+4,500				
−4,500				

Cash flows: no effect

A	=	L	+	OE
+4,500				
−4,500				

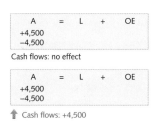

↑ Cash flows: +4,500

Note that the recovery of a bad debt, like the write off of a bad debt, affects only balance sheet accounts. The net effect of the two entries is a debit to Cash and a credit to Allowance for Doubtful Accounts for $4,500. Accounts Receivable is debited and later credited for two reasons. First, the company must reverse the write off. Second, Kids Online did pay, so the accounts receivable account in the general ledger and Kids Online's account in the subsidiary ledger, if a subsidiary ledger is used, should show this payment as it will need to be considered in deciding what credit to give to Kids Online in the future.

Summary of Allowance Method

In summary, there are three types of transactions that you may need to record when valuing accounts receivable using the allowance method:

1. Estimates of uncollectible accounts receivable are recorded as adjusting entries at the end of the period by debiting Bad Debts Expense and crediting Allowance for Doubtful Accounts. The amount to record can be calculated using either the percentage of sales approach or the percentage of receivables approach.
2. Write offs of actual uncollectible accounts are recorded in the next accounting period by debiting Allowance for Doubtful Accounts and crediting Accounts Receivable.
3. Later recoveries, if any, are recorded in two separate entries. The first reverses the write off by debiting Accounts Receivable and crediting Allowance for Doubtful Accounts. The second records the normal collection of the account by debiting Cash and crediting Accounts Receivable.

These entries are summarized in the following T accounts:

Accounts Receivable		Allowance for Doubtful Accounts	
Beginning balance	Cash collections	Write offs	Beginning balance
Credit sales	Write offs		Later recoveries
Later recoveries			Bad debt adjusting entry
Ending balance			Ending balance

ACCOUNTING IN ACTION: ACROSS THE ORGANIZATION INSIGHT

More and more businesses are turning to collection agencies to pursue their bad debts. And these agencies are using tougher and more creative tactics to extract payment. They scour websites like Facebook and Craigslist to track down people who haven't paid their bills. Collection agencies are generally not allowed to make threats, call clients repeatedly, or be overly aggressive. If people have no means to pay and can't negotiate with the collection agency, the biggest problem they will likely face is damage to their credit report. Still, unless consumers pay their debts, the calls from collection agents are unlikely to stop. Agencies are becoming more effective, with the development of statistical models that use historical information from debt collection records, combined with socioeconomic and other demographic information, to predict which indebted consumers are more likely to pay and thus focus their efforts on these people.

Source: Carly Weeks, "Collection Agencies: The New Big Brother?" *The Globe and Mail*, May 11, 2009.

Why would a business choose to use a collection agency to follow up on late accounts instead of pursuing them internally?

BEFORE YOU GO ON . . .

Review It

1. How does the allowance method ensure that expenses are properly matched with revenues?
2. Explain the differences between the percentage of receivables and percentage of sales approaches.
3. How do write offs and subsequent recoveries affect profit and the net realizable value of the accounts receivable when they are recorded?

Do It

The unadjusted trial balance at December 31 for Woo Wholesalers Co. shows the following selected information:

	Debit	Credit
Accounts receivable	$120,000	
Allowance for doubtful accounts		$ 2,000
Net credit sales		820,000

(a) Prepare the adjusting journal entry to record bad debts expense for each of the following *independent* situations:

1. Using the percentage of receivables approach, Woo estimates uncollectible accounts to be as follows: 0–30 days, $85,000, 5% uncollectible; 31–60 days, $25,000, 15% uncollectible; and over 60 days, $10,000, 25% uncollectible.
2. Using the percentage of sales approach, Woo estimates uncollectible accounts to be 1% of net credit sales.

(b) Calculate the net realizable value of Woo's accounts receivable for each of the above situations.

Action Plan

- Percentage of receivables: Apply percentages to the receivables in each age category to determine total estimated uncollectible accounts. The total amount determined in the aging schedule is the ending balance required in the allowance account, not the amount of the adjustment. Use the existing balance in the allowance account to determine the required adjusting entry.
- Percentage of sales: Apply the percentage to net credit sales to determine estimated bad debts expense—the adjusting entry amount. Ignore the balance in the allowance for doubtful accounts.
- Net realizable value is equal to the balance in Accounts Receivable minus the balance in Allowance for Doubtful Accounts after the journal entry to record bad debts expense has been recorded.

Solution

(a) 1. Bad Debts Expense ($10,500[1] – $2,000)	8,500	
Allowance for Doubtful Accounts		8,500
To record estimate of uncollectible accounts.		
[1]($85,000 × 5%) + ($25,000 × 15%) + ($10,000 × 25%) = $10,500		
2. Bad Debts Expense ($820,000 × 1%)	8,200	
Allowance for Doubtful Accounts		8,200
To record estimate of uncollectible accounts.		

(b) 1. Net Realizable Value = Accounts Receivable – Allowance for Doubtful Accounts
= [$120,000 – ($2,000 + $8,500)]
= $109,500

2. Net Realizable Value = Accounts Receivable – Allowance for Doubtful Accounts
= [$120,000 – ($2,000 + $8,200)]
= $109,800

Related exercise material: BE8–5, BE8–6, BE8–7, BE8–8, BE8–9, E8–4, E8–5, E8–6, and E8–7.

The Navigator

Notes Receivable

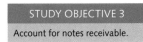

STUDY OBJECTIVE 3

Account for notes receivable.

Credit may also be granted in exchange for a formal credit instrument known as a promissory note. A **promissory note** is a written promise to pay a specified amount of money on demand or at a definite time. Promissory notes may be used (1) when individuals and companies lend or borrow money, (2) when the amount of the transaction and the credit period are longer than normal limits, or (3) in the settlement of accounts receivable.

In a promissory note, the party making the promise to pay is called the maker. The party to whom payment is to be made is called the payee. In the note shown in Illustration 8-6, Higly Inc. is the maker and Wolder Company is the payee. To Wolder Company, the promissory note is a note receivable. To Higly Inc. it is a note payable.

Illustration 8-6

Promissory note

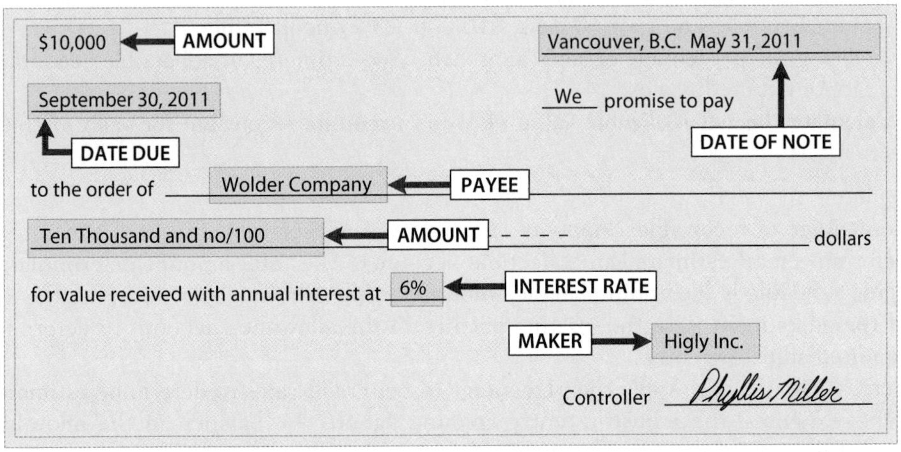

A promissory note might also contain other details such as whether any security is pledged as collateral for the loan and what happens if the maker defaults (does not pay).

A note receivable is a formal promise to pay an amount that bears interest from the time it is issued until it is due. An account receivable is an informal promise to pay that bears interest only after its due date. Because it is less formal, it does not have as strong a legal claim as a note receivable. Most accounts receivable are due within a short period of time, usually 30 days, while a note can extend over longer periods of time.

There are also similarities between notes and accounts receivable. Both are credit instruments. Both can be sold to another party. Both are valued at their net realizable values. The basic issues in accounting for notes receivable are the same as those for accounts receivable, as follows:

1. Recognizing notes receivable
2. Disposing of notes receivable

Recognizing Notes Receivable

To illustrate the basic entries for notes receivable, we will use the $10,000, four-month, 6% promissory note shown in Illustration 8-6. Assuming that Higly Inc. wrote the note in settlement of an account receivable, Wolder Company makes the following entry for the receipt of the note:

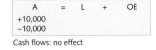

A	=	L	+	OE
+10,000				
−10,000				

Cash flows: no effect

May 31	Notes Receivable—Higly	10,000	
	Accounts Receivable—Higly		10,000
	To record acceptance of Higly note.		

If a note is exchanged for cash instead of an account receivable, the entry is a debit to Notes Receivable and a credit to Cash for the amount of the loan.

The note receivable is recorded at its principal value (the value shown on the face of the note). No interest revenue is reported when the note is accepted because, according to the revenue recognition principle, revenue is not recognized until it is earned. Interest is earned (accrued) as time passes.

Recording Interest

As we learned in Chapter 3, the basic formula for calculating interest on an interest-bearing note is the following:

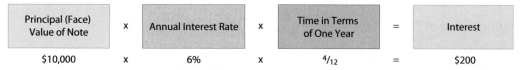

Principal (Face) Value of Note	x	Annual Interest Rate	x	Time in Terms of One Year	=	Interest
\$10,000	x	6%	x	4/12	=	\$200

Illustration 8-7
Formula for calculating interest

The interest rate specified in a note is an annual rate of interest. There are many factors that affect the interest rate. You will learn more about that in a finance course. Interest rates may also be fixed for the term of the note or may change over the term. In this textbook, we will always assume that the rate remains fixed for the term.

The time factor in the above formula gives the fraction of the year that the note has been outstanding. As we did in past chapters, to keep it simple we will assume that interest is calculated in months rather than days. Illustration 8-7 shows the calculation of interest revenue for Wolder Company and interest expense for Higly Inc. for the term of the note.

If Wolder Company's year end was June 30, the following adjusting journal entry would be required to accrue interest for the month of June:

June 30	Interest Receivable	50	
	Interest Revenue (\$10,000 × 6% × 1/12)		50
	To accrue interest on Higly note receivable.		

A	=	L	+	OE
+50				+50

Cash flows: no effect

Notice that interest on a note receivable is not debited to the Notes Receivable account. Instead, a separate account for the interest receivable is used. Since the note is a formal credit instrument, its recorded value stays the same as its face value.

Valuing Notes Receivable

Like accounts receivable, notes receivable are reported at their net realizable value. Each note must be analyzed to determine how likely it is to be collected. If eventual collection is doubtful, bad debts expense and an allowance for doubtful notes must be recorded in the same way as for accounts receivable. Some companies use only one allowance account for both accounts and notes, and call it Allowance for Doubtful Accounts.

Disposing of Notes Receivable

Notes are normally held to their maturity date, at which time the principal plus any unpaid interest is collected. This is known as honouring (paying) the note. Sometimes, the maker of the note defaults and an adjustment to the accounts must be made. This is known as dishonouring (not paying) the note.

Honouring of Notes Receivable

A note is honoured when it is paid in full at its maturity date. The amount due at maturity is the principal of the note plus interest for the length of time the note is outstanding (assuming interest is due at maturity rather than monthly). If Higly Inc. honours the note when it is due on September 30—the maturity date—the entry by Wolder Company to record the collection is:

A	=	L	+	OE
+10,200				+150
−10,000				
−50				

Cash flows: +10,200

Sep. 30	Cash	10,200	
	Notes Receivable—Higly		10,000
	Interest Revenue		150
	Interest Receivable		50
	To record collection of Higly note.		

Recall that one month of interest revenue, \$50 (\$10,000 × 6% × $^1/_{12}$), was accrued on June 30, Wolder's year end. Consequently, only three months of interest revenue, \$150 (\$10,000 × 6% × $^3/_{12}$), is recorded in this period.

Dishonouring of Notes Receivable

A **dishonoured note** is a note that is not paid in full at maturity. Since a dishonoured note receivable is no longer negotiable, the Notes Receivable account must be reduced by the principal of the note. The payee still has a claim against the maker of the note for both the principal and any unpaid interest and will transfer the amount owing to an Accounts Receivable account if there is hope that the amount will eventually be collected.

To illustrate, assume that on September 30 Higly Inc. says that it cannot pay at the present time but Wolder Company expects eventual collection. Wolder would make the following entry at the time the note is dishonoured:

A	=	L	+	OE
+10,200				+150
−10,000				
−50				

Cash flows: no effect

Sep. 30	Accounts Receivable—Higly	10,200	
	Notes Receivable—Higly		10,000
	Interest Revenue		150
	Interest Receivable		50
	To record dishonouring of Higly note where collection is expected.		

Wolder will continue to follow up with Higly. If the amount owing is eventually collected, Wolder will simply debit Cash and credit Accounts Receivable. If Wolder decides at a later date that it will never collect this amount from Higly, Wolder will write off the account receivable in the same way we learned earlier in the chapter—debit Allowance for Doubtful Accounts, and credit Accounts Receivable.

On the other hand, Wolder could directly write the note off on September 30 if it decided there was no hope of collection. Assuming Wolder uses one allowance account for both accounts and notes, it would record the following:

A	=	L	+	OE
+10,050				
−10,000				
−50				

Cash flows: no effect

Sep. 30	Allowance for Doubtful Accounts	10,050	
	Notes Receivable—Higly		10,000
	Interest Receivable		50
	To record dishonouring of Higly note where collection is not expected.		

No interest revenue is recorded, because collection will not occur. The interest receivable that previously had been accrued is also written off.

BEFORE YOU GO ON . . .

Review It

1. Explain the differences between an account receivable and a note receivable.
2. How is interest calculated for a note receivable?
3. At what value are notes receivable reported on the balance sheet?
4. Explain the difference between honouring and dishonouring a note receivable.

Do It

On May 1, Gambit Stores accepts from J. Nyznyk a $3,400, three-month, 5% note in settlement of Nyznyk's overdue account. Interest is due at maturity. Gambit has a June 30 year end. (a) What are the entries made by Gambit on May 1, June 30, and on the maturity date of August 1, assuming Nyznyk pays the note at that time? (b) What is the entry on August 1 if Nyznyk does not pay the note and collection is not expected in the future?

Action Plan

- Calculate the accrued interest. The formula is: Principal (face) value × annual interest rate × time in terms of one year.
- Record the interest accrued on June 30 to follow revenue recognition criteria. Use Interest Receivable, not Notes Receivable, for accrued interest.
- If the note is honoured, calculate the interest accrued after June 30 and the total interest on the note. Record the interest accrued and the collection of the note and the total interest.
- If the note is dishonoured, record the transfer of the note and any interest earned to an accounts receivable account if eventual collection is expected or to an allowance account if collection is not expected.

Solution

(a) May 1	Notes Receivable—J. Nyznyk	3,400	
	Accounts Receivable—J. Nyznyk		3,400
	To replace account receivable with 5% note receivable, due August 1.		
Jun. 30	Interest Receivable	28	
	Interest Revenue ($3,400 × 5% × $^2/_{12}$)		28
	To record interest earned to June 30.		
Aug. 1	Cash	3,442	
	Interest Receivable		28
	Notes Receivable—J. Nyznyk		3,400
	Interest Revenue ($3,400 × 5% × $^2/_{12}$)		14
	To record collection of Nyznyk note plus interest.		
(b) Aug. 1	Allowance for Doubtful Accounts	3,428	
	Interest Receivable		28
	Notes Receivable—J. Nyznyk		3,400
	To record dishonouring of Nyznyk note as collection is not expected.		

Related exercise material: BE8–10, BE8–11, BE8–12, E8–8, and E8–9.

The Navigator

Statement Presentation and Management of Receivables

STUDY OBJECTIVE 4

Demonstrate the presentation, analysis, and management of receivables.

The way receivables are presented in the financial statements is important because receivables are directly affected by how a company recognizes its revenue and bad debts expense. In addition, these reported numbers are critical for analyzing a company's liquidity and how well it manages its receivables. In the next sections, we will discuss the presentation, analysis, and management of receivables.

Presentation

Each of the major types of receivables should be identified in the balance sheet or in the notes to the financial statements. Other receivables include interest receivable, loans or advances to employees, and recoverable sales and income taxes. These receivables are generally classified and reported as separate items in the current or noncurrent sections of the balance sheet, according to their due dates. Notes receivable may also be either current assets or long-term assets, depending on their due dates.

If the balance sheet is presented in order of decreasing liquidity, current receivables are reported following cash and short-term investments, as shown in Research In Motion's balance sheet. Research In Motion (RIM) uses the term "trade receivables." Recall from the beginning of the chapter that trade receivables includes both accounts and notes receivable resulting from sales transactions. If current notes receivable are shown separately, they are often listed before accounts receivable because notes are more easily converted to cash.

The presentation of receivables in current assets for Research In Motion Limited is shown below:

RESEARCH IN MOTION LIMITED
Balance Sheet (partial)
February 28, 2009
(in U.S. thousands)

Current assets	
Cash and cash equivalents	$ 835,546
Short-term investments	682,666
Trade receivables	2,112,117
Other receivables	157,728
Inventory	682,400
Other current assets	187,257
Deferred income tax asset	183,872
	$4,841,586

In Note 1 to its financial statements, RIM states that its trade receivables include invoiced and accrued revenue and are presented net of an allowance for doubtful accounts of $2,100 thousand. The company also tells us that the allowance for doubtful accounts reflects estimates of probable losses in trade receivables. RIM explains that when it becomes aware of a specific customer's inability to meet its financial obligations, it records a specific bad debt provision to reduce the customer's related trade receivable to its estimated net realizable value. If the circumstances of specific customers change, RIM could then adjust its estimates of the recoverability of its trade receivables balances.

Traditionally, only the net amount of receivables had to be disclosed. It was not required to report both the gross amount of receivables and the allowance for doubtful accounts, either in the statement or in the notes to the financial statements. But if a company had a significant risk of uncollectible accounts or other problems with receivables, it was required to disclose this possibility in the notes to the financial statements. RIM discloses that for the majority of its products, its sales depend on several significant customers and on large, complex contracts. With the introduction of International Financial Reporting Standards, additional disclosures will be required. Companies will have to disclose a reconciliation of changes to the allowance account during the period, which will include items such as the beginning and ending balances of the allowance as well as the amount of write offs and recoveries.

In the income statement, bad debts expense is reported in the operating expenses section. RIM reports that in fiscal 2009, bad debt expense was $24,000 thousand. In fiscal 2008, it had a bad debt recovery (the opposite of an expense) of $26,000 thousand. A recovery of bad debt expenses in 2008 would mean that RIM overestimated its bad debts expense in fiscal 2007 and thus it reversed the expense in fiscal 2008. This shows just how difficult it can be to accurately estimate uncollectible accounts.

Analysis

Managers need to carefully watch the relationships between sales, accounts receivable, and cash collections. If sales increase, then accounts receivable are also expected to increase. But an unusually high increase in accounts receivable might signal trouble. Perhaps the company increased its sales by loosening its credit policy, and these receivables may be difficult or impossible to collect. The company could also end up with higher costs because of the increase in sales since it may need more cash to pay for inventory and salaries.

Recall that the ability to pay obligations as they come due is measured by a company's liquidity. How can we tell if a company's management of its receivables is helping or hurting the company's liquidity? One way of doing this is to calculate a ratio called the **receivables turnover ratio**. This ratio measures the number of times, on average, that receivables are collected during the period. It is calculated by dividing net credit sales by average gross receivables during the year.

Unfortunately, companies rarely report the amount of net sales made on credit in their financial statements. As a result, net sales (including both cash and credit sales) is used as a substitute. In addition, because some companies do not publicly report their gross accounts receivable, net accounts receivable must be used. As long as the components that are used to calculate a ratio are the same for all companies being compared, however, the comparison is fair.

In Illustration 8-8, the substitute figures of total revenue and net accounts receivable were used to calculate the 2009 receivables turnover for Forzani (dollars in thousands). We have calculated this ratio using Forzani's net accounts receivable, even though Forzani reported its gross receivables in note 16(h), because information on 2008 gross accounts receivable was not available.

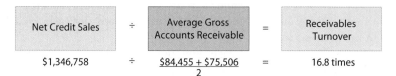

Illustration 8-8
Receivables turnover

Net Credit Sales	÷	Average Gross Accounts Receivable	=	Receivables Turnover
$1,346,758	÷	$\frac{\$84,455 + \$75,506}{2}$	=	16.8 times

The result indicates an accounts receivable turnover ratio of 16.8 times per year for Forzani. The higher the turnover ratio, the more liquid the company's receivables are.

A popular variation of the receivables turnover ratio is to convert it into the number of days it takes the company to collect its receivables. This ratio, called the **collection period**, is calculated by dividing 365 days by the receivables turnover, as shown for Forzani in Illustration 8-9.

Illustration 8-9
Collection period

Days in Year	÷	Receivables Turnover	=	Collection Period
365 days	÷	16.8	=	21.7 days

This means that in fiscal 2009, Forzani collected its receivables, on average, in approximately 21.7 days. Bell Aliant, in our feature story, states that the vast majority of its consumer customers pay on or before the due date but that it takes about 50 to 60 days to collect from businesses. The result is an overall average of between 43 and 45 days.

The collection period is often used to judge how effective a company's credit and collection policies are. The general rule is that the collection period should not be much longer than the credit term period (i.e., the time allowed for payment). Accounts receivable are basically an interest-free loan to the customer, so the faster they are collected, the better.

Both the receivables turnover and the collection period are useful for judging how efficiently a company converts its credit sales to cash. Remember that these measures should also be compared with industry averages, and with previous years.

In addition, these measures should also be analyzed along with other information about a company's liquidity, including the current ratio and inventory turnover. For example, low receivables may result in a low current ratio, which might make the company look like it has poor liquidity. But the receivables may be low because they are turning over quickly. In general, the faster the turnover, the more reliable the current ratio is for assessing liquidity.

The collection period can also be used to assess the length of a company's operating cycle. Recall from Chapter 4 that the operating cycle is the time it takes to go from cash to cash in producing revenues. In a merchandising company the operating cycle may be measured by determining the average time that it takes to purchase inventory, sell it on account, and then collect cash from customers. In Chapter 6, we learned how to calculate days sales in inventory, which is the average age of the inventory on hand. The combination of the collection period and days sales in inventory is a useful way to measure the length of a company's operating cycle. Using the number of days sales in inventory calculated in Chapter 6, this calculation is shown in Illustration 8-10 for Forzani.

Illustration 8-10 →
Operating cycle

Days Sales in Inventory	+	Collection Period	=	Operating Cycle in Days
130 days	+	21.7 days	=	151.7 days

This means that in fiscal 2009 it took 151.7 days on average from the time Forzani purchased its inventory until it collected cash.

Accelerating Cash Receipts from Receivables

If a company sells on credit, it has to wait until the customer pays the receivable before it has cash available to pay for such items as inventory and operating expenses. As credit sales and receivables increase in size and significance, waiting for receivables to be collected increases costs because the company cannot use the revenue from the sale until cash is collected. If a company can collect cash more quickly from its receivables, it can shorten the cash-to-cash operating cycle discussed in the previous section.

There are two typical ways to collect cash more quickly from receivables: using the receivables to secure a loan and selling the receivables.

Loans Secured by Receivables

One of the most common ways to speed up cash flow from accounts receivable is to go to a bank and borrow money using accounts receivable as collateral. While this does have a cost (interest has to be paid to the bank on the loan), the cash is available for the company to use earlier. The loan can then be repaid as the receivables are collected. Generally, banks are willing to give financing of up to 75% of receivables that are less than 90 days old. Quite often, these arrangements occur through an operating line of credit, which is discussed in Chapter 10.

Sale of Receivables

Companies also frequently sell their receivables to another company for cash. There are three reasons for the sale of receivables. The first is their size. To be competitive, sellers often give financing to purchasers of their goods to encourage the sale of the product. But the companies may not want to hold large amounts of receivables. As a result, many major companies in the automobile, truck, equipment, computer, and appliance industries have created wholly owned captive finance companies that accept responsibility for accounts receivable financing. An example is Ford Credit Canada, owned by the Ford Motor Company of Canada.

Second, receivables may be sold because they are the only reasonable source of cash. When money is tight, companies may not be able to borrow money in the usual credit markets. Even if credit is available, the cost of borrowing may be too high.

A final reason for selling receivables is that billing and collection are often time-consuming and costly. It is often easier for a retailer to sell its receivables to another party with expertise in billing and collection matters. Credit card companies, such as Visa and MasterCard, specialize in billing and collecting accounts receivable.

Factoring. One way to accelerate receivables collection is by sale to a factor. A **factor** is a finance company or bank that buys receivables from businesses and then collects the cash directly from the customer. If the customer does not pay, the business is usually responsible for reimbursing the factor for the uncollected amounts. This is known as selling receivables on a recourse basis.

Securitization of Receivables. An increasingly common transaction is to sell receivables to investors in return for cash through a process called **securitization**. Receivables are sold to an independent trust that holds them as an investment. This converts the receivables into securities of the trust, which is why the term "securitization of receivables" is used. In some cases, the transfer is treated as a sale of receivables; in other cases, it is treated as a secured loan.

The differences between factoring and securitization are that securitization involves many investors and the cost is lower, the receivables are of higher quality, and the seller usually continues to be involved with collecting the receivables. In factoring, the sale is usually to only one company, the cost is higher, the receivables quality is lower, and the seller does not normally have any involvement with collecting the receivables.

For such companies as Canadian National Railway and Bell Aliant, securitization of receivables is one method of using their receivables to obtain cash. Each of these companies reports details of the securitization of its receivables in the notes to its financial statements.

ACCOUNTING IN ACTION: BUSINESS INSIGHT

During the financial crisis in the fall of 2008, Canada's federal government introduced a program to buy up to $125 billion in mortgages from banks. The Insured Mortgage Purchase Program worked well; the country's banks weathered the crisis with few problems. But some analysts think the banks may have sold too many loans to the government. After all, securitization is considered a reason for the decline in lending standards that led to the U.S. subprime mortgage crisis. Canadian banks have securitized about $275 billion worth of mortgages through government programs, including the IMPP—one-quarter of the total outstanding mortgages. The programs have kept mortgage rates low and the housing market active, and have been a source of big gains for the banks. However, as banks securitize more of their insured mortgages, are they weakening their balance sheets? By the summer of 2009, insured mortgages made up just 6% of total assets held by Canadian banks, down from 10% a decade earlier. However, the pace of mortgage securitization was expected to slow as the cost of bank borrowing dropped and banks kept more mortgage loans on their books.

Source: Tara Perkins, "Ottawa Mortgage Aid May cost Banks," *The Globe and Mail Report on Business*, July 10, 2009.

What was the benefit to the banks of securitizing their mortgage receivables?

BEFORE YOU GO ON . . .

Review It

1. Explain where and how accounts and notes receivable are reported on the balance sheet.
2. Where is bad debts expense reported on the income statement?
3. What do the receivables turnover and collection period reveal?
4. Why do companies want to accelerate cash receipts from receivables?

Related exercise material: BE8–13, BE8–14, BE8–15, E8–3, E8–10, E8–11, E8–12, and E8–13.

The Navigator

Demonstration Problem

WILEY PLUS

Demonstration Problems

On February 28, Dylan Co. had the following balances in select accounts:

Accounts Receivable	$200,000
Allowance for Doubtful Accounts (credit)	12,500

Selected transactions for Dylan Co. follow. Dylan's year end is June 30.

Mar. 1	Sold $20,000 of merchandise to Potter Company, terms n/30.
1	Accepted Juno Company's $16,500, six-month, 6% note for the balance due on account.
11	Potter Company returned $600 worth of goods.
13	Made Dylan Co. credit card sales for $13,200.
30	Received payment in full from Potter Company.
Apr. 13	Received collections of $8,200 on Dylan Co. credit card sales. Added interest charges of 18% to the remaining balance.
May 10	Wrote off as uncollectible $15,000 of accounts receivable.
June 30	Dylan uses the percentage of receivables approach to estimate uncollectible accounts. Estimated uncollectible accounts are determined to be $20,000 at June 30.
30	Recorded the interest accrued on the Juno Company note.
July 16	One of the accounts receivable written off in May pays the amount due, $4,000, in full.
Sept. 1	Collected cash from Juno Company in payment of the March 1 note receivable.

Instructions

(a) Prepare the journal entries for the transactions. Dylan Co. uses a periodic inventory system.

(b) Open T accounts for Accounts Receivable and the Allowance for Doubtful Accounts, and post the relevant journal entries to these accounts. Calculate the balance in these accounts at June 30 and at September 1.

(c) Calculate the net realizable value of the accounts receivable at June 30 and September 1.

Solution to Demonstration Problem

(a)

Mar. 1	Accounts Receivable—Potter	20,000	
	Sales		20,000
	To record sale on account.		
1	Notes Receivable—Juno	16,500	
	Accounts Receivable—Juno		16,500
	To record acceptance of Juno Company note.		
11	Sales Returns and Allowances	600	
	Accounts Receivable—Potter		600
	To record return of goods.		
13	Accounts Receivable	13,200	
	Sales		13,200
	To record company credit card sales.		
30	Cash ($20,000 – $600)	19,400	
	Accounts Receivable—Potter		19,400
	To record collection of account receivable.		
Apr. 13	Cash	8,200	
	Accounts Receivable		8,200
	To record collection of credit card accounts receivable.		

Action Plan

- Record receivables at the invoice price.
- Recognize that sales returns and allowances reduce the amount received on accounts receivable.
- Calculate interest by multiplying the interest rate by the face value by the part of the year that has passed.
- Record write offs of accounts and recoveries of accounts written off only in balance sheet accounts.
- Consider any existing balance in the allowance account when making the adjustment for uncollectible accounts.
- Recognize any remaining interest on notes receivable when recording the collection of a note.

13	Accounts Receivable [($13,200 – $8,200) × 18% × $^1/_{12}$]	75	
	Interest Revenue		75
	To record interest on amount due.		
May 10	Allowance for Doubtful Accounts	15,000	
	Accounts Receivable		15,000
	To record write off of accounts receivable.		
June 30	Bad Debts Expense ($20,000 + $2,500)	22,500	
	Allowance for Doubtful Accounts		22,500
	To record estimate of uncollectible accounts.		
30	Interest Receivable ($16,500 × 6% × $^4/_{12}$)	330	
	Interest Revenue		330
	To record interest earned.		
July 16	Accounts Receivable	4,000	
	Allowance for Doubtful Accounts		4,000
	To reverse write off of account receivable.		
16	Cash	4,000	
	Accounts Receivable		4,000
	To record collection of account receivable.		
Sept. 1	Cash [$16,500 + ($16,500 × 6% × $^6/_{12}$)]	16,995	
	Interest Revenue ($16,500 × 6% × $^2/_{12}$)		165
	Interest Receivable		330
	Note Receivable		16,500
	To record collection of note receivable plus interest.		

(b)

Accounts Receivable

Feb. 28	Bal.	200,000	16,500
		20,000	600
		13,200	19,400
		75	8,200
			15,000
June 30	Bal.	173,575	
		4,000	4,000
Sept. 1	Bal.	173,575	

Allowance for Doubtful Accounts

		15,000	Feb. 28	Bal.	12,500
June 30	Bal.	2,500			
			June 30	Adj.	22,500
			June 30	Bal.	20,000
					4,000
			Sept. 1	Bal.	24,000

(c)

	June 30	Sept. 1
Accounts receivable	$173,575	$173,575
Less: Allowance for doubtful accounts	20,000	24,000
Net realizable value	$153,575	$149,575

The Navigator

Summary of Study Objectives

1. ***Record accounts receivable transactions.*** Accounts receivable are recorded at the invoice price. They are reduced by sales returns and allowances, and sales discounts. Accounts receivable subsidiary ledgers are used to keep track of individual account balances. When interest is charged on a past-due receivable, this interest is added to the accounts receivable balance and is recognized as interest revenue. Sales using non-bank credit cards result in a receivable, net of the credit card charges, from the credit card company; sales using company credit cards result in a receivable from the customer.

2. ***Calculate the net realizable value of accounts receivable and account for bad debts.*** The allowance method is used to match expected bad debts expense against sales revenue in the period when the sales occur. There are two approaches that can be used to estimate the bad debts: (a) percentage of receivables, or (b) percentage of sales. The percentage of receivables approach emphasizes determining the correct net realizable value of the accounts receivable. An aging schedule is usually used with the percentage of receivables approach where percentages are applied to different categories of accounts receivable to determine the allowance for doubtful accounts. The percentage of sales approach emphasizes achieving the most accurate matching of expenses to revenues. A percentage is applied to credit sales to determine the bad debt expense. The allowance is deducted from gross accounts receivable to report accounts receivable at their net realizable value in the balance sheet.

3. ***Account for notes receivable.*** Notes receivable are recorded at their principal, or face, value. Interest is earned from the date the note is issued until it matures and must be recorded in the correct accounting period. Interest receivable is recorded in a separate account from the note. Like accounts receivable, notes receivable are reported at their net realizable value.

Notes are normally held to maturity. At that time, the principal plus any unpaid interest is due and the note is removed from the accounts. If a note is not paid at maturity, it is said to be dishonoured. If eventual collection is still expected, an account receivable replaces the note receivable and any unpaid interest. Otherwise, the note must be written off.

4. ***Demonstrate the presentation, analysis, and management of receivables.*** Each major type of receivable should be identified in the balance sheet or in the notes to the financial statements. It is desirable to report the gross amount of receivables and the allowance for doubtful accounts/notes. Bad debts expense is reported in the income statement as an operating expense.

The liquidity of receivables can be evaluated by calculating the receivables turnover and collection period ratios. The receivables turnover is calculated by dividing net credit sales by average gross accounts receivable. This ratio measures how efficiently the company is converting its receivables into sales. The collection period converts the receivables turnover into days, dividing 365 days by the receivables turnover ratio. It shows the number of days, on average, it takes a company to collect its accounts receivable. The combination of the collection period and days sales in inventory is a useful way to measure the length of a company's operating cycle.

There are two additional ways to obtain cash from receivables: using the receivables to secure a loan and selling the receivables either to a factor or by securitizing them.

Glossary

WILEY PLUS Glossary
Key Term Matching Activity

Accounts receivable Amounts owed by customers on account. (p. 436)

Aging schedule A list of accounts receivable organized by the length of time they have been unpaid. (p. 443)

Allowance method A method of accounting for bad debts that involves estimating uncollectible accounts at the end of each period. (p. 441)

Bad debts expense An expense account to record uncollectible receivables. (p. 440)

Balance sheet approach Another name for the percentage of receivables approach. (p. 443)

Collection period The average number of days that receivables are outstanding. It is calculated by dividing 365 days by the receivables turnover. (p. 453)

Dishonoured note A note that is not paid in full at maturity. (p. 450)

Factor A finance company or bank that buys receivables from businesses and then collects the payments directly from the customers. (p. 455)

Income statement approach Another name for the percentage of sales approach. (p. 444)

Net realizable value The net amount of receivables expected to be received in cash; calculated by deducting the allowance for doubtful accounts from gross receivables. (p. 440)

Notes receivable Claims for which formal instruments of credit are issued as evidence of the debt. (p. 436)

Percentage of receivables approach An approach to estimating uncollectible accounts where the allowance for doubtful accounts is calculated as a percentage of receivables. (p. 442)

Percentage of sales approach An approach to estimating uncollectible accounts where bad debts expense is calculated as a percentage of net credit sales. (p. 444)

Promissory note A written promise to pay a specified amount of money on demand or at a definite time. (p. 448)

Receivables turnover ratio A measure of the liquidity of receivables, calculated by dividing net credit sales by average gross accounts receivable. (p. 453)

Securitization The conversion of assets such as receivables into securities that are then sold to investors in return for cash. (p. 455)

Trade receivables Accounts and notes receivable that result from sales transactions. (p. 436)

Self-Study Questions

WILEY PLUS Quizzes

Answers are at the end of the chapter.

(SO 1) AP 1. On June 15, Patel Company sells merchandise on account to Bullock Co. for $1,000, terms 2/10, n/30. On June 20, Bullock returns merchandise worth $300 to Patel. On June 24, payment is received from Bullock for the balance due. What is the amount of cash received?
(a) $680
(b) $686
(c) $700
(d) $980

(SO 2) AP 2. Sanderson Company has a debit balance of $5,000 in Allowance for Doubtful Accounts before any adjustments are made. Based on an aging of its accounts receivable at the end of the period, the company estimates that $60,000 of its receivables are uncollectible. The amount of bad debts expense that should be reported for this accounting period is:
(a) $5,000.
(b) $55,000.
(c) $60,000.
(d) $65,000.

(SO 2) AP 3. On January 1, 2011, the Allowance for Doubtful Accounts has a credit balance of $18,000. During 2011, $30,000 of uncollectible accounts receivable were written off. An aging schedule indicates that uncollectible accounts are $20,000 at the end of 2011. What is the required adjustment to Bad Debt Expense at December 31, 2011?
(a) $2,000
(b) $8,000
(c) $20,000
(d) $32,000

4. Net sales for the month are $800,000 and bad debts are expected to be 1.5% of net sales. The company uses the percentage of sales approach. If Allowance for Doubtful Accounts has a credit balance of $15,000 before adjustment, what is the balance in the allowance account after adjustment? (SO 2) AP
(a) $15,000
(b) $23,000
(c) $27,000
(d) $12,000

5. On January 1, 2011, Allowance for Doubtful Accounts had a credit balance of $35,000. In 2011, $30,000 of uncollectible accounts receivable were written off. On December 31, 2011, the company had accounts receivable of $850,000. Experience indicates that 3% of total receivables will become uncollectible. The adjusting journal entry that would be recorded for bad debts expense on December 31, 2011, would be: (SO 2) AP

(a) Allowance for Doubtful Accounts	20,500	
Accounts Receivable		20,500
(b) Bad Debt Expense	30,000	
Accounts Receivable		30,000
(c) Bad Debt Expense	25,500	
Allowance for Doubtful Accounts		25,500
(d) Bad Debt Expense	20,500	
Allowance for Doubtful Accounts		20,500

6. On July 1, Sorenson Co. accepts a $1,000, four-month, 8% promissory note in settlement of an account with Parton Co. Sorenson has a September 30 fiscal year end. The adjusting entry to record interest on August 31 is: (SO 3) AP

(a) Interest Receivable	20	
Interest Revenue		20
(b) Interest Receivable	80	
Interest Revenue		80
(c) Notes Receivable	80	
Unearned Interest Revenue		80
(d) Interest Receivable	60	
Interest Revenue		60

(SO 3) AP 7. Schlicht Co. holds Osgrove Inc.'s $10,000, four-month, 9% note. If no interest has been accrued when the note is collected, the entry made by Schlicht Co. is:

(a) Cash	10,300	
Notes Receivable		10,300
(b) Cash	10,900	
Interest Revenue		900
Notes Receivable		10,000
(c) Accounts Receivable	10,300	
Notes Receivable		10,000
Interest Revenue		300
(d) Cash	10,300	
Notes Receivable		10,000
Interest Revenue		300

(SO 4) K 8. Accounts and notes receivable are reported in the current assets section of the balance sheet at:
(a) net realizable value.
(b) carrying amount.
(c) lower of cost and net realizable value.
(d) full value.

9. Moore Company had net credit sales of $800,000 in the year and a cost of goods sold of $500,000. The balance in Accounts Receivable at the beginning of the year was $100,000 and at the end of the year it was $150,000. What were the receivables turnover and collection period ratios, respectively? (SO 4) AP
(a) 4.0 and 91 days
(b) 5.3 and 69 days
(c) 6.4 and 57 days
(d) 8.0 and 46 days

10. Which statement about International Financial Reporting Standards is correct? (SO 4) K
(a) Accounts receivable must be presented before Cash on the Balance Sheet.
(b) Companies will be required to disclose the beginning and ending balances in the Allowance for Doubtful Accounts as well as the write offs during the year.
(c) Companies must use the percentage of receivables approach to estimate uncollectible accounts.
(d) All trade receivables must be included in current assets.

Questions

(SO 1) K 1. Why are accounts receivable and notes receivable sometimes called trade receivables?

(SO 1) C 2. (a) What are the advantages of using an accounts receivable subsidiary ledger? (b) Describe the relationship between the general ledger control account and the subsidiary ledger.

(SO 1) K 3. Under what circumstances is interest normally recorded for an account receivable?

(SO 1) C 4. Ashley Dreher is confused about how a retail company should record a credit card sale. She thinks it does not matter if the customer used a bank credit card, a nonbank credit card, or a company credit card—the retail company should always debit Accounts Receivable because the customer is not paying in cash. Is Ashley correct? Explain.

(SO 2) C 5. Rod Ponach is the new credit manager for ACCT Company. He has told management there will be no bad debts in the future because he will do a complete credit check on each customer before the company makes a sale on credit to the customer. Do you think Rod can completely eliminate bad debts for the company? Discuss.

6. Explain the allowance method of accounting for bad debts. How does this method result in the matching of expenses with revenues? (SO 2) K

7. (a) What is the purpose of the account Allowance for Doubtful Accounts? (b) Although the normal balance of this account is a credit balance, it sometimes has a debit balance. Explain how this can happen. (SO 2) C

8. Why is the bad debts expense that is reported in the income statement usually not the same amount as the allowance for doubtful accounts amount reported in the balance sheet? (SO 2) K

9. Explain the difference between the percentage of receivables and the percentage of sales approaches in estimating uncollectible accounts. (SO 2) C

10. Explain why the percentage of receivables approach is also called the balance sheet approach and the percentage of sales approach is also called the income statement approach. (SO 2) K

(SO 2) C 11. Which approach is a preferable method to estimate uncollectible accounts—percentage of receivables or percentage of sales?

(SO 2) C 12. Soo Eng cannot understand why net realizable value does not decrease when an uncollectible account is written off under the allowance method. Clarify this for Soo Eng.

(SO 2) C 13. When an account receivable that was written off is later collected, two journal entries are usually made. Explain why.

(SO 3) K 14. Explain how notes receivable and accounts receivable are the same and how they are different.

(SO 3) C 15. Why might a company prefer to have a note receivable instead of an account receivable?

(SO 3) C 16. Danielle does not understand why a note receivable is not immediately recorded at its maturity value (principal plus interest). After all, you know you are going to collect both the principal and the interest and you know how much each will be. Explain to Danielle why notes are not recorded at their maturity value.

(SO 3) C 17. Explain how recording interest revenue differs for accounts receivable and notes receivable.

18. What does it mean if a note is dishonoured? What are the alternatives for the payee in accounting for a dishonoured note? (SO 3) C

19. Saucier Company has accounts receivable, notes receivable due in three months, notes receivable due in two years, an allowance for doubtful accounts, sales taxes recoverable, and income tax receivable. How should the receivables be reported on the balance sheet? (SO 4) C

20. The president proudly announces that her company's liquidity has improved. Its acid-test ratio increased substantially this year. Does an increase in the acid-test ratio always indicate improved liquidity? What other ratio(s) might you review to determine whether or not the increase in the acid-test ratio is an improvement in the company's financial health? (SO 4) C

21. Canadian Worldwide Communications Co. receivables turnover was 5.8 times in 2010 and 6.3 times in 2011. Has the company's receivables management improved or worsened? (SO 4) C

22. Why do companies sometimes sell their receivables? (SO 4) K

23. What is the difference between factoring and securitizing receivables? (SO 4) C

Brief Exercises

BE8–1 Seven transactions follow. For each transaction, indicate if the transaction increases, decreases, or has no effect on (a) accounts receivable, (b) notes receivable, (c) total assets, and (d) owner's equity. Use the following format, in which the first transaction is given as an example:

Identify impact of transaction on receivables, total assets, and owner's equity.
(SO 1) K

Transaction:	(a) Accounts Receivable	(b) Notes Receivable	(c) Total Assets	(d) Owner's Equity
1. Performed services on account for a customer.	Increase	No effect	Increase	Increase
2. A customer paid cash for services to be provided next month.				
3. Performed services for a customer in exchange for a note.				
4. Collected cash from the customer in 1 above.				
5. Performed services for a customer for cash.				
6. Extended a customer's account for three months by accepting a note in exchange for it.				
7. Performed services for a customer who had paid in advance.				

Record accounts receivable transactions.
(SO 1) AP

BE8–2 Record the following transactions on the books of Essex Co.:

(a) On July 1, Essex Co. sold merchandise on account to Cambridge Inc. for $15,000, terms 2/10, n/30. The cost of the merchandise sold was $9,500. Essex uses a perpetual inventory system.
(b) On July 3, Cambridge Inc. returned merchandise worth $2,500 to Essex Co. The original cost of the merchandise was $1,580. The merchandise was returned to inventory.
(c) On July 10, Cambridge Inc. paid for the merchandise.

Record accounts receivable transactions.
(SO 1) AP

BE8–3 Record the following transactions on the books of Low Co:

(a) On August 1, Low Co. sold merchandise on account to High Inc. for $25,000, terms 2/10, n/30. Low uses a periodic inventory system.
(b) On August 5, High Inc. returned merchandise worth $4,500 to Low Co.
(c) On September 30, Low Co. charged High Inc. one month's interest for the overdue account. Low charges 12% on overdue accounts. (Round calculation to the nearest dollar.)
(d) On October 4, High Inc. paid the amount owing to Low Co.

Record credit card transactions.
(SO 1) AP

BE8–4 Stewart Department Store accepted a nonbank card in payment of a $400 purchase of merchandise on July 11. The credit card company charges a 3% fee. (a) What entry should Stewart Department Store make? (b) What if the customer had used a Visa credit card instead of a nonbank credit card? Assume Visa also charges a 3% fee. (c) What entry should Stewart Department Store record if the customer had used a Stewart Department Store credit card instead of a nonbank credit card?

Record bad debts using percentage of receivables approach.
(SO 2) AP

BE8–5 Groleskey Co. uses the percentage of receivables approach to record bad debts expense. It estimates that 4% of total accounts receivable will become uncollectible. Accounts receivable are $300,000 at the end of the year. The allowance for doubtful accounts has a credit balance of $2,500.

(a) Prepare the adjusting entry to record bad debts expense for the year ended December 31.
(b) If the allowance for doubtful accounts had a debit balance of $1,500 instead of a credit balance of $2,500, what amount would be reported for bad debts expense?

Complete aging schedule and record bad debts expense.
(SO 2) AP

BE8–6 Refer to BE8–5. Groleskey Co. decides to refine its estimate of uncollectible accounts by preparing an aging schedule. Complete the following schedule and prepare the adjusting journal entry using this estimate. Assume Allowance for Doubtful Accounts has a credit balance of $2,500.

Number of Days Outstanding	Accounts Receivable	Estimated % Uncollectible	Estimated Uncollectible Accounts
0–30 days	$184,000	1%	
31–60 days	60,000	4%	
61–90 days	36,000	10%	
Over 90 days	20,000	20%	
Total	$300,000		

Record bad debts using percentage of sales approach.
(SO 2) AP

BE8–7 Qinshan Co. uses the percentage of sales approach to record bad debts expense. It estimates that 1.5% of net credit sales will become uncollectible. Credit sales are $950,000 for the year ended April 30, 2011; sales returns and allowances are $60,000; sales discounts are $20,000; and the allowance for doubtful accounts has a credit balance of $6,000. Prepare the adjusting entry to record bad debts expense in 2011.

Record write off and compare net realizable value.
(SO 2) AP

BE8–8 At the end of 2010, Searcy Co. has an allowance for doubtful accounts of $36,000. On January 24, 2011, when it has accounts receivable of $650,000, Searcy Co. learns that its $8,000 receivable from Hutley Inc. is not collectible. Management authorizes a write off.

(a) Record the write off.

(b) What is the net realizable value of the accounts receivable (1) before the write off, and (2) after the write off?

BE8–9 Assume the same information as in BE8–8. Hutley's financial difficulties are over. On June 4, 2011, Searcy Co. receives a payment in full of $8,000 from Hutley Inc. Record this transaction.

Record recovery of account written off.
(SO 2) AP

BE8–10 Rocky Ridge Co. has three outstanding notes receivable at its December 31, 2010, fiscal year end. For each note, calculate (a) total interest revenue, (b) interest revenue to be recorded in 2010, and (c) interest revenue to be recorded in 2011.

Calculate interest on notes receivable.
(SO 3) AP

Issue Date	Term	Principal	Interest Rate
1. July 31, 2010	9 months	$15,000	7%
2. September 1, 2010	6 months	44,000	8%
3. November 1, 2010	15 months	30,000	6%

BE8–11 On March 31, 2011, Raja Co. sold merchandise on account to Opal Co. for $24,000, terms n/30. Raja uses a perpetual inventory system and the merchandise had a cost of $14,500. On May 1, 2011, Opal gave Raja a five-month, 7% promissory note in settlement of the account. Interest is to be paid at maturity. On October 1, Opal paid the note and accrued interest. Record the above transactions for Raja Co. Raja Co. has a May 31 fiscal year end and adjusts its accounts annually.

Record notes receivable transactions.
(SO 3) AP

BE8–12 Lee Company accepts a $27,000, three-month, 7% note receivable in settlement of an account receivable on June 1, 2011. Interest is to be paid at maturity. Lee Company has a December 31 year end and adjusts its accounts annually.

Record notes receivable transactions.
(SO 3) AP

(a) Record (1) the issue of the note on June 1 and (2) the settlement of the note on September 1, assuming the note is honoured.
(b) Repeat part (a) assuming that the note is dishonoured but eventual collection is expected.
(c) Repeat part (a) assuming that the note is dishonoured and eventual collection is not expected.

BE8–13 Chant Co. lent Sharp Inc. $100,000 cash in exchange for a five-year, 4% note on July 1, 2010. Interest is payable quarterly on January 1, April 1, July 1, and October 1 each year. Chant Co. has a December 31 year end.

Record notes receivable transactions and indicate statement presentation.
(SO 3, 4) AP

(a) Record Chant's entries related to the note to January 1, 2011.
(b) What amounts related to this note will be reported on Chant's December 31, 2010, financial statements?

BE8–14 WAF Company's general ledger included the following accounts at November 30, 2011:

Prepare current assets section.
(SO 4) AP

Accounts payable	$145,500
Accounts receivable	109,000
Allowance for doubtful accounts	6,950
Bad debts expense	35,970
Cash	74,000
GST recoverable	21,850
Interest receivable	2,500
Interest revenue	10,000
Merchandise inventory	110,800
Note receivable—due April 23, 2012	50,000
Note receivable—due May 21, 2015	150,000
Prepaid expenses	15,300
Short-term investments	80,500

Prepare the current assets section of the balance sheet.

Calculate and interpret ratios. (SO 4) AN

BE8–15 The financial statements of Maple Leaf Foods Inc. report sales of $5,242,602 thousand for the year ended December 31, 2008. Accounts receivable are $139,144 thousand at the end of the year, and $202,285 thousand at the beginning of the year. Calculate Maple Leaf's receivables turnover and collection period. If the company's receivables turnover and collection period in the previous year were 25.8 and 14.1 days, respectively, has the company's liquidity improved or weakened?

Exercises

Identify impact and record accounts receivable transactions. (SO 1) AP

E8–1 Links Costumes uses a perpetual inventory system. Selected transactions for April and June follow:

Apr. 6	Sold merchandise costing $3,000 to Pumphill Theatre for $6,500, terms 2/10, n/30.
8	Pumphill returned $500 of the merchandise. This merchandise had originally cost Links $235 and was returned to inventory.
16	Pumphill paid Links the amount owing.
17	Sold merchandise costing $2,525 to EastCo Productions for $5,500, terms 1/10, n/30.
18	EastCo returned $400 of the merchandise because it was damaged. The merchandise had originally cost Links $185. Links scrapped the merchandise.
June 17	Added interest charges for one month to the amount owning by EastCo. Links charges 18% on outstanding receivables.
20	EastCo paid the amount owing.

Instructions

(a) For each of these transactions indicate if the transaction has increased (+) or decreased (–) cash, accounts receivable, inventory, and owner's equity and by how much. If the item is not changed, write NE to indicate there is no effect. Use the following format, in which the first one has been done for you as an example.

Transaction Date	Cash	Accounts Receivable	Inventory	Owner's Equity
April 6	NE	+ $6,500	– $3,000	+ $3,500

(b) Prepare journal entries to record the above transactions.

Record accounts receivable transactions. Post to subsidiary and general ledgers. (SO 1) AP

E8–2 Transactions follow for the Adventure Sports Co. store and three of its customers in the company's first month of business:

Mar. 2	Andrew Noren used his Adventure Sports credit card to purchase $575 of merchandise.
4	Andrew returned $75 of merchandise for credit.
5	Elaine Davidson used her Adventure Sports credit card to purchase $380 of merchandise.
8	Erik Smistad purchased $421 of merchandise and paid for it in cash.
17	Andrew Noren used his Adventure Sports credit card to purchase an additional $348 of merchandise.
19	Elaine Davidson made a $100 payment on her credit card account.
22	Erik Smistad used his Adventure Sports credit card to purchase $299 of merchandise.
27	Andrew Noren paid the amount owing on his March 2 purchase.
29	Elaine Davidson used her Adventure Sports credit card to purchase $310 of merchandise.

Instructions

(a) Record the above transactions. Adventure Sports uses a periodic inventory system.
(b) Set up general ledger accounts for the Accounts Receivable control account and for the Accounts Receivable subsidiary ledger accounts. Post the journal entries to these accounts.
(c) Prepare a list of customers and the balances of their accounts from the subsidiary ledger. Prove that the total of the subsidiary ledger is equal to the control account balance.

E8–3 Krazy Hair Salon accepts its own credit card, as well as debit cards, and bank and nonbank credit cards. Krazy is charged 3.5% for all bank credit card transactions, 4.25% for all nonbank credit card transactions, and $0.50 per transaction for all debit card transactions. In October and November 2011, the following summary transactions occurred:

Record credit card transactions and indicate statement presentation.
(SO 1, 4) AP

Oct.	15	Performed services totalling $15,000 for customers who used Krazy credit cards.
	20	Performed services totalling $7,500 for customers who used Visa credit cards.
	30	Performed services totalling $2,000 for customers who used nonbank credit cards.
	31	Performed services totalling $5,000 for customers who used debit cards (100 transactions).
Nov.	15	Collected $9,000 on Krazy credit cards.
	14	Collected the amount owing from the nonbank credit card companies for the October 30 transactions.
	30	Added interest charges of 24% to outstanding Krazy credit card balances.

Instructions

(a) Record the above transactions for Krazy Hair Salon.
(b) Using these transactions, prepare a multi-step income statement for Krazy Hair Salon for the two months ended November 30.

E8–4 The ledger of Assen Company at December 31, 2011, the end of the current year, shows Accounts Receivable $180,000; Allowance for Doubtful Accounts $2,200 (credit); Sales $1,420,000; Sales Returns and Allowances $50,000; and Sales Discounts $20,000.

Record bad debts using two approaches; calculate net realizable value.
(SO 2) AP

Instructions

(a) Record the adjusting entry at December 31, 2011, assuming bad debts are estimated to be (1) 10% of accounts receivable, and (2) 1.5% of net sales.
(b) Calculate the net realizable value of the accounts receivable for each approach to estimating uncollectible accounts in (a) above.
(c) Assume instead that the Allowance for Doubtful Accounts had a debit balance of $2,600 at December 31, 2011. What is bad debt expense for 2011, and what is the net realizable value of the accounts receivable December 31, 2011, assuming bad debts are estimated to be (1) 10% of accounts receivable, and (2) 1.5% of net sales?

E8–5 Grevina Company has accounts receivable of $185,000 at March 31, 2011. An analysis of the accounts shows the following:

Prepare aging schedule and record bad debts.
(SO 2) AP

Month of Sale	Balance
March	$130,000
February	25,200
January	17,000
October, November, and December	12,800
	$185,000

Credit terms are 2/10, n/30. On April 1, 2010, the Allowance for Doubtful Accounts had a credit balance of $16,700. During the year, the company wrote off accounts receivable of $20,000 as uncollectible. The company uses the percentage of receivables approach and an aging schedule to estimate uncollectible accounts. The company's percentage estimates of bad debts are as follows:

Number of Days Outstanding	Estimated % Uncollectible
0–30	2%
31–60	10%
61–90	30%
Over 90	50%

Instructions

(a) Prepare an aging schedule to determine the total estimated uncollectible accounts at March 31, 2011.
(b) Prepare the adjusting entry at March 31 to record bad debts expense.
(c) What is the net realizable value of the accounts receivable at March 31, 2011?

Determine missing amounts.
(SO 1, 2) AP

E8–6 Wilton Corporation reported the following information in its general ledger at December 31:

Accounts Receivable

Beg. bal.	9,000	28,000
	(a)	(b)
End. bal.	(c)	

Sales

	30,000

Allowance for Doubtful Accounts

	Beg. bal.	900
500		(d)
	End. bal.	(e)

Bad Debts Expense

(d)	

All sales were on account. At the end of the year, uncollectible accounts were estimated to total $1,000 based on an aging schedule.

Instructions

Using your knowledge of receivables transactions, determine the missing amounts. (*Hint*: You may find it helpful to reconstruct the journal entries.)

Record bad debts, write off, and recovery; calculate net realizable value.
(SO 2) AP

E8–7 On December 31, 2010, Jacey Co. estimated that 4% of its $550,000 of accounts receivable would become uncollectible. Prior to the recording of the bad debts adjusting entry, the Allowance for Doubtful Accounts had a debit balance of $1,200. On May 21, 2011, the company determined that Robert Worthy's $1,850 account and Samir Dusaki's $3,450 account were uncollectible and wrote off the two accounts. Jacey's accounts receivable were $575,000 prior to recording the write offs. On July 11, 2011, Dusaki paid his account that had been written off on May 21. On July 11, 2011, Jacey's accounts receivable were $521,000 prior to recording the cash receipt from Dusaki.

Instructions

(a) Prepare the journal entries on December 31, 2010, May 21, 2011, and July 11, 2011.
(b) Post the journal entries to Allowance for Doubtful Accounts and calculate the new balance after each entry.
(c) Calculate the net realizable value of accounts receivable both before and after writing off the two accounts on May 21, 2011.
(d) Calculate the net realizable value of the accounts receivable both before and after recording the cash receipt from Dusaki on July 11, 2011.

E8–8 Passera Supply Co. has the following transactions:

Record notes receivable transactions.
(SO 3) AP

Nov. 1	Loaned $48,000 cash to A. Morgan on a one-year, 8% note.
15	Sold goods to H. Giorgi on account for $9,000, terms n/30. The goods cost Passera $5,500. Passera uses the perpetual inventory system.
Dec. 1	Sold goods to Wright, Inc., receiving an $18,000, three-month, 6% note. The goods cost Passera $11,000.
15	H. Giorgi was unable to pay her account. Giorgi gave Passera a six-month, 7% note in settlement of her account.
31	Accrued interest revenue on all notes receivable. Interest is due at maturity.
Mar. 1	Collected the amount owing on the Wright note.
Jun. 15	H. Giorgi defaults on the note. Future payment is not expected.

Instructions

Record the transactions for Passera Supply Co. (Round calculations to the nearest dollar.)

E8–9 The following are notes receivable transactions for Rather Co.:

Record notes receivable transactions.
(SO 3) AP

May 1	Received a $10,500, six-month, 5% note from Jioux Company in settlement of an accounts receivable. Interest is due at maturity.
June 30	Accrued interest on the Jioux note, at Rather's year end. Adjustments are recorded annually.
July 31	Lent $3,000 cash to an employee, Noreen Irvine, receiving a three-month, 6% note. Interest is due at the end of each month.
Aug. 31	Received the interest due from Ms. Irvine.
Sep. 30	Received the interest due from Ms. Irvine.
Oct. 31	Received payment in full for the employee note from Ms. Irvine.
Nov. 1	Jioux Company defaults on its note. Rather expects to collect the amount owing in January.

Instructions

Record the transactions for Rather Co. (Round calculations to the nearest dollar.)

E8–10 Ni Co. has the following notes receivable outstanding at December 31, 2011:

Record notes receivable transactions and indicate statement presentation.
(SO 3, 4) AP

Issue Date	Term	Principal	Interest Rate
1. August 31, 2010	2 years	$15,000	4%
2. October 1, 2010	18 months	46,000	5%
3. February 1, 2011	1 year	32,000	4%
4. May 31, 2011	5 years	22,000	6%
5. October 31, 2011	7 months	9,000	5%

For notes with terms of one year or longer, interest is payable on the first day of each month, for interest earned the previous month. For notes with terms less than one year, interest is payable at maturity.

Instructions

(a) Calculate the interest revenue that Ni Co. will report on its income statement for the year ended December 31, 2011. Indicate where this will be presented on the income statement. (Round calculations to the nearest dollar.)

(b) Calculate the amounts related to these notes that will be reported on Ni Co.'s balance sheet at December 31, 2011. Indicate where they will be presented. Assume all required interest payments have been received on time. (Round calculations to the nearest dollar.)

Record bad debts, prepare partial balance sheet, and calculate ratios.
(SO 2, 4) AP

E8–11 In its first year of operations, AJS Company had sales of $3 million (all on credit) and cost of goods sold of $1,750,000. Sales allowances of $100,000 were given on substandard merchandise. During the year the company collected $2.4 million cash on account. At year end, December 31, 2011, the credit manager estimates that 5% of the accounts receivables will become uncollectible.

At December 31, 2011, the balances in selected other accounts were:

Accounts payable	$350,000
Cash	85,000
Interest receivable	1,125
Interest revenue	2,250
Merchandise inventory	325,000
Notes receivable, due April 10, 2014	45,000
Short-term investments	50,000
Supplies	10,000
Unearned sales revenue	25,000

Instructions

(a) Prepare the journal entry to record the estimated uncollectibles.
(b) Prepare the current assets section of the balance sheet for AJS Company at December 31, 2011.
(c) Calculate the receivables turnover and collection period. (Remember that this is the end of the first year of business.)

Calculate ratios and comment.
(SO 4) AN

E8–12 The following information (in millions) was taken from the December 31 financial statements of Canadian National Railway Company:

	2008	2007	2006
Accounts receivable, gross	$ 939	$ 397	$ 711
Allowance for doubtful accounts	26	27	19
Accounts receivable, net	913	370	692
Revenues	8,482	7,897	7,929
Total current assets	1,756	1,048	1,336
Total current liabilities	1,892	1,590	2,114

Instructions

(a) Calculate the 2008 and 2007 current ratios.
(b) Calculate the receivables turnover and average collection period for 2008 and 2007.
(c) Are accounts receivable a material component of the company's current assets?
(d) Comment on any improvement or weakening in CN's liquidity and its management of accounts receivable.

Discuss sale of receivables.
(SO 4) C

E8–13 Refer to E8–12. In the notes to its financial statements, Canadian National Railway Company reports that it has a revolving agreement to sell eligible freight trade and other receivables up to a maximum of $600 million of receivables outstanding at any point in time. At December 31, 2008, the company had sold $71 million of these receivables, compared with $588 million at December 31, 2007, and $393 million at December 31, 2006. CN has retained the responsibility for servicing, administering, and collecting the freight receivables sold.

Instructions

Explain why CN, a financially stable company, securitizes (sells) a portion of its receivables. Explain the impact of amounts securitized on the accounts receivable shown on the balance sheet.

Problems: Set A

Record accounts receivable and bad debts transactions; show balance sheet presentation.
(SO 1, 2) AP

P8–1A At December 31, 2010, Bordeaux Co. reported the following information on its balance sheet:

Accounts receivable	$480,000
Less: Allowance for doubtful accounts	33,600

During 2011, the company had the following transactions related to receivables:

1. Sales on account, $1,700,000
2. Sales returns and allowances, $250,000
3. Collections of accounts receivable, $1,500,000
4. Write offs of accounts considered uncollectible, $55,000
5. Recovery of accounts previously written off as uncollectible, $6,750

Instructions

(a) Prepare the summary journal entries to record each of these five transactions.
(b) Enter the January 1, 2011, balances in the Accounts Receivable and Allowance for Doubtful Accounts general ledger accounts, post the entries to the two accounts, and determine the balances.
(c) Prepare the journal entry to record bad debts expense for 2011. Uncollectible accounts are estimated at 7% of accounts receivable.
(d) Calculate the net realizable value of accounts receivable at December 31, 2011.
(e) Show the balance sheet presentation of the receivables as at December 31, 2011.

Taking It Further For several years, Bordeaux Co. has estimated uncollectible accounts at 7% of accounts receivable. Discuss whether or not the company should continue to do this at December 31, 2011.

Record accounts receivable and bad debts transactions; show financial statement presentation.
(SO 1, 2) AP

P8–2A At the beginning of the current period, Huang Co. had a balance of $100,000 in Accounts Receivable and a $7,000 credit balance in Allowance for Doubtful Accounts. In the period, it had net credit sales of $400,000 and collections of $361,500. It wrote off accounts receivable of $10,500 as uncollectible. However, a $1,750 account written off as uncollectible was recovered before the end of the current period. Based on an aging schedule, uncollectible accounts are estimated to be $8,000 at the end of the period.

Instructions

(a) Record sales and collections in the period.
(b) Record the write off of uncollectible accounts in the period.
(c) Record the recovery of the account written off as uncollectible in the period.
(d) Record the bad debts expense adjusting entry for the period.
(e) Show the balance sheet presentation of the receivables at the end of the period.
(f) What is the amount of bad debts expense on the income statement for the period?
(g) Now assume that Huang Co. uses the percentage of sales approach instead of the percentage of receivables approach to estimate uncollectible accounts. Repeat (d) through (f) assuming Huang estimates 2.25% of net credit sales will become uncollectible.

Taking It Further Should Huang Co. use the percentage of receivables approach or the percentage of sales approach to estimating uncollectible accounts? Explain.

Calculate bad debt amounts and answer questions.
(SO 2) AP

P8–3A Information on Hohenberger Company for 2011 follows:

Total credit sales	$1,000,000
Accounts receivable at December 31	400,000
Uncollectible accounts written off	17,500
Uncollectible accounts later recovered (after write off but before year end)	2,500

Instructions

(a) What amount of bad debts expense will Hohenberger Company report if it does not use the allowance method?
(b) Assume that Hohenberger Company decides to estimate its uncollectible accounts using the allowance method and an aging schedule. Uncollectible accounts are estimated to be $24,000. What amount of bad debts expense will Hohenberger Company record if Allowance for Doubtful Accounts had an opening balance of $20,000 on January 1, 2011?
(c) Assume that Hohenberger Company decides to estimate its uncollectible accounts using the allowance method and estimates its bad debts expense at 2.25% of credit sales. What amount of bad debts expense will Hohenberger Company record if Allowance for Doubtful Accounts had an opening balance of $20,000 on January 1, 2011?
(d) Assume the same facts as in (b) except that the Allowance for Doubtful Accounts had a $12,000 balance on January 1, 2011. What amount of bad debts expense will Hohenberger record?
(e) How does the amount of accounts written off during the period affect the amount of bad debts expense recorded at the end of the period if a company is using the allowance method?
(f) How does the collection of an account that had previously been written off affect the net realizable value of accounts receivable?

Taking It Further What are the advantages of using the allowance method of accounting for bad debts?

Prepare aging schedule and record bad debts and explain method.
(SO 2) AP

P8–4A NewWest uses the allowance method to estimate uncollectible accounts receivable. The company produced the following information from aging its accounts receivable at year end:

		Number of Days Outstanding			
	Total	0–30	31–60	61–90	91–120
Accounts receivable	$520,000	$240,000	$120,000	$100,000	$60,000
Estimated % uncollectible		1.5%	7%	10%	30%
Estimated uncollectible accounts					

The unadjusted balance in Allowance for Doubtful Accounts is a credit of $14,000.

Instructions

(a) Complete the aging schedule and calculate the total estimated uncollectible accounts.
(b) Record the bad debts adjusting entry using the information determined in (a).
(c) In the following year, $21,000 of the outstanding accounts receivable is determined to be uncollectible. Record the write off of the uncollectible accounts.
(d) The company collects $3,900 of the $21,000 of accounts that were determined to be uncollectible in (c). The company also expects to collect an additional $500. Record the journal entry (or entries) to restore the accounts receivable and the cash collected. Collection of the $500 is expected in the near future.
(e) Explain how using the allowance method matches expenses with revenues.

Taking It Further What are the advantages and disadvantages to the company of using an aging schedule to estimate uncollectible accounts, as compared with estimating uncollectible accounts as 10% of total accounts receivable?

Prepare aging schedule and record bad debts.
(SO 2) AP

P8–5A An aging analysis of Hagiwara Company's accounts receivable at December 31, 2010 and 2011, showed the following:

Number of Days Outstanding	Estimated % Uncollectible	December 31 2011	December 31 2010
0–30 days	2.5%	$115,000	$145,000
31–60 days	6.0%	35,000	63,000
61–90 days	18.0%	45,000	38,000
Over 90 days	35.0%	80,000	24,000
Total		$275,000	$270,000

Additional information:

1. At December 31, 2010, the unadjusted balance in Allowance for Doubtful Accounts was a credit of $4,800.
2. In 2011, $26,500 of accounts were written off as uncollectible and $1,500 of accounts previously written off were recovered.

Instructions

(a) Prepare an aging schedule to calculate the estimated uncollectible accounts at December 31, 2010, and at December 31, 2011.

(b) Record the following transactions:

1. The adjusting entry on December 31, 2010
2. The write off of uncollectible accounts in 2011
3. The collection of accounts previously written off
4. The adjusting entry on December 31, 2011

(c) Calculate the net realizable value of Hagiwara's accounts receivable at December 31, 2010, and December 31, 2011.

Taking It Further What are the implications of the changes in the age of the receivables from 2010 to 2011?

Calculate allowance for doubtful accounts and bad debts; show financial statement presentation.
(SO 2) AP

P8–6A Sucha Company operates in an industry that has a high rate of bad debts. On August 31, 2011, before any year-end adjustments, the balance in Sucha's Accounts Receivable account was $312,500 and Allowance for Doubtful Accounts had a debit balance of $7,500. The credit manager closely watches the collection of the accounts receivable and has prepared the following information at August 31, 2011:

Days Account Outstanding	Amount	Probability of Collection
Less than 16 days	$177,500	97%
Between 16 and 30 days	57,500	92%
Between 31 and 45 days	40,000	80%
Between 46 and 60 days	20,000	75%
Between 61 and 75 days	10,000	40%
Over 75 days	7,500	10%

Instructions

(a) Using the aging method of estimating the percentage of receivables that are uncollectible, what is the appropriate balance for Allowance for Doubtful Accounts at August 31, 2011?

(b) Show how accounts receivable will be presented on the August 31, 2011, balance sheet.

(c) What is the bad debt expense that will be reported in the income statement for the year?

Taking It Further On December 15, 2011, Sucha writes off all of the $7,500 amount that had been over 75 days old at August 31, 2011. Should the company go back and adjust the Allowance for Doubtful Accounts and the Bad Debt Expense reported on the August 31, 2011, financial statements? Explain.

Determine missing amounts.
(SO 2) AN

P8–7A Kadakus and Company reported the following information in its general ledger at August 31:

Accounts Receivable

Beg. bal. 854,000	(b)
(a)	(c)
4,200	(d)
End. bal. 927,500	

Sales

	(f)

Allowance for Doubtful Accounts

	Beg. bal. 73,300
(c)	(e)
	(b)
	End. bal. 79,600

Bad Debts Expense

52,500	

All sales were made on account. Bad debts expense was estimated as 1% of sales.

Instructions

Determine the missing amounts in Kadakus and Company's accounts. State what each of these amounts represents. You will not be able to determine the missing items in alphabetical order. (To solve this problem, it might help if you reconstruct the journal entries.)

Taking It Further Explain the differences between bad debt expense and the allowance for doubtful accounts.

Identify impact of accounts receivable and bad debts transactions; determine statement presentation.
(SO 1, 2, 4) AP

P8–8A Bassano Company uses the percentage of sales approach to record bad debts expense for its monthly financial statements and the percentage of receivables approach for its year-end financial statements. Bassano Company has an October 31 fiscal year end, closes temporary accounts annually, and uses a perpetual inventory system.

On August 31, 2011, after completing its month-end adjustments, it had accounts receivable of $74,500, a credit balance of $2,980 in Allowance for Doubtful Accounts, and bad debts expense of $9,860. In September and October, the following occurred:

September

1. Sold $56,300 of merchandise on account; the cost of the merchandise was $25,335.
2. A total of $900 of the merchandise sold on account was returned. These customers were issued credit memos. The cost of the merchandise was $400 and it was returned to inventory.
3. Collected $59,200 cash on account from customers.
4. Interest charges of $745 were charged to outstanding accounts receivable.
5. As part of the month-end adjusting entries, recorded bad debts expense of 2% of net credit sales for the month.

October

1. Credit sales in the month were $63,900; the cost of the merchandise was $28,700.
2. Received $350 cash from a customer whose account had been written off in July.
3. Collected $58,500 cash, in addition to the cash collected in (2) above, from customers on account.
4. Wrote off $7,500 of accounts receivable as uncollectible.
5. Interest charges of $710 were charged to outstanding accounts receivable.
6. Recorded the year-end adjustment for bad debts. Uncollectible accounts were estimated to be 4% of accounts receivable.

Instructions

(a) For each of these transactions, indicate if the transaction has increased (+) or decreased (–) Cash, Accounts Receivable, Allowance for Doubtful Accounts, Inventory, Total Assets, and Owner's Equity and by how much. If the item is not changed, write NE to indicate there is no effect. Use the following format, in which the first one has been done for you as an example.

Transaction	Cash	Accounts Receivable	Allowance for Doubtful Accounts	Inventory	Total Assets	Owner's Equity
September:						
1.	NE	+ $56,300	NE	– $25,335	+ $30,965	+ $30,965

(b) Show how accounts receivable will appear on the October 31, 2011, balance sheet.
(c) What amount will be reported as bad debts expense on the income statement for the year ended October 31, 2011?

Taking It Further Discuss the appropriateness of Bassano using the percentage of sales approach to estimating uncollectible accounts for its monthly financial statements and the percentage of receivables approach for its year-end financial statements. The monthly financial statements are used by Bassano's management and are not distributed to anyone outside of the company.

P8–9A Bleumortier Company has a March 31 fiscal year end and adjusts accounts annually. Selected transactions in the year included the following:

Record receivables transactions.
(SO 1, 3) AP

Jan. 2 Sold $18,000 of merchandise to Brooks Company, terms n/30. The cost of the goods sold was $12,000. Bleumortier uses the perpetual inventory system.
Feb. 1 Accepted an $18,000, four-month, 6% promissory note from Brooks Company for the balance due. (See January 2 transaction.) Interest is payable at maturity.
15 Sold $13,400 of merchandise costing $8,800 to Gage Company and accepted Gage's two-month, 6% note in payment. Interest is payable at maturity.
26 Sold $8,000 of merchandise to Mathias Co., terms n/30. The cost of the merchandise sold was $5,400.
Mar. 31 Accepted a $8,000, two-month, 7% note from Mathias Co. for its balance due. Interest is payable at maturity. (See February 26 transaction.)
31 Accrued interest at year end.
Apr. 15 Collected the Gage note in full. (See February 15 transaction.)
May 31 Mathias Co. dishonours its note of March 31. It is expected that Mathias will eventually pay the amount owed.
June 1 Collected Brooks Company note in full. (See February 1 transaction.)
July 13 Sold $5,000 merchandise costing $3,300 to Tritt Inc. and accepted Tritt's $5,000, three-month, 7% note for the amount due, with interest payable at maturity.
Oct. 13 The Tritt Inc. note was dishonoured. (See July 13 transaction.) Tritt Inc. is bankrupt and there is no hope of future settlement.

Instructions

Record the above transactions. (Round calculations to the nearest dollar.)

Taking It Further What are the advantages and disadvantages of Bleumortier Company accepting notes receivable from its customers?

P8–10A Tardif Company adjusts its books monthly. On September 30, 2011, notes receivable include the following:

Record note receivable transactions; show balance sheet presentation.
(SO 1, 3, 4) AP

Issue Date	Maker	Principal	Interest	Term
Aug. 1, 2010	RJF Inc.	$19,000	4.5%	2.5 years
Mar. 31, 2011	RES Co.	17,000	5.0%	7 months
May 31, 2011	IMG Ltd.	17,500	5.5%	18 months
Aug. 31, 2011	DRA Co.	6,000	8.5%	2 months
Sept. 30, 2011	MGH Corp.	20,500	6.0%	16 months

Interest is payable on the first day of each month for notes with terms of one year or longer. Interest is payable at maturity for notes with terms less than one year. In October, the following transactions were completed:

Oct. 1 Received payment of the interest due from RJF Inc.
1 Received payment of the interest due from IMG Ltd.
31 Received notice that the DRA note had been dishonoured. (Assume that DRA is expected to pay in the future.)
31 Collected the amount owing from RES Co.

Instructions

(a) Calculate the balance in the Interest Receivable and Notes Receivable accounts at September 30, 2011.
(b) Record the October transactions and the October 31 adjusting entry for accrued interest receivable.
(c) Enter the balances at October 1 in the receivables accounts, and post the entries to the receivables accounts.
(d) Show the balance sheet presentation of the interest and notes receivables accounts at October 31.

(e) How would the journal entry on October 31 be different if DRA were not expected to pay in the future?

Taking It Further The interest rate for the DRA note is higher than the other notes. Why might that have been the case?

Prepare assets section of balance sheet; calculate and interpret ratios.
(SO 4) AN

P8–11A Tocksfor Company's general ledger included the following selected accounts (in thousands) at September 30, 2011:

Accounts payable	$1,077.3
Accounts receivable	590.4
Accumulated depreciation—equipment	858.7
Allowance for doubtful accounts	35.4
Bad debts expense	91.3
Cash	395.6
Cost of goods sold	660.4
Equipment	1,732.8
Interest revenue	19.7
Merchandise inventory	630.9
Notes receivable—due May 15, 2012	96.0
Notes receivable—due in 2015	191.1
Prepaid expenses and deposits	20.1
Sales	4,565.5
Sales discounts	31.3
Short-term investments	194.9
Supplies	21.7
Unearned sales revenue	56.3

Additional information:

1. On September 30, 2010, Accounts Receivable was $611.1 thousand and the Allowance for Doubtful Accounts was $36.6 thousand.
2. The receivables turnover was 8.3 the previous year.

Instructions

(a) Prepare the assets section of the balance sheet.
(b) Calculate the receivables turnover and average collection period. Compare these results with the previous year's results and comment on any trends.

Taking It Further What other information should Tocksfor consider when analyzing its receivables turnover and average collection period?

Comment on approach; calculate and interpret ratios.
(SO 4) AN

P8–12A Presented here is selected financial information (in millions) from the 2008 financial statements of Rogers Communications Inc. and Shaw Communications Inc.:

	Rogers	Shaw
Sales	$11,335	$3,104.9
Allowance for doubtful accounts, beginning of year	151	15.2
Allowance for doubtful accounts, end of year	163	15.4
Accounts receivable balance (net), beginning of year	1,245	155.5
Accounts receivable balance (net), end of year	1,403	188.1

Instructions

(a) In Shaw's notes to its financial statements, it states that the company considers factors such as the number of days the subscriber account is past due, the company's past collection history, and changes in business circumstances when estimating its bad debts. Is Shaw using the percentage of receivables or sales approach to determining uncollectible accounts? Explain.

(b) Calculate the receivables turnover and average collection period for both companies. Comment on the difference in their collection experiences.

Taking It Further Shaw has an August 31 fiscal year end; Rogers has a December 31 fiscal year end. Does this affect our ability to compare the receivables turnover and average collection period between the two companies? Explain.

P8–13A The following ratios are available for Satellite Mechanical:

Evaluate liquidity.
(SO 4) AN

	2011	2010	2009
Current ratio	2.0 to 1	1.6 to 1	1.4 to 1
Acid-test ratio	1.1 to 1	0.8 to 1	0.7 to 1
Receivables turnover	7.3 times	10.1 times	10.3 times
Inventory turnover	6.3 times	6.1 times	6.4 times

Instructions

(a) Calculate the collection period, days sales in inventory, and operating cycle in days for each year.
(b) Has Satellite Mechanical's liquidity improved or weakened over the three-year period? Explain.

Taking It Further At the beginning of 2011, the owner of Satellite Mechanical decided to eliminate sales discounts because she thought it was costing the company too much money. The terms of credit sales were changed from 2/10, n/30 to n/30. Evaluate this decision.

Problems: Set B

P8–1B At December 31, 2010, Underwood Imports reported the following information on its balance sheet:

Record accounts receivable and bad debts transactions; show balance sheet presentation.
(SO 1, 2) AP

Accounts receivable	$1,990,000
Less: Allowance for doubtful accounts	119,400

During 2011, the company had the following transactions related to receivables:

1. Sales on account, $5,200,000
2. Sales returns and allowances, $80,000
3. Collections of accounts receivable, $5,400,000
4. Interest added to overdue accounts, $400,000
5. Write offs of accounts deemed uncollectible, $130,000
6. Recovery of bad debts previously written off as uncollectible, $50,400

Instructions

(a) Prepare the summary journal entries to record each of these six transactions.
(b) Enter the January 1, 2011, balances in the Accounts Receivable and Allowance for Doubtful Accounts general ledger accounts, post the entries to the two accounts, and determine the balances.
(c) Record bad debts expense for 2011. Uncollectible accounts are estimated at 6% of accounts receivable.
(d) Calculate the net realizable value of accounts receivable at December 31, 2011.
(e) Show the balance sheet presentation of accounts receivable at December 31, 2011.

Taking It Further For several years, Underwood Imports has estimated uncollectible accounts at 6% of accounts receivable. Discuss whether or not the company should continue to do this at December 31, 2011.

Record accounts receivable and bad debts transactions; show financial statement presentation.
(SO 1, 2) AP

P8–2B At the beginning of the current period, Fassi Co. had a balance of $800,000 in Accounts Receivable and a $44,000 credit balance in Allowance for Doubtful Accounts. In the period, it had net credit sales of $1,900,000 and collections of $2,042,000. It wrote off accounts receivable of $58,000. However, a $4,000 account written off as uncollectible was recovered before the end of the current period. Based on an aging schedule, uncollectible accounts are estimated to be $36,000 at the end of the period.

Instructions

(a) Record sales and collections in the period.
(b) Record the write off of uncollectible accounts in the period.
(c) Record the recovery of the uncollectible account in the period.
(d) Record the bad debts expense adjusting entry for the period.
(e) Show the balance sheet presentation of the accounts receivable at the end of the period.
(f) What is the bad debts expense on the income statement for the period?
(g) Now assume that Fassi Co. uses the percentage of sales approach instead of the percentage of receivables approach to estimate uncollectible accounts. Repeat (d) through (f) assuming Fassi estimates 1.25% of the credit sales will become uncollectible.

Taking It Further Should Fassi Co. use the percentage of receivables approach or the percentage of sales approach to estimating uncollectible accounts? Explain.

Calculate bad debt amounts and answer questions.
(SO 2) AP

P8–3B Information for Tisipai Company in 2011 follows:

Total net credit sales	$3,300,000
Accounts receivable at December 31	1,250,000
Accounts receivable written off	48,000
Accounts receivable later recovered	8,000

Instructions

(a) What amount will Tisipai Company report for bad debts expense if it does not use the allowance method of accounting for uncollectible accounts?
(b) Assume instead that Tisipai Company decides to use the allowance method and estimates its uncollectible accounts to be $52,000 based on an aging schedule. What amount of bad debts expense will Tisipai record if Allowance for Doubtful Accounts had an opening balance of $30,000 on January 1, 2011?
(c) Assume instead that Tisipai Company decides to estimate its uncollectible accounts using 1.5% of net credit sales. What amount of bad debts expense will Tisipai record if Allowance for Doubtful Accounts had an opening balance of $30,000 on January 1, 2011?
(d) Assume the same facts as in (b), except that there is a $2,250 credit balance in Allowance for Doubtful Accounts before recording the adjustment. What amount of bad debts expense will the company record?
(e) How does the write off of an uncollectible account affect the net realizable value of accounts receivable?
(f) Why use an Allowance for Doubtful Accounts instead of directly reducing Accounts Receivable when recording bad debts expense?

Taking It Further Why should companies use the allowance method of accounting for uncollectible accounts?

Prepare aging schedule and record bad debts and comment.
(SO 2) AP

P8–4B Imagine Co. uses the allowance method to estimate uncollectible accounts receivable. The computer produced the following aging of the accounts receivable at year end:

		Number of Days Outstanding			
	Total	0–30	31–60	61–90	91–120
Accounts receivable	$192,500	$110,000	$50,000	$20,000	$12,500
Estimated % uncollectible		1.5%	5%	15%	20%
Estimated uncollectible accounts					

The unadjusted balance in Allowance for Doubtful Accounts is a debit of $5,000.

Instructions

(a) Complete the aging schedule and calculate the total estimated uncollectible accounts from the above information.

(b) Record the bad debts adjusting entry using the above information.

(c) In the following year, $11,900 of the outstanding accounts receivable is determined to be uncollectible. Record the write off of the uncollectible accounts.

(d) The company collects $2,100 of the $11,900 of accounts receivable that were determined to be uncollectible in (c). No further amounts are expected to be collected. Prepare the journal entry (or entries) to record the recovery of this amount.

(e) Comment on how your answers to parts (a) to (d) would change if Imagine Co. used a percentage of total accounts receivable of 8% instead of aging the accounts receivable.

Taking It Further What are the advantages for the company of aging the accounts receivable rather than applying a percentage to total accounts receivable?

P8–5B An aging analysis of Hake Company's accounts receivable at December 31, 2010 and 2011, showed the following:

Prepare aging schedule and record bad debts.

(SO 2) AP

Number of Days Outstanding	Estimated % Uncollectible	December 31 2011	December 31 2010
0–30 days	3%	$190,000	$220,000
31–60 days	6%	40,000	105,000
61–90 days	12%	65,000	40,000
Over 90 days	24%	75,000	25,000
Total		$370,000	$390,000

Additional information:

1. At December 31, 2010, the unadjusted balance in Allowance for Doubtful Accounts was a debit of $4,200.
2. In 2011, $25,500 of accounts were written off as uncollectible and $2,500 of accounts previously written off were recovered.

Instructions

(a) Prepare an aging schedule to calculate the estimated uncollectible accounts at December 31, 2010, and at December 31, 2011.

(b) Record the following transactions:

1. The adjusting entry on December 31, 2010
2. The write off of uncollectible accounts in 2011
3. The collection of accounts previously written off
4. The adjusting entry on December 31, 2011

(c) Calculate the net realizable value of Hake's accounts receivable at December 31, 2010, and December 31, 2011.

Taking It Further What are the implications of the changes in the age of accounts receivable from 2010 to 2011?

Calculate allowance for doubtful accounts and bad debts; show financial statement presentation.
(SO 2) AP

P8–6B Paderewski Company operates in an industry that has a high rate of bad debts. On October 31, 2011, before any year-end adjustments, the balance in Paderewski's Accounts Receivable account was $625,000 and Allowance for Doubtful Accounts had a credit balance of $35,000. The credit manager closely watches the collection of the accounts receivable and has prepared the following information at October 31, 2011:

Days Account Outstanding	Amount	Probability of Collection
Less than 16 days	$355,000	97%
Between 16 and 30 days	115,000	92%
Between 31 and 45 days	80,000	80%
Between 46 and 60 days	40,000	75%
Between 61 and 75 days	20,000	40%
Over 75 days	15,000	10%

Instructions

(a) Using the aging method of estimating the percentage of receivables that are uncollectible, what is the appropriate balance for Allowance for Doubtful Accounts at October 31, 2011?
(b) Show how accounts receivable will be presented on the October 31, 2011, balance sheet.
(c) What is the bad debt expense that will be reported in the income statement for the year?

Taking It Further On December 15, 2011, Paderewski collects the $15,000 amount that had been over 75 days old at October 31, 2011. Should the company go back and adjust the Allowance for Doubtful Accounts and the Bad Debt Expense reported on the October 31, 2011, financial statements? Explain.

Determine missing amounts.
(SO 2) AN

P8–7B Armadillo and Company reported the following information in its general ledger at July 31:

Accounts Receivable

Debit		Credit
Beg. bal.	320,000	2,442,450
	(a)	(d)
	(b)	2,250
End. bal.	(c)	

Sales

Debit	Credit
	(a)

Allowance for Doubtful Accounts

Debit		Credit
	Beg. bal.	(e)
25,450		(b)
		(f)
	End. bal.	30,400

Bad Debts Expense

Debit	Credit
(f)	

All sales were made on account. At the beginning of the year, uncollectible accounts were estimated to be 7% of accounts receivable. At the end of the year, uncollectible accounts were estimated to be 8% of accounts receivable.

Instructions

Determine the missing amounts in Armadillo and Company's accounts. State what each of these amounts represents. You will not be able to determine the missing items in alphabetical order. (To solve this problem, it might help if you reconstruct the journal entries.)

Taking It Further Explain the difference between bad debt expense and the allowance for doubtful accounts.

Identify impact of accounts receivable and bad debts transactions; determine statement presentation.
(SO 1, 2, 4) AP

P8–8B Assiniboia Co. uses the percentage of sales approach to record bad debts expense for its monthly financial statements and the percentage of receivables approach for its year-end financial statements. Assiniboia Co. has a May 31 fiscal year end, closes temporary accounts annually, and uses the perpetual inventory system.

On March 31, 2011, after completing its month-end adjustments, it had accounts receivable of $89,200, a credit balance of $4,930 in Allowance for Doubtful Accounts, and a debit balance in Bad Debts Expense of $19,880. In April and May, the following occurred:

April

1. Sold $64,600 of merchandise on credit. The cost of the merchandise was $35,530.
2. Accepted $800 of returns on the merchandise sold on credit. These customers were issued credit memos. The merchandise had a cost of $440 and was discarded because it was damaged.
3. Collected $69,200 cash on account from customers.
4. Interest charges of $1,645 were charged to outstanding accounts receivable.
5. As part of the month-end adjusting entries, recorded bad debts expense of 3% of net credit sales for the month.

May

1. Credit sales were $76,600. The cost of the merchandise was $42,130.
2. Received $450 cash from a customer whose account had been written off in March.
3. Collected $78,500 cash, in addition to the cash collected in (2) above, from customers on account.
4. Wrote off $9,580 of accounts receivable as uncollectible.
5. Interest charges of $1,570 were charged to outstanding accounts receivable.
6. Recorded the year-end adjustment for bad debts. Uncollectible accounts were estimated to be 6% of accounts receivable.

Instructions

(a) For each of these transactions, indicate if the transaction has increased (+) or decreased (–) Cash, Accounts Receivable, Allowance for Doubtful Accounts, Inventory, Total Assets, and Owner's Equity and by how much. If the item is not changed, write NE to indicate there is no effect. Use the following format, in which the first one has been done for you as an example.

Transaction	Cash	Accounts Receivable	Allowance for Doubtful Accounts	Inventory	Total Assets	Owner's Equity
April:						
1.	NE	+ $64,600	NE	– $35,530	+ $29,070	+ $29,070

(b) Show how accounts receivable will appear on the May 31, 2011, balance sheet.

(c) What amount will be reported as bad debts expense on the income statement for the year ended May 31, 2011?

Taking It Further Discuss the appropriateness of Assiniboia using the percentage of sales approach to estimating uncollectible accounts for its monthly financial statements and the percentage of receivables approach for its year-end financial statements. The monthly financial statements are used by Assiniboia's management and are not distributed to anyone outside of the company.

P8–9B On January 1, 2010, Vu Co. had an $18,000, five-month, 5% notes receivable from Annabelle Company dated October 31, 2009. Interest receivable of $150 was accrued on the note on December 31, 2009. Vu Co. has a December 31 fiscal year end and adjusts its accounts annually. In 2010, the following selected transactions occurred:

Record receivables transactions.
(SO 1, 2, 3) AP

Jan. 2	Sold $15,000 of merchandise costing $8,200 to George Company, terms 2/10, n/30. Vu Co. uses the perpetual inventory system.
Feb. 1	Accepted George Company's $15,000, three-month, 6% note for the balance due. (See January 2 transaction.) Interest is due at maturity.
Mar. 31	Received payment in full from Annabelle Company for the amount due.
May 1	Collected George Company note in full. (See February 1 transaction.)
25	Accepted Avery Inc.'s $9,000, two-month, 6% note in settlement of a past-due balance on account. Interest is payable monthly.
June 25	Received one month's interest from Avery Inc. on its note. (See May 25 transaction.)
July 25	The Avery Inc. note was dishonoured. (See May 25 transaction.) Avery Inc. is bankrupt and future payment is not expected.

Oct. 1 Loaned Emily Haworth, an employee, \$6,000 on a four-month, 8% note. Interest is due at maturity.
Nov. 30 Gave MRC Corp a \$5,000 cash loan and accepted MRC's four-month, 4.5% note.
Dec. 1 Emily Haworth left for a job at another company. Vu Co. asked her to immediately pay the note receivable. (See October 1 transaction.) Emily told the company that she does not have the money to do so.
31 Accrued interest is recorded on any outstanding notes at year end.

Instructions

Record the above transactions.

Taking It Further Do you think the note receivable from Emily Haworth should be written off as at the year end? If not, do you think interest should be accrued on this note receivable at year end?

Record note receivable transactions; show balance sheet presentation.
(SO 3, 4) AP

P8–10B Ouellette Co. adjusts its books monthly. On June 30, 2011, notes receivable include the following:

Issue Date	Maker	Principal	Term	Interest
May 1, 2010	ALD Inc.	\$ 6,000	3 years	4.0%
October 31, 2010	KAB Ltd.	10,000	15 months	5.0%
January 31, 2011	BFF Co.	15,000	6 months	5.5%
May 31, 2011	DNR Co.	4,800	2 months	8.75%
June 30, 2011	MJH Corp.	9,000	8 months	5.0%

Interest is payable on the first day of each month for notes with terms of one year or longer. Interest is payable at maturity for notes with terms less than one year. In July, the following transactions were completed:

July 1 Received payment of the interest due from ALD Inc.
2 Received payment of the interest due from KAB Ltd.
31 Collected the full amount on the BFF Co. note.
31 Received notice that the DNR Co. note has been dishonoured. Assume that DNR Co. is expected to pay in the future.

Instructions

(a) Calculate the balance in the Interest Receivable and Notes Receivable accounts at June 30, 2011.
(b) Record the July transactions and the July 31 adjusting entry for accrued interest receivable.
(c) Enter the balances at July 1 in the receivables accounts. Post the entries to the receivables accounts.
(d) Show the balance sheet presentation of the receivables accounts at July 31, 2011.
(e) How would the journal entry on July 31 be different if DNR Co. were not expected to pay in the future?

Taking It Further The interest rate for the DNR note is higher than the other notes. Why might that be the case?

Prepare assets section of balance sheet; calculate and interpret ratios.
(SO 4) AN

P8–11B Norlandia Saga Company's general ledger included the following selected accounts (in thousands) at November 30, 2011:

Accounts payable	\$ 546.2
Accounts receivable	311.4
Accumulated depreciation—equipment	471.7
Allowance for doubtful accounts	14.8
Bad debts expense	43.6
Cash	417.1
Cost of goods sold	353.0
Equipment	924.2

Interest revenue	10.7
Merchandise inventory	336.5
Notes receivable—due in 2012	51.2
Notes receivable—due in 2015	101.9
Prepaid expenses and deposits	19.3
Sales	2,823.8
Sales discounts	18.5
Short-term investments	224.6
Supplies	15.9
Unearned sales revenue	40.2

Additional information:

1. On November 30, 2010, Accounts Receivable was $271.7 thousand and the Allowance for Doubtful Accounts was $13.6 thousand.
2. The receivables turnover was 9.1 the previous year.

Instructions

(a) Prepare the assets section of the balance sheet.
(b) Calculate the receivables turnover and average collection period. Compare these results with the previous year's results and comment on any trends.

Taking It Further What other information should Norlandia Saga consider when analyzing its receivables turnover and average collection period?

P8–12B Presented here is selected financial information from the 2008 financial statements of Nike (in U.S. millions) and Adidas (in Euro millions):

Calculate and interpret ratios. (SO 4) AN

	Nike	Adidas
Sales	$18,627.0	€10,794
Allowance for doubtful accounts, Jan. 1	71.5	111
Allowance for doubtful accounts, Dec. 31	78.4	119
Accounts receivable balance (net), Jan. 1	2,494.7	1,459
Accounts receivable balance (net), Dec. 31	2,795.3	1,624

Instructions

Calculate the receivables turnover and average collection period for both companies and compare the two companies. Comment on the difference in the two companies' collection experiences.

Taking It Further Adidas' financial statements are prepared using Euros, while Nike uses U.S. dollars. How does this affect our ability to compare sales between the two companies? Receivables turnover and collection period?

P8–13B The following ratios are available for Western Roofing:

Evaluate liquidity. (SO 4) AN

	2011	2010	2009
Current ratio	1.6 to 1	2.0 to 1	1.9 to 1
Acid-test ratio	0.8 to 1	1.3 to 1	1.2 to 1
Receivables turnover	10.6 times	8.9 times	9.0 times
Inventory turnover	7.3 times	7.6 times	7.5 times

Instructions

(a) Calculate the collection period, days sales in inventory, and operating cycle for each year.
(b) Has Western Roofing's liquidity improved or weakened over the three-year period? Explain.

Taking It Further At the beginning of 2011, the owner of Western Roofing decided to start offering customers a sales discount for early payment. The terms of credit sales were changed from n/30 to 2/10, n/30. Evaluate this decision.

Continuing Cookie Chronicle

(*Note:* This is a continuation of the Cookie Chronicle from Chapters 1 through 7.)

Natalie has been approached by one of her friends, Curtis Lesperance. Curtis runs a coffee shop where he sells specialty coffees, and prepares and sells muffins and cookies. He is very anxious to buy one of Natalie's fine European mixers because he would then be able to prepare larger batches of muffins and cookies. Curtis, however, cannot afford to pay for the mixer for at least 30 days. He has asked Natalie if she would be willing to sell him the mixer on credit.

Natalie comes to you for advice and asks the following questions:

1. Curtis has given me a set of his most recent financial statements. What calculations should I do with the data from these statements and what questions should I ask him after I have analyzed the statements? How will this information help me decide if I should extend credit to Curtis?
2. Is there another alternative than extending credit to Curtis for 30 days?
3. If, instead of extending credit to Curtis for 30 days, I have Curtis sign a promissory note and he is unable to pay at the end of the agreement term, will having that signed promissory note really make any difference?
4. I am thinking seriously about being able to have my customers use credit cards. What are some of the advantages and disadvantages of letting my customers pay by credit card? Are there differences in the types of credit cards that my customers can use?

The following transactions occur in June and July 2011:

June 1	After much thought, Natalie sells a mixer to Curtis for $1,050 (the cost of the mixer is $551). Curtis signs a two-month, 8.5% promissory note. Curtis can repay the note at any time before the due date with interest accruing to the date of payment.
30	Curtis calls Natalie. He expects to pay the amount outstanding in the next week or so.
July 15	Natalie receives a cheque from Curtis in payment of his balance owing plus interest that has accrued.

Instructions

(a) Answer Natalie's questions.
(b) Prepare journal entries for the transactions that occurred in June and July.

BROADENING YOUR PERSPECTIVE

Financial Reporting and Analysis

Financial Reporting Problem

BYP8–1 The receivables turnover, collection period, and operating cycle for The Forzani Group Ltd. were calculated in this chapter, based on the company's financial statements for the 2009 fiscal year. These consolidated financial statements are presented in Appendix A.

Instructions

(a) Calculate Forzani's receivables turnover, collection period, and operating cycle for the 2008 fiscal year. At the end of the company's 2007 fiscal year, it reported accounts receivable of $65,543 thousand and inventory of $302,207 thousand. You will have to use the net realizable value reported for accounts receivable for 2007 and 2008 because the company did not disclose the allowance amount prior to 2009 (see note 16 (c) to the 2009 financial statements).

(b) Comment on any significant differences you observe between the ratios for 2009 (as calculated in the chapter) and 2008 (as calculated by you above).

(c) In Note 1 to the 2009 financial statements, Forzani describes itself as "Canada's largest retailer of sporting goods." Large retailers sell goods to the general public and would not normally allow you to negotiate credit terms with them when you buy a pair of running shoes. How do you think their receivables arise? Would they be from Visa or MasterCard sales? Could they be from Forzani's own credit card (if it issues its own)? How can you find this out? Which types of sales described in note 2 (h) and note 16 (c) are most likely to be transacted "on account"?

(d) Note 16 (c) to the 2009 financial statements discusses credit risks associated with receivables. Why do you think they include a breakdown of the aging of overdue accounts and the balance of the allowance for doubtful accounts?

(e) A substantial portion of receivables is shown to be overdue, by even more than 60 days. This seems inconsistent with the textbook's calculation of the average collection period as much less than 60 days. The figures provided by management on page 46 of the "Management's Discussion and Analysis" section in the 2009 Annual Report show an average collection period of 121 days—much more than 60 days. The difference appears to be due to the text using all sales and not just "credit" sales (sales "on account"). Given management's figure for average receivables days outstanding for 2009, what percentage of "wholesale" revenues reported in the statement of operations appear to have been transacted "on account"?

Interpreting Financial Statements

BYP8–2 Suncor Energy Inc. reported the following information (in millions) in its financial statements for the fiscal years 2006 through 2008:

	2008	2007	2006
Operating revenues (assume all credit)	$18,336	$15,020	$13,798
Cash and cash equivalents	660	569	521
Accounts receivable (gross)	1,584	1,441	1,054
Allowance for doubtful accounts	4	3	4
Inventories	909	1012	589
Other current assets	88	141	142
Total current liabilities	3,529	3,156	2,158

Additional detail about Suncor's receivables includes the following:

The company had a securitization program in place to sell to a third party, on a revolving, fully serviced, and limited recourse basis, up to $170 million of accounts receivable having a maturity of 45 days or less. As at December 31, 2008, no outstanding accounts receivable had been sold under the program and the program had been allowed to expire.

Industry averages are as follows: current ratio, 1.3:1; acid-test ratio, 0.8:1; receivables turnover, 10.6 times; and average collection period, 34 days.

Instructions

(a) Calculate the current ratios, acid-test ratios, receivables turnover ratios, and average collection periods for fiscal 2008 and 2007. Comment on Suncor's liquidity for each of the years and compare it with that of the industry.

(b) In 2008, Suncor's dollar amount of its allowance for doubtful accounts was the same as it was in 2006. Comment on the relevance of this as a percentage of accounts receivable.
(c) What are the advantages of having a securitization program to sell accounts receivable? Why might Suncor have allowed its securitization program to expire?

Critical Thinking

Collaborative Learning Activity

Note to instructor: Additional instructions and material for this group activity can be found on the Instructor Resource Site.

WILEY PLUS
Working in Groups

BYP8–3 In this group activity, you will work in pairs to review the following two approaches to estimate bad debts:

1. Percentage of sales
2. Percentage of receivables

Instructions

(a) In your pair, each select one of the above approaches. Temporarily leave your partner and join the "expert" group for that approach.
(b) In the "expert" group, use the handout given to you by your instructor and discuss your approach. Ensure that each group member thoroughly understands it.
(c) Return to your partner and explain your approach.
(d) You may be asked by your instructor to write a short quiz on this topic.

Communication Activity

WILEY PLUS
Writing Handbook

BYP8–4 Toys for Big Boys sells snowmobiles, personal watercraft, ATVs, and the like. Recently, the credit manager of Toys for Big Boys retired. The sales staff threw him a big retirement party—they were glad to see him go because they felt his credit policies restricted their selling ability. The sales staff convinced management that there was no need to replace the credit manager since they could handle this responsibility in addition to their sales positions.

Management was thrilled at year end when sales doubled. However, accounts receivable quadrupled and cash flow halved. The company's average collection period increased from 30 days to 120 days.

Instructions

In a memo to management, explain the financial impact of allowing the sales staff to manage the credit function. Has the business assumed any additional credit risk? What would you recommend the company do to better manage its increasing accounts receivable?

Ethics Case

BYP8–5 The controller of Proust Company has completed draft financial statements for the year just ended and is reviewing them with the president. As part of the review, he has summarized an aging schedule showing the basis of estimating uncollectible accounts using the following percentages: 0–30 days, 5%; 31–60 days, 10%; 61–90 days, 30%; 91–120 days, 50%; and over 120 days, 80%. The president of the company, Suzanne Bros, is nervous because the bank expects the company to sustain a growth rate for profit of at least 5% each year over the next two years—the remaining term of its bank loan. The profit growth for the past year was much more than 5% because of certain special orders with high margins, but those orders will not be repeated next year, so it will be very hard to achieve even the same profit next year, and even more difficult to grow it another 5%. It would be easier to show an increase next year if the past year's reported profit had been a little lower. President Bros recalls from her college accounting course that bad debts expense is based on certain estimates subject to judgement. She suggests that the controller increase the estimate percentages, which will increase the amount of the required bad debts expense adjustment and therefore lower profit for last year so that it will be easier to show a better growth rate next year.

WILEY PLUS
Ethics in Accounting

Instructions

(a) Who are the stakeholders in this case?
(b) Does the president's request create an ethical dilemma for the controller?
(c) Should the controller be concerned with Proust Company's reported profit growth rate in estimating the allowance? Explain your answer.

"All About You" Activity

BYP8–6 In the "All About You" feature, you learned about interest rates charged on credit cards and some of the advantages and disadvantages of credit cards. To get the most from your credit card and to save money, you need to understand the features of your credit card and how interest is charged on credit cards.

Instructions

Go to the Financial Consumer Agency of Canada's publication "Credit Cards and You: Getting the Most from Your Credit Card" at **http://www.fcac-acfc.gc.ca/eng/publications/CreditCardsYou/PDFs/GetMost-eng.pdf** and answer the following questions:

(a) Identify any benefits and risks of credit cards that were not previously identified in the answer to the feature's question.
(b) Credit cards provide interest-free loans on the purchase of goods, as long as you pay your bill in full by the end of the grace period. What is the grace period? The Canadian government brought in regulations that require a minimum grace period of 21 days. Assuming you used a credit card to purchase your textbooks on September 15, your statement date is October 7 and the grace period is 21 days. How many days is the interest-free period?
(c) There is no interest-free period on cash advances or balance transfers on credit cards. What is a cash advance? What is a balance transfer?
(d) Suppose you have one month left in the semester and you take a $1,000 cash advance on your credit card on April 1 to cover your living expenses until you get your first paycheque from your summer job on May 15. The interest rate on your credit card is 19%. Assuming that is the only charge on your credit card, calculate the interest you will be charged assuming you pay your bill in full on May 15. (*Hint:* Go to page 12 of the above publication on the website to see how interest is calculated.)

(e) Go to the Financial Consumer Agency of Canada's interactive tool "Credit Card Payment Calculator." (*Hint:* To find the Credit Card Payment Calculator, go to http://www.fcac-acfc.gc.ca/ and click on "For Consumers," then click on "Interactive Tools," and then click on the credit card icon.)

1. For option A, assume you have a credit card balance of $1,000, the interest rate is 19%, and the minimum monthly payment is $10 or 3%, whichever is greater.
2. For option B, assume the same information as in part 1, but you make an additional monthly payment of $10.
3. For option C assume the same information as in part 1, but you make a monthly payment of $100.

For each of the options a, b, and c, calculate how long it will take to pay off the credit card, assuming there are no additional purchases made, and calculate the total amount of interest paid.

ANSWERS TO CHAPTER QUESTIONS

Answers to Accounting in Action Insight Questions

All About You Insight, p. 439

Q: Should you use credit cards or not?

A: Credit cards can make your life easier, as long as they are used properly. They certainly have advantages: (1) they provide interest-free loans on the purchase of goods, as long as you pay your bill in full by the end of the grace period; (2) monthly credit card statements provide detailed records of all transactions, payments, and returned merchandise; and (3) many transactions, such as Internet purchases, are difficult or impossible to carry out without a credit card.

However, credit cards also have disadvantages: (1) if you do not pay your bill in full every month, expect to pay a very high interest rate on the unpaid balance; (2) they are so easy to use that you might start buying items without thinking about whether you really need them—and can afford them; and (3) credit cards can be stolen, which might damage your credit rating.

Across the Organization Insight, p. 446

Q: Why would a business choose to use a collection agency to follow up on late accounts instead of pursuing them internally?

A: Managers need to make decisions about the best way to use their staff. Many companies, particularly small ones, do not have enough staff to pursue uncollectible accounts. Collection agencies are specialists at following up on late accounts. They use methods that many companies do not have the expertise or the time to use and thus often collect accounts that a company wasn't able to collect. Even though the collection agency may keep a substantial portion of the accounts it collects, for companies that lack the expertise and staff to do so, it is better to receive part of the account than none of it.

Business Insight, p. 455

Q: What was the benefit to the banks of securitizing their mortgage receivables?
A: By securitizing their mortgages receivable, banks were able to raise cash at a time when credit was very tight. This allowed banks to keep their lending rates low and to continue to extend credit to people who were interested in purchasing houses at a time when prices were depressed.

Answer to Forzani Review It Question 1, p. 439

In Note 2 (h) on revenue recognition, The Forzani Group Ltd. states that it earns revenue on both sales to customers in stores and sales to, and service fees from, franchise stores and others. Forzani also states that revenue is recognized on sales to franchise stores at the time of shipment. These sales to franchise stores are probably on credit. Forzani would therefore record a receivable from the franchise store when the merchandise is shipped.

Answers to Self-Study Questions

1. b 2. d 3. d 4. c 5. d 6. a 7. d 8. a 9. c 10. b

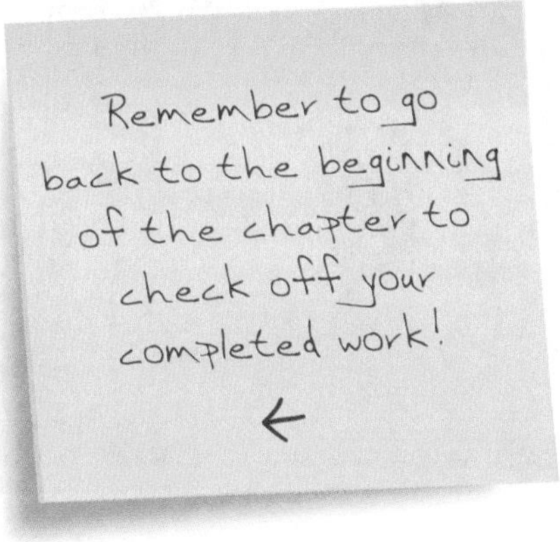
Remember to go
back to the beginning
of the chapter to
check off your
completed work!

CHAPTER 9
LONG-LIVED ASSETS

THE NAVIGATOR

- ☐ Understand *Concepts for Review*
- ☐ Read *Feature Story*
- ☐ Scan *Study Objectives*
- ☐ Read *Chapter Preview*
- ☐ Read text and answer *Before You Go On*
- ☐ Work *Demonstration Problems*
- ☐ Review *Summary of Study Objectives*
- ☐ Answer *Self-Study Questions*
- ☐ Complete assignments

CONCEPTS FOR REVIEW:

Before studying this chapter, you should understand or, if necessary, review:

a. Expense recognition criteria (Ch. 3, pp. 120–121).

b. What depreciation is, and how to make adjustments for it. (Ch. 3, pp. 125–126).

c. Non-current assets and the classified balance sheet (Ch. 4, pp. 194–195).

MEASURING VALUE: WHAT'S A HISTORIC BUILDING WORTH?

Montreal, Que.—For a college or university, the buildings where classes and other activities take place are some of its most important assets. Look around the campus of your own school. Where did the money for these buildings come from and what was their cost? Who pays to maintain them and how is the cost of repairs and maintenance recorded? How did the college choose its method of depreciation? And how much are the buildings worth?

For Dawson College in Montreal, the first of these questions is easy. The provincial government financed the 1982 purchase of its current building, the historic former Mother House of the Congrégation de Notre-Dame, at a cost of $12.2 million. With this purchase and subsequent renovations and expansions, Dawson's facilities included the former Mother House and the college's Selby pavilion from 1988 until 1997, when they were consolidated under one roof at the former Mother House.

As for the second question, again, the provincial government pays for most of Dawson's expenses. Established in 1969 as the first English-language institution in Quebec's network of CEGEPs (which are the equivalents of Grades 12 and 13), Dawson receives an annual allocation of about $1.5 million to cover any needed repairs or renovations, explains controller Guy Veilleux. It has also received lump sums from the government for specific projects, such as the $37-million renovations done after the building was purchased, a $10-million expansion in 1990–91, another $23-million expansion that took place from 1995 to 1997, and yet another costing $10 million in 2006–07. In addition, the government allocates specific funds for equipment purchases and renovations required when it revises programs.

How the cost of the buildings should be allocated or depreciated has been a complicated problem. "For years, there was no depreciation of buildings or equipment in our books," says Mr. Veilleux. Until the early 2000s, special accounting principles for government entities did not require accrual accounting. When the public sector accounting principles changed to require accrual accounting, the government and other public institutions began recognizing the depreciation of their physical assets.

In 2000–01, the government instructed its CEGEPs to calculate depreciation retroactively from 1995–96 using the diminishing-balance method. By 2011, Dawson's building will have been depreciated to about 33% of its book value, using a 3% depreciation rate.

How much the buildings are worth now is the trickiest question. "The value of the building is not the cost. The value of the building that we show on the financial statements is the municipal value for 1996 plus the cost of the acquisitions since then, and less the accumulated depreciation over the years," says Mr. Veilleux. However, since the former Mother House is a designated heritage site, some would deem it to be priceless.

The Navigator

STUDY OBJECTIVES:

After studying this chapter, you should be able to:

1. Determine the cost of property, plant, and equipment.
2. Explain and calculate depreciation.
3. Explain the factors that cause changes in periodic depreciation and calculate revisions.
4. Account for the disposal of property, plant, and equipment.
5. Calculate and record depreciation of natural resources.
6. Identify the basic accounting issues for intangible assets and goodwill.
7. Illustrate the reporting and analysis of long-lived assets.

The Navigator

PREVIEW OF CHAPTER 9

For organizations such as Dawson College, making the right decisions about long-lived assets is critical because these assets represent huge investments. Organizations must make decisions about what assets to acquire, how to account for them, and when to dispose of them.

In this chapter, we address these and other issues surrounding long-lived assets. Our discussions will focus on three types of long-lived assets: (1) property, plant, and equipment; (2) natural resources; and (3) intangible assets.

The chapter is organized as follows:

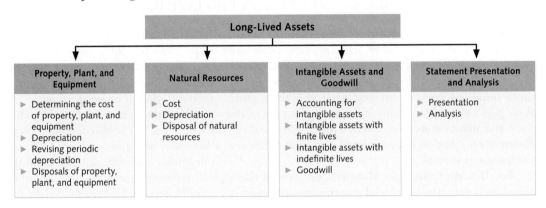

Long-Lived Assets

Property, Plant, and Equipment
- Determining the cost of property, plant, and equipment
- Depreciation
- Revising periodic depreciation
- Disposals of property, plant, and equipment

Natural Resources
- Cost
- Depreciation
- Disposal of natural resources

Intangible Assets and Goodwill
- Accounting for intangible assets
- Intangible assets with finite lives
- Intangible assets with indefinite lives
- Goodwill

Statement Presentation and Analysis
- Presentation
- Analysis

Property, Plant, and Equipment

Alternative terminology Property, plant, and equipment are also commonly known as *fixed assets*; *land, building, and equipment*; or *capital assets*.

Property, plant, and equipment are long-lived assets that the company owns and uses for the production and sale of goods or services to consumers. They have three characteristics. They (1) have a physical substance (a definite size and shape), (2) are used in the operations of the business, and (3) are not intended for sale to customers. An item of property, plant, and equipment is recognized (recorded) as an asset if it is probable that the company will receive future economic benefits from the item.

In the following sections, we will learn about determining the cost of property, plant, and equipment; the depreciation of property, plant, and equipment; and the accounting for disposals of property, plant, and equipment.

Determining the Cost of Property, Plant, and Equipment

STUDY OBJECTIVE 1

Determine the cost of property, plant, and equipment.

The cost of an item of property, plant, and equipment includes the following:

1. The purchase price, plus any non-refundable taxes, less any discounts or rebates
2. The expenditures necessary to bring the asset to the location and condition necessary to make it ready for its intended use

If there are obligations to dismantle, remove, or restore the asset when it is retired, an initial estimate of these costs is also included in the cost of the long-lived asset. These are known as **asset retirement costs**. Accounting for these costs can be complex and we will leave that discussion to a future accounting course. But you should be aware that the cost of some property, plant, and equipment items includes the cost of retiring the asset. For simplicity, we will assume asset retirement costs are equal to zero in the examples in this text.

Alternative terminology Asset retirement costs are also called *decommissioning costs*.

All of these costs are capitalized (recorded as property, plant, and equipment), rather than expensed, if it is probable that the company will receive an economic benefit in the future from the asset. Determining which costs to include in a long-lived asset account and which costs not to include is very important. Costs that benefit only the current period are expensed. Such costs are called **operating expenditures**. Costs that benefit future periods are included in a long-lived asset account. These costs are called **capital expenditures**.

For example, the cost to purchase an asset is recorded as a capital expenditure, because the asset will benefit future periods. In addition, the insurance paid on the same asset as it is shipped to the company should also be capitalized because the insurance during transit benefits more than just the current period. It is considered a necessary expenditure to get the asset to its required location and ready for use.

Subsequent to acquisition, the same distinction exists between capital and operating expenditures. For example, once the asset is in use, insurance benefits only the current period and is treated as an expense. But major expenditures that are incurred once the asset is in use that increase the life of the asset or its productivity are capitalized. We will discuss expenditures subsequent to acquisition in more depth later in the chapter.

Property, plant, and equipment are often subdivided into four classes:

1. Land, such as a building site
2. Land improvements, such as driveways, parking lots, fences, and underground sprinkler systems
3. Buildings, such as stores, offices, factories, and warehouses
4. Equipment, such as store checkout counters, cash registers, coolers, office furniture, factory machinery, and delivery equipment

Determining the cost of each of the major classes of property, plant, and equipment is explained in the following sections.

Land

The cost of land includes (1) the purchase price, (2) closing costs such as surveying and legal fees, and (3) the costs of preparing the land for its intended use, such as the removal of old buildings, clearing, draining, filling, and grading. All of these costs (less any proceeds from salvaged materials) are debited to the Land account.

To illustrate, assume that the Budovitch Manufacturing Company purchases real estate for $100,000 cash. The property contained an old warehouse that is removed at a net cost of $6,000 ($7,500 to remove it less $1,500 received for materials from the warehouse that were salvaged and later sold). Additional expenditures include the legal fee of $3,000. The cost of the land is $109,000, calculated as follows:

Land	
Cash price of property	$100,000
Net cost of removing warehouse ($7,500 – $1,500)	6,000
Legal fee	3,000
Cost of land	$109,000

When recording the acquisition, Land is debited for $109,000 and Cash is credited for $109,000 (assuming the costs were paid in cash). Land is a unique long-lived asset. Its cost is not depreciated—allocated over its useful life—because land has an unlimited useful life.

Land Improvements

Land improvements are structural additions made to land, such as driveways, sidewalks, fences, and parking lots. Land improvements, unlike land, decline in service potential over time, and require maintenance and replacement. Because of this, land improvements are recorded separately from land and are depreciated over their useful lives.

Many students confuse the cost to get land ready for its intended use with land improvements. They think, for example, that removing an old building or grading the land is "improving" the land, and thus incorrectly reason that these costs should be considered land improvements. When classifying costs, it is important to remember that one-time costs required for getting the land ready to use are always charged to the Land account, not the Land Improvement account.

Buildings

All costs that are directly related to the purchase or construction of a building are debited to the Buildings account. When a building is purchased, these costs include the purchase price and closing costs (e.g., legal fees). The costs of making a building ready to be used as intended can include expenditures for remodelling, and for replacing or repairing the roof, floors, electrical wiring, and plumbing. These costs are also debited to Buildings.

When a new building is built, cost includes the contract price plus payments for architects' fees, building permits, and excavation costs. The interest costs of financing the construction project are also included in the asset's cost when a significant amount of time is needed to get the building ready to be used. In these circumstances, interest costs are considered to be as necessary as materials and labour are. Only the interest costs that occur during the construction period are included, however. After construction is finished, future interest payments on funds that were borrowed to finance the cost of the constructed building are debited to Interest Expense.

Equipment

The "equipment" classification is a broad one that can include delivery equipment, office equipment, machinery, vehicles, furniture and fixtures, and other similar assets. The cost of these assets includes the purchase price; freight charges and insurance during transit that are paid by the purchaser; and the costs of assembling, installing, and testing the equipment. These costs are treated as capital expenditures because they benefit future periods.

Such annual costs as motor vehicle licences and insurance on company trucks and cars are treated as operating expenditures because they are recurring expenditures that do not benefit future periods.

To illustrate, assume that 1 Stop Florists purchases a used delivery truck on January 1, 2011, for $24,500 cash. Related expenditures include painting and lettering, $500; a motor vehicle licence, $80; and a one-year insurance policy, $2,600. The cost of the delivery truck is $25,000, calculated as follows:

Delivery Truck	
Cash price	$24,500
Painting and lettering	500
Cost of delivery truck	$25,000

The cost of the motor vehicle licence is recorded as an expense and the cost of the insurance policy is recorded as a prepaid asset. The entry to record the purchase of the truck and related expenditures, assuming they were all paid for in cash, is as follows:

A	=	L	+	OE
+25,000				−80
+2,600				
−27,680				

Cash flows: −27,680

Jan. 1	Delivery Truck	25,000	
	Licence Expense	80	
	Prepaid Insurance	2,600	
	Cash		27,680
	To record purchase of delivery truck and related expenditures.		

Allocating Cost to Multiple Assets and Significant Components

Alternative terminology A basket purchase is also known as a *lump sum purchase*.

Multiple Assets. Property, plant, and equipment are often purchased together for a single price. This is known as a **basket purchase**. We need to know the cost of each individual asset in order to journalize the purchase, and later calculate the depreciation of each asset. When a basket purchase occurs, we determine individual costs by allocating the total price paid for the group of assets to each individual asset based on its relative fair value.

To illustrate, assume Sega Company acquired a building and a parcel of land on July 31 for $300,000, paying $50,000 cash and incurring a mortgage payable for the balance. The land was recently appraised at $120,000. The building was appraised at $200,000. The $300,000 cost should be allocated based on fair values (i.e., appraised values), as shown in Illustration 9-1.

	Fair value	Allocated Percentage	Allocated Cost
Land	$120,000	37.5% ($120,000 ÷ $320,000)	$112,500 ($300,000 × 37.5%)
Building	200,000	62.5% ($200,000 ÷ $320,000)	187,500 ($300,000 × 62.5%)
Totals	$320,000	100.0%	$300,000

Illustration 9-1

Allocating cost in a basket purchase

The journal entry to record this purchase is as follows:

July 31	Land	112,500	
	Building	187,500	
	Cash		50,000
	Mortgage Payable		250,000
	To record purchase of land and building, with costs allocated based on appraised values of $120,000 and $200,000, respectively.		

A	=	L	+	OE
+112,500		+250,000		
+187,500				
−50,000				

Cash flows: −50,000

Significant Components. When an item of property, plant, and equipment includes components with a cost that is significant relative to its total cost, the cost of the item must be allocated to its different components. This is necessary so that each component can be depreciated separately over the different useful lives or possibly by using different depreciation methods. For example, it may be appropriate to depreciate elements such as aircraft engines separately from the rest of the aircraft instead of doing one depreciation calculation for the entire aircraft. The SAS Group, an airline in Europe, depreciates its aircraft over an estimated useful life of 20 years and its engine components over an estimated useful life of 8 years. This is known as **component depreciation.**

Separating the cost of the entire asset into its significant components can be accomplished using the same process to allocate cost illustrated above for a basket purchase. The asset's total cost would be allocated to the significant components based on the components' relative fair values. The calculations would be similar to those in Illustration 9-1.

Component accounting is a new requirement for Canadian companies, resulting from the change to International Financial Reporting Standards (IFRS). Implementing it will likely require more detailed accounting records than many Canadian companies may have maintained under Canadian accounting standards. For simplicity, we will assume in this text that all of the components of the depreciable asset have the same useful life, and we will depreciate assets as a whole.

BEFORE YOU GO ON . . .

Review It

1. What are the three characteristics of property, plant, and equipment?
2. What types of costs are capitalized for property, plant, and equipment?
3. Explain the difference between operating and capital expenditures.
4. Under what circumstances is it necessary to divide up the cost among different assets or components of an asset?
5. What is the cost of each type of capital asset that The Forzani Group Ltd. reports in Note 5 to its balance sheet? The answer to this question is at the end of the chapter.

Do It

Assume that factory machinery is purchased on November 6 for $10,000 cash and a $40,000 note payable. Related cash expenditures include insurance during shipping, $500; the annual insurance policy, $750; and installation and testing, $1,000. Prepare the journal entry to record these expenditures.

Action Plan

- Capitalize expenditures that are made to get the machinery ready for its intended use.
- Expense operating expenditures that benefit only the current period, or are recurring costs.

Solution

Factory Machinery	
Purchase price	$50,000
Insurance during shipping	500
Installation and testing	1,000
Cost of machinery	$51,500

The entry to record the purchase and related expenditures is:

Nov. 6	Factory Machinery	51,500	
	Prepaid Insurance	750	
	Cash ($10,000 + $500 + $750 + $1,000)		12,250
	Note Payable		40,000
	To record purchase of factory machinery and related expenditures.		

The Navigator

Related exercise material: BE9–1, BE9–2, BE9–3, BE9–4, and E9–1.

Depreciation

STUDY OBJECTIVE 2

Explain and calculate depreciation.

Under IFRS, companies have two models they can choose between to account for their property, plant, and equipment: the cost model or the revaluation model. The cost model is by far the more commonly used method, and is the method Canadian companies used prior to IFRS. The cost model is also required under Canadian GAAP for Private Enterprises.

The **cost model** records property, plant, and equipment at cost of acquisition. After acquisition, depreciation is recorded each period and the assets are carried at cost less accumulated depreciation. We will cover the cost model in the following sections of the chapter and refer briefly to the revaluation model in a later section.

As we learned in Chapter 3, depreciation is the systematic allocation of the cost of a long-lived asset, such as property, plant, and equipment, over the asset's useful life. The cost is allocated to expense over the asset's useful life because the asset is used to help generate revenue over that period of time. Assets are depreciated over their useful lives even if the use of the asset is not directly related to earning revenue.

You will recall that depreciation is recorded through an adjusting journal entry that debits Depreciation Expense and credits Accumulated Depreciation. Depreciation expense is an operating expense on the income statement. Accumulated depreciation appears on the balance sheet as a contra account to the related asset account. This contra asset account is similar in purpose to the one used in Chapter 8 for the allowance for doubtful accounts. Both contra accounts reduce assets to their carrying values: *net realizable value* for accounts receivable, and *carrying amount* for property, plant, and equipment.

It is important to understand that depreciation is a process of cost allocation, not a process of determining an asset's real value. Illustration 9-2 shows this. Under the cost model, an increase in an asset's fair value is not relevant because property, plant, and equipment are not for resale. (Fair values are only relevant if an impairment loss has occurred, which we will discuss later in the chapter.) As a result, the carrying amount of property, plant, or equipment (cost less accumulated depreciation) may be very different from its fair value. We saw this in our feature story, where Dawson College's former Mother House building has a carrying amount much lower than its fair value.

Illustration 9-2

Depreciation as an allocation concept

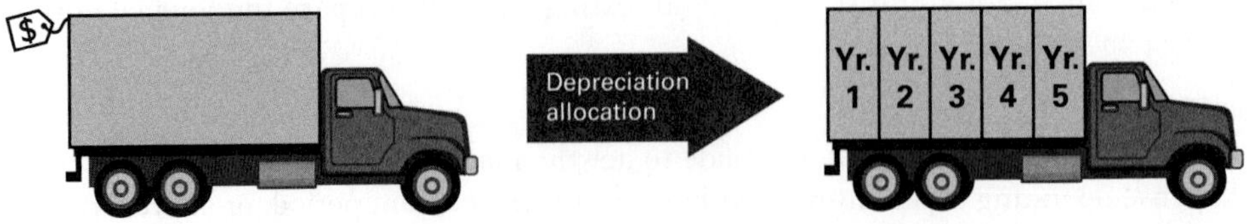

It is also important to understand that depreciation does not result in the accumulation of cash to replace the asset. The balance in Accumulated Depreciation only represents the total amount of the asset's cost that has been allocated to expense so far. It is not a cash fund. Cash is neither increased nor decreased by the adjusting entry to record depreciation.

During a depreciable asset's useful life, its revenue-producing ability declines because of physical factors such as wear and tear, and economic factors such as obsolescence. For example, a company may replace a truck because it is physically worn out. On the other hand, companies replace computers long before they are physically worn out because improvements in hardware and software have made the old computer obsolete.

You will recall from Chapter 4 that we can expect to see companies using a variety of terms as Canadian public companies start following IFRS. Under IFRS, it is typical to use the term "depreciation" for property, plant, and equipment, and "amortization" for intangible assets. Under Canadian GAAP for Private Enterprises it is acceptable to use either "amortization" or "depreciation" when allocating the cost of property, plant, and equipment. We have followed the IFRS practice in this textbook. We have also adopted the IFRS practice of using the term "carrying amount" instead of "book value." Both of these terms are acceptable under Canadian accounting standards. We will point out a number of other terminology choices related to long-lived assets in this chapter.

Factors in Calculating Depreciation

In Chapter 3, we learned that depreciation expense was calculated by dividing the cost of a depreciable asset by its useful life. At that time, we assumed the asset's residual value was zero. In this chapter, we will now include a residual value when calculating depreciation. Consequently, there are now three factors that affect the calculation of depreciation:

1. Cost. The factors that affect the cost of a depreciable asset were explained earlier in this chapter. Remember that the cost of property, plant, and equipment includes the purchase price plus all costs necessary to get the asset ready for use. We also saw that cost includes an initial estimate of the retirement costs, if there are any.
2. Useful life. **Useful life** is (a) the period of time over which an asset is expected to be available for use or (b) the number of units of production (such as machine hours) or units of output that are expected to be obtained from an asset. Useful life is an estimate based on such factors as the asset's intended use, its expected need for repair and maintenance, and how vulnerable it is to wearing out or becoming obsolete. The company's past experience with similar assets often helps in estimating the expected useful life.
3. Residual value. **Residual value** is the estimated amount that a company would currently obtain from disposing of the asset if the asset were already as old as it will be, and in the condition it is expected to be in, at the end of its useful life. Residual value is not depreciated, since the amount is expected to be recovered at the end of the asset's useful life.

Alternative terminology Residual value is sometimes called *salvage value*.

Illustration 9-3 summarizes these three factors.

Illustration 9-3
Three factors in calculating depreciation

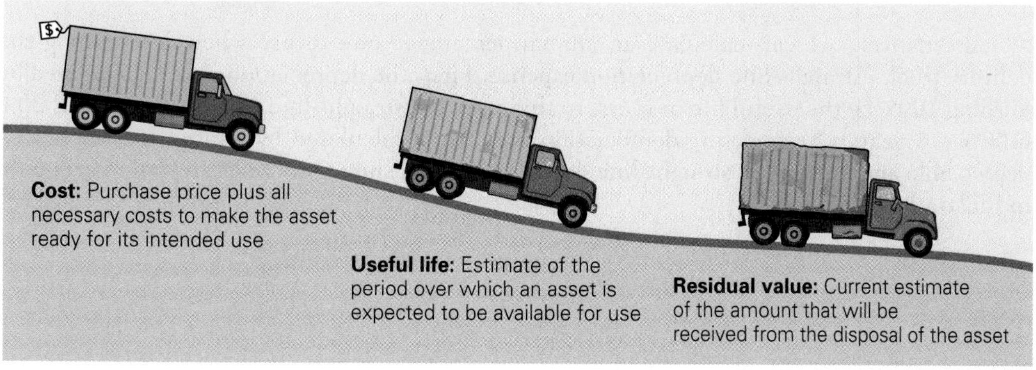

$
Cost: Purchase price plus all necessary costs to make the asset ready for its intended use
Useful life: Estimate of the period over which an asset is expected to be available for use
Residual value: Current estimate of the amount that will be received from the disposal of the asset

Depreciation Methods

Depreciation is generally calculated using one of the following methods:

1. Straight-line
2. Diminishing-balance
3. Units-of-production

How do companies choose which of the three depreciation methods to use? Management must choose the method that best matches the estimated pattern in which the asset's future economic benefits are expected to be consumed. The depreciation method must be reviewed at least once a year. If the expected pattern of consumption of the future economic benefits has changed, the depreciation method must be changed. The estimated useful life and residual values must also be reviewed each year.

However, changing methods makes it more difficult to compare the results of one year with another, and so the change must be justifiable. We will discuss how to account for changes in depreciation methods later in the chapter.

To learn how to calculate the three depreciation methods and to compare them, we will use the following data for the small delivery truck bought by 1 Stop Florists on January 1, 2011:

Cost (as shown on page 492)	$ 25,000
Estimated residual value	$2,000
Estimated useful life (in years)	5
Estimated useful life (in kilometres)	200,000

Straight-Line. The straight-line method was first defined in Chapter 3. We will define it again here, this time including the impact of a residual value on the calculation. The **straight-line method** of calculating depreciation has two steps. First, residual value is deducted from the asset's cost to determine an asset's **depreciable amount**—the total amount that can be depreciated. Second, the depreciable amount is divided by the asset's useful life to calculate the annual depreciation expense.

The depreciation expense will be the same for each year of the asset's useful life if the cost, the useful life, and the residual value do not change. The calculation of depreciation expense in the first year for 1 Stop Florists' delivery truck is shown in Illustration 9-4.

Illustration 9-4

Formula for straight-line method

Cost	−	Residual Value	=	Depreciable Amount
$25,000	−	$2,000	=	$23,000
Depreciable Amount	÷	Estimated Useful Life	=	Annual Depreciation Expense
$23,000	÷	5 years	=	$4,600

Alternatively, we can calculate an annual percentage rate to use when determining the delivery truck's straight-line depreciation expense. First, the depreciation rate is calculated by dividing 100% by the useful life in years. In this case, the straight-line depreciation rate is 20% (100% ÷ 5 years). Second, the depreciation expense is calculated by multiplying the asset's depreciable amount by the straight-line depreciation rate shown in the depreciation schedule in Illustration 9-5.

Illustration 9-5

Straight-line depreciation schedule

1 STOP FLORISTS Straight-Line Depreciation Schedule								
							End of Year	
Year	Depreciable Amount	×	Depreciation Rate	=	Depreciation Expense		Accumulated Depreciation	Carrying Amount
								$25,000
2011	$23,000		20%		$ 4,600		$ 4,600	20,400
2012	23,000		20%		4,600		9,200	15,800
2013	23,000		20%		4,600		13,800	11,200
2014	23,000		20%		4,600		18,400	6,600
2015	23,000		20%		4,600		23,000	2,000
					$23,000			

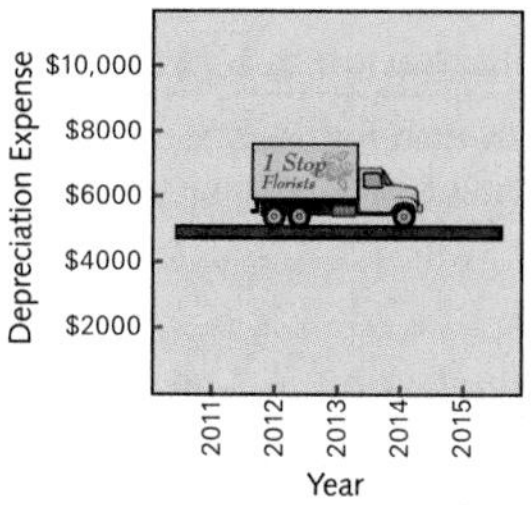

Note that the depreciation expense of $4,600 is the same each year. Also note that the column total for depreciation expense is equal to the asset's depreciable amount, and that the carrying amount at the end of the useful life is equal to the estimated $2,000 residual value.

What happens when an asset is purchased during the year, rather than on January 1 as in our example? In that case, it is necessary to pro-rate the annual depreciation for the part of the year that the asset was used. If 1 Stop Florists' delivery truck was ready to be used on April 1, 2011, the truck would be depreciated for nine months in 2011 (April through December). The depreciation for 2011 would be $3,450 ($23,000 × 20% × $^9/_{12}$). Note that depreciation is normally rounded to the nearest month. Since depreciation is an estimate, calculating it to the nearest day gives a false sense of accuracy.

To keep things simple, some companies establish a policy for partial-period depreciation, rather than calculating depreciation monthly. Companies may choose to record a full year's depreciation in the year of acquisition and none in the year of disposal. Others may record a half year's depreciation in the year of acquisition and a half year's depreciation in the year of disposal. Whatever policy is chosen for partial-year depreciation, the impact is not significant in the long run if the policy is used consistently.

The straight-line method of depreciation has been the most popular method for Canadian companies, in part because it is simple to apply. But with the change to IFRS, the depreciation method used must be consistent with the pattern in which the economic benefits from owning the asset are expected to be consumed. Therefore, it is appropriate to use the straight-line method when the asset is used quite uniformly throughout its useful life. Examples of assets that deliver their benefit primarily as a function of time include office furniture and fixtures, buildings, warehouses, and garages for motor vehicles.

Diminishing-Balance. The **diminishing-balance method** produces a decreasing annual depreciation expense over the asset's useful life. It is called the "diminishing-balance" method because the periodic depreciation is calculated based on the asset's carrying amount, which diminishes each year because accumulated depreciation increases. Annual depreciation expense is calculated by multiplying the carrying amount at the beginning of the year by the depreciation rate. The depreciation rate remains constant from year to year, but the rate is applied to a carrying amount that declines each year.

Alternative terminology The diminishing-balance method is also sometimes called the *declining-balance* method.

The carrying amount for the first year is the asset's cost, because the balance in Accumulated Depreciation at the beginning of the asset's useful life is zero. In the following years, the carrying amount is the difference between cost and the accumulated depreciation at the beginning of the year. Unlike the other depreciation methods, the diminishing-balance method does not use depreciable amount. Residual value is not used in determining the amount that the diminishing-balance depreciation rate is applied to. Residual value does, however, limit the total depreciation that can be taken. Depreciation stops when the asset's carrying amount equals its estimated residual value.

The diminishing-balance method can be applied using different rates, which results in varying speeds of depreciation. You will find rates such as one time (single), two times (double), and even three times (triple) the straight-line rate of depreciation. A depreciation rate that is often used is double the straight-line rate. This method is referred to as the double diminishing-balance method.

Helpful Hint The straight-line rate is determined by dividing 100% by the estimated useful life. In 1 Stop Florist's case, it is 100% ÷ 5 = 20%.

If 1 Stop Florists uses the double diminishing-balance method, the depreciation rate is 40% (2 × the straight-line rate of 20%). Illustration 9-6 shows the calculation of depreciation on the delivery truck for the first year.

Illustration 9-6 Formula for double diminishing-balance method

Carrying Amount at Beginning of Year	×	Straight-Line Rate × 2	=	Annual Depreciation Expense
$25,000	×	40%	=	$10,000

The depreciation schedule under this method is given in Illustration 9-7.

Illustration 9-7 Double diminishing-balance depreciation schedule

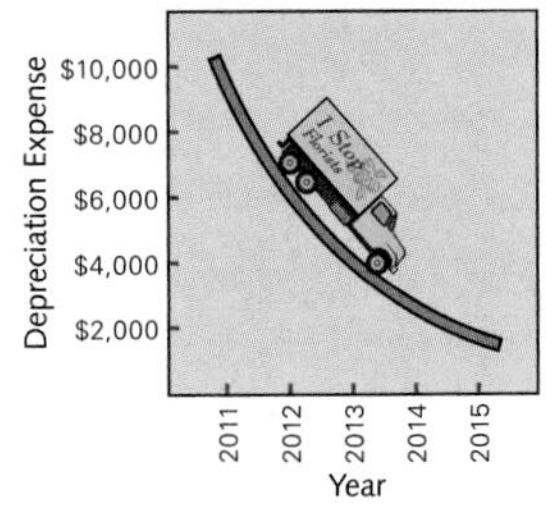

1 STOP FLORISTS
Double Diminishing-Balance Depreciation Schedule

						End of Year	
Year	Carrying Amount Beginning of Year	×	Depreciation Rate	=	Depreciation Expense	Accumulated Depreciation	Carrying Amount
							$25,000
2011	$25,000		40%		$10,000	$10,000	15,000
2012	15,000		40%		6,000	16,000	9,000
2013	9,000		40%		3,600	19,600	5,400
2014	5,400		40%		2,160	21,760	3,240
2015	3,240		40%		1,240*	23,000	2,000
					$23,000		

* The calculation of $1,296 ($3,240 × 40%) is adjusted to $1,240 so that the carrying amount will equal the residual value.

When an asset is purchased during the year, it is necessary to pro-rate the diminishing-balance depreciation in the first year, based on time. For example, if 1 Stop Florists had purchased the delivery truck on April 1, 2011, the depreciation for 2011 would be $7,500 ($25,000 × 40% × $^9/_{12}$) if depreciation is calculated monthly. The carrying amount for calculating depreciation in 2012 would then become $17,500 ($25,000 – $7,500). The depreciation for 2012 would be $7,000 ($17,500 × 40%). Future calculations would follow from these amounts until the carrying amount equalled the residual value.

Returning to Illustration 9-7, which assumes the asset was bought at the start of the year, you can see that the delivery truck is 70% depreciated ($16,000 ÷ $23,000) at the end of the second year. Under the straight-line method, it would be 40% depreciated ($9,200 ÷ $23,000) at that time.

Regardless of the method that is used, the total amount of depreciation over the life of the delivery truck is $23,000—the depreciable amount. In early years, however, diminishing-balance depreciation expense will be higher than the straight-line depreciation expense, and in later years it will be less than the straight-line expense. Methods such as the diminishing-balance method that produce higher depreciation expense in the early years than in the later years are known as *accelerated* depreciation methods.

Managers must choose the diminishing-balance, or another accelerated method, if the company receives more economic benefit in the early years of the asset's useful life than in the later years. That is, this method is used if the asset, for example, has higher revenue-producing ability in its early years, or if the asset is expected to become less useful over time. Dawson College, in the feature story, uses the diminishing-balance method of depreciation for its buildings. It uses a depreciation rate of 3%, which means that its buildings are depreciated over an average useful life of 33⅓ years.

Alternative terminology The units-of-production method is often called the *units-of-activity method.*

Units-of-Production. As indicated earlier, useful life can be expressed in ways other than time. In the **units-of-production method**, useful life is either the estimated total units of production or total expected use from the asset, not the number of years that the asset is expected to be used. The units-of-production method is ideal for equipment whose activity can be measured in units of output, such as kilometres driven or hours in use. The units-of-production method is generally not suitable for buildings or furniture, because depreciation of these assets is more a result of time than of use.

In this method, the total units of production for the entire useful life are estimated. This amount is divided into the depreciable amount (cost – residual value) to determine the depreciable amount per unit. The depreciable amount per unit is then multiplied by the actual units of production during the year to calculate the annual depreciation expense.

To illustrate, assume that the 1 Stop Florists' delivery truck is driven 30,000 kilometres in the first year of a total estimated life of 200,000 kilometres. Illustration 9-8 shows the calculation of depreciation expense in the first year.

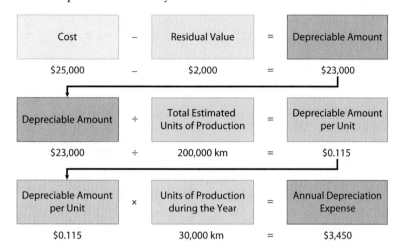

Illustration 9-8
Formula for units-of-production method

Cost	–	Residual Value	=	Depreciable Amount
$25,000	–	$2,000	=	$23,000

Depreciable Amount	÷	Total Estimated Units of Production	=	Depreciable Amount per Unit
$23,000	÷	200,000 km	=	$0.115

Depreciable Amount per Unit	×	Units of Production during the Year	=	Annual Depreciation Expense
$0.115		30,000 km	=	$3,450

Illustration 9-9 shows the units-of-production depreciation schedule, using assumed units of production (kilometres driven) for the later years.

Illustration 9-9
Units-of-production depreciation schedule

1 STOP FLORISTS
Units-of-Production Depreciation Schedule

Year	Units of Production	×	Depreciable Cost/Unit	=	Depreciation Expense	End of Year Accumulated Depreciation	End of Year Carrying Amount
							$25,000
2011	30,000		$0.115		$ 3,450	$ 3,450	21,550
2012	60,000		$0.115		6,900	10,350	14,650
2013	40,000		$0.115		4,600	14,950	10,050
2014	50,000		$0.115		5,750	20,700	4,300
2015	20,000		$0.115		2,300	23,000	2,000
	200,000				$23,000		

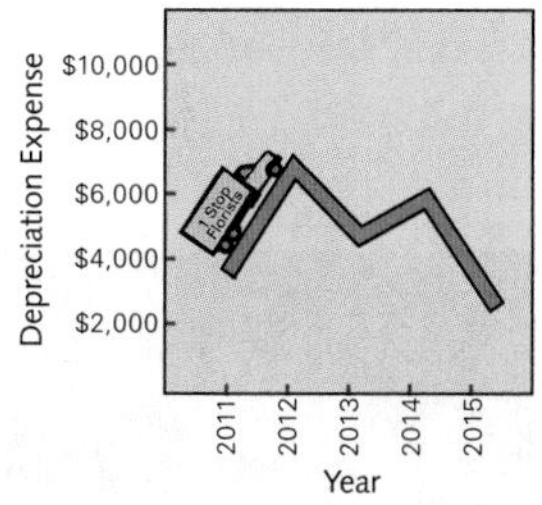

In the example in Illustration 9-9, the total actual units of production equal the original estimated total units of production of 200,000 kilometres. But in most real-life situations, the total actual units of production do not exactly equal the total estimated units of production. This means that the final year's depreciation will have to be adjusted—as we saw in the diminishing-balance method in Illustration 9-7—so that the ending carrying amount is equal to the estimated residual value.

This method is easy to apply when assets are purchased during the year. The actual units of production already show how much the asset was used during the year. Therefore, the depreciation calculations do not need to be adjusted for partial periods as is done in the straight-line and diminishing-balance methods.

The units-of-production method is used for assets whose activity can be measured in units of output. But it can only be used if it is possible to make a reasonable estimate of total activity. Later in this chapter, we will see that this method is widely used to depreciate natural resources. The units-of-production method results in the best matching of expenses with revenues when the asset's productivity varies significantly from one period to another.

Comparison of Depreciation Methods

Illustration 9-10 presents a comparison of annual and total depreciation expense for 1 Stop Florists under each of the three depreciation methods. In addition, if we assume for simplicity that profit before deducting depreciation expense is $50,000 for each of the five years, we can clearly see the impact that the choice of method has on profit.

Illustration 9-10

Comparison of depreciation methods

	Straight-Line		Double Diminishing-Balance		Units-of-Production	
Year	Depreciation Expense	Profit	Depreciation Expense	Profit	Depreciation Expense	Profit
2011	$ 4,600	$ 45,400	$ 10,000	$ 40,000	$ 3,450	$ 46,550
2012	4,600	45,400	6,000	44,000	6,900	43,100
2013	4,600	45,400	3,600	46,400	4,600	45,400
2014	4,600	45,400	2,160	47,840	5,750	44,250
2015	4,600	45,400	1,240	48,760	2,300	47,700
	$23,000	$227,000	$23,000	$227,000	$23,000	$227,000

Recall that straight-line depreciation results in the same amount of depreciation expense and therefore profit each year. Diminishing-balance depreciation results in a higher depreciation expense in early years, and therefore lower profit, and a lower depreciation expense and higher profit in later years. Results with the units-of-production method vary, depending on how much the asset is used each year. While the depreciation expense and profit will be different each year for each method, *total* depreciation expense and *total* profit after the five-year period are the same for all three methods.

The balance sheet is also affected by the choice of depreciation method because accumulated depreciation is increased by depreciation expense and owner's equity is increased by profit. There is no impact on cash flow because depreciation does not involve cash.

As explained earlier, management should choose the method that best matches the estimated pattern in which the asset's economic benefits are expected to be consumed. If the economic benefit of owning an asset is fairly consistent over time, the straight-line method is appropriate. The diminishing-balance method is appropriate if the company receives more economic benefit in the early years of the asset's useful life than in the later years. The units-of-production method is appropriate for assets whose usage varies over time. Because companies have more than one type of asset, they often use more than one depreciation method.

ACCOUNTING IN ACTION: BUSINESS INSIGHT

Why does Morris Formal Wear use the units-of-production method for its tuxedos? The reason is that the Ottawa-based family business wants to track wear and tear on each of its 5,200 tuxedos individually. Each tuxedo has its own bar code. When a tux is rented, a clerk runs its code across an electronic scanner. At year end, the computer adds up the total rentals for each of the tuxedos, then divides this number by expected total use to calculate the rate. For instance, on a two-button black tux, Morris expects a life of 30 rentals. In one year, the tux was rented 13 times. The depreciation rate for that period was 43% (13 ÷ 30) of the depreciable cost.

Is the units-of-production method the best depreciation method for Morris Formal Wear to use for its tuxedos or would you recommend another method?

Depreciation and Income Tax

The Canada Revenue Agency (CRA) allows companies to deduct a specified amount of depreciation expense when they calculate their taxable income. As we have just learned, for accounting purposes, a company must choose the depreciation method that best reflects the pattern in which the asset's future economic benefits are consumed. The CRA does not permit a choice among the three depreciation methods. Instead, the CRA requires taxpayers to use the single diminishing-balance method on the tax return, regardless of what method is used in the financial statements.

In addition, the CRA does not allow taxpayers to estimate the useful lives of assets or depreciation rates. Assets are grouped into various classes and maximum depreciation rates for each class are specified. Depreciation allowed for income tax purposes is calculated on a class (group) basis and is called **capital cost allowance (CCA)**. Capital cost allowance is an optional deduction from taxable income, but depreciation expense is not optional in calculating profit. Consequently, you may see a company deduct depreciation on its income statement, which is required by generally accepted accounting principles, but not deduct CCA for income tax purposes.

Helpful Hint Depreciation for accounting purposes is usually different from depreciation for income tax purposes.

BEFORE YOU GO ON . . .

Review It

1. What is the relationship, if any, between depreciation and (a) cost allocation, (b) asset valuation, and (c) cash accumulation?
2. Explain the factors that are used to calculate depreciation.
3. How are annual depreciation and profit different each year over the useful life of an asset, and in total after the entire life of an asset, under each of the three depreciation methods?
4. When a company chooses a depreciation method, what should it base its decision on?

Do It

On October 1, 2011, Iron Mountain Ski Company purchases a new snow grooming machine for $52,000. The machine is estimated to have a five-year useful life and a $4,000 residual value. It is also estimated to have a total useful life of 6,000 hours. It is used 1,000 hours in the year ended December 31, 2011, and 1,300 hours in the year ended December 31, 2012. How much depreciation expense should Iron Mountain Ski record in each of 2011 and 2012 under each depreciation method: (a) straight-line, (b) double diminishing-balance, and (c) units-of-production?

Action Plan

- Under straight-line depreciation, annual depreciation expense is equal to the depreciable amount (cost less residual value) divided by the estimated useful life.
- Under double diminishing-balance depreciation, annual depreciation expense is equal to double the straight-line rate of depreciation times the asset's carrying amount at the beginning of the year. Residual values are ignored in this method.
- Under the straight-line and diminishing-balance methods, the annual depreciation expense must be pro-rated if the asset is purchased during the year.
- Under units-of-production depreciation, the depreciable amount per unit is equal to the total depreciable amount divided by the total estimated units of production. The annual depreciation expense is equal to the depreciable amount per unit times the actual usage in each year.

Solution

	2011	2012
Straight-line	$2,400	$ 9,600
Double diminishing-balance	5,200	18,720
Units-of-production	8,000	10,400

(a) Straight-line: ($52,000 – $4,000) ÷ 5 years = $9,600 per year
2011: $9,600 × $\frac{3}{12}$ = $2,400
(b) Double diminishing-balance: 100% ÷ 5 years = 20% straight-line rate
20% × 2 = 40% double diminishing-balance rate
2011: $52,000 × 40% × $\frac{3}{12}$ = $5,200
2012: ($52,000 – $5,200) × 40% = $18,720
(c) Units-of-production: ($52,000 – $4,000) ÷ 6,000 hours = $8.00 per hour
2011: 1,000 × $8.00 = $8,000
2012: 1,300 × $8.00 = $10,400

Related exercise material: BE9–5, BE9–6, BE9–7, BE9–8, BE9–9, E9–2, E9–3, E9–4, and E9–5.

The Navigator

Revising Periodic Depreciation

STUDY OBJECTIVE 3

Explain the factors that cause changes in periodic depreciation and calculate revisions.

Recall that the three factors that affect the calculation of depreciation are the asset's cost, useful life, and residual value. During the useful life of a long-lived asset, the annual depreciation expense needs to be revised if there are changes to any of these factors. Depreciation therefore needs to be revised if there are (1) capital expenditures during the asset's useful life, (2) impairments in the asset's fair value, (3) changes in the asset's fair value when using the revaluation model, and/or (4) changes in the appropriate depreciation method, or in the asset's estimated useful life or residual value. In the following sections, we discuss each of these items and then show how to revise depreciation calculations.

Capital Expenditures during Useful Life

Earlier in the chapter, we learned that companies can have both operating and capital expenditures when a long-lived asset is purchased. Similarly, during the useful life of a long-lived asset, a company may incur costs for ordinary repairs, or for additions or improvements.

Ordinary repairs are costs to *maintain* the asset's operating efficiency and expected productive life. Motor tune-ups and oil changes, repainting a building, or replacing worn-out gears on machinery are examples of ordinary repairs. These costs are frequently fairly small amounts that occur regularly. They may also be larger, infrequent amounts, but if they simply restore an asset to its prior condition, they are considered an ordinary repair. Such repairs are debited to Repair (or Maintenance) Expense as they occur. Ordinary repairs are operating expenditures.

Additions and improvements are costs that are incurred to *increase* the asset's operating efficiency, productive capacity, or expected useful life. These costs are usually large and happen less often. Additions and improvements that add to the future cash flows associated with that asset are not expensed as they occur—they are capitalized. As capital expenditures, they are generally debited to the appropriate property, plant, or equipment account, or to the specific component of that asset. The capital expenditure will be depreciated over the remaining life of the original structure or the useful life of the addition, if the capital expenditure's useful life does not depend on the original asset's useful life. Additions and improvements can therefore change an asset's annual depreciation, compared with the original depreciation estimate.

In our feature story, Dawson College spent $37 million on renovations and $43 million on three expansions. According to the explanation just given, these would be treated as capital expenditures and would have resulted in revisions to the college's depreciation of its buildings.

Impairments

As noted earlier in the chapter, under the cost model, the carrying amount of property, plant, and equipment is cost less any accumulated depreciation since its acquisition. And, as already discussed, the carrying amount of property, plant, and equipment is rarely the same as its fair value. Remember that the fair value is normally not relevant since property, plant, and equipment are not purchased for resale, but rather for use in operations over the long term.

While it is accepted that long-lived assets such as property, plant, and equipment may be undervalued on the balance sheet, it is not appropriate if property, plant, and equipment are overvalued. Property, plant, and equipment are considered impaired if the asset's carrying amount exceeds its **recoverable amount** (the higher of the asset's fair value less costs to sell, or its value in use). If this is the case, an impairment loss must be recorded. An **impairment loss** is the amount by which the asset's carrying amount exceeds its recoverable amount.

Companies are required to review their assets regularly for possible impairment or do so whenever a change in circumstances affects an asset's recoverable amount. For example, if a machine has become obsolete, or if the market for a product made by a machine has dried up or has become very competitive, there is a strong possibility that an impairment loss exists. Management is then required to estimate the machine's recoverable amount.

To illustrate the writedown of a long-lived asset, assume that on December 31, Piniwa Company reviews its equipment for possible impairment. The equipment has a cost of $800,000 and accumulated depreciation of $200,000. The equipment's recoverable amount is currently $500,000. The amount of the impairment loss is determined by comparing the asset's carrying amount with its recoverable amount as follows:

Carrying amount ($800,000 – $200,000)	$600,000
Recoverable amount	500,000
Impairment loss	$100,000

The journal entry to record the impairment is:

Dec. 31	Impairment Loss	100,000	
	Accumulated Depreciation—Equipment		100,000
	To record impairment loss on equipment.		

A	=	L	+	OE
−100,000				−100,000

Cash flows: no effect

Assuming that the asset will continue to be used in operations, the impairment loss is reported on the income statement as part of operating profit rather than as "other expense." Often the loss is combined with depreciation expense on the income statement. An accumulated depreciation account is credited for the impairment loss, not the asset account; recording the loss this way keeps a record of the asset's original cost.

We had previously defined an asset's carrying amount as its cost less accumulated depreciation. This is still the case, but the Accumulated Depreciation account can now include more than just the depreciation recorded on the asset to date. It will also include impairment losses, if there have been any. Future depreciation calculations will need to be revised because of the reduction in the asset's carrying amount.

International Financial Reporting Standards allow the reversal of a previously recorded impairment loss. Under IFRS, at each year end, the company must determine whether or not an impairment loss still exists by measuring the asset's recoverable amount. If this recoverable amount exceeds the current carrying amount, then a reversal is recorded. The reversal for an asset is limited to the amount required to increase the asset's carrying amount to what it would have been if the impairment loss had not been recorded. The reversal will result in additional revisions to depreciation calculations. Canadian GAAP for Private Enterprises does not permit companies to reverse a previously recorded impairment.

Cost Model versus Revaluation Model

As previously mentioned, under IFRS, companies can choose to account for their property, plant, and equipment under either the cost model or the revaluation model. We have used the cost model in this chapter because it is used by almost all companies. Only about 3% of companies reporting under IFRS use the revaluation model. The revaluation model is allowed under IFRS mainly because it is particularly useful in countries that experience high rates of inflation or for companies in certain industries, such as investment or real estate companies, where fair values are more relevant than cost.

Under the **revaluation model**, the carrying amount of property, plant, and equipment is its fair value less any accumulated depreciation less any subsequent impairment losses. This model can be applied only to assets whose fair value can be reliably measured, and revaluations must be carried out often enough that the carrying amount is not materially different from the asset's fair value at the balance sheet date. As the accounting in the revaluation model is relatively complex, and because so few companies use this model, we will not cover this model in this textbook and leave further discussion of it to a later accounting course.

Changes in Depreciation Method, Estimated Useful Life, or Residual Value

As previously explained, the depreciation method used should be consistent with the pattern in which the asset's future economic benefits are expected to be consumed by the company. The appropriateness of the method should be reviewed at least annually in case there has been a change in the expected pattern. Management must also review its estimates of the useful life and residual value of the company's depreciable assets at least at each year end. If wear and tear or obsolescence indicates that the estimates are too low or too high, estimates should be changed. If the depreciation method, estimated useful life, or residual values are changed, this will cause a revision to the depreciation calculations.

Revised Depreciation Calculations

All of the above discussed factors will result in a revision to the depreciation calculation. In each case, the revision is made for current and future years only. The revision is not made retroactively for past periods. Thus, when a change in depreciation is made, (1) there is no correction of previously recorded depreciation expense, and (2) depreciation expense for current and future years is revised. The rationale for this treatment is that the original calculation made in the past was based on the best information available at that time. The revision is based on new information that should affect only future periods. In addition, if past periods were often restated, users would feel less confident about financial statements.

To calculate the new annual depreciation expense, we must first calculate the asset's carrying amount at the time of the change. This is equal to the asset's original cost minus the accumulated depreciation to date, plus any capital expenditures, minus any impairment in value. We must also determine if the original depreciation method, residual value, and useful life are still appropriate. If not, we must determine which method is now appropriate, and the revised residual value and useful life.

To illustrate how to revise depreciation, assume that 1 Stop Florists decides on December 31, 2014—before recording its depreciation for 2014—to extend the estimated useful life of its truck by one more year (to December 31, 2016) because of its good condition. As a result of using the truck an extra year, the estimated residual value is expected to decline from its original estimate of \$2,000 to \$700. Assume that the company has been using straight-line depreciation and determines this is still the appropriate method. Recall that the truck was purchased on January 1, 2011, for \$25,000 and originally had an estimated useful life of five years.

The carrying amount at December 31, 2014—before recording depreciation for 2014—is \$11,200 [\$25,000 − (3 × \$4,600)]. This is also the amount shown in Illustration 9-5 as the carrying amount at December 31, 2013. The remaining useful life of three years is calculated by taking the original useful life of five years, subtracting the three years where depreciation has already been recorded, and adding the additional estimated years of useful life—in this case one year. The new annual depreciation is \$3,500, calculated as in Illustration 9-11.

Illustration 9-11

Formula for revised straight-line depreciation

Carrying Amount at Time of Change in Estimate	−	Revised Residual Value	=	Remaining Depreciable Amount at Time of Change in Estimate
\$11,200	−	\$700	=	\$10,500

Remaining Depreciable Amount at Time of Change in Estimate	÷	Remaining Estimated Useful Life	=	Revised Annual Depreciation Expense
\$10,500	÷	3 years	=	\$3,500

As a result of the revision to the truck's estimated useful life and residual value, 1 Stop Florists will record depreciation expense of \$3,500 on December 31 of 2014, 2015, and 2016. The company will not go back and change the depreciation for 2011, 2012, and 2013. Accumulated depreciation will now equal \$24,300 [(\$4,600 × 3) + (\$3,500 × 3)] at the end of the six-year useful life instead of the $23,000 that was originally calculated. The $1,300 increase in accumulated depreciation is because the estimated residual value was revised and decreased by $1,300 ($2,000 – $700).

If the units-of-production depreciation method is used, the calculation is the same as we just saw except that the remaining useful life is expressed as units rather than years. If the diminishing-balance method is used, the revised rate would be applied to the carrying amount at the time of the change in estimate. The rate must be revised because the useful life has changed.

In our feature story, we are told that in 2000–01, Dawson College retroactively calculated depreciation from 1995–96. Based on what you have just learned, this retroactive change would appear to be incorrect. However, the retroactive change in 2000–01 was the result of recording depreciation for the first time. Before this, Dawson had not recorded depreciation. This type of change is known as a change in accounting policy. Changes in accounting policy usually apply to past periods.

ACCOUNTING IN ACTION: ACROSS THE ORGANIZATION INSIGHT

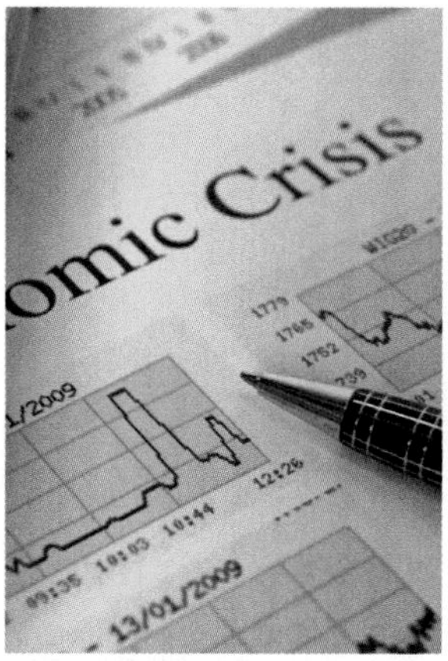

The 2008 global financial crisis had a significant impact on the forest industry, a 2009 PricewaterhouseCoopers study found. Canadian producers described 2008 as the worst economic downturn in recent history. The onset of the global financial crisis and reduction in demand resulted in inventory increases and reductions in sales volumes for the last half of the year. Nearly every segment of the industry experienced significant drops in demand, which led to a buildup in inventory and shrinking prices for the products. This resulted in many companies recording writedowns and asset impairments as they looked to restructure and clean up their balance sheets. The total loss for the 11 Canadian companies included in the global survey rose 355% to $4.04 billion, compared with a loss of $889 million in 2007. The top 100 forest, paper, and packaging companies worldwide recorded total losses of US$8 billion in 2008, compared with profits of US$13.8 billion in 2007.

Source: Brenda Bouw, "Global forest earnings slide into red," *The Globe and Mail*, June 25, 2009.

What parts of an organization are responsible for determining if an impairment loss should be recorded?

BEFORE YOU GO ON . . .

Review It

1. Under what circumstances will depreciation need to be revised?
2. What are the differences between operating and capital expenditures?
3. What is an impairment loss? How is it calculated?
4. What are the differences between the cost and revaluation models?
5. Are revisions of depreciation made to prior periods, future periods, or both? Explain.

Do It

On August 1, 1996, just after its year end, Fine Furniture Company purchased a building for $500,000. The company used straight-line depreciation to allocate the cost of this building, estimating a residual value of $50,000 and a useful life of 30 years. After 15 years of use, on August 1, 2011, the company was forced to replace the roof at a cost of $25,000 cash. The residual value was expected to remain at $50,000 but the total useful life was now expected to increase to 40 years. Prepare journal entries to record (a) depreciation for the year ended July 31, 2011; (b) the cost of the addition on August 1, 2011; and (c) depreciation for the year ended July 31, 2012.

Action Plan

- Understand the difference between an operating expenditure (benefits only the current period) and a capital expenditure (benefits future periods).
- To revise annual depreciation, calculate the carrying amount (cost less accumulated depreciation) at the revision date. Note that the cost of any capital expenditure will increase the carrying amount of the asset to be depreciated.

- Subtract any revised residual value from the carrying amount at the time of the change in estimate (plus the capital expenditure in this case) to determine the depreciable amount.
- Allocate the revised depreciable amount over the remaining (not total) useful life.

Solution

(a)

July 31, 2011	Depreciation Expense [($500,000 – $50,000) ÷ 30]	15,000	
	Accumulated Depreciation—Building		15,000
	To record annual depreciation expense.		

(b)

Aug. 1, 2011	Building	25,000	
	Cash		25,000
	To record replacement of roof.		

(c)

Cost:	$500,000
Less: Accumulated depreciation $15,000 per year × 15 years	225,000
Carrying amount before replacement of roof, August 1, 2011	275,000
Add: Capital expenditure (roof)	25,000
Carrying amount after replacement of roof, August 1, 2011	300,000
Less: Revised residual value	50,000
Revised depreciable amount	250,000
Divide by: Remaining useful life (40 – 15)	÷25 years
Revised annual depreciation	$ 10,000

July 31, 2012	Depreciation Expense	10,000	
	Accumulated Depreciation—Building		10,000
	To record revised annual depreciation expense.		

The Navigator

Related exercise material: BE9–10, BE9–11, E9–6, E9–7, and E9–8.

Disposals of Property, Plant, and Equipment

STUDY OBJECTIVE 4

Account for the disposal of property, plant, and equipment.

Companies dispose of property, plant, or equipment that is no longer useful to them. Illustration 9-12 shows three methods of disposal.

Illustration 9-12

Methods of property, plant, and equipment disposal

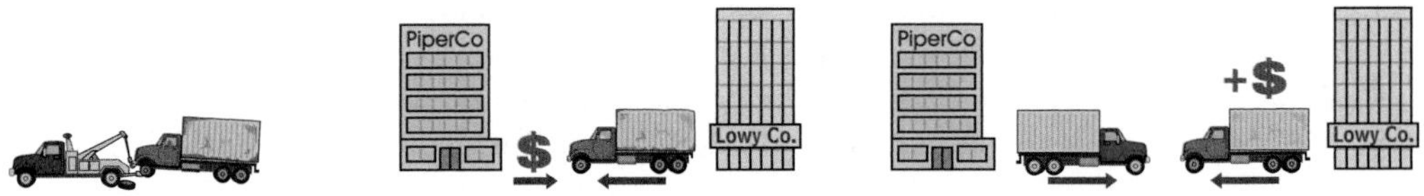

Retirement — Equipment is scrapped or discarded.

Sale — Equipment is sold.

Exchange — Existing equipment is traded for new equipment.

Steps in Recording Disposals of Property, Plant, and Equipment

Whatever the disposal method, a company must take the following four steps to record the retirement, sale, or exchange of the property, plant, or equipment:

Step 1: Update Depreciation.

Depreciation must be recorded over the entire period of time an asset is available for use. Therefore, if the disposal occurs in the middle of an accounting period, depreciation must be updated for the fraction of the year since the last time adjusting entries were recorded up to the date of disposal. Depreciation is recorded even if the asset is not in use, unless it is fully depreciated.

Step 2: Calculate the Carrying Amount.

Calculate the carrying amount at the date of disposal after updating the accumulated depreciation for any partial year depreciation calculated in Step 1 above:

Cost − Accumulated Depreciation = Carrying Amount

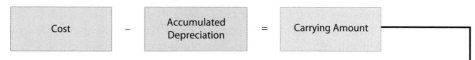

Step 3: Calculate the Gain or Loss.

Determine the amount of the gain or loss on disposal, if any, by comparing the proceeds received from the disposal with the carrying amount at the date of disposal:

Proceeds − Carrying Amount = Gain (Loss)

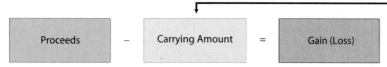

If the proceeds of the sale are more than the carrying amount of the property, plant, or equipment, there is a gain on disposal. If the proceeds of the sale are less than the carrying amount of the asset sold, there is a loss on disposal.

Step 4: Record the Disposal.

Record the disposal, removing the asset's cost and the accumulated depreciation from the accounts. The Accumulated Depreciation account is decreased by the balance in the account, which is the total amount of depreciation and any impairment losses that have been recorded for the asset up to its disposal date. This is the same amount that was used to calculate the carrying amount in Step 2 above. Record the proceeds (if any) and the gain or loss on disposal (if any). Gains on disposal are recorded as credits because credits increase owner's equity; losses on disposal are recorded as debits because debits decrease owner's equity.

Dr. Cash (or other account)
Dr. Accumulated Depreciation
Dr. Loss on Disposal OR Cr. Gain on Disposal
Cr. Property, plant, or equipment account

Gains and losses are reported in the operating section of a multiple-step income statement. Why? Recall that depreciation expense is an estimate. Loss results when the annual depreciation expense has not been sufficient so that the carrying amount at the date of disposal is equal to the proceeds. Gains are caused because annual depreciation expense has been too high, so the carrying amount at the date of disposal is less than the proceeds. Thus gains and losses are basically just adjustments to depreciation expense and should be recorded in the same section of the income statement.

Retirement of Property, Plant, and Equipment

Instead of being sold or exchanged, some assets are simply retired at the end of their useful lives. For example, some productive assets used in manufacturing may have highly specialized uses and consequently have no market when the company no longer needs the asset. In this case, the asset is simply retired.

When an asset is retired, there are no proceeds on disposal. The Accumulated Depreciation account is decreased (debited) for the full amount of depreciation taken over the life of the asset. The asset account is reduced (credited) for the asset's original cost. Even if the carrying amount equals zero, a journal entry is still required to remove the asset and its related depreciation account from the books, as shown in the following example.

To illustrate the retirement of a piece of property, plant, and equipment, assume that on August 1, 2011, Baseyev Enterprises retires its printing equipment, which cost $31,200. At the time of purchase, on August 1, 2007, the printing equipment was expected to have a four-year useful life and no residual value. Baseyev used straight-line depreciation and the annual depreciation expense was $7,800 per year ($31,200 ÷ 4) or $650 per month ($7,800 ÷ 12). The balance in the account Accumulated Depreciation at Baseyev's year end, December 31, 2010, was $26,650 ($650/month × 41 months). Straight-line depreciation for the seven months from December 31, 2010, to August 1, 2011, is $4,550 ($650/month × 7 months).

To update the depreciation since the last time that adjusting journal entries were made, which would have been at Baseyev's year end, December 31, 2010, a journal entry to record the seven months of depreciation is made, as follows:

A	=	L	+	OE
−4,550				−4,550

Cash flows: no effect

Aug. 1	Depreciation Expense	4,550	
	Accumulated Depreciation—Printing Equipment		4,550
	To record depreciation expense for the first 7 months of 2011.		

After this journal entry is posted, the balance in Accumulated Depreciation is $31,200 ($26,650 + $4,550). The printing equipment is now fully depreciated with a carrying amount of zero (cost of $31,200 – accumulated depreciation of $31,200).

The entry to record the retirement of the printing equipment is:

A	=	L	+	OE
+31,200 −31,200				

Cash flows: no effect

Aug. 1	Accumulated Depreciation—Printing Equipment	31,200	
	Printing Equipment		31,200
	To record retirement of fully depreciated printing equipment.		

What happens if a company is still using a fully depreciated asset? In this case, the asset and its accumulated depreciation continue to be reported on the balance sheet, without further depreciation, until the asset is retired. Reporting the asset and related depreciation on the balance sheet informs the reader of the financial statements that the asset is still being used by the company. Once an asset is fully depreciated, even if it is still being used, no additional depreciation should be taken. Accumulated depreciation on a piece of property, plant, and equipment can never be more than the asset's cost.

If a piece of property, plant, and equipment is retired before it is fully depreciated and no residual value is received, a loss on disposal occurs. Assume that Baseyev Enterprises retires its printing equipment on January 1, 2011. The loss on disposal is calculated by subtracting the asset's carrying amount from the proceeds that are received. In this case, there are no proceeds and the carrying amount is $4,550 (cost of $31,200 – accumulated depreciation of $26,650), resulting in a loss of $4,550:

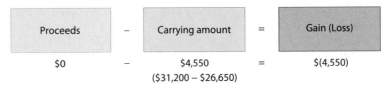

Proceeds	–	Carrying amount	=	Gain (Loss)
$0	–	$4,550 ($31,200 – $26,650)	=	$(4,550)

The entry to record the retirement of equipment is as follows:

A	=	L	+	OE
+26,650 −31,200				−4,550

Cash flows: no effect

Jan. 1	Accumulated Depreciation—Printing Equipment	26,650	
	Loss on Disposal	4,550	
	Printing Equipment		31,200
	To record retirement of printing equipment at a loss.		

You should also note that there will never be a gain when an asset is retired. The proceeds are always zero and therefore can never be greater than the carrying amount of the retired asset.

Sale of Property, Plant, and Equipment

In a disposal by sale, the four steps listed earlier are followed. Both gains and losses on disposal are common when an asset is sold. Only by coincidence will the asset's carrying amount and fair value (the proceeds) be the same when the asset is sold. We will illustrate the sale of office furniture at both a gain and a loss in the following sections.

Gain on Disposal. To illustrate a gain, assume that on April 1, 2011, Baseyev Enterprises sells office furniture for $15,000 cash. The office furniture had originally been purchased on January 1, 2007, at a cost of $60,200. At that time, it was estimated that the office furniture would have a residual value of $5,000 and a useful life of five years.

The first step is to update any unrecorded depreciation. Annual depreciation using the straight-line method is $11,040 [($60,200 − $5,000) ÷ 5]. The entry to record the depreciation expense and update accumulated depreciation for the first three months of 2011 is as follows:

Apr. 1	Depreciation Expense ($11,040 × $^3/_{12}$)	2,760	
	Accumulated Depreciation—Office Furniture		2,760
	To record depreciation expense for the first 3 months of 2011.		

A	=	L	+	OE
−2,760				−2,760

Cash flows: no effect

The second step is to calculate the carrying amount on April 1, 2011. Accumulated depreciation of $46,920 is calculated using four years (January 1, 2007 to December 31, 2010) at $11,040/year plus $2,760 for 2011.

Cost	−	Accumulated Depreciation	=	Carrying Amount
$60,200	−	$46,920 [($11,040 × 4) + $2,760]	=	$13,280

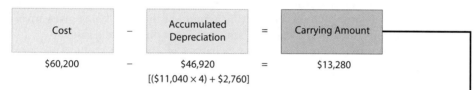

The third step is to calculate the gain or loss on disposal. A $1,720 gain on disposal is determined as follows:

Proceeds	−	Carrying Amount	=	Gain (Loss)
$15,000	−	$13,280	=	$1,720

The fourth step is the entry to record the sale of the office furniture as follows:

Apr. 1	Cash	15,000	
	Accumulated Depreciation—Office Furniture	46,920	
	Gain on Disposal		1,720
	Office Furniture		60,200
	To record the sale of office furniture at a gain.		

A	=	L	+	OE
+15,000 +46,920 −60,200				+1,720

↑ Cash flows: +15,000

Notice that the carrying amount of $13,280 does not appear in the journal entry. Instead, the asset's cost ($60,200) and the total accumulated depreciation ($46,920) are used. Remember the carrying amount is simply a number calculated to determine the gain or loss. It is not an account and cannot be debited or credited.

Loss on Disposal. Assume that instead of selling the office furniture for $15,000, Baseyev sells it for $9,000. In this case, a loss of $4,280 is calculated as follows:

Proceeds	−	Carrying Amount	=	Gain (Loss)
$9,000	−	$13,280	=	$(4,280)

The entry to record the sale of the office furniture is as follows:

A	=	L	+	OE
+9,000				−4,280
+46,920				
−60,200				

↑ Cash flows: +9,000

Apr. 1	Cash	9,000	
	Accumulated Depreciation—Office Furniture	46,920	
	Loss on Disposal	4,280	
	Office Furniture		60,200
	To record the sale of office furniture at a loss.		

As previously explained, the loss on disposal is the result of not recording enough depreciation expense prior to selling the asset.

Exchanges of Property, Plant, and Equipment

An exchange of assets is recorded as the purchase of a new asset and the sale of an old asset. Typically a **trade-in allowance** on the old asset is given toward the purchase price of the new asset. An additional cash payment is usually also required for the difference between the trade-in allowance and the stated purchase price (list price) of the new asset. The trade-in allowance amount, however, is often affected by price concessions for the new asset and therefore rarely reflects the fair value of the asset that is given up. Consequently, as fair value is what matters, trade-in allowances are ignored for accounting purposes.

Instead of using the stated purchase price, the new asset is recorded at the fair value of the asset given up plus any cash paid (or less any cash received). Instead of using the trade-in allowance, the fair value of the asset given up is used to calculate the gain or loss on the asset being given up. A loss results if the carrying amount of the asset being given up is more than its fair value. A gain results if the carrying amount is less than its fair value.

Thus, the procedure to account for exchanges of assets is as follows:

Step 1: Update any unrecorded depreciation expense on the asset being given up to the date of the exchange.
Step 2: Calculate the carrying amount of the asset being given up (cost – accumulated depreciation).
Step 3: Calculate any gain or loss on disposal [fair value – carrying amount = gain (loss)].
Step 4: Record the exchange as follows:

- Remove the cost and the accumulated depreciation of the asset that is given up.
- Record any gain or loss on disposal.
- Record the new asset at the fair value of the old asset plus any cash paid (or less any cash received).
- Record the cash paid or received.

To illustrate an exchange of long-lived assets, assume that Chilko Company exchanged old computers for new computers on October 1, 2011. The original cost of the old computers was $61,000 on January 1, 2009. Depreciation was calculated using the straight-line method, over a three-year useful life, with an estimated residual value of $1,000. The fair value of the old computers on October 1, 2011, is $5,000.

The list price of the new computers was $51,000. Chilko received an $8,000 trade-in allowance from the computer retailer for the old computers and paid $43,000 cash ($51,000 – $8,000) for the new computers. Chilko's year end is December 31.

The first step is to update the depreciation on the old computers for the nine months ended October 1, 2011. Annual depreciation expense is $20,000 [($61,000 – $1,000) ÷ 3], so depreciation for nine months is $15,000 ($20,000 × $^9/_{12}$).

A	=	L	+	OE
−15,000				−15,000

Cash flows: no effect

Oct. 1	Depreciation Expense	15,000	
	Accumulated Depreciation—Computers		15,000
	To record depreciation expense for the first 9 months of 2011.		

After this entry is posted, the balance in Accumulated Depreciation on October 1, 2011, is $55,000 [$20,000 (in 2009) + $20,000 (in 2010) + $15,000 (in 2011)]. The accumulated depreciation can also be calculated as follows: $20,000 × 2.75 years = $55,000. Be sure to watch the dates and time periods carefully when calculating partial period depreciation: thus, the ".75" is for the nine months of depreciation in the current year.

On October 1, 2011, the carrying amount is $6,000 (cost of $61,000 – accumulated depreciation of $55,000). The loss on disposal on the old computers is determined by comparing the carrying amount with the fair value, which represents the proceeds in this situation:

Proceeds (Fair Value of Old Computers)	–	Carrying Amount (Old Computers)	=	Gain (Loss)
$5,000	–	$6,000 ($61,000 – $55,000)	=	$(1,000)

The entry to record the exchange of computers is as follows:

Oct. 1	Computers (new)	48,000	
	Accumulated Depreciation—Computers (old)	55,000	
	Loss on Disposal	1,000	
	Computers (old)		61,000
	Cash		43,000
	To record exchange of computers, plus cash.		

A	=	L	+	OE
+48,000				−1,000
+55,000				
−61,000				
−43,000				

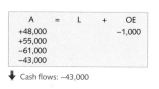

Cash flows: −43,000

Note that the exchange of computers is not netted. That is, it is shown as a separate increase and decrease to the general ledger account Computers. The cost of the new computers ($48,000) is determined by the fair value of the old computers ($5,000) plus the cash paid ($43,000). The list price of $51,000 and the trade-in allowance of $8,000 are ignored in determining the real cost of the new computers.

In some situations, the exchange lacks commercial substance or else the fair values of the asset acquired, or the asset given up, cannot be determined. In such cases, the new long-lived asset is recorded at the carrying amount of the old asset that was given up, plus any cash paid (or less any cash received). Carrying amount is used in these circumstances because the new asset is basically substituted or swapped for the old asset. As the carrying amount of the old asset is used for the carrying amount of the new asset, and the exchange has therefore not changed the operations of the business significantly, no gain or loss is recorded.

BEFORE YOU GO ON . . .

Review It

1. What is the proper way to account for the retirement, sale, or exchange of a piece of property, plant, and equipment?
2. What is the formula to calculate a gain or loss on disposal?
3. What is the procedure to account for an exchange of assets?

Do It

Overland Trucking has a truck that was purchased on January 1, 2007, for $80,000. The truck had been depreciated on a straight-line basis with an estimated residual value of $5,000 and an estimated useful life of five years. Overland has a December 31 year end. Assume each of the following four independent situations:

1. On January 1, 2012, Overland retires the truck.
2. On May 1, 2011, Overland sells the truck for $9,500 cash.
3. On October 1, 2011, Overland sells the truck for $9,500 cash.
4. On November 1, 2011, Overland exchanges the old truck, plus $60,000 cash, for a new truck. The old truck has a fair value of $9,500. The new truck has a list price of $70,000, but the dealer will give Overland a $10,000 trade-in allowance on the old truck.

Prepare the journal entry to record each of these situations.

Action Plan

- Update any unrecorded depreciation for dispositions during the fiscal year.
- Compare the proceeds with the asset's carrying amount to determine if there has been a gain or loss.
- Record any proceeds received and any gain or loss. Remove both the asset and any related accumulated depreciation from the accounts.
- Determine the cash paid in an exchange situation as the difference between the list price and the trade-in allowance.
- Record the cost of the new asset in an exchange situation as the fair value of the asset given up, plus the cash paid.

Solution

$$\frac{\$80,000 - \$5,000}{5 \text{ years}} = \$15,000 \text{ annual depreciation exspence}$$

$$\$15,000 \div 12 = \$1,250 \text{ per month}$$

1. Retirement of truck:

Jan. 1, 2012	Accumulated Depreciation ($1,250 × 60 months)	75,000	
	Loss on Disposal [$0 – ($80,000 – $75,000)]	5,000	
	Truck		80,000
	To record retirement of truck.		

2. Sale of truck for $9,500 on May 1, 2011:

May 1, 2011	Depreciation Expense ($1,250 × 4 months)	5,000	
	Accumulated Depreciation		5,000
	To record depreciation for 4 months.		
	Cash	9,500	
	Accumulated Depreciation—Truck ($1,250 × 52 months)	65,000	
	Loss on Disposal [$9,500 – ($80,000 – $65,000)]	5,500	
	Truck		80,000
	To record sale of truck at a loss.		

3. Sale of truck for $9,500 on Oct. 1, 2011:

Oct. 1, 2011	Depreciation Expense ($1,250 × 9 months)	11,250	
	Accumulated Depreciation		11,250
	To record depreciation for 9 months.		
	Cash	9,500	
	Accumulated Depreciation—Truck ($1,250 × 57 months)	71,250	
	Gain on Disposal [$9,500 – ($80,000 – $71,250)]		750
	Truck		80,000
	To record sale of truck at a gain.		

4. Exchange of truck on Nov. 1, 2011:

Nov. 1, 2011	Depreciation Expense ($1,250 × 10 months)	12,500	
	Accumulated Depreciation		12,500
	To record depreciation for 10 months.		
	Truck (new) ($9,500 + $60,000)	69,500	
	Accumulated Depreciation—Truck ($1,250 × 58 months)	72,500	
	Gain on Disposal [$9,500 – ($80,000 – $72,500)]		2,000
	Truck (old)		80,000
	Cash ($70,000 – $10,000)		60,000
	To record exchange of trucks, plus cash.		

The Navigator

Related exercise material: BE9–12, BE9–13, BE9–14, E9–9, and E9–10.

Natural Resources

STUDY OBJECTIVE 5
Calculate and record depreciation of natural resources.

Natural resources consist of standing timber and underground deposits of oil, gas, and minerals. Canada is rich in natural resources, ranging from the towering rainforests in coastal British Columbia to one of the world's largest nickel deposits in Voisey's Bay, Labrador. These long-lived assets have two characteristics that make them different from other long-lived assets: (1) they are physically extracted in operations such as mining, cutting, or pumping; and (2) only an act of nature can replace them. Because of these characteristics, natural resources are sometimes called *wasting assets*.

Natural resources are tangible assets, similar to property, plant, and equipment. A key distinction between natural resources and property, plant, and equipment is that natural resources physically lose substance, or deplete, as they are used. For example, there is less of a tract of timberland (a natural resource) as the timber is cut and sold. When we use equipment, its physical substance remains the same regardless of the product it produces.

Cost

The cost of a natural resource is determined in the same way as the cost of property, plant, and equipment and includes all expenditures necessary in acquiring the resource and preparing it for its intended use. These costs are often referred to as acquisition, exploration, and development costs. The cost of a natural resource also includes the estimated future removal and site restoration cleanup costs, which are often large. Restoration costs are usually required in order to return the resource as closely as possible to its natural state at the end of its useful life.

As discussed earlier in the chapter, accounting for asset retirement costs and the allocation of these costs over the useful life of the natural resource is complicated. Further discussion of these concepts is left to an intermediate accounting course. Accounting for exploration and development costs is also very complex. We will, however, look at how the acquisition cost of a natural resource is allocated over its useful life in the next section.

Depreciation

The units-of-production method (learned earlier in the chapter) is generally used to calculate the depreciation of wasting assets. Under the units-of-production method, the total cost of the natural resource minus its residual value is divided by the number of units estimated to be in the resource. The result is a depreciable amount per unit of product. The depreciable amount per unit is then multiplied by the number of units extracted, to determine the annual depreciation expense.

Alternative terminology Depreciation for natural resources is frequently called *depletion* because the assets physically deplete as the resource is extracted.

To illustrate, assume that Rabbit Lake Company invests $5.5 million in a mine that is estimated to have 10 million tonnes of uranium and a $200,000 residual value. In the first year, 800,000 tonnes of uranium are extracted. Illustration 9-13 shows the formulas and calculations.

Cost	−	Residual Value	=	Depreciable Amount
$5,500,000	−	$200,000	=	$5,300,000
Depreciable Amount	÷	Total Estimated Units of Production	=	Depreciable Amount per Unit
$5,300,000	÷	10,000,000 t	=	$0.53
Depreciable Amount per Unit	×	Number of Units Extracted and Sold during the Year	=	Annual Depreciation Expense
$0.53	×	800,000 t	=	$424,000

Illustration 9-13
Formula for units-of-production method for natural resources

The depreciation expense for the amount of the resource that has been extracted is initially charged (debited) to an inventory account, a current asset. Note that this is not the same as depreciation for property, plant, and equipment, which is recorded as an expense. Depreciation on natural resources is accounted for in this way because the resource extracted is available for sale—similar to merchandise that has been purchased or manufactured for sale, as we learned in Chapter 5.

The entry to record depreciation of the uranium mine for Rabbit Lake Company's first year of operation, ended December 31, 2011, is as follows:

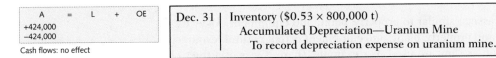

A	=	L	+	OE
+424,000				
−424,000				

Cash flows: no effect

Dec. 31	Inventory ($\$0.53 \times 800{,}000$ t)	424,000	
	Accumulated Depreciation—Uranium Mine		424,000
	To record depreciation expense on uranium mine.		

All costs of extracting the natural resource—both current production costs such as labour and depreciation of the natural resource—are recorded as inventory. When sold, the inventory costs are transferred to cost of goods sold and matched with the period's revenue. In other words, the depreciation is charged to the income statement only in the period in which the related goods are sold. Depreciation related to goods not yet sold remains in inventory and is reported as a current asset.

For example, assume that Rabbit Lake Company does not sell all of the 800,000 tonnes of uranium extracted in 2011. It sells 700,000 tonnes and stores 100,000 tonnes for later sale. In this situation, Rabbit Lake Company would include $371,000 (700,000 × $0.53) in the cost of the resource sold on its income statement. As mentioned before, the cost of labour and other production costs related to the goods sold would also be included in the cost of the resource sold on the income statement. The remaining depreciation of $53,000 ($424,000 – $371,000) is for the 100,000 tonnes kept for later sale and will be included in inventory in the current assets section of the company's balance sheet.

Like depreciation for property, plant, and equipment, the depreciation of a natural resource needs to be revised if there are capital expenditures during the useful life. Also, the depreciable amount per unit of a natural resource needs to be revised whenever the estimated total units of the resource have changed as a result of new information. Natural resources such as oil and gas deposits and some metals have provided the greatest challenges. Estimates of the total units (also called reserves) of these natural resources are mostly knowledgeable guesses and may be revised whenever more information becomes available.

Natural resources must also be reviewed and tested for impairment annually or more frequently whenever circumstances make this appropriate. For example, Rabbit Lake Company would need to test the uranium mine for impairment if there was a significant and permanent decline in the selling price of uranium. If there is impairment, the uranium mine must be written down to its fair value, an impairment loss must be recorded, and current and future depreciation needs to be revised accordingly.

Disposal of Natural Resources

At disposal, just as with property, plant, and equipment, any unrecorded depreciation must be updated for the portion of the year up to the date of the disposal. Then proceeds are recorded, the cost and the accumulated depreciation of the natural resource are removed, and a gain or loss, if any, is recorded. As mentioned earlier, there may also be site restoration costs at this time, but we leave the accounting for these costs to a future accounting course.

BEFORE YOU GO ON . . .

Review It

1. How is depreciation expense calculated for natural resources?
2. Explain how depreciation expense can be both an asset (inventory) and an expense (cost of goods sold).
3. Why might a company need to revise the depreciation of a natural resource?

Do It

High Timber Company invests $14 million in a tract of timber land. It is estimated to have 10 million cunits (1 cunit = 100 cubic feet) of timber and a $500,000 residual value. In the first year, 40,000 cunits of timber are cut, and 30,000 of these cunits are sold. Calculate depreciation for High Timber's first year of operations and allocate it between inventory and cost of goods sold.

Action Plan

- Use units-of-production depreciation for natural resources.
- Calculate the depreciable amount per unit by dividing the total cost minus the estimated residual value by the total estimated units.
- Multiply the depreciable amount per unit by the number of units cut to determine the total depreciation.
- Allocate the depreciation related to the units that have been cut but not yet sold to inventory.
- Allocate the depreciation related to the units that have been cut and sold to expense.

Solution

1. Depreciable amount per unit: ($14,000,000 – $500,000) ÷ 10,000,000 cunits = $1.35 per cunit
2. Total depreciation for the year: $1.35 per cunit × 40,000 cunits cut = $54,000
3. Depreciation allocated to inventory: $1.35 per cunit × 10,000 cunits on hand = $13,500
4. Depreciation allocated to expense: $1.35 per cunit × 30,000 cunits sold = $40,500

Related exercise material: BE9–15 and E9–11.

The Navigator

Intangible Assets and Goodwill

STUDY OBJECTIVE 6

Identify the basic accounting issues for intangible assets and goodwill.

Similar to property, plant, and equipment, and natural resources, intangible assets provide economic benefits in future periods. They are used to produce products or provide services over these periods and are not intended for sale to customers. However, unlike property, plant, and equipment, and natural resources, which are **tangible assets** because they have a physical substance, **intangible assets** involve rights, privileges, and competitive advantages that have no physical substance. In other words, they are not physical things. Many companies' most valuable assets are intangible. Some widely known intangibles are Alexander Graham Bell's patent on the telephone, the franchises of Tim Hortons, the trade name of President's Choice, and the trademark CBC.

An intangible asset must be identifiable, which means it must meet one of the two following criteria: (1) it can be separated from the company and sold, whether or not the company intends to do so, or (2) it is based on contractual or legal rights, regardless of whether or not it can be separated from the company. Since goodwill cannot be separated from a company and sold, there are differences in the accounting for goodwill versus other intangible assets.

Accounting for Intangible Assets

Like tangible assets (property, plant, and equipment, and natural resources), intangible assets are recorded at cost. Cost includes all the costs of acquisition and other costs that are needed to make the intangible asset ready for its intended use—including legal fees and similar charges.

As with tangible assets, companies have a choice of following the cost model or the revaluation model when accounting for intangible assets subsequent to acquisition. The majority of companies use the cost model for all long-lived assets. So we will leave further study of the revaluation model, as it applies to intangible assets, for a later accounting course.

Under the cost model, if an intangible asset has a finite (limited) life, its cost must be systematically allocated over its useful life. We called this "depreciation" when discussing tangible assets. With intangible assets, we use the term **amortization**.

For an intangible asset with a finite life, its **amortizable amount** (cost less residual value) should be allocated over the shorter of the (1) estimated useful life and (2) legal life. Intangible assets, by their nature, rarely have any residual value, so the amortizable amount is normally equal to the cost. In addition, the useful life of an intangible asset is usually shorter than its legal life, so useful life is most often used as the amortization period.

When a company estimates the useful life of an intangible asset, it must consider factors such as how long the company expects to use the asset, obsolescence, demand, and other factors that can make the intangible asset ineffective at helping to earn revenue. For example, a patent on a computer chip may have a legal life of 20 years, but with technology changing as rapidly as it does, the chip's useful life may be only four or five years maximum.

Amortization begins as soon as the asset is ready to be used as intended by management. Similar to depreciation, the company must use the amortization method that best matches the pattern with which the asset's future economic benefits are expected to be consumed. If that pattern cannot be determined reliably, the straight-line method should be used.

Just as land is considered to have an indefinite life, there are also intangible assets with indefinite life. An intangible asset is considered to have an indefinite (unlimited) life when, based on an analysis of all of the relevant factors, there is no foreseeable limit to the period over which the intangible asset is expected to generate net cash inflows for the company. If an intangible has an indefinite life, it is not amortized.

As with tangible assets, all intangible assets must be reviewed and tested for impairment. Intangible assets with indefinite lives are tested more frequently for impairments than are intangible assets with finite lives. Indefinite-life intangible assets should be tested for impairment at least once a year.

Recall from earlier in this chapter that there is impairment if the asset's recoverable amount falls below its carrying amount. If any impairment is evident, the intangible asset is written down to its recoverable amount and an impairment loss recorded. Under IFRS, an impairment loss cannot be reversed for goodwill, but it can be for other intangible assets.

Similar to tangible assets, the amortization is revised if there are changes in cost, or useful life, or an impairment loss. The revision is accounted for in the current and future periods; retroactive adjustments are not recorded.

At disposal, just as with tangible assets, the carrying amount of the intangible asset is removed, and a gain or loss, if any, is recorded.

Intangible Assets with Finite Lives

Examples of intangible assets with finite lives include patents and copyrights. We also include research and development costs in this section because these costs often lead to the creation of patents and copyrights.

Patents

A **patent** is an exclusive right issued by the Canadian Intellectual Property Office of Industry Canada that allows the patent holder to manufacture, sell, or otherwise control an invention for a period of 20 years from the date of the application. A patent cannot be renewed. But the legal life of a patent may be extended if the patent holder obtains new patents for improvements or other changes in the basic design.

The initial cost of a patent is the price paid to acquire it. After it has been acquired, legal costs are often incurred. There is a saying that "A patent is only as good as the money you're prepared to spend defending it," which is very true. Companies such as Microsoft, Verizon, Dell, and Hewlett Packard are frequently sued for patent infringement. About 80% of patent suits are against large technology and financial companies.

Legal costs to successfully defend a patent in an infringement suit are considered necessary to prove the patent's validity. They are added to the Patent account and amortized over the patent's remaining life.

The cost of a patent should be amortized over its 20-year legal life or its useful life, whichever is shorter. As mentioned earlier, the useful life should be carefully assessed by considering whether the patent is likely to become ineffective at contributing to revenue before the end of its legal life.

Copyrights

A **copyright** is granted by the Canadian Intellectual Property Office, giving the owner an exclusive right to reproduce and sell an artistic or published work. Copyrights extend for the life of the creator plus 50 years. Generally, a copyright's useful life is significantly shorter than its legal life.

The cost of a copyright consists of the cost of acquiring and defending it. The cost may only be the fee paid to register the copyright, or it may amount to a great deal more if a copyright infringement suit is involved.

ACCOUNTING IN ACTION: ALL ABOUT YOU

Canadian copyright laws have not undergone a major reform for over 10 years. The Internet and other new technologies have changed the way in which we produce and access copyright material. In 1998, the first MP3 player, which could store up to one hour of music, was introduced in the market. Today a device that is smaller than a credit card can hold thousands of songs, videos, and photographs. It has been argued that Canadian copyright law needs to be updated to give Canadian creators and consumers the tools they need to participate in the digital marketplace and to foster innovation. On July 20, 2009, the federal government launched nationwide consultations to solicit Canadians' opinions on the issue of copyright following two failed attempts by the Canadian government to change the copyright law. Proposed amendments included a $500 fine for downloading copyrighted material from the Internet for personal use and a fine of up to $20,000 for breaking digital locks on DVDs or uploading copyrighted material for file-sharing.

Source: Government of Canada's Copyright Consultations website, available at: http://copyright.econsultation.ca; Kate Kennedy and Chris Selley, "A users guide to the copyright bill," *Macleans* magazine, June 16, 2008.

Is it important that the copyrights of artists, writers, musicians, and the entertainment industry be protected?

Research and Development Costs

Research and development (R&D) costs are not intangible assets by themselves. But they may lead to patents and copyrights, new processes, and new products. Many companies spend large sums of money on research and development in an ongoing effort to develop new products or processes. Microsoft spends almost $10 billion a year on R&D—significantly more than any other company in the world.

Research and development costs present two accounting problems: (1) it is sometimes difficult to determine the costs related to specific projects; (2) it is also hard to know the extent and timing of future benefits. As a result, accounting distinguishes between research costs and development costs.

Research is original, planned investigation that is done to gain new knowledge and understanding. All research costs should be expensed when they are incurred.

Development is the use of research findings and knowledge for a plan or design before the start of commercial production. Development costs with probable future benefits should be capitalized. In addition, all of the following conditions must be met for development costs to be capitalized:

- Management must have the technical feasibility, intention, and ability to complete the intangible asset and use or sell it.
- A future market must be defined.
- Adequate resources must exist to complete the project.
- Management must be able to measure the costs related to the development of the intangible asset.

If any of these conditions are not met, the development costs must be expensed. Illustration 9-14 shows the distinction between research and development.

Illustration 9-14

Distinction between research and development

Research | **Development**

Research – Examples

- Laboratory research aimed at the discovery of new knowledge
- Searching for ways to use new research findings or other knowledge
- Forming concepts and designs of possible product or process alternatives

Development – Examples

- Testing in search or evaluation of product or process alternatives
- Design, construction, and testing of pre-production prototypes and models
- Design of tools, jigs, moulds, and dies involving new technology

Intangible Assets with Indefinite Lives

An intangible asset is considered to have an indefinite life when there is no foreseeable limit to the length of time over which the asset is expected to generate cash. Examples of intangible assets with indefinite lives include trademarks and trade names, franchises, and licences. Intangible assets do not always fit perfectly in a specific category. Sometimes trademarks, trade names, franchises, or licences do have finite lives. In such cases, they would be amortized over the shorter of their legal or useful lives. It is more usual, however, for these intangible assets, along with goodwill, to have indefinite lives.

Trademarks, Trade Names, and Brands

A **trademark** or **trade name** is a word, phrase, jingle, or symbol that identifies a particular enterprise or product. Trade names like President's Choice, KFC, Nike, Big Mac, the Blue Jays, and TSN create immediate brand recognition and generally help the sale of a product or service. Each year, Interbrands ranks the world's best brands. In 2008, it ranked Coca-Cola as the most successful brand in the world. There were only two Canadian companies included in the list of the 100 most successful global brands in 2008: Thomson Reuters, ranked 44th, and BlackBerry (from Research In Motion Ltd.), ranked 73rd.

The creator can get an exclusive legal right to the trademark or trade name by registering it with the Canadian Intellectual Property Office. This registration gives continuous protection. It may be renewed every 15 years, as long as the trademark or trade name is in use. In most cases, companies continuously renew their trademarks or trade names. In such cases, as long as the trademark or trade name continues to be marketable, it will have an indefinite useful life.

If the trademark or trade name is purchased, the cost is the purchase price. If the trademark or trade name is developed internally rather than purchased, it cannot be recognized as an intangible asset on the balance sheet. The reason is that expenditures on internally developed trademarks or brands cannot be distinguished from the cost of developing the business as a whole. The cost cannot be separately measured.

Franchises and Licences

When you purchase a Civic from a Honda dealer, fill up your gas tank at the corner Mohawk station, or buy coffee from Tim Hortons, you are dealing with franchises. The Forzani Group also uses franchises to sell its products, including Sports Experts, Intersport, Atmosphere, Econosports, RnR, Tech Shop/Pegasus, Nevada Bob's Golf, and Hockey Experts.

A **franchise** is a contractual arrangement under which the franchisor grants the franchisee the right to sell certain products, to provide specific services, or to use certain trademarks or trade names, usually inside a specific geographic area. Another type of franchise is granted by a government body that allows a company to use public property in performing its services. Examples are the use of city streets for a bus line or taxi service; the use of public land for telephone, power, and cable lines; and the use of airwaves for radio or TV broadcasting. Such operating rights are called **licences**.

When costs can be identified with the acquisition of the franchise or licence, an intangible asset should be recognized. These rights have indefinite lives and are not amortized.

Annual payments, which are often in proportion to the franchise's total sales, are sometimes required under a franchise agreement. These payments are called **royalties** and are recorded as operating expenses in the period in which they are incurred.

Goodwill

Goodwill represents the value of all the favourable attributes that relate to a company. These include exceptional management, a desirable location, good customer relations, skilled employees, high-quality products, fair pricing policies, and harmonious relations with labour unions. Unlike other assets, which can be sold individually in the marketplace, goodwill cannot be sold individually as it is part of the business as a whole. It cannot be separated from the company, nor is it based on legal rights.

If goodwill can be identified only with the business as a whole, how can it be determined? An accountant could try to put a dollar value on the attributes (exceptional management, a desirable location, and so on), but the results would be very subjective. Subjective valuations would not contribute to the reliability of financial statements. For this reason, internally generated goodwill is not recognized as an asset.

Goodwill is recorded only when there is a purchase of an entire business, at which time an independent valuation can be determined. The cost of goodwill is measured by comparing the cost paid to purchase the entire business with the fair value of its net assets (assets less liabilities). If the cost is greater than these net identifiable assets, then the purchaser has paid for something that is not identifiable, that cannot be separated and sold—goodwill. In this situation, because a transaction has occurred, the cost of the purchased goodwill can be measured and therefore recorded as an asset.

Because goodwill has an indefinite life, just as the company has an indefinite life, it is not amortized. Since goodwill is measured using the company's fair value—a value that can easily change—it must be tested regularly for impairment just like other intangible assets with indefinite lives. Both goodwill and indefinite life intangible assets must be tested annually for impairment regardless of whether there is any indication of impairment. This is different than finite-life intangible assets, which are assessed for indications of impairment at the end of each year, and are tested only if the assessment shows that an impairment may exist.

Impairment losses on goodwill are never reversed, even if the value of the company increases after the impairment loss has been recognized. But IFRS does allow for reversals of impairment losses on both finite-life and other indefinite-life intangible assets if their value increases in the future.

BEFORE YOU GO ON . . .

Review It

1. What are the similarities and differences between accounting for intangible and tangible assets?
2. Give some examples of intangible assets in your everyday surroundings.
3. What are the differences between the amortization policy for intangible assets with finite lives and the policy for those with indefinite lives?
4. What are the differences between the treatment of impairment losses for (a) intangible assets with finite lives, (b) intangible assets with indefinite lives, and (c) goodwill?

Do It

Dummies 'R' Us Company purchased a copyright to a new book series for $15,000 cash on August 1, 2010. The books are expected to have a saleable life of three years. One year later, the company spends an additional $6,000 cash to successfully defend this copyright in court. The company's year end is July 31. Record (a) the purchase of the copyright on August 1, 2010; (b) the year-end amortization at July 31, 2011; (c) the legal costs incurred on August 1, 2011; and (d) the year-end amortization at July 31, 2012.

Action Plan

- Amortize intangible assets with finite lives over the shorter of their useful life and legal life (the legal life of a copyright is the life of the author plus 50 years).
- Treat costs to successfully defend an intangible asset as a capital expenditure because they benefit future periods.
- Revise amortization for additions to the cost of the asset, using the carrying amount at the time of the addition and the remaining useful life.

Solution

(a)

Aug. 1, 2010	Copyright	15,000	
	Cash		15,000
	To record purchase of copyright.		

(b)

July 31, 2011	Amortization Expense ($15,000 ÷ 3)	5,000	
	Accumulated Amortization—Copyright		5,000
	To record amortization expense.		

(c)

Aug. 1, 2011	Copyright	6,000	
	Cash		6,000
	To record costs incurred to defend copyright.		

(d)

July 31, 2012	Amortization Expense	8,000[1]	
	Accumulated Amortization—Copyright		8,000
	To record revised amortization expense.		

1 $15,000 – $5,000 + $6,000 = $16,000 carrying amount; $16,000 carrying amount ÷ 2 years remaining = $8,000

The Navigator

Related exercise material: BE9–16, E9–12, E9–13, and E9–14.

Statement Presentation and Analysis

STUDY OBJECTIVE 7

Illustrate the reporting and analysis of long-lived assets.

Presentation

Property, plant, and equipment, and natural resources are often combined and reported in the balance sheet as "property, plant, and equipment" or "capital assets." Intangible assets are listed separately, after property, plant, and equipment. Goodwill must be disclosed separately. Other intangibles can be grouped under the caption "intangible assets" for reporting purposes.

For assets that are depreciated or amortized, the balances and accumulated depreciation and/or amortization should be disclosed in the balance sheet or notes. In addition, the depreciation and amortization methods that are used must be described. The amount of depreciation and amortization expense for the period should also be disclosed. For assets that are not depreciated or amortized, the carrying amount of each major type of asset should be disclosed in the balance sheet or notes.

Companies must also disclose their impairment policy in the notes to the financial statements. Impairment losses, if any, should be shown on a separate line on the income statement, with the details disclosed in a note.

The following is an excerpt from Enerflex Systems' 2008 balance sheet:

ENERFLEX SYSTEMS LTD.
Balance Sheet (partial)
December 31, 2008
(in thousands)

ENERFLEX

Assets	
Rental equipment (note 3)	$ 88,641
Property, plant, and equipment (note 3)	70,130
Intangible assets	7,812
Goodwill	126,146

Enerflex provides additional details on the long-lived assets in the notes to its financial statements. For example, note 3 discloses the cost, accumulated depreciation, and carrying amount of Enerflex Systems' property, plant, and equipment, which include land, buildings, equipment, assets under construction, and assets held for sale, and its rental equipment.

Another note, Enerflex Systems' summary of significant accounting policies, further discloses the depreciation methods that are used and the estimated useful lives of the company's long-lived assets. This note also states that major renewals and improvements in rental equipment and property, plant, and equipment are capitalized. It also includes information on Enerflex Systems' policies on testing its long-lived assets for impairment. Rental equipment and property, plant, and equipment are assessed for impairment whenever changes in events or changes in circumstances indicate that the asset's carrying amount may not be recovered. Intangible assets and goodwill are assessed for impairment at least annually. The company did not record any impairment losses in 2008.

Under IFRS, companies such as Enerflex will also have to disclose if they are using the cost or the revaluation model for each class of assets, and include a reconciliation of the carrying amount at the beginning and end of the period for each class of long-lived assets in the notes to the financial statements. This means they must show all of the following for each class of long-lived assets: (1) additions, (2) disposals, (3) depreciation or amortization, (4) impairment losses, and (5) reversals of impairment losses. If a company uses the revaluation model, it must also disclose any increases or decreases from revaluations as well as other information about the revaluation.

Analysis

Typically, long-lived assets are a substantial portion of a company's total assets. We will use two ratios to assess the profitability of total assets: asset turnover and return on assets.

Asset Turnover

The **asset turnover** ratio indicates how efficiently a company uses its assets; that is, how many dollars of sales are generated by each dollar that is invested in assets. It is calculated by dividing net sales by average total assets. If a company is using its assets efficiently, each dollar of assets will create a high amount of sales. When we compare two companies in the same industry, the one with the higher asset turnover is operating more efficiently. The asset turnover ratio for fiscal 2009 for The Forzani Group ($ in thousands) is calculated in Illustration 9-15.

Illustration 9-15
Asset turnover

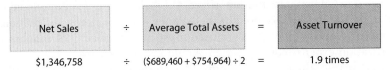

Net Sales	÷	Average Total Assets	=	Asset Turnover
$1,346,758	÷	($689,460 + $754,964) ÷ 2	=	1.9 times

The asset turnover ratio shows that each dollar invested in assets produced $1.90 in sales for Forzani. This ratio varies greatly among different industries—from those that have a large investment in assets (e.g., utility companies) to those that have much less invested in assets (e.g., service companies). Asset turnover ratios, therefore, should only be compared for companies that are in the same industry.

Return on Assets

The **return on assets** ratio measures overall profitability. This ratio is calculated by dividing profit by average total assets. The return on assets ratio indicates the amount of earnings that is generated by each dollar invested in assets. A high return on assets indicates a profitable company. Illustration 9-16 shows the return on assets for Forzani ($ in thousands).

Illustration 9-16
Return on assets

Profit	÷	Average Total Assets	=	Return on Assets
$29,325	÷	($689,460 + $754,964) ÷ 2	=	4.1%

Forzani's return on assets was 4.1% for 2009. As with other ratios, the return on assets should be compared with previous years, with other companies in the same industry, and with industry averages, to determine how well the company has performed.

BEFORE YOU GO ON . . .

Review It

1. How are long-lived assets reported on the financial statements?
2. What information related to long-lived assets is disclosed in the notes to the financial statements?
3. What is the purpose of the asset turnover and return on assets ratios?

The Navigator

Related exercise material: BE9–17, BE9–18, BE9–19, E9–15, and E9–16.

Demonstration Problem 1

WILEY PLUS
Demonstration Problems

DuPage Company purchases a factory machine at a cost of $17,500 on June 1, 2011. The machine is expected to have a residual value of $1,500 at the end of its four-year useful life on May 31, 2015. DuPage has a December 31 year end.

During its useful life, the machine is expected to be used for 10,000 hours. Actual annual use was as follows: 1,300 hours in 2011; 2,800 hours in 2012; 3,300 hours in 2013; 1,900 hours in 2014; and 700 hours in 2015.

Instructions

Prepare depreciation schedules for the following methods: (a) straight-line, (b) units-of-production, and (c) diminishing-balance using double the straight-line rate.

Solution to Demonstration Problem 1

(a) Straight-Line Method

Year	Depreciable Amount	×	Depreciation Rate	=	Depreciation Expense	End of Year Accumulated Depreciation	End of Year Carrying Amount
							$17,500
2011	$16,000[a]		25%[b] × 7/12		$2,333	$ 2,333	15,167
2012	16,000		25%		4,000	6,333	11,167
2013	16,000		25%		4,000	10,333	7,167
2014	16,000		25%		4,000	14,333	3,167
2015	16,000		25% × 5/12		1,667	16,000	1,500

[a] $17,500 – $1,500 = $16,000

[b] 100% ÷ 4 years = 25%

(b) Units-of-Production Method

Year	Units of Production	×	Depreciable Amount/Unit	=	Depreciation Expense	End of Year Accumulated Depreciation	End of Year Carrying Amount
							$17,500
2011	1,300		$1.60[a]		$2,080	$ 2,080	15,420
2012	2,800		1.60		4,480	6,560	10,940
2013	3,300		1.60		5,280	11,840	5,660
2014	1,900		1.60		3,040	14,880	2,620
2015	700		1.60		1,120	16,000	1,500

[a] $17,500 – $1,500 = $16,000 depreciable amount ÷ 10,000 total units = $1.60/unit

(c) Diminishing-Balance Method

Year	Carrying Amount Beginning of Year	×	Depreciation Rate (25% × 2)	=	Depreciation Expense	End of Year Accumulated Depreciation	End of Year Carrying Amount End of Year
							$17,500
2011	$17,500		50% × 7/12		$5,104	$ 5,104	12,396
2012	12,396		50%		6,198	11,302	6,198
2013	6,198		50%		3,099	14,401	3,099
2014	3,099		50%		1,549	15,950	1,550
2015	1,550		50%		50[a]	16,000	1,500

[a] Adjusted to $50 so that the carrying amount at the end of the year is not less than the residual value.

Action Plan

- Deduct the residual value in the straight-line and units-of-production methods, but not in the diminishing-balance method.
- In the diminishing-balance method, the depreciation rate is applied to the carrying amount (cost – accumulated depreciation). The residual value is not used in the calculations except to make sure the carrying amount is not reduced below the residual value.
- When the asset is purchased during the year, the first year's depreciation for the straight-line and diminishing-balance methods must be adjusted for the part of the year that the asset is owned. No adjustment is required for the units-of-production method. In the straight-line method, the final year must also be adjusted.
- Depreciation should never reduce the asset's carrying amount below its estimated residual value.

The Navigator

Demonstration Problem 2

On January 1, 2008, Skyline Limousine Co. purchased a specialty limo for $78,000. The vehicle is being amortized by the straight-line method using a four-year service life and a $4,000 residual value. The company's fiscal year ends on December 31.

WILEY PLUS Demonstration Problems

Instructions

Prepare the journal entry or entries to record the disposal of the limo, assuming that it is:

(a) retired on January 1, 2012.
(b) sold for $15,000 on July 1, 2011.
(c) traded in on a new limousine on January 1, 2011, for a trade-in allowance of $25,000 and cash of $52,000. The fair value of the old vehicle on January 1, 2011, was $20,000.

Action Plan

- Update the depreciation to the date of the disposal for any partial period.
- Determine the asset's carrying amount at the time of disposal.
- Calculate any gain or loss by comparing proceeds with the carrying amount.
- Remove the asset's carrying amount by debiting accumulated depreciation (for the total depreciation to the date of disposal) and crediting the asset account for the cost of the asset. Record proceeds and any gain or loss.
- Ignore trade-in allowances.
- Record the new asset in an exchange situation at the fair value of the asset given up, plus the cash paid.

The Navigator

Solution to Demonstration Problem 2

$$\frac{\$78{,}000 - \$4{,}000}{4 \text{ years}} = \$18{,}500 \text{ annual depreciation expense}$$

(a)

Jan. 1, 2012	Accumulated Depreciation ($18,500 × 4 years)	74,000	
	Loss on Disposal [$0 – ($78,000 – $74,000)]	4,000	
	Limo		78,000
	To record retirement of limo.		

(b)

July 1, 2011	Depreciation Expense ($18,500 × $^6/_{12}$)	9,250	
	Accumulated Depreciation		9,250
	To record depreciation for 6 months.		
	Cash	15,000	
	Accumulated Depreciation ($18,500 × 3.5 years)	64,750	
	Gain on Disposal [$15,000 – ($78,000 – $64,750)]		1,750
	Limo		78,000
	To record sale of limo.		

(c)

Jan. 1, 2011	Limo (new) ($20,000 + $52,000)	72,000	
	Accumulated Depreciation ($18,500 × 3 years)	55,500	
	Loss on Disposal [$20,000 – ($78,000 – $55,500)]	2,500	
	Limo (old)		78,000
	Cash		52,000
	To record exchange of limousines, plus cash.		

Summary of Study Objectives

1. ***Determine the cost of property, plant, and equipment.*** The cost of property, plant, and equipment includes all costs that are necessary to acquire the asset and make it ready for its intended use. All costs that benefit future periods (i.e., capital expenditures) are included in the cost of the asset. When applicable, cost also includes asset retirement costs. When multiple assets are purchased in one transaction, or when an asset has significant components, the cost is allocated to each individual asset or component using their relative fair values.

2. ***Explain and calculate depreciation.*** After acquisition, assets are accounted for using the cost model or the revaluation model. Depreciation is recorded and assets are carried at cost less accumulated depreciation. Depreciation is the allocation of the cost of a long-lived asset to expense over its useful life (i.e., service life) in a rational and systematic way. Depreciation is not a process of valuation and it does not result in an accumulation of cash. There are three commonly used depreciation methods:

Method	Effect on Annual Depreciation	Calculation
Straight-line	Constant amount	(Cost – residual value) ÷ estimated useful life (in years)
Diminishing-balance	Diminishing amount	Carrying amount at beginning of year × diminishing-balance rate
Units-of-production	Varying amount	(Cost – residual value) ÷ total estimated units of production × actual activity during the year

Each method results in the same amount of depreciation over the asset's useful life. Depreciation expense for income tax purposes is called capital cost allowance (CCA). The single diminishing-balance method is required and depreciation rates are prescribed.

3. ***Explain the factors that cause changes in periodic depreciation and calculate revisions.*** A revision to depreciation will be required if there are (1) capital expenditures during the asset's useful life, (2) impairments in the asset's fair value, (3) changes in the asset's fair value when using the revaluation model, and/or (4) changes in the appropriate depreciation method, estimated useful life, or residual value. An impairment loss must be recorded if the recoverable amount is less than the carrying amount. Impairment losses can be reversed in future periods if the recoverable amount increases. Revisions of periodic depreciation are made in present and future periods, not retroactively. The new annual depreciation is determined by using the depreciable amount (carrying amount less the revised residual value), and the remaining useful life, at the time of the revision.

4. ***Account for the disposal of property, plant, and equipment.*** The accounting for the disposal of a piece of property, plant, or equipment through retirement or sale is as follows:

(a) Update any unrecorded depreciation.
(b) Calculate the carrying amount.
(c) Calculate any gain (proceeds > carrying amount) or loss (proceeds < carrying amount) on disposal.
(d) Remove the asset and accumulated depreciation accounts at the date of disposal. Record the proceeds received and the gain or loss, if any.

An exchange of assets is recorded as the purchase of a new asset and the sale of an old asset. The new asset is recorded at the fair value of the asset given up plus any cash paid (or less any cash received). The fair value of the asset given up is compared with its carrying amount to calculate the gain or loss. If the fair value of the new asset or the asset given up cannot be determined, the new long-lived asset is recorded at the carrying amount of the old asset that was given up, plus any cash paid (or less any cash received).

5. ***Calculate and record depreciation of natural resources.*** The units-of-production method of depreciation is generally used for natural resources. The depreciable amount per unit is calculated by dividing the total depreciable amount by the number of units estimated to be in the resource. The depreciable amount per unit is multiplied by the number of units that have been extracted to determine the annual depreciation. The depreciation and any other costs to extract the resource are recorded as inventory until the resource is sold. At that time, the costs are transferred to cost of resource sold on the income statement. Revisions to depreciation will be required for capital expenditures during the asset's useful life, for impairments, and for changes in the total estimated units of the resource.

6. ***Identify the basic accounting issues for intangible assets and goodwill.*** The accounting for tangible and intangible assets is much the same. Intangible assets are reported at cost, which includes all expenditures necessary to prepare the asset for its intended use. An intangible asset with a finite life is amortized over the shorter of its useful life or legal life, usually on a straight-line basis, and must be assessed for impairment annually. Intangible assets with indefinite lives and goodwill are not amortized and are tested at least annually for impairment. Impairment losses on goodwill are never reversed.

7. ***Illustrate the reporting and analysis of long-lived assets.*** It is common for property, plant, and equipment, and natural resources to be combined under the heading "Property, Plant, and Equipment." Intangible assets with finite and indefinite lives are sometimes combined under the heading "Intangible Assets" or are listed separately. Goodwill must be presented separately. Either on the balance sheet or in the notes, the cost of the major classes of long-lived assets is presented. Accumulated depreciation (if the asset is depreciable) and carrying amount must be disclosed either in the balance sheet or in the notes. The depreciation and amortization methods and rates, as well as the annual depreciation expense, must also be indicated. The company's impairment policy and any impairment losses should be described and reported. Under IFRS, companies must include a reconciliation of the carrying amount at the beginning and end of the period for each class of long-lived assets and whether the cost or revaluation model is used.

The asset turnover ratio (net sales ÷ average total assets) is one measure that is used by companies to show how efficiently they are using their assets to generate sales revenue. A second ratio, return on assets (profit ÷ average total assets), calculates how profitable the company is in terms of using its assets to generate profit.

Glossary

WILEY PLUS Glossary
Key Term Matching Activity

Additions and improvements Costs that are incurred to increase the operating efficiency, productive capacity, or expected useful life of property, plant, or equipment. (p. 502)

Amortizable amount The cost of a finite-life intangible asset to be amortized less its residual value. (p. 516)

Amortization The systemic allocation of the amortizable amount of a finite-life intangible asset over its useful life. (p. 515)

Asset retirement costs The cost to dismantle, remove, or restore an asset when it is retired. (p. 490)

Asset turnover A measure of how efficiently a company uses its total assets to generate sales. It is calculated by dividing net sales by average total assets. (p. 521)

Basket purchase The acquisition of a group of assets for a single price. Individual asset costs are determined by allocating relative fair values. (p. 492)

Capital cost allowance (CCA) The depreciation of long-lived assets that is allowed by the *Income Tax Act* for income tax purposes. It is calculated on a class (group) basis and mainly uses the diminishing-balance method with maximum rates specified for each class of assets. (p. 501)

Capital expenditures Expenditures related to long-lived assets that benefit the company over several accounting periods. (p. 490)

Component depreciation Calculating depreciation separately for the different significant components of an item of property, plant, and equipment. Used when the useful life of the component is different from the useful life of the other components or the asset as a whole. (p. 493)

Copyright An exclusive right granted by the federal government allowing the owner to reproduce and sell an artistic or published work. (p. 517)

Cost model A model of accounting for a long-lived asset that carries the asset at its cost less accumulated depreciation or amortization and any impairment losses. (p. 494)

Depreciable amount The cost of a depreciable asset (property, plant, and equipment, or natural resources) less its residual value. (p. 496)

Diminishing-balance method A depreciation method that applies a constant rate to the asset's diminishing carrying amount. This method produces a decreasing annual depreciation expense over the useful life of the asset. (p. 498)

Franchise A contractual arrangement under which the franchisor grants the franchisee the right to sell certain products, offer specific services, or use certain trademarks or trade names, usually inside a specific geographical area. (p. 519)

Goodwill The amount paid to purchase another company that is more than the fair value of the company's net identifiable assets. (p. 519)

Impairment loss The amount by which an asset's carrying amount exceeds its recoverable amount. (p. 503)

Intangible assets Rights, privileges, and competitive advantages that result from owning long-lived assets that have no physical substance. (p. 515)

Land improvements Structural additions to land that have limited useful lives, such as paving, fencing, and lighting. (p. 491)

Licences Operating rights to use public property, granted by a government agency to a company. (p. 519)

Natural resources Long-lived tangible assets, such as standing timber and underground deposits of oil, gas, and minerals, that are physically extracted and are only replaceable by an act of nature. (p. 513)

Operating expenditures Expenditures that benefit only the current period. They are immediately charged against revenues as expenses. (p. 490)

Ordinary repairs Expenditures to maintain the operating efficiency and productive life of the unit. (p. 502)

Patent An exclusive right issued by the federal government that enables the recipient to manufacture, sell, or otherwise control an invention for a period of 20 years from the date of the application. (p. 517)

Property, plant, and equipment Identifiable, long-lived tangible assets, such as land, land improvements, buildings, and equipment, that the company owns and uses for the production and sale of goods or services. (p. 490)

Recoverable amount The higher of the asset's fair value, less costs to sell, and its value in use. (p. 503)

Research and development (R&D) costs Expenditures that may lead to patents, copyrights, new processes, and new products. (p. 517)

Residual value The estimated amount that a company would currently obtain from disposing of the asset if the asset were already as old as it will be, and in the condition it is expected to be in, at the end of its useful life. (p. 496)

Return on assets An overall measure of profitability that indicates the amount of profit that is earned from each dollar invested in assets. It is calculated by dividing profit by average total assets. (p. 522)

Revaluation model A long-lived asset is carried at its fair value less accumulated depreciation or amortization and any impairment losses. (p. 504)

Royalties Recurring payments that may be required under a franchise agreement and are paid by the franchisee to the franchisor for services provided (e.g., advertising, purchasing), and are often proportionate to sales. (p. 519)

Straight-line method A depreciation method in which an asset's depreciable amount is divided by its estimated useful life. This method produces the same periodic depreciation for each year of the asset's useful life. (p. 496)

Tangible assets Long-lived resources that have physical substance, are used in the operations of the business, and are not intended for sale to customers. Tangible assets include property, plant, and equipment and natural resources. (p. 515)

Trade-in allowance A price reduction offered by the seller when a used asset is exchanged for a new asset as part of the deal. (p. 510)

Trademark (trade name) A word, phrase, jingle, or symbol that distinguishes or identifies a particular enterprise or product. (p. 518)

Units-of-production method A depreciation method in which useful life is expressed in terms of the total estimated units of production or use expected from the asset. Depreciation expense is calculated by multiplying the depreciable amount per unit (cost less residual value divided by total estimated activity) by the actual activity that occurs during the year. (p. 499)

Useful life The period of time over which an asset is expected to be available for use, or the number of units of production (such as machine hours) or units of output that are expected to be obtained from an asset. (p. 495)

Self-Study Questions

WILEY PLUS Quizzes

Answers are at the end of the chapter.

(SO 1) AP 1. Asura Company purchased land, a building, and equipment for a package price of $200,000. The land's fair value at the time of acquisition was $75,000. The building's fair value was $80,000. The equipment's fair value was $50,000. What costs should be debited to the three accounts Land, Building, and Equipment, respectively?
(a) $66,667, $66,667, and $66,666
(b) $73,171, $78,049, and $48,780
(c) $75,000, $80,000, and $50,000
(d) $200,000, $0, and $0

(SO 2) AP 2. Cuso Company purchased equipment on January 1, 2010, at a total cost of $40,000. The equipment has an estimated residual value of $10,000 and an estimated useful life of five years. If the straight-line method of depreciation is used, what is the amount of accumulated depreciation at December 31, 2011, the end of the second year of the asset's life?
(a) $6,000
(b) $12,000
(c) $18,000
(d) $24,000

(SO 2) AP 3. Kant Enterprises purchases a truck for $33,000 on July 1, 2011. The truck has an estimated residual value of $3,000, and an estimated useful life of five years, or a total distance of 300,000 kilometres. If 50,000 kilometres are driven in 2011, what amount of depreciation expense would Kant record at December 31, 2011, assuming it uses the units-of-production method?
(a) $2,500
(b) $3,000
(c) $5,000
(d) $5,333

4. Refer to the data for Kant Enterprises in question 3. If Kant uses the double diminishing-balance method of depreciation, what amount of depreciation expense would it record at December 31, 2011? (SO 2) AP
(a) $6,000
(b) $6,600
(c) $12,000
(d) $13,200

5. Which of the following is true? When there is a change in estimated useful life and/or residual value: (SO 3) K
(a) the depreciation of past years should be corrected.
(b) the depreciation of current and future years should be revised.
(c) only the depreciation of future years should be revised.
(d) depreciation does not need to be changed because it is an estimate.

6. Oviatt Company sold equipment for $10,000. At that time, the equipment had a cost of $45,000 and accumulated depreciation of $30,000. Oviatt should record a: (SO 4) AP
(a) $5,000 loss on disposal.
(b) $5,000 gain on disposal.
(c) $15,000 loss on disposal.
(d) $15,000 gain on disposal.

7. St. Laurent Company exchanged an old machine with a carrying amount of $39,000 and a fair value of $35,000 for a new machine. The new machine had a list price of $47,500. St. Laurent was offered a trade-in allowance of $37,500, and paid $10,000 cash in the exchange. At what amount should the new machine be recorded on St. Laurent's books? (SO 4) AP
(a) $35,000

(b) $45,000
(c) $47,000
(d) $49,000

(SO 5) AP 8. On April 1, 2010, Shady Tree Farm Company purchased a Christmas tree farm that has an estimated 100,000 harvestable Christmas trees. The purchase price was $500,000 and the tree farm is expected to have an estimated residual value of $50,000. During the first year of operations, ended January 31, 2011, Shady Tree Farm cut and sold 10,000 trees. What amount of depreciation should be included in cost of goods sold for the year ended January 31?
(a) $37,500
(b) $40,500
(c) $45,000
(d) $50,000

9. Pierce Company had $150,000 of development costs in its laboratory that were related to a patent granted on January 2, 2011. On July 31, 2011, Pierce paid $35,000 for legal fees in a successful defence of the patent. The total amount debited to Patents through July 31, 2011, should be: (SO 9) AP
(a) $35,500.
(b) $150,000.
(c) $185,000.
(d) None of the above.

10. WestJet Airlines Ltd. reported net sales of $2,550 million, profit of $178 million, and average total assets of $3,132 million in 2008. What are WestJet's return on assets and asset turnover? (SO 7) AP
(a) 0. 81% and 5.7 times
(b) 5.7% and 1.2 times
(c) 7.0% and 5.7 times
(d) 5.7% and 0.81 times

Questions

(SO 1) C 1. What are the three characteristics of property, plant, and equipment? When are they recorded as assets?

(SO 1) C 2. What are the three components of the cost of property, plant, and equipment?

(SO 1) C 3. Deer Fern Company purchases equipment and incurs a number of expenditures before it is ready to use the equipment. Give two examples of operating expenditures and two examples of capital expenditures that the company might incur on new equipment and explain how these expenditures would be recorded and why.

(SO 1) C 4. What are land improvements? Should the cost of clearing and grading land be recorded as a land improvement cost or not? Explain.

(SO 1) C 5. Jacques asks why the total cost in a basket purchase has to be allocated to the individual assets. For example, if we purchase land and a building for $250,000, why can we not just debit an account called Land and Building for $250,000? Answer his questions.

(SO 2) C 6. Some people believe that the fair values of property, plant, and equipment are more relevant than the asset's cost for decisions made by such users as creditors, investors, and managers. Why then is the cost model acceptable and more widely used than the revaluation model?

(SO 2) C 7. What is the purpose of depreciation? What are some common misunderstandings about depreciation?

8. Cecile is studying for her next accounting exam. She asks for your help on two questions: (a) What is residual value? (b) How is residual value used in calculating depreciation in each of the depreciation methods? Answer her questions. (SO 2) K

9. Contrast the effects of the three depreciation methods on (1) depreciation expense, (2) profit, (3) accumulated depreciation, and (4) carrying amount in each of the following: (a) in the early years of an asset's life, and (b) over the total life of the asset. (SO 2) C

10. What factors should be considered when choosing a depreciation method? When revising a depreciation method? (SO 2, 3) C

11. Ralph has a plan to reduce the amount of income taxes that will have to be paid on his company's profit. He has decided to calculate depreciation expense using very low estimated useful lives on his property, plant, and equipment. Will Ralph's plan work? (SO 2) C

12. Explain the difference between operating expenditures and capital expenditures during an asset's useful life and describe the accounting treatment of each. (SO 3) C

13. What factors restrict the ability of companies to use the revaluation model and in what circumstances is it significantly more useful than the cost model? (SO 3) C

14. What factors contribute to an impairment loss? In what circumstances, if any, is a company allowed to write up its property, plant, and equipment? (SO 3) C

(SO 3) C 15. In the third year of an asset's four-year useful life, the company decides that the asset will have a six-year service life. Should prior periods be restated because of the revised depreciation? Explain why or why not.

(SO 4) C 16. If equipment is sold in the middle of a fiscal year, why does depreciation have to be updated for the partial period? Doesn't the subsequent journal entry to record the sale remove the accumulated depreciation from the books anyway?

(SO 4) C 17. Ewing Company owns a machine that is fully depreciated but is still being used. How should Ewing account for this asset and report it in the financial statements?

(SO 4) K 18. How is a gain or loss on the sale of an item of property, plant, or equipment calculated? Is the calculation the same for an exchange of a piece of property, plant, or equipment?

(SO 5) K 19. Describe the similarities and differences between natural resources and property, plant, and equipment.

(SO 5) C 20. Why is the units-of-production method used frequently to calculate depreciation for natural resources? Why is the term "depletion" often used instead of "depreciation?"

(SO 5) C 21. Under what circumstances is the depreciation of natural resources recorded as a current asset under inventory rather than as an expense?

22. What are the characteristics of an intangible asset? (SO 6) C

23. Heflin Company has been amortizing its finite-life intangible assets over their legal life. The company's accountant argues this is appropriate because an intangible asset's legal life is known with certainty, but its useful life is subjective. Why is this not correct, and what impact might it have on the company's financial statements? (SO 6) C

24. Bob Leno, a business student, is working on a case problem for one of his classes. In this problem, the company needs to raise cash to market a new product it has developed. Saul Cain, an engineering student, takes one look at the company's balance sheet and says, "This company has an awful lot of goodwill. Why don't you recommend that they sell some of it to raise cash?" How should Bob respond to Saul's suggestion? (SO 6) C

25. How should long-lived assets be reported on the balance sheet and income statement? What information should be disclosed in the notes to the financial statements? (SO 7) K

26. What information do the asset turnover and return on assets ratios show about a company? (SO 7) C

Brief Exercises

BE9–1 The following costs were incurred by Shumway Company in purchasing land: cash price, $75,000; removal of old building, $5,000; legal fees, $2,500; clearing and grading, $3,500; installation of fence, $3,000. (a) What is the cost of the land? (b) What is the cost of the land improvements?

Determine cost of land and land improvements.
(SO 1) AP

BE9–2 Mabasa Company incurs the following costs in purchasing equipment: invoice price, $31,350; installation, $650; testing, $1,000; one-year insurance policy, $2,000. What is the cost of the equipment?

Determine cost of equipment.
(SO 1) AP

BE9–3 In the space provided, indicate whether each of the following items is an operating expenditure (O) or a capital expenditure (C):

Identify operating and capital expenditures.
(SO 1) K

(a) ___ Repaired building roof, $1,500
(b) ___ Replaced building roof, $27,500
(c) ___ Purchased building, $480,000
(d) ___ Purchased supplies, $350
(e) ___ Purchased truck, $55,000
(f) ___ Purchased oil and gas for truck, $125
(g) ___ Rebuilt engine on truck, $5,000
(h) ___ Replaced tires on truck, $600
(i) ___ Estimated retirement cost of plant, $1,000,000
(j) ___ Added new wing to building, $250,000
(k) ___ Painted interior of building, $1,500
(l) ___ Paid insurance on equipment in transit, $550

Record basket purchase.
(SO 1) AP

BE9–4 Rainbow Company purchased land, a building, and equipment on January 2, 2011, for $800,000. The company paid $200,000 cash and signed a mortgage note payable for the remainder. Management's best estimate of the value of the land was $255,000, of the building, $510,000, and of the equipment, $85,000. Record the purchase.

Calculate straight-line depreciation.
(SO 2) AP

BE9–5 On January 2, 2011, Mabasa Company acquires equipment at a cost of $33,000. The equipment is expected to have a residual value of $3,000 at the end of its three-year useful life. Calculate the depreciation using the straight-line method (a) for each year of the equipment's life, and (b) in total over the equipment's life. Mabasa has a December 31 fiscal year end.

Calculate diminishing-balance depreciation.
(SO 2) AP

BE9–6 Depreciation information for Mabasa Company is given in BE9–5. Use the diminishing-balance method and assume the diminishing-balance depreciation rate is double the straight-line rate. Calculate the depreciation expense (a) for each year of the equipment's life, and (b) in total over the equipment's life.

Calculate units-of-production depreciation.
(SO 2) AP

BE9–7 Speedy Taxi Service uses the units-of-production method in calculating depreciation on its taxicabs. Each cab is expected to be driven 525,000 kilometres. Taxi 10 cost $35,000 and is expected to have a residual value of $350. Taxi 10 is driven 110,000 kilometres in 2010, and 155,000 kilometres in 2011. Calculate the depreciation expense for each year.

Calculate partial-year straight-line depreciation.
(SO 2) AP

BE9–8 Depreciation information for Mabasa Company is given in BE9–5. Assuming the equipment was purchased on March 5, 2011, calculate the depreciation using the straight-line method (a) for each year of the truck's life, and (b) in total over the truck's life. The company pro-rates depreciation to the nearest month.

Calculate partial-year diminishing-balance depreciation.
(SO 2) AP

BE9–9 Depreciation information for Mabasa Company is given in BE9–5. Assuming the equipment was purchased on March 5, 2011, calculate the depreciation using the double diminishing-balance method (a) for each year of the truck's life, and (b) in total over the truck's life. Assume the company has a policy of recording a half year's depreciation in the year of acquisition and a half year's depreciation in the year of disposal.

Record impairment loss.
(SO 3) AP

BE9–10 AMMA Phone Company owns machinery that cost $90,000 and has accumulated depreciation of $54,000. The machinery's recoverable amount is $30,000. Record the impairment loss.

Calculate revised depreciation.
(SO 3) AP

BE9–11 On January 2, 2008, Lapointe Company purchased equipment for $60,000. At that time, the equipment was estimated to have a useful life of seven years and a residual value of $4,000. On January 3, 2011, Lapointe upgrades the equipment at a cost of $9,000. Lapointe estimates that the equipment will now have a total useful life of nine years and a residual value of $3,000. The company uses straight-line depreciation and has a December 31 fiscal year end. Calculate the 2011 depreciation expense.

Record disposal by retirement.
(SO 4) AP

BE9–12 On January 3, 2011, Ruiz Company retires its delivery equipment, which cost $37,000. No residual value is received. Prepare journal entries to record the transaction if (a) accumulated depreciation is also $37,000 on this delivery equipment, and (b) the accumulated depreciation is $33,500 instead of $37,000. Ruiz has a December 31 fiscal year end.

Record disposal by sale.
(SO 4) AP

BE9–13 Wiley Company sells office equipment on September 30, 2011, for $21,000 cash. The office equipment was purchased on January 5, 2008, at a cost of $72,000, and had an estimated useful life of five years and an estimated residual value of $2,000. Adjusting journal entries are made annually at the company's year end, December 31. Prepare the journal entries to (a) update depreciation to September 30, 2011, (b) record the sale of the equipment, and (c) record the sale of the equipment if Wiley Company received $15,000 cash for it.

BE9–14 Subramanian Company has machinery with an original cost of $95,000 and, as at December 31, 2010, accumulated depreciation of $78,000. On January 7, 2011, Subramanian exchanges the machinery, plus $62,000 cash, for new machinery. The old machinery has a fair value of $14,000. The dealer gave Subramanian an $18,000 trade-in allowance on the old machinery. Record the January 7, 2011, journal entry for the machinery exchange.

Record disposal by exchange of machinery.
(SO 4) AP

BE9–15 Cuono Mining Co. purchased a mine for $8 million that is estimated to have 25 million tonnes of ore and a residual value of $500,000. In the first year, 7 million tonnes of ore are extracted and 6.5 million tonnes are sold.

Record depreciation and show balance sheet presentation for natural resources.
(SO 5) AP

(a) Record the depreciation and the cost of the ore extracted for the first year, ended August 31, 2011.
(b) Show how the mine and the ore on hand are reported on the balance sheet on August 31, 2011.

BE9–16 Surkis Company purchases a patent for $180,000 cash on January 2, 2011. Its legal life is 20 years and its estimated useful life is 9 years. On January 5, 2012, Surkis paid $25,000 cash to successfully defend the patent in court.

Record acquisition, legal expenditure, and amortization for patent.
(SO 6) AP

(a) Record the purchase of the patent on January 2, 2011.
(b) Record amortization expense for the year ended December 31, 2011.
(c) Record the legal costs on January 5, 2012.
(d) Calculate amortization expense for 2012.

BE9–17 Indicate whether each of the following items is property, plant, and equipment (write "PPE"), a natural resource ("NR"), or an intangible asset ("I"). If the item does not fit any of these categories, write "NA" (not applicable) in the space provided.

Identify and classify long-lived assets.
(SO 7) K

(a) ___ Building
(b) ___ Cost of goods sold
(c) ___ Franchise
(d) ___ Goodwill
(e) ___ Inventory
(f) ___ Land
(g) ___ Licence right
(h) ___ Mining machinery
(i) ___ Natural gas deposit
(j) ___ Note receivable, due in 3 months
(k) ___ Parking lot
(l) ___ Patent
(m) ___ Supplies
(n) ___ Trademark

BE9–18 Canadian Tire Corporation, Limited reports the following selected information about long-lived assets at December 31, 2008 (in millions):

Prepare partial balance sheet.
(SO 7) AP

Accumulated depreciation—buildings	$ 787.1
Accumulated depreciation—fixtures and equipment	434.5
Accumulated depreciation—leasehold improvements	143.5
Buildings	2,347.2
Fixtures and equipment	645.3
Goodwill	70.7
Land	727.9
Leasehold improvements	460.5
Mark's Work Wearhouse store brands and banners	50.4
Mark's Work Wearhouse franchise agreements and locations	8.0
Other property, plant, and equipment	574.0

Mark's Work Wearhouse store brands, banners, and franchises are considered to have indefinite lives. Prepare a partial balance sheet for Canadian Tire.

Calculate ratios.
(SO 7) AP

BE9–19 Agrium Inc., a global agricultural nutrients producer that is headquartered in Calgary, Alberta, reports the following in its 2008 financial statements (in US millions):

Net sales	$10,268	Total assets, December 31, 2008	$9,818
Profit	1,322	Total assets, December 31, 2007	5,832

Calculate Agrium's return on assets and asset turnover for 2008.

Exercises

Classify expenditures.
(SO 1) AP

E9–1 The following expenditures related to property, plant, and equipment were made by Pascal Company:

1. Paid $45,000 for a new delivery truck.
2. Paid $450 to have the company name and advertising slogan painted on the new truck.
3. Paid the $75 motor vehicle licence fee on the new truck.
4. Paid $900 for a one-year accident insurance policy on the new delivery truck.
5. Paid $300,000 for a new plant site.
6. Paid $4,000 in legal fees on the purchase of the plant site.
7. Paid $6,600 to demolish an old building on the plant site; residual materials were sold for $1,700.
8. Paid $4,700 for grading the plant site.
9. Paid $17,500 in architect fees for work on the new plant.
10. Paid $5,600 interest during the construction of the new plant.
11. Paid $17,500 for paving the parking lots and driveways on the plant site.
12. Paid $18,000 for the installation of new factory machinery.
13. Paid $200 for insurance to cover potential damage to the new factory machinery while it was in transit.
14. Estimated it would cost $25,000 for restoration when the company is finished using the plant site.

Instructions

(a) Explain what types of costs should be included in determining the cost of property, plant, and equipment.
(b) List the numbers of the preceding transactions, and beside each number write the account title that the expenditure should be debited to.

Record basket purchase and calculate depreciation.
(SO 1, 2) AP

E9–2 Hohenberger Farms purchased real estate for $1,150,000. It paid $350,000 cash and incurred a mortgage payable for the balance. Legal fees of $10,000 were paid in cash. The real estate included land that was appraised at $720,000, buildings appraised at $420,000, and fences and other land improvements appraised at $60,000. The buildings have an estimated useful life of 40 years and a $20,000 residual value. Land improvements have an estimated 15-year useful life and no residual value.

Instructions

(a) Calculate the cost that should be allocated to each asset purchased.
(b) Record the purchase of the real estate.
(c) Calculate the annual depreciation expense for the buildings and land improvements assuming Hohenberger Farms uses straight-line depreciation.

Calculate cost and depreciation; recommend method.
(SO 1, 2) AP

E9–3 Randell Equipment Repair purchased machinery on March 15, 2011, for $75,000. The company also paid the following amounts: $1,000 for delivery charges; $200 for insurance while the machine was in transit; $1,800 for a one-year insurance policy; and $2,800 for testing and installation. The machine was ready for use on April 1, 2011, but the company did not start using it until May 1, 2011.

Randell will depreciate the machinery over 10 years with no residual value. It expects to consume the machinery's future economic benefits evenly over the useful life. The company has a December 31 fiscal year end.

Instructions

(a) Calculate the cost of the machinery.
(b) When should the company begin depreciating the machinery: March 15, April 1, or May 1? Why?
(c) Which depreciation method should the company use? Why?
(d) Calculate the depreciation on the machinery for 2011 and 2012.

E9–4 Intercity Bus Lines purchases a bus on January 2, 2010, at a cost of $410,000. Over its five-year useful life, the bus is expected to be driven 500,000 kilometres and to have a residual value of $10,000. The company has a December 31 fiscal year end.

Calculate depreciation using three methods; recommend method.
(SO 2) AP

Instructions

(a) Calculate depreciation under the straight-line method for 2010 and 2011.
(b) Calculate the depreciation expense under the diminishing-balance method using double the straight-line rate, for 2010 and 2011.
(c) Calculate the depreciation expense under the units-of-production method, assuming the actual distance driven was 44,800 kilometres in 2010 and 60,300 kilometres in 2011.
(d) Based on this information, which depreciation method should the company use? Why?

E9–5 Sitrus Company purchased a new machine on October 4, 2010, at a cost of $86,000. The company estimated that the machine will have a residual value of $12,000. The machine is expected to be used for 10,000 working hours during its four-year life. Sitrus Company has a December 31 year end and pro-rates depreciation to the nearest month. The actual machine usage was: 500 hours in 2010; 2,800 hours in 2011; 2,900 hours in 2012; 2,600 hours in 2013; and 1,300 hours in 2014.

Prepare depreciation schedules and answer questions.
(SO 2) AP

Instructions

(a) Prepare a depreciation schedule for the life of the asset under each of the following methods:
    1. straight-line,
    2. diminishing-balance using double the straight-line rate, and
    3. units-of-production.
(b) Which method results in the highest depreciation expense over the life of the asset?
(c) Which method results in the highest cash flow over the life of the asset?

E9–6 Bisor Company has a December 31 year end and uses straight-line depreciation for all property, plant, and equipment. On July 1, 2007, the company purchased equipment for $500,000. The equipment had an expected useful life of 10 years and no residual value.

Record depreciation and impairment.
(SO 3) AP

On December 31, 2010, after recording annual depreciation, Bisor reviewed its equipment for possible impairment. Bisor determined that the equipment has a recoverable amount of $225,000. It is not known if the recoverable amount will increase or decrease in the future.

Instructions

(a) Prepare journal entries to record the purchase of the asset on July 1, 2007, and to record depreciation expense on December 31, 2007, and December 31, 2010.
(b) Determine if there is an impairment loss at December 31, 2010, and if any, prepare a journal entry to record it.
(c) Calculate depreciation expense for 2011 and the carrying amount of the equipment at December 31, 2011.
(d) Assume that the equipment is assessed again for impairment at December 31, 2011, and that the company determines the recoverable amount is $240,000. Should Bisor make an adjustment to reflect the increase in the recoverable amount? Explain why or why not.

Calculate and record revised depreciation.
(SO 3) AP

E9–7 Lindy Weink, the new controller of Lafrenière Company, has reviewed the expected useful lives and residual values of selected depreciable assets at December 31, 2010 (depreciation for 2010 has not been recorded yet). Her findings are as follows:

Type of	Date		Total Useful Life in Years		Residual Value	
Asset	Acquired	Cost	Current	Proposed	Current	Proposed
Building	Jan. 1, 1999	$800,000	20	25	$40,000	$65,000
Equipment	Jan. 1, 2009	120,000	5	4	5,000	3,500

After discussion, management agrees to accept Lindy's proposed changes. All assets are depreciated by the straight-line method. Lafrenière Company has a December 31 year end.

Instructions

(a) For each asset, calculate the annual depreciation expense for 2009 and the carrying amount at December 31, 2009.
(b) For each asset, calculate the annual depreciation expense for 2010 and the carrying amount at December 31, 2010.
(c) For each asset, calculate the annual depreciation expense for 2011 and the carrying amount at December 31, 2011.

Record asset addition and depreciation.
(SO 3) AP

E9–8 Mactaquac Company purchased a piece of high-tech equipment on July 1, 2009, for $60,000 cash. The equipment was expected to last four years and have a residual value of $8,000. Mactaquac uses straight-line depreciation and its fiscal year end is June 30.

On July 1, 2010, Mactaquac purchased and installed a new part on the equipment that is expected to significantly increase the equipment's productivity. Mactaquac paid $10,000 cash for the part. It paid an additional $1,000 for the installation and testing of this part. The equipment is expected to last six years in total now and to have a revised residual value of $6,000.

Instructions

(a) Record the annual depreciation of the equipment on June 30, 2010.
(b) Record the purchase of the part, and its installation and testing, on July 1, 2010.
(c) Record the annual depreciation of the equipment on June 30, 2011.
(d) Calculate the carrying amount of the equipment on June 30, 2011, after recording the annual depreciation.

Record disposal of property, plant, and equipment.
(SO 4) AP

E9–9 Here are some transactions of Surendal Company for 2011. Surendal Company uses straight-line depreciation and has a December 31 year end.

Jan. 2 Scrapped a piece of equipment that originally cost $8,000 and was fully depreciated.
Feb. 28 Retired a piece of machinery that was purchased on January 1, 2002, for $54,000. The machinery had an expected useful life of 10 years with no residual value.
Aug. 1 Received $2,000 cash from the sale of office equipment that was purchased on January 1, 2009. The equipment cost $10,980 and was amortized over an expected useful life of three years with no residual value.
Dec. 1 Traded in an old delivery truck for a new delivery truck, receiving a $10,000 trade-in allowance and paying $35,000 cash. The old delivery truck had been purchased on December 1, 2004, at a cost of $30,000. The estimated useful life was eight years and the estimated residual value was $6,000. The fair value of the old delivery truck was $7,000 on December 1, 2011.

Instructions

(a) For each of these disposals, prepare a journal entry to record depreciation from January 1, 2011, to the date of disposal, if required.
(b) For each these disposals, indicate if the disposal has increased (+) or decreased (–) Cash, Equipment, Accumulated Depreciation, total property, plant, and equipment (PP&E), and profit, and by how much. If the item is not changed, write "NE" to indicate there is no effect. Use the following format, in which the first one has been done for you as an example.

Transaction	Cash	Equipment	Accumulated Depreciation	Total PP&E	Total Assets	Owner's Equity	Profit
Jan. 2	NE	–$8,000	–$8,000	NE	NE	NE	NE

(c) Prepare the journal entry to record each of the disposals.

E9–10 On January 3, 2008, Hamir Company purchased computer equipment for $32,000. Hamir planned to keep the equipment for four years, and expected the equipment would then be sold for $2,000. On January 5, 2011, Hamir sold the computer equipment for $6,500.

Calculate gain or loss on disposal under different depreciation methods and comment.
(SO 4) AP

Instructions

(a) Calculate the depreciation expense for 2008, 2009, and 2010 under (1) the straight-line method and (2) the double diminishing-balance method.
(b) Calculate the gain or loss on disposal if Hamir had used (1) the straight-line method and (2) the double diminishing-balance method.
(c) Explain why the gain or loss on disposal is not the same under the two depreciation methods.
(d) Calculate the total depreciation expense plus the loss or minus the gain under (1) the straight-line method and (2) the double diminishing-balance method. Comment on your findings.

E9–11 On July 1, 2011, Phillips Inc. invests $1.3 million in a mine that is estimated to have 800,000 tonnes of ore. The company estimates that the property will be sold for $100,000 when production at the mine has ended. During the last six months of 2011, 100,000 tonnes of ore are mined and sold. Phillips has a December 31 fiscal year end.

Record depreciation for natural resources; show financial statement presentation; comment on potential impairment.
(SO 5) AP

Instructions

(a) Explain why the units-of-production method is often used for depreciating natural resources.
(b) Record the 2011 depreciation.
(c) Show how the mine and any related accounts are reported on the December 31, 2011, income statement and balance sheet.
(d) Assume that the selling price of ore has dropped significantly after December 31, 2011. By June 30, 2012, it is $1.40 per tonne. Does this indicate that the mine may be impaired? Why?

E9–12 An accounting co-op student encountered the following situations at Chin Company:

Apply accounting concepts.
(SO 1, 2, 6) AP

1. During the year, Chin Company purchased land and paid legal fees on the purchase. The land had an old building, which was demolished. The land was then cleared and graded. Construction of a new building will start next year. All of these costs were included in the cost of land. The student decided that this was incorrect, and prepared a journal entry to put the cost of removing the building and clearing and grading the land in land improvements and the legal fees in legal fee expense.
2. The student learned that Chin is depreciating its buildings and equipment, but not its land. The student could not understand why land was not included, so she prepared journal entries to depreciate all of the company's property, plant, and equipment for the current year end.
3. The student decided that Chin's amortization policy on its intangible assets is wrong. The company is currently amortizing its patents but not its trademarks. The student fixed that for the current year end by adding trademarks to her adjusting entry for amortization. She told a fellow student that she felt she had improved the consistency of the company's accounting policies by making these changes.
4. One of the buildings that Chin uses has a zero carrying amount but a substantial fair value. The co-op student felt that leaving the carrying amount at zero did not benefit the financial information's users—especially the bank—and wrote the building up to its fair value. After all, she reasoned, you write down assets if fair values are lower. She feels that writing them up if their fair value is higher is yet another example of the improved consistency that her employment has brought to the company's accounting practices.

Instructions

Explain whether or not the co-op student's accounting treatment in each of the above situations follows generally accepted accounting principles. If it does not, explain why and what the appropriate accounting treatment should be.

Record acquisition, amortization, and impairment of intangible assets.
(SO 6) AP

E9–13 On December 31, 2010, Erhart Company owned the following intangible assets:

1. Goodwill purchased on August 21, 2003, for $360,000.
2. A patent purchased on January 1, 2009, for $225,000. When the patent was purchased, it had an estimated useful life of five years and a legal life of 20 years.

In 2011, Erhart had the following transactions related to intangible assets:

Jan. 2	Incurred legal fees of $22,500 to successfully defend the patent.
Apr. 1	Purchased a 10-year franchise, which expires on April 1, 2021, for $250,000.
July 1	Purchased a trademark with an indefinite expected life for $335,000.
Nov. 1	Incurred research costs of $185,000.
Dec. 31	Reviewed each intangible asset for impairments. Determined that the recoverable amount of the goodwill had declined to $300,000.

Instructions

(a) Record these transactions. All incurred costs were for cash.
(b) Record any necessary amortization and impairment losses on December 31, 2011. Erhart has not previously recorded any impairment losses on its intangible assets.

Determine balance sheet and income statement presentation for intangible assets and goodwill.
(SO 6) AP

E9–14 Whiteway Company has a December 31 fiscal year end. Selected information follows for Whiteway Company for three independent situations as at December 3, 2011:

1. Whiteway purchased a patent from Hopkins Inc. for $400,000 on January 1, 2008. The patent expires on January 1, 2018. Whiteway has been amortizing it over its legal life. During 2011, Whiteway determined that the patent's economic benefits would not last longer than six years from the date of acquisition.
2. Whiteway has a trademark that had been purchased in 2007 for $250,000. During 2010, the company spent $50,000 on a lawsuit that successfully defended the trademark. On December 31, 2011, it was assessed for impairment and the recoverable amount was determined to be $275,000.
3. In 2009, Whiteway purchased another business and paid $70,000 in excess of the fair value of the net identifiable assets of that business. This goodwill was assessed for impairment as at December 31, 2010, and December 31, 2011. The recoverable amount was determined to be $55,000 at December 31, 2010, and $80,000 at December 31, 2011.

Instructions

(a) For each of these assets, determine the amount that will be reported on Whiteway's December 31, 2010 and 2011, balance sheets.
(b) For each of these assets, determine what, if anything, will be recorded on Whiteway's 2011 income statement. Be specific about the account name and the amount.

Classify long-lived assets; prepare partial balance sheet.
(SO 7) AP

E9–15 BCE Inc. reported the following selected information as at December 31, 2008 (in millions):

Accumulated amortization—finite-life intangible assets	$ 3,050
Accumulated depreciation—buildings	1,570
Accumulated depreciation—machinery and equipment	4,567
Accumulated depreciation—other property, plant, and equipment	133
Accumulated depreciation—satellites	562
Accumulated depreciation—telecommunications assets	28,264
Depreciation and amortization expense	3,269
Buildings	3,459

Cash and cash equivalents	$ 363
Common shares	13,525
Finite-life intangible assets	5,747
Goodwill	5,659
Indefinite-life intangible assets	3,697
Land	77
Machinery and equipment	7,009
Other long-term assets	2,625
Other property, plant, and equipment	333
Plant under construction	1,099
Satellites	1,395
Telecommunications assets	41,131

Instructions

(a) Identify in which financial statement (balance sheet or income statement) and which section (e.g., current assets) each of the above items should be reported.
(b) Prepare the tangible and intangible assets sections of the balance sheet as at December 31, 2008.

E9–16 Suncor Energy Inc. reported the following information for the fiscal years ended December 31, 2008, and December 31, 2007 (in millions):

Calculate asset turnover and return on assets.
(SO 7) AN

	Dec. 31, 2008	Dec. 31, 2007
Net revenues	$30,089	$18,565
Profit	2,137	2,983
Total assets, end of year	32,528	24,509
Total assets, beginning of year	24,509	18,759

Instructions

(a) Calculate Suncor's asset turnover and return on assets for the two years.
(b) Comment on what the ratios reveal about Suncor Energy Inc.'s effectiveness in using its assets to generate revenues and produce profit.

Problems: Set A

P9–1A In 2011, Kadlec Company had the following transactions related to the purchase of a property. All transactions were for cash unless otherwise stated.

Record property transactions.
(SO 1) AP

Jan.	12	Purchased real estate for a future plant site for $220,000, paying $55,000 cash and signing a note payable for the balance. On the site, there was an old building and the fair values of the land and building were $210,000 and $30,000, respectively. The old building will be demolished and a new one built.
	16	Paid $4,500 for legal fees on the real estate purchase.
	31	Paid $25,000 to demolish the old building to make room for the new plant.
Feb.	13	Received $7,500 for residual materials from the demolished building.
	28	Graded and filled the land in preparation for the construction for $8,000.
Mar.	14	Paid $35,000 in architect fees for the building plans.
	31	Paid the local municipality $15,000 for building permits.
Apr.	22	Excavation costs for the new building were $17,000.
May	1	Construction on the new building began.
June	15	Received a bill for $300,000 from the building contractor for half of the cost of the new building. Paid $75,000 in cash and signed a note payable for the balance.
Sept.	14	Received a bill for the remaining $300,000 owed to the building contractor for the construction of the new building. Paid $100,000 cash and signed a note payable for the balance.

Oct. 12 Paved the parking lots, driveways, and sidewalks for $42,000.
15 Installed a fence for $8,000.
20 Building was ready for use. Interest costs while the building was under construction amounted to $6,700.
Nov. 30 Kadlec moved in and began using the building.
Dec. 31 Interest costs after the building was in use amounted to $2,800.

Instructions

(a) Record the above transactions.
(b) Determine the cost of the land, land improvements, and building that will appear on Kadlec's December 31, 2011, balance sheet.

Taking It Further Should Kadlec record depreciation on this property in 2011? If yes, on which assets and as of when should it start recording depreciation?

Calculate partial period depreciation.
(SO 2) AP

P9–2A In recent years, Flatboard Company purchased two machines. Various depreciation methods were selected. Information on the machines is summarized here:

Machine	Acquired	Cost	Residual Value	Useful Life in Years	Depreciation Method
1	Mar. 2, 2008	$392,000	$ 8,000	10	Straight-line
2	Oct. 25, 2010	120,000	20,000	8	Single diminishing-balance

Instructions

(a) If Flatboard has a policy of recording depreciation to the nearest month, calculate the amount of accumulated depreciation on each machine at December 31, 2011. Round your answers to the nearest dollar.
(b) If Flatboard has a policy of recording a half year's depreciation in the year of acquisition and disposal, calculate the amount of accumulated depreciation on each machine at December 31, 2011. Round your answers to the nearest dollar.
(c) Which policy should Flatboard follow in the year of acquisition: recording depreciation to the nearest whole month or recording a half year of depreciation?

Taking It Further Should Flatboard consider recording depreciation to the nearest day? Why or why not?

Determine cost; calculate and compare depreciation under different methods.
(SO 1, 2) AP

P9–3A Whiteline Company purchased a machine on account on September 3, 2009, at an invoice price of $204,000. On September 4, 2009, it paid $10,400 for delivery of the machine. A one-year, $1,975 insurance policy on the machine was purchased on September 6, 2009. On September 20, 2009, Whiteline paid $8,600 for installation and testing of the machine. The machine was ready for use on October 1, 2009.

Whiteline estimates that the machine's useful life will be four years, with a residual value of $13,000. It also estimates that, in terms of activity, the machine's useful life will be 90,000 units. Whiteline has a December 31 fiscal year end and records depreciation to the nearest month. Assume that actual usage is as follows: 6,000 units in 2009; 27,450 units in 2010; 22,950 units in 2011; 20,100 units in 2012; and 13,500 units in 2013.

Instructions

(a) Determine the cost of the machine.
(b) Prepare depreciation schedules for the life of the asset under the following assumptions:

1. Whiteline uses the straight-line method of depreciation.
2. Whiteline uses the diminishing-balance method at double the straight-line rate.
3. Whiteline uses the units-of-production method.

(c) Which method would result in the highest profit in 2009? Over the life of the asset?
(d) Which method would result in the highest cash flow in 2009? Over the life of the asset?

Taking It Further Assume instead that, when Whiteline purchased the machine, it had a legal obligation to ensure that the machine was recycled at the end of its useful life. Assume the cost of doing this is significant. Would this have had an impact on the answers to (a) and (b) above? Explain.

P9–4A Arnison Company had the following selected transactions related to property, plant, and equipment in 2011:

Account for operating and capital expenditures, and asset impairments.
(SO 1, 3) AP

Jan. 12 All of the company's light bulbs were converted to energy-efficient bulbs for $2,200. Arnison expects that this will save money on its utility bills in the future.
Feb. 24 An air conditioning system in the factory was installed for $75,000.
Mar. 6 A fee of $5,400 was paid to paint machinery that had started to rust.
May 17 Safety training was given to factory employees on using the machinery at a cost of $3,100.
July 19 Windows broken in a labour dispute (not covered by insurance) were replaced for $5,900.
Aug. 21 Paid $26,000 to convert the company's trucks from gasoline to propane. Arnison expects this will substantially reduce the trucks' future operating costs, but it will not extend the trucks' useful lives.
Sept. 20 The exhaust system in a delivery vehicle was repaired for $2,700.
Oct. 25 New parts were added to a machine for $20,000. Arnison expects this will increase the machine's useful life by four years.
Nov. 9 The tires on two delivery vehicles were replaced for $1,200.
Dec. 31 After recording annual depreciation, Arnison reviewed its property, plant, and equipment for possible impairment. Arnison determined the following:

1. Land that originally cost $200,000 had previously been written down to $125,000 in 2008 as a result of a decline in the recoverable amount. The current recoverable amount of the land is $220,000.
2. The recoverable amount of equipment that originally cost $150,000 and has accumulated depreciation of $62,500 is $50,000.

Instructions

(a) For each of these transactions, indicate if the transaction has increased (+) or decreased (–) Land, Buildings, Equipment, Accumulated Depreciation, total property, plant, and equipment (PP&E), and profit, and by how much. If the item is not changed, write "NE" to indicate there is no effect. Use the following format, in which the first one has been done for you as an example.

Transaction	Land	Buildings	Equipment	Accumulated Depreciation	Total PP&E	Profit
Jan. 12	NE	NE	NE	NE	NE	–$2,200

(b) Prepare journal entries to record the above transactions. All transactions are paid in cash.

Taking It Further Assume that Arnison also purchases a new machine with an expected useful life of 12 years. Assume also that the machine's engine will need to be replaced every four years. Which useful life should Arnison use when calculating depreciation on the machine? Explain.

P9–5A At the beginning of 2006, Bérubé Company acquired equipment costing $1.2 million. It was estimated at that time that this equipment would have a useful life of 10 years and a residual value of $100,000. Bérubé uses the straight-line method of depreciation and has a December 31 year end.

Record impairment and calculate revised depreciation.
(SO 3) AP

On December 31, 2010, after recording the annual depreciation expense, Bérubé determined that the equipment's recoverable amount was $400,000. In 2011, Bérubé determined that the equipment's useful life will remain as originally estimated but that the equipment would have no residual value at the end of its useful life.

Instructions

(a) Calculate the depreciation expense for the years 2006 to 2010 and accumulated depreciation at December 31, 2010.
(b) Record the impairment loss on December 31, 2010.
(c) Would you expect Bérubé's depreciation expense to increase or decrease in 2011 after recording the impairment loss? Explain why.
(d) Calculate depreciation expense for the years 2011 to 2015. Assume no further impairments or recoveries.
(e) What will accumulated depreciation and the equipment's carrying amount be at the end of its useful life?

Taking It Further What factors could cause a decline in the recoverable amount of equipment?

Record acquisition, depreciation, impairment, and disposal of land and building.
(SO 2, 3, 4) AP

P9–6A NW Tool Supply Company purchased land and a building on May 1, 2009, for $385,000. The company paid $115,000 in cash and signed a 5% note payable for the balance. At that time, it was estimated that the land was worth $150,000 and the building, $235,000. The building was estimated to have a 25-year useful life with a $35,000 residual value. The company has a December 31 year end and uses the single diminishing-balance depreciation method for buildings. The following are related transactions and adjustments during the next three years.

2009	
Dec. 31	Recorded annual depreciation.
31	Paid the interest owing on the note payable.
2010	
Feb. 17	Paid $225 to have the furnace cleaned and serviced.
Dec. 31	Recorded annual depreciation.
31	Paid the interest owing on the note payable.
31	The land and building were tested for impairment. The land had a recoverable amount of $120,000 and the building, $240,000.
2011	
Jan. 31	Sold the land and building for $320,000 cash: $110,000 for the land and $210,000 for the building.
Feb. 1	Paid the note payable and interest owing.

Instructions

(a) Record the above transactions and adjustments, including the purchase on May 1, 2009.
(b) What factors may have been responsible for the impairment?
(c) Assume instead that the company sold the land and building on October 31, 2011, for $400,000 cash: $160,000 for the land and $240,000 for the building. Record the journal entries to record the sale.

Taking It Further How might management determine what is the recoverable amount of the land and buildings at each year end? Would the company need to test the assets for impairment every year?

Calculate and compare depreciation and gain or loss on disposal under straight-line and diminishing-balance methods.
(SO 1, 2, 4) AP

P9–7A Forristal Farms purchased a piece of equipment on December 28, 2008, for $91,500. The equipment had an estimated useful life of five years and a residual value of $7,500. Management is considering the merits of using the double diminishing-balance method of depreciation versus the straight-line method. Management feels that the straight-line method will have a more favourable impact on the income statement.

Instructions

(a) Calculate depreciation for the equipment for 2009 to 2013 under (1) the straight-line method, and (2) the diminishing-balance method, using double the straight-line rate.
(b) Assume that the equipment is sold on January 3, 2013, for $15,000.
1. Calculate the gain or loss on the sale of the equipment, under (a) the straight-line method, and (b) the diminishing-balance method.
2. Prepare a schedule to show the overall impact of the total depreciation expense combined with the gain or loss on sale over the life of the asset under each method of depreciation. (Consider the total effect on profit over the asset's life.) Compare this with the difference between the asset's purchase price and the proceeds received from its sale. Comment on your results.

Taking It Further What factors should influence management's choice of depreciation method?

Record acquisition, depreciation, and disposal of equipment.
(SO 2, 4) AP

P9–8A Express Co. purchased delivery equipment on March 1, 2009, for $65,000 on account. The equipment had an estimated useful life of five years, with a residual value of $5,000. The equipment is disposed of on September 30, 2011. Express Co. uses the straight-line method of depreciation and calculates depreciation for partial periods to the nearest month. The company has an August 31 year end.

Instructions

(a) Record the acquisition of the delivery equipment on March 1, 2009.
(b) Record depreciation at August 31, 2009, 2010, and 2011.
(c) Record the disposal on September 30, 2011, under the following assumptions:
1. It was scrapped with no residual value.
2. It was sold for $30,000.
3. It was sold for $40,000.
4. It was traded for new delivery equipment with a list price of $87,000. Express was given a trade-in allowance of $32,000 on the old delivery equipment and paid the balance in cash. Express determined the old equipment's fair value to be $28,000 at the date of the exchange.

Taking It Further What are the arguments in favour of recording gains and losses on disposals of property, plant, and equipment as part of profit from operations? What are the arguments in favour of recording them as non-operating items?

Record property, plant, and equipment transactions; prepare partial financial statements.
(SO 2, 4, 7) AP

P9–9A At January 1, 2011, Hamsmith Corporation reported the following property, plant, and equipment accounts:

Accumulated depreciation—buildings	$31,100,000
Accumulated depreciation—equipment	27,000,000
Buildings	48,700,000
Equipment	75,000,000
Land	10,000,000

Hamsmith uses straight-line depreciation for buildings and equipment and its fiscal year end is December 31. The buildings are estimated to have a 50-year useful life and no residual value; the equipment is estimated to have a 10-year useful life and no residual value. Interest on the notes is payable or collectible annually on the anniversary date of the issue.

During 2011, the following selected transactions occurred:

Apr. 1 Purchased land for $2.2 million. Paid $550,000 cash and issued a three-year, 6% note for the balance.
May 1 Sold equipment for $150,000 cash. The equipment cost $1.4 million when originally purchased on January 1, 2003.
June 1 Sold land for $1.8 million. Received $450,000 cash and accepted a three-year, 5% note for the balance. The land cost $700,000.
July 1 Purchased equipment for $1.1 million cash.
Dec. 31 Retired equipment that cost $500,000 when purchased on December 31, 2001.

Instructions

(a) Record the above transactions.
(b) Record any adjusting entries required at December 31, 2011.
(c) Prepare the property, plant, and equipment section of Hamsmith's balance sheet at December 31, 2011.

Taking It Further The owner of Hamsmith suggests the company should start using the revaluation model, not the cost model, for property, plant, and equipment now that it is following International Financial Reporting Standards. Comment on this suggestion.

Correct errors in recording intangible asset transactions.
(SO 6) AP

P9–10A Due to rapid turnover in the accounting department, several transactions involving intangible assets were improperly recorded by Riley Co. in the year ended December 31, 2011:

1. Riley developed a new manufacturing process early in the year, incurring research and development costs of $160,000. Of this amount, 45% was considered to be development costs that could be capitalized. Riley recorded the entire $160,000 in the Patents account and amortized it using a 15-year estimated useful life.
2. On July 1, 2011, Riley purchased a small company and, as a result of the purchase, recorded goodwill of $400,000. Riley recorded a half year's amortization on the goodwill in 2011 based on a 40-year useful life.
3. The company purchased a trademark for $47,500. Shortly thereafter, it was sued for trademark infringement. At the end of the year, Riley determined that the recoverable amount of the trademark was $35,000. Riley did not record an impairment loss because it is hopeful that the recoverable amount will rebound next year after the conclusion of a legal case defending the company's right to use this trademark.
4. Several years ago, Riley paid $70,000 for a licence to be the exclusive Canadian distributor of a Danish beer. In 2008, Riley determined there was an impairment of $40,000 in the value of the licence and recorded the loss. In 2011, because of a change in consumer tastes, the value of the licence increased to $80,000. Riley recorded the $50,000 increase in the licence's value by crediting Gain on Licence Fair Value and debiting the licence account. Management felt the company should consistently record increases and decreases in value.
5. The company made an $8,000 charitable donation on December 31, 2011, which it debited to goodwill.

Instructions

Prepare the journal entries that are needed to correct the errors made during 2011.

Taking It Further The majority of the intangible assets reported on a balance sheet have been purchased as opposed to being internally generated. Why? What happens to the cost of an internally generated intangible asset if it is not recorded as an asset?

Record intangible asset transactions; prepare partial balance sheet.
(SO 6, 7) AP

P9–11A The intangible assets reported by Ip Company at December 31, 2010, follow:

Patent #1	$70,000	
Less: Accumulated amortization	14,000	$ 56,000
Copyright #1	$48,000	
Less: Accumulated amortization	28,800	19,200
Goodwill		210,000
Total		$285,200

Patent #1 was acquired in January 2009 and has an estimated useful life of 10 years. Copyright #1 was acquired in January 2006 and also has an estimated useful life of 10 years. The following cash transactions may have affected intangible assets during the year 2011:

Jan. 2	Paid $22,400 of legal costs to successfully defend Patent #1 against infringement by another company.
June 30	Developed a new product, incurring $220,000 in research costs and $60,000 in development costs, which were paid in cash. Patent #2 was granted for the product on July 1. Its estimated useful life is equal to its legal life of 20 years.
Sept. 1	Paid $21,000 to an Olympic athlete to appear in commercials advertising the company's products. The commercials will air in September.
Oct. 1	Acquired a second copyright for $16,000 cash. Copyright #2 has an estimated useful life of eight years.
Dec. 31	Determined the recoverable amount of the goodwill to be $245,000. The company had originally paid $250,000 for the goodwill in 2008. In 2009, the company had recorded a $40,000 impairment loss on the goodwill. There is no indication that the patents and copyrights were impaired.

Instructions

(a) Record the above transactions.
(b) Prepare any adjusting journal entries required at December 31, 2011.
(c) Prepare the intangible assets section of the balance sheet at December 31, 2011.

Taking It Further Since intangible assets do not have physical substance, why are they considered to be assets?

P9–12A Yount Mining Company has a December 31 fiscal year end. The following information related to its Gough Alexander mine is available:

Record natural resource transactions; prepare partial financial statements. (SO 3, 5, 7) AP

1. Yount purchased the Gough Alexander mine on March 31, 2010, for $2.6 million cash. On the same day, modernization of the mine was completed at a cash cost of $260,000. It is estimated that this mine will yield 560,000 tonnes of ore. The mine's estimated residual value is $200,000. Yount expects it will extract all the ore, and then close and sell the mine site in four years.
2. During 2010, Yount extracted and sold 120,000 tonnes of ore from the mine.
3. At the beginning of 2011, Yount reassessed its estimate of the remaining ore in the mine. Yount estimates that there is still 550,000 tonnes of ore in the mine at January 1, 2011. The estimated residual value remains at $200,000.
4. During 2011, Yount extracted and sold 100,000 tonnes of ore from the mine.

Instructions

(a) Prepare the 2010 and 2011 journal entries for the above, including any year-end adjustments.
(b) Show how the Gough Alexander mine will be reported on Yount's December 31, 2011, income statement and balance sheet.

Taking It Further If the total estimated amount of units that will be produced (extracted) changes during the life of the natural resource, is it still appropriate to use the units-of-production method? Explain.

P9–13A Andruski Company and Brar Company both manufacture in-line skates. They reported the following information at December 31, 2011 (in thousands):

Calculate ratios and comment. (SO 7) AN

	Andruski Company	Brar Company
Net sales	$449.0	$1,464.1
Profit	15.5	84.8
Total assets, start of year	589.6	1,288.5
Total assets, end of year	561.9	1,324.4

Instructions

(a) For each company, calculate the asset turnover and return on assets ratios. Round your answers to two decimal points.
(b) Based on your results in part (a), compare the two companies by commenting on how effective they are at using their assets to generate sales and produce profit.

Taking It Further What other information would be useful in comparing these two companies?

Problems: Set B

Record property transactions. (SO 1) AP

P9–1B In 2011, Weisman Company had the following transactions related to the purchase of a property. All transactions are for cash unless otherwise stated.

Feb.	7	Purchased real estate for $275,000, paying $75,000 cash and signing a note payable for the balance. The site had an old building on it and the fair value of the land and building were $270,000 and $30,000, respectively. Weisman intends to demolish the old building and construct a new building on the site.
	9	Paid legal fees of $5,500 on the real estate purchase on February 7.
	15	Paid $11,000 to demolish the old building and make the land ready for the construction of the apartment building.
	17	Received $4,000 from the sale of material from the demolished building.
	25	Graded and filled the land in preparation for the building construction at a cost of $9,000.
Mar.	2	Architect's fees on the apartment building were $18,000.
	15	Excavation costs were $15,000. Construction began on March 20.
Aug.	31	The full cost for construction of the apartment building was $650,000. Paid $170,000 cash and signed a note payable for the balance.
Sept.	3	Paid $12,000 for sidewalks and a parking lot for the building.
	10	Building was ready for use. Purchased a one-year insurance policy on the finished building for $2,500.
	11	Interest costs while the building was under construction amounted to $6,500.
Oct.	31	Moved into the building and began using it.
Dec.	31	Interest costs after the building was completed and rented to tenants amounted to $17,500.

Instructions

(a) Record the above transactions.
(b) Determine the cost of the land, land improvements, and building that will appear on Weisman's December 31, 2011, balance sheet.

Taking It Further Should Weisman record depreciation on this property in 2011? If yes, on which assets and as of when should it start calculating depreciation?

Calculate partial period depreciation. (SO 2) AP

P9–2B In recent years, Tarcher Company purchased two machines and uses a different method of depreciation for each. Information on the machines is as follows:

Machine	Acquired	Cost	Residual Value	Useful Life in Years	Depreciation Method
1	Feb. 5, 2009	$ 97,880	$8,000	7	Straight-line
2	Sept. 25, 2010	168,000	9,000	10	Diminishing-balance

The company uses double the straight-line rate for the diminishing-balance method.

Instructions

(a) If Tarcher has a policy of recording depreciation to the nearest month, calculate the amount of accumulated depreciation on each machine at December 31, 2011. Round your answers to the nearest dollar.
(b) If Tarcher has a policy of recording a half year of depreciation in the year of acquisition and disposal, calculate the amount of accumulated depreciation on each machine at December 31, 2011. Round your answers to the nearest dollar.
(c) Which policy should Tarcher follow: recording depreciation to the nearest month in the year of acquisition or recording a half year of depreciation in the year of acquisition?

Taking It Further How would Tarcher's choice of how to record depreciation in the year of acquisition affect depreciation calculations if Tarcher used the units-of-production method to amortize the machines?

P9–3B Orange-Circle Company purchased a machine on account on April 6, 2009, at an invoice price of $360,000. On April 7, 2009, it paid $2,000 for delivery of the machine. A one-year, $3,175 insurance policy on the machine was purchased on April 9, 2009. On April 22, 2009, Orange-Circle paid $6,400 for installation and testing of the machine. The machine was ready for use on April 30, 2009.

Determine cost; calculate and compare depreciation under different methods.

(SO 1, 2) AP

Orange-Circle estimates that the machine's useful life will be five years, with a residual value of $23,000. Orange-Circle estimates that the machine's useful life, in terms of activity, will be 165,000 units. Orange-Circle has a December 31 fiscal year end and records depreciation to the nearest month. Assume actual usage is as follows: 25,500 units in 2009; 36,000 units in 2010; 34,500 units in 2011; 31,500 units in 2012; 28,500 units in 2013; and 9,000 units in 2014.

Instructions

(a) Determine the cost of the machine.
(b) Prepare a depreciation schedule for the life of the asset under each of the following assumptions:
1. Orange-Circle uses the straight-line method of depreciation.
2. Orange-Circle uses the diminishing-balance method at double the straight-line rate.
3. Orange-Circle uses the units-of-production method.

(c) Which method would result in the lowest profit in 2009? Over the life of the asset?
(d) Which method would result in the lowest cash flow in 2009? Over the life of the asset?

Taking It Further Assume instead that at the time Orange-Circle purchased the machine, it had a legal obligation to ensure that the machine was recycled at the end of its useful life. Assume the cost of doing this is significant. Would this have had an impact on the answers to (a) and (b) above? Explain.

P9–4B Sugden Company had the following selected transactions related to property, plant, and equipment in 2011:

Account for operating and capital expenditures and asset impairments.

(SO 1, 3) AP

Jan. 22 Performed an annual safety inspection on the equipment for $4,600.
Apr. 10 Installed a conveyor belt system in the factory for $95,000, which is expected to increase efficiency and allow the company to produce more products each year.
May 6 Replaced carpets in the main reception area and hallways for $15,500.
July 20 Repaired a machine for $10,000. An employee had used incorrect material in the machine, which resulted in a complete breakdown.
Aug. 7 Overhauled machinery that originally cost $100,000 for $35,000. This increased the machinery's expected useful life by three years.
15 Trained several new employees to operate the company's machinery at a cost of $1,900.
Nov. 6 Added an elevator and ramps to a building owned by the company to make it wheelchair accessible for $120,000.
28 Replaced the tires on several company vehicles for $5,000.

Dec. 31 After recording annual depreciation, Sugden reviewed its property, plant, and equipment for possible impairment. Sugden determined the following:

1. The recoverable amount on equipment that originally cost $200,000 and has accumulated depreciation of $75,000 is $90,000.
2. Land that originally cost $575,000 had previously been written down to $480,000 as a result of an impairment in 2008. Circumstances have changed, and the land's recoverable amount is $620,000.

Instructions

(a) For each of these transactions, indicate if the transaction has increased (+) or decreased (–) Land, Buildings, Equipment, Accumulated Depreciation, total property, plant, and equipment (PP&E), and profit, and by how much. If the item is not changed, write "NE" to indicate there is no effect. Use the following format, in which the first one has been done for you as an example.

Transaction	Land	Buildings	Equipment	Accumulated Depreciation	Total PP&E	Profit
Jan. 22	NE	NE	NE	NE	NE	–$4,600

(b) Prepare journal entries to record the above transactions. All transactions are on account.

Taking It Further Assume that Sugden also purchased a new machine with an expected useful life of 15 years and that the machine's engine will need to be replaced every five years. Which useful life should Sugden use when calculating depreciation on the machine? Explain.

Record impairment and calculate revised depreciation. (SO 3) AP

P9–5B On January 4, 2007, Harrington Company acquired equipment costing $375,000. It was estimated at that time that this equipment would have a useful life of 10 years and a residual value of $15,000. Harrington uses the straight-line method of depreciation and has a December 31 year end.

On December 31, 2010, after recording the annual depreciation expense, Harrington determined that the equipment's recoverable amount was $155,000. In 2011, Harrington also determined that the equipment's useful life would be 7 years in total, instead of the previously estimated 10. The residual value is still expected to be $15,000 at the end of the equipment's useful life.

Instructions

(a) Calculate the depreciation expense for the years 2007 to 2010 and accumulated depreciation at December 31, 2010.
(b) Record the impairment loss on December 31, 2010.
(c) Would you expect Harrington's depreciation expense to increase or decrease in 2011 after recording the impairment loss? Explain why.
(d) Calculate depreciation expense for each of 2011, 2012, and 2013.
(e) What should the equipment's accumulated depreciation and carrying amount be at the end of its useful life?

Taking It Further What factors could cause a decline in the recoverable amount on equipment? Why might this also reduce the equipment's estimated useful life?

Record acquisition, depreciation, impairment, and disposal of land and buildings. (SO 1, 2, 3, 4) AP

P9–6B SE Parts Supply Company purchased land and a building on August 1, 2009, for $595,000. It paid $200,000 in cash and signed a 5% note payable for the balance. The company estimated the land was worth $340,000 and building, $255,000. The building was estimated to have a 40-year useful life with a $15,000 residual value. The company has a December 31 year end and uses the straight-line depreciation method for buildings. The following are related transactions and adjustments during the next three years.

2009

Dec. 31 Recorded annual depreciation.

31 Paid the interest owing on the note payable.

2010
May 21 Paid $2,000 to fix the roof.
31 Recorded annual depreciation.
31 Paid the interest owing on the note payable.
31 The land and building were tested for impairment. The land had a recoverable amount of $280,000 and the building, $249,000.

2011
Mar. 31 Sold the land and building for $480,000 cash: $250,000 for the land and $230,000 for the building.
Apr. 1 Paid the note payable and interest owing.

Instructions

(a) Record the above transactions and adjustments, including the acquisition on August 1, 2009.
(b) What factors may have been responsible for the impairment?
(c) Assume instead that the company sold the land and building on November 30, 2011, for $650,000 cash: $390,000 for the land and $260,000 for the building. Record the journal entries to record the sale.

Taking It Further How might management determine the recoverable amount of the land and buildings at each year end? Does the company need to test the assets for impairment every year?

P9–7B Rapid Transportation Ltd. purchased a new bus on January 5, 2010, at a cost of $254,000. The bus has an estimated useful life of three years with a residual value of $40,000. Management is contemplating the merits of using the units-of-production method of depreciation instead of the straight-line method, which it currently uses.

Calculate and compare depreciation and gain or loss on disposal under straight-line and units-of-production methods.
(SO 2, 4) AP

Under the units-of-production method, management estimates a total estimated useful life of 450,000 kilometres: 175,000 kilometres driven in 2010; 152,000 kilometres in 2011; and 123,000 kilometres in 2012.

Instructions

(a) Calculate depreciation for the life of the bus using (1) the straight-line method and (2) the units-of-production method. Rapid Transportation has a December 31 fiscal year end.
(b) Assume that the bus is sold on December 30, 2011, for $100,000.
1. Calculate the gain or loss on the sale of the bus under (a) the straight-line method and (b) the units-of-production method. (*Hint*: Round the depreciable cost per unit to four decimals.)
2. Prepare a schedule to show the overall impact of the total depreciation expense combined with the gain or loss on sale for the two-year period under each method of depreciation. (Consider the total effect on profit over the two-year period.) Compare this with the difference between the asset's purchase price and the proceeds received from its sale. Comment on your results.

Taking It Further What factors should influence management's choice of depreciation method?

P9–8B Walker Co. purchased office furniture on February 1, 2009, for $85,000 on account. At that time, it was expected to have a useful life of five years and a $1,000 residual value. The furniture was disposed of on October 26, 2011, when the company moved to new premises. Walker Co. uses the straight-line method of depreciation and calculates depreciation for partial periods to the nearest month. The company has a September 30 year end.

Record acquisition, depreciation, and disposal of furniture.
(SO 2, 4) AP

Instructions

(a) Record the acquisition of the office furniture on February 1, 2009.
(b) Record depreciation for each of 2009, 2010, and 2011.
(c) Record the disposal on October 26, 2011, under the following assumptions:

1. It was scrapped and has no residual value.
2. It was sold for $50,000.
3. It was sold for $40,000.
4. It was traded for new office furniture with a catalogue price of $113,000. Walker Co. was given a trade-in allowance of $45,000 on the old office furniture and paid the balance in cash. Walker Co. determined that the old office furniture's fair value was $38,000 at the date of the exchange.

Taking It Further What are the arguments in favour of recording gains and losses on disposals of property, plant, and equipment as part of profit from operations? What are the arguments in favour of recording them as non-operating items?

Record property, plant, and equipment transactions; prepare partial financial statements.
(SO 2, 4, 7) AP

P9–9B At January 1, 2011, Jaina Company reported the following property, plant, and equipment accounts:

Accumulated depreciation—buildings	$12,100,000
Accumulated depreciation—equipment	15,000,000
Buildings	28,500,000
Equipment	48,000,000
Land	4,000,000

Jaina uses straight-line depreciation for buildings and equipment, and its fiscal year end is December 31. The buildings are estimated to have a 50-year life and no residual value; the equipment is estimated to have a 10-year useful life and no residual value. Interest on all notes is payable or collectible at maturity on the anniversary date of the issue.

During 2011, the following selected transactions occurred:

Apr.	1	Purchased land for $1.9 million. Paid $475,000 cash and issued a 10-year, 6% note for the balance.
May	1	Sold equipment that cost $750,000 when purchased on January 1, 2004. The equipment was sold for $350,000 cash.
June	1	Sold land purchased on June 1, 1993, for $1.2 million. Received $380,000 cash and accepted a 6% note for the balance. The land cost $300,000.
July	1	Purchased equipment for $1 million on account, terms n/60.
Dec.	31	Retired equipment that cost $470,000 when purchased on December 31, 2001.

Instructions

(a) Record the above transactions.
(b) Record any adjusting entries required at December 31, 2011.
(c) Prepare the property, plant, and equipment section of Jaina's balance sheet at December 31, 2011.

Taking It Further The owner of Jaina Company suggests the company should start using the revaluation model, not the cost model, for property, plant, and equipment now that it is following International Financial Reporting Standards. Comment on this suggestion.

Correct errors in recording intangible asset transactions.
(SO 6) AP

P9–10B Due to rapid employee turnover in the accounting department, the following transactions involving intangible assets were recorded in a questionable way by Hahn Company in the year ended August 31, 2011:

1. Hahn developed an electronic monitoring device for running shoes. It incurred research costs of $70,000 and development costs with probable future benefits of $45,000. It recorded all of these costs in the Patent account.
2. The company registered the patent for the monitoring device developed in transaction 1. Legal fees and registration costs totalled $21,000. These costs were recorded in the Legal Fees Expense account.
3. The company successfully fought a competitor in court, defending its patent. It incurred $38,000 of legal fees. These costs were recorded in the Legal Fees Expense account.

4. The company recorded $5,750 of annual amortization on the patent over its legal life of 20 years [($70,000 + $45,000 = $115,000) ÷ 20 years]. The patent's expected economic life is five years. Assume that for amortization purposes, all costs occurred at the beginning of the year.
5. At the end of the year, Hahn tested the patent for impairment and found that its recoverable amount of $110,000 exceeded its carrying amount of $109,250 ($115,000 – $5,750). Since Hahn follows the cost model, it did not record an entry.

Instructions

Prepare the journal entries that are needed to correct the errors made during 2011.

Taking It Further The majority of the intangible assets reported on a balance sheet have been purchased as opposed to being internally generated. Why? What happens to the cost of an internally generated intangible asset if it is not recorded as an asset?

Record intangible asset transactions; prepare partial balance sheet.

(SO 6, 7) AP

P9–11B The intangible assets section of Ghani Corporation's balance sheet at December 31, 2010, is as follows:

Copyright #1	$36,000	
Less: Accumulated amortization	24,000	$ 12,000
Trademark		54,000
Goodwill		125,000
Total		$191,000

The copyright was acquired in January 2009 and has an estimated useful life of three years. The trademark was acquired in January 2007 and is expected to have an indefinite useful life. The following cash transactions may have affected intangible assets during 2011:

Jan. 2	Paid $7,000 in legal costs to successfully defend the trademark against infringement by another company.
July 1	Developed a new product, incurring $210,000 in research costs and $50,000 in development costs. A patent was granted for the product on July 1, and its useful life is equal to its legal life.
Aug. 1	Paid $60,000 to a popular hockey player to appear in commercials advertising the company's products. The commercials will air in September and October.
Oct. 1	Acquired a second copyright for $180,000. The new copyright has an estimated useful life of three years.
Dec. 31	The company determined the recoverable amount of the trademark and goodwill to be $65,000, and $90,000, respectively. There was no indication that any of the patents or copyrights were impaired.

Instructions

(a) Prepare journal entries to record the transactions.
(b) Prepare any adjusting journal entries required at December 31, 2011.
(c) Prepare the intangible assets section of the balance sheet at December 31, 2011.

Taking It Further Since intangible assets do not have physical substance, why are they considered to be assets?

Record equipment, note payable, and natural resource transactions; prepare partial financial statements.

(SO 2, 5, 7) AP

P9–12B Cypress Timber Company has a December 31 fiscal year end. The following information related to its Westerlund tract of timber land is available:

1. Cypress purchased a 50,000-hectare tract of timber land at Westerlund on June 7, 2010, for $50 million, paying $10 million cash and signing a 7% mortgage payable for the balance. Principal payments of $8 million and the annual interest on the mortgage are due each December 31. It is estimated that this tract will yield 1 million tonnes of timber. The timber tract's estimated residual value is $2 million. Cypress expects it will cut all the trees and then sell the Westerlund site in five years.

2. On June 26, 2010, Cypress purchased and installed weighing equipment at the Westerlund timber site for $196,000 cash. The weighing equipment will be amortized on a straight-line basis over an estimated useful life of seven years with no residual value. Cypress has a policy of recording depreciation for partial periods to the nearest month. The weighing equipment will be scrapped after the Westerlund site is harvested.
3. In 2010, Cypress cut and sold 110,000 tonnes of timber.
4. In 2011, Cypress cut and sold 240,000 tonnes of timber.

Instructions

(a) Prepare the 2010 and 2011 journal entries for the above, including any year-end adjustments.
(b) Show how property, plant, and equipment, natural resources, and related accounts will be reported on Cypress's December 31, 2011, income statement and balance sheet.

Taking It Further If the total estimated amount of units that will be produced (extracted) changes during the life of the natural resource, is it still appropriate to use the units-of-production method? Explain.

Calculate ratios and comment. (SO 7) AN

P9–13B STAD Company and STHN Company, two companies that manufacture sea kayaks, reported the following information in 2011 (in millions):

	STAD Company	STHN Company
Net sales	$341.7	$9,411.5
Profit	12.8	672.6
Total assets, January 1, 2011	264.5	4,429.9
Total assets, December 31, 2011	234.0	5,343.9

Instructions

(a) For each company, calculate the asset turnover and return on assets ratios. Round your answer to two decimals.
(b) Based on your results in part (a), compare the two companies by commenting on how effective they are at using their assets to generate sales and produce profit.

Taking It Further What, if anything, complicates your ability to compare the two companies?

Continuing Cookie Chronicle

(*Note:* This is a continuation of the Cookie Chronicle from Chapters 1 through 8.)

Natalie is thinking of buying a van that will only be used for business. The cost of the van is estimated at $27,200. Natalie would spend an additional $2,500 to have the van painted. As well, she wants the back seat of the van removed so that she will have lots of room to transport her mixer inventory and baking supplies. The cost of taking out the back seat and installing shelving units is estimated at $1,500. She expects the van to last about five years and to be driven for 200,000 km. The annual cost of vehicle insurance will be $1,440. Natalie estimates that at the end of the five-year useful life, the van will sell for $6,600. Assume that she will buy the van on August 15, 2011, and it will be ready for use on September 1, 2011.

Natalie is concerned about the impact of the van's cost on her income statement and balance sheet. She has come to you for advice on calculating the van's depreciation.

Instructions

(a) Determine the cost of the van.
(b) Prepare schedules for each method of depreciation: (1) straight-line (similar to the one in Illustration 9-5), (2) double diminishing-balance (Illustration 9-7), and (3) units-of-production (Illustration 9-9). For units of production, it is estimated that the van will be driven as follows: 15,000 km in 2011, 45,000 km in 2012, 50,000 km in 2013, 45,000 km in 2014, 35,000 km in 2015, and 10,000 km in 2016. Recall that Cookie Creations has a December 31 year end.
(c) What impact will each method of depreciation have on Natalie's balance sheet at December 31, 2011? What impact will each method have on Natalie's income statement in 2011?
(d) What impact will each method of depreciation have on Natalie's income statement in total over the van's five-year useful life?
(e) Which method of depreciation would you recommend that Natalie use? Why?

BROADENING YOUR PERSPECTIVE

Financial Reporting and Analysis

Financial Reporting Problem

BYP9–1 Refer to the financial statements and the Notes to Consolidated Statements for The Forzani Group Ltd., which are reproduced in Appendix A.

Instructions

(a) Identify the following amounts for the company's long-lived assets (capital assets, goodwill and other intangibles, and other assets) at February 1, 2009: (1) cost, (2) accumulated depreciation (amortization), and (3) carrying amount (net book value).
(b) What was the amount of cash used to buy capital assets during the 2009 fiscal year? (*Hint*: Look at the statement of cash flows to determine this amount.)
(c) What depreciation methods are used by Forzani for financial reporting purposes (see note 2 to the financial statements)? What was the amount of depreciation (amortization) expense reported in the statement of operations for fiscal 2009?
(d) What expected useful life does the company use to calculate the depreciation (amortization) on the "furniture, fixtures, equipment, software and automotive" grouping of capital assets?
(e) What types of intangible assets does Forzani have?
(f) Did the company report any impairment losses in 2009 related to capital assets? How does Forzani determine if an impairment loss needs to be recorded?

Interpreting Financial Statements

BYP9–2 Maple Leaf Foods is Canada's largest food processor, serving customers across North America and internationally. Near the end of 2006, the company announced that it was going to restructure its meat processing business. In management's discussion and analysis in the 2008 annual report, it identifies expansion of capacity at the Brandon, Manitoba, pork processing plant as a major milestone achieved in 2008. The cash flow statement identifies "additions to property and equipment" of $206 million in 2008, some of which was for the Brandon expansion. However, some of the "expansion of capacity" involved only adding an extra shift (i.e., running the equipment and staffing the operations for 16 hours per day instead of just 8 hours per day).

Instructions

(a) How should Maple Leaf account for additions to property and equipment at the Brandon, Manitoba, pork processing plant?
(b) Identify and discuss advantages and disadvantages of three different possible depreciation methods for Maple Leaf Foods' pork processing facilities. Which method would you recommend that Maple Leaf use to depreciate the Brandon plant? Which method would you recommend for the equipment? Explain your reason for choosing the method(s) you did.
(c) Would you still choose the same depreciation method(s) in (b) if the plant moved to a three-shift operation (24 hours per day)? If you do choose the same depreciation method, how would the amount of annual depreciation expense be affected by the change to a three-shift operation compared with a double-shift operation?

Critical Thinking

Collaborative Learning Activity

Note to instructor: Additional instructions and material for this group activity can be found on the Instructor Resource Site.

WILEY PLUS
Working in Groups

BYP9–3 In this group activity, you will review the following three depreciation methods:

1. Straight-line
2. Diminishing-balance
3. Units-of-production.

Instructions

(a) Your instructor will divide the class into "home" groups with three members in each "home" group. Each member of your "home" group will choose one of the above methods and then move to the "expert" group for that method.
(b) In the "expert" group, you will be given a handout explaining your method of depreciation. As a group, discuss the handout and ensure that each group member thoroughly understands that method.
(c) Return to your "home" group and explain your method to the other students in the group.
(d) You may be asked by your instructor to write a short quiz on this topic

Communication Activity

BYP9–4 Long Trucking Corporation is a medium-sized publicly owned trucking company with trucks that are driven across North America. The company owns large garages and equipment to repair and maintain the trucks. Ken Bond, the controller, knows that long-lived assets are reviewed annually for impairment. Ken records an impairment loss of $100,000 and the loss appears on the income statement for the current fiscal year. Jason Long, the company president, reviews the financial statements and wants more information from Ken about the impairment loss.

WILEY PLUS
Writing Handbook

Instructions

Write a memo to Jason Long that explains (1) what might have caused the impairment loss, (2) the journal entry required for the impairment loss, and (3) how this writedown will affect Long Trucking's balance sheet and income statement in future years.

Ethics Case

BYP9–5 Finney Container Company has been seeing sales go down for its main product, non-biodegradable plastic cartons. Although some expenses have also reduced in line with the reduced revenues, there has been a decrease in profit because some expenses, such as depreciation, have not reduced. The company uses the straight-line depreciation method.

WILEY PLUS
Ethics in Accounting

The president, Philip Shapiro, recalling his college accounting classes, instructs his controller to lengthen the estimated asset lives used for depreciation calculations in order to reduce annual depreciation expense and increase profit. The president's compensation includes an annual bonus based on the amount of net profit reported in the income statement.

A processing line of automated plastic extruding equipment that was purchased for $2.9 million in January 2009 was originally estimated to have a useful life between five and nine years. Therefore, the company used the middle of that estimate, or seven years, as the useful life, and a residual value of $100,000, to calculate the annual straight-line depreciation for the first two years. However, the president now wants the equipment's estimated useful life to be changed to nine years (total), and to continue using the straight-line method.

The controller is hesitant to make the change, believing it is unethical to increase profit in this way. The president says, "Hey, the useful life is only an estimate. Besides, I've heard that our competition uses a nine-year estimated life on its production equipment. You want the company results to be competitive, don't you? So maybe we were wrong the first time and now we are getting it right. Or you can tell the auditors that we think maybe the equipment will last longer now that we are not using it as much."

Instructions

(a) Who are the stakeholders in this situation?
(b) Is the suggested change in asset life unethical, or simply a shrewd business practice by a sharp president?
(c) What would be the impact of the president's proposed change on profit in the year of the change?

"All About You" Activity

BYP9–6 In the "All About You" feature, you learned about actions that have been taken to toughen Canada's copyright law and the radical changes in technology that are driving the need to update the law. You have recently graduated from a music program and have composed two songs that you believe a recording artist may produce. You are wondering how you can best get copyright protection for your songs.

Instructions

Go to the Canadian Intellectual Property Office website at http://www.cipo.ic.gc.ca and search for its publication "A Guide to Copyrights."

Answer the following questions:

(a) What is a copyright and to what does copyright apply?
(b) How can you obtain a copyright for your songs and what do you have to do to be protected?
(c) What are the benefits to you of getting copyright registration for your songs?
(d) How and where do you register a copyright?
(e) Section 55 of the *Copyright Act* is the section that applies to registering the copyrights for the songs that you have written. How much is the registration fee if you file the application on-line?
(f) Should the registration fee for the copyright be recorded as an asset?
(g) What is infringement of copyright? Provide a specific example of infringement.
(h) Whose responsibility is it for policing the use of your songs once you have registered the copyright?

ANSWERS TO CHAPTER QUESTIONS

Answers to Accounting in Action Insight Questions

Business Insight, p. 500

Q: Is the units-of-production method the best depreciation method for Morris Formal Wear to use for its tuxedos or would you recommend another method?

A: Since Morris Formal Wear wants to track wear and tear on each of its tuxedos, the units-of-production depreciation method is the best choice. Rental tuxedos are the type of long-lived asset that will physically wear out with use much faster than they would become obsolete due to changing tuxedo styles. By keeping track of how many times each tuxedo has been used, instead of just how old they are, the company can make better decisions about when to replace the tuxedos.

Across the Organization, p. 505

Q: What parts of an organization are responsible for determining if an impairment loss should be recorded?

A: The accounting department would work closely with the operations department to determine if there might be an impairment. In many companies, the operations department is responsible for forecasting demand and then monitoring sales to determine if its forecasts are accurate and if it needs to adjust production plans. Thus the operations department would be a valuable source of information to the accounting department in determining if an impairment exists.

All About You Insight, p. 517

Q: Is it important that the copyrights of artists, writers, musicians, and the entertainment industry be protected?

A: Just as it is important that you as an individual be compensated in your career, it is important that individuals in artistic, music, entertainment, and literary careers be compensated fairly for their creativity. Without fair compensation, Canada's creativity and innovation will be discouraged. Without copyright protection, it may be difficult to ensure that appropriate individuals are fairly compensated and companies may not be willing to invest in creative ventures if the work is not protected.

Answer to Forzani Review It Question 5, p. 493

Forzani reports (in thousands) land, \$3,173; buildings, \$20,928; building on leased land, \$4,583; furniture, fixtures, equipment, software, and automotive, \$243,564; leasehold improvements, \$260,030; and construction in progress, \$14,029.

Answers to Self-Study Questions

1. b 2. b 3. c 4. b 5. b 6. a 7. b 8. c 9. c 10. d

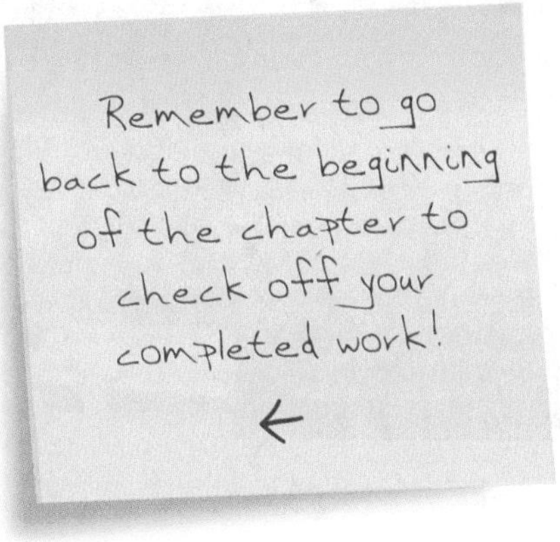
Remember to go
back to the beginning
of the chapter to
check off your
completed work!

CHAPTER 10
CURRENT LIABILITIES AND PAYROLL

THE NAVIGATOR

- [ ] Understand *Concepts for Review*
- [ ] Read *Feature Story*
- [ ] Scan *Study Objectives*
- [ ] Read *Chapter Preview*
- [ ] Read text and answer *Before You Go On*
- [ ] Work *Demonstration Problem*
- [ ] Review *Summary of Study Objectives*
- [ ] Answer *Self-Study Questions*
- [ ] Complete assignments

CONCEPTS FOR REVIEW:

Before studying this chapter, you should understand or, if necessary, review:

a. How to make adjusting entries for unearned revenue (Ch. 3, p. 127) and accrued expenses. (Ch. 3, pp. 130–132)

b. The importance of liquidity in evaluating the financial position of a company. (Ch. 4, pp. 200–201)

c. How to account for sales discounts. (Ch. 5, p. 257)

d. Accounting for notes receivable. (Ch. 8, pp. 448–451)

Even Small Companies Have Big Payroll Obligations

A big portion of any organization's current liabilities is its payroll obligations: employees' salaries or wages, and any related deductions for things like the Canada Pension Plan, Employment Insurance, and income taxes. Then there are health care taxes, workers' compensation premiums, and any taxable benefits the employer offers. Depending on the size and reach of the business, there are up to 185 different pieces of legislation and regulations that a payroll person would have to keep up to date with, points out Steven Van Alstine, Vice President, Compliance Programs and Services, at the Canadian Payroll Association (CPA). This includes the federal *Income Tax Act* and *Employment Insurance Act*, provincial workers' compensation regulations, employment standards, health tax acts, and so on. "It is difficult, certainly if you're a new small business, being faced with myriad different requirements or legislation," he says. "It is a little daunting when you think, as a new business owner, 'What do I have to do?'"

No doubt, accounting for this liability can be a challenge for smaller businesses. Of the CPA's 14,000 members, 65% to 70% are organizations with 200 or fewer employees, says Van Alstine. But several resources are available to help them. For about one third of people working in payroll, payroll is their sole responsibility, he continues. But for the remaining two thirds, it's only a part of their responsibilities, which likely include such functions as human resources or accounts payable. The CPA is an information source for people who don't handle payroll on a full-time basis. "We are a support for those individuals who may be the sole payroll person within the organization," he says. Consultants are on hand to answer questions by phone and guide payroll staff through the process.

The CPA offers a certification program for payroll professionals. In addition, it offers "Learning Payroll" courses. The association also has a "Setting Up a New Payroll" checklist that lists various resources and forms an employer may need and where to locate them, including those specific to provinces.

The Canada Revenue Agency also has tools available to help employers with their payroll, including an on-line payroll deduction calculator, which many may think does the job for them. However, as Van Alstine points out, "The employer needs to know that those are the deductions for the employee."

Those lacking the necessary qualifications and skills to properly account for payroll may hire a CPA-certified professional, a bookkeeper, or an accounting firm to take over the paperwork. Or they may outsource the whole payroll function to a service provider like Ceridian or ADP. The benefits to employers include reduced costs, partly because they use the service provider's technology rather than setting up their own system. They also don't have to service the technology and update it, though they are still responsible for their day-to-day payroll administration.

Payroll is a liability that needs proper administration no matter what the size of the business is. After all, a company's employees are its greatest asset.

The Navigator

STUDY OBJECTIVES:

After studying this chapter, you should be able to:

1. Account for determinable or certain current liabilities.
2. Account for estimated liabilities.
3. Account for contingencies.
4. Determine payroll costs and record payroll transactions.
5. Prepare the current liabilities section of the balance sheet.
6. Calculate mandatory payroll deductions (Appendix 10A).

The Navigator

PREVIEW OF CHAPTER 10

Whether it is a huge company such as one of Canada's chartered banks, or a small business such as your local convenience store, every company has current liabilities. As explained in Chapter 4, current liabilities are obligations that are expected to be settled within one year from the balance sheet date or in the company's normal operating cycle. Obligations that are expected to be paid after one year or longer are classified as long-term liabilities. We explain current liabilities in this chapter and long-term liabilities in Chapter 15. Payroll creates current liabilities and affects almost every company. It is also explained in this chapter.

The chapter is organized as follows:

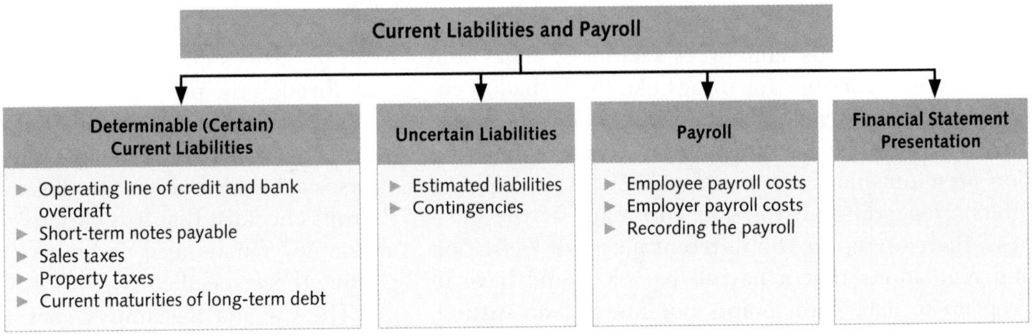

Determinable (Certain) Current Liabilities

STUDY OBJECTIVE 1

Account for determinable or certain current liabilities.

In Chapter 1, we defined liabilities as present obligations, arising from past events, to make future payments of assets or services. A future commitment is not considered a liability unless an obligation also exists. For example, a company may have made a commitment to purchase an asset in the future, but the obligation normally arises only when the goods are delivered or if the company has entered into an irrevocable agreement. Thus, an essential characteristic of a liability is the existence of a *present* obligation.

Sometimes there is a great deal of uncertainty regarding whether or not a liability exists. Even if it is certain that the liability exists, then sometimes we are not certain as to whom we owe, how much we owe, or when we owe. We will discuss this type of liability in the sections on estimated liabilities and contingencies.

In this section of the chapter, we will discuss liabilities where there is no uncertainty about their existence, amount, or timing. Liabilities with a known amount, payee, and due date are often referred to as **determinable liabilities**.

Alternative terminology Determinable liabilities are also referred to as *certain liabilities* or *known liabilities*.

Examples of determinable current liabilities include bank indebtedness from operating lines of credit, and notes payable, accounts payable, sales taxes payable, unearned revenue, and current maturities of long-term debt. This category also includes accrued liabilities such as property taxes, payroll, and interest.

The entries for many of these liabilities have been explained in previous chapters, including the entries for accounts payable and unearned revenues. We will discuss the accounting for other types of current liabilities in this section, including bank indebtedness from an operating line of credit, notes payable, sales taxes payable, property taxes payable, and current maturities of long-term debt. Payroll and employee benefits payable are also examples of determinable liabilities, but as the accounting for payroll is complex, we discuss it in a separate section of this chapter.

Operating Line of Credit and Bank Overdraft

Operating Line of Credit

Current assets (such as accounts receivable) do not always turn into cash at the exact time that current liabilities (such as accounts payable) must be paid. Consequently, most companies have an **operating line of credit** at their bank to help them manage temporary cash shortfalls. This means that the company has been pre-authorized by the bank to borrow money when it is needed, up to a pre-set limit.

Security, called **collateral**, is usually required by the bank as protection in case the company is unable to repay the loan. Collateral normally includes some, or all, of the company's current assets (e.g., accounts receivable or inventories); investments; or property, plant, and equipment. The Forzani Group Ltd. has a $250-million operating line of credit that is "collateralized by general security agreements against all existing and future acquired assets of the Company." Forzani refers to it as a "revolving credit facility" as opposed to an "operating line of credit."

Money borrowed through a line of credit is normally borrowed on a short-term basis, and is repayable immediately upon request—that is, on demand—by the bank. In reality, repayment is rarely demanded without notice. A line of credit makes it very easy for a company to borrow money. It does not have to make a call or visit its bank to actually arrange the transaction. The bank simply covers any cheques written in excess of the bank account balance, up to the approved credit limit.

Bank Overdraft

Some companies have a negative (credit), or overdrawn, cash balance at year end. This amount is usually called *bank indebtedness*, *bank overdraft*, or *bank advances*. No special entry or account is required to record the overdrawn amount. The Cash account has a credit balance because the dollar amount of cheques written exceeded the dollar amount of deposits. The credit balance in Cash is reported as a current liability with an appropriate note disclosure.

Interest is usually charged on the overdrawn amount at a floating rate, such as prime plus a specified percentage. The **prime rate** is the interest rate that banks charge their best customers. This rate is usually increased by a specified percentage according to the company's risk profile.

Short-Term Notes Payable

The line of credit described above is similar to a **note payable**. Notes payable are obligations in the form of written promissory notes. In Chapter 8, we discussed notes receivable and included an illustration of a promissory note. You will recall that the payee has a note receivable and the maker of the note has a note payable.

Notes payable may be used instead of accounts payable. This gives the lender proof of the obligation in case legal action is needed to collect the debt. Accounts and notes payable that result from purchase transactions (i.e., amounts owed to suppliers) are often called **trade payables**. Notes payable are also frequently issued to meet short-term financing needs.

Helpful hint Notes payable are the opposite of notes receivable, and the accounting is similar.

Notes are issued for varying periods. If they are due for payment within one year of the balance sheet date, they are classified as current liabilities. Most notes are interest-bearing, with interest due monthly or at maturity.

To illustrate the accounting for notes payable, assume that Kok Co. borrows $100,000 from the local Caisse Populaire on March 1 for four months, at an interest rate of 6%. The note matures on July 1 and interest, along with the principal amount of the note, is payable at maturity.

Kok makes the following journal entry when it signs the note and receives the $100,000:

Mar. 1	Cash	100,000	
	Note Payable		100,000
	To record issue of four-month, 6% note to Caisse Populaire.		

A	=	L	+	OE
+100,000		+100,000		

↑ Cash flows: +100,000

Interest accrues over the life of the note; therefore, interest expense must be recorded in the period when the borrowed money is used. Also, at year end, all liabilities (all obligations) must be recorded. If Kok Co. has a March 31 year end, then the interest owing at the end of March must be recorded. An adjusting entry is made to recognize interest expense and interest payable of $500 ($100,000 × 6% × $^{1}/_{12}$) at March 31. Recall from Chapter 3 that interest is calculated by multiplying the principal amount by the annual interest rate by the fraction of the year in the accrual.

The adjusting entry is:

A	=	L	+	OE
		+500		−500

Cash flows: no effect

Mar. 31	Interest Expense	500	
	Interest Payable		500
	To accrue interest to March 31.		

In the March 31 financial statements, the current liabilities section of the balance sheet will show notes payable of $100,000 and interest payable of $500. In addition, interest expense of $500 will be reported as other expenses in the income statement. Interest payable is shown separately from the note payable.

At maturity (July 1), Kok Co. must pay the face value of the note ($100,000) plus $2,000 interest ($100,000 × 6% × $^4/_{12}$). One month ($500) of this interest has already been accrued. Interest must also be updated for $1,500 ($100,000 × 6% × $^3/_{12}$) for the three additional months—April through June—since interest was last recorded. This can be done in one compound entry or in separate journal entries as follows:

A	=	L	+	OE
		+1,500		−1,500

Cash flows: no effect

A	=	L	+	OE
−102,000		−100,000		
		−2,000		

↓ Cash flows: −102,000

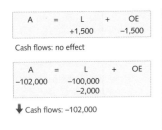

July 1	Interest Expense	1,500	
	Interest Payable		1,500
	To accrue interest for April, May, and June.		
1	Note Payable	100,000	
	Interest Payable ($500 + $1,500)	2,000	
	Cash ($100,000 + $2,000)		102,000
	To record payment of Caisse Populaire note and accrued interest.		

Sales Taxes

As a consumer, you are well aware that you pay sales taxes on many of the products you buy at retail stores. For the retail store, sales taxes collected from customers are a liability because the company has an obligation to pay the amount collected to the appropriate government body.

Sales taxes are expressed as a percentage of the sales price. As discussed in earlier chapters and in Appendix B, sales taxes usually take the form of the federal Goods and Services Tax (GST) and Provincial Sales Tax (PST). In Quebec, the provincial sales tax is called the Quebec Sales Tax (QST). The GST is 5% across Canada. Provincial sales tax rates vary from 0% to 10% across the country.

At the time of writing, in British Columbia, Ontario, Newfoundland and Labrador, Nova Scotia, and New Brunswick, the PST and GST have been or were about to be combined into one 13% Harmonized Sales Tax (HST). It was also expected that Saskatchewan and Manitoba would decide to harmonize their sales taxes in the near future. Alberta, Yukon, Northwest Territories, and Nunavut do not have PST. Quebec and Prince Edward Island are the only two provinces with a separate provincial sales tax system, where there are currently no thoughts of harmonizing with the federal sales tax.

Whether GST, PST, or HST, the retailer collects the tax from the customer when the sale occurs. The retailer then pays (remits) the sales taxes collected to the designated federal and provincial collecting authorities. In the case of GST, HST, and QST, collections may be offset against payments. In such cases, only the net amount owing or recoverable must be paid or refunded. Depending on the size of the retailer, the sales taxes must be sent to the government monthly, quarterly or, for very small companies, annually.

The amount of the sale and the amount of the sales tax collected are usually rung up separately on the cash register. The cash register readings are then used to credit sales or services and the correct sales taxes payable accounts. For example, if the March 25 cash register reading for Comeau Company, in New Brunswick, shows sales of $10,000 and Harmonized Sales Tax of $1,300 ($10,000 × 13% HST rate), the entry is as follows:

Mar. 25	Cash	11,300	
	Sales		10,000
	HST Payable		1,300
	To record sales and sales taxes.		

A	=	L	+	OE
+11,300		+1,300		+10,000

↑ Cash flows: +11,300

Comeau Company does not report the sales taxes collected from customers as revenue; sales taxes collected from customers are a liability. Comeau Company serves only as a collection agent for the government. When Comeau Company remits (pays) these sales taxes to the appropriate government collecting authorities, the HST Payable account is debited and Cash is credited.

Some businesses include sales taxes in the selling price. They do not separate sales taxes from the price of the goods sold. In these businesses, however, sales taxes must still be recorded separately from sales revenues. To find the sales amount, the total receipts are divided by 100% plus the sales tax percentage.

To illustrate, assume that Comeau Company's total receipts of $11,300 include HST. The total receipts from the sale are equal to 100% of the sales amount plus 13% of sales, or 1.13 times the sales amount, which gives $11,300. We can use algebra to calculate the sales amount as follows: $11,300 ÷ 1.13 = $10,000. The HST of $1,300 can be found by multiplying the sales amount by the sales tax rate ($10,000 × 13% = $1,300).

Helpful hint If sales taxes are included in the sales price, then the sales tax collected is equal to the selling price × the sales tax percentage *divided by 100% plus the sales tax percentage.*

Currently, in two provinces, the provincial sales tax is charged on the total selling price plus GST. For example, in Prince Edward Island a $100 sale is subject to $5 GST ($100 × 5%) and $10.50 PST [($100 + $5) × 10%]. The escalated sales tax rate is 15.5% [($5 + $10.50) ÷ $100] rather than 15% (5% GST + 10% PST). Quebec also charges QST on the selling price plus GST. It is important to be careful when getting sales tax amounts from total receipts because of the different rate combinations across Canada.

Property Taxes

Businesses that own property pay property taxes. These taxes are charged by the municipal governments, and are calculated at a specified rate for every $100 of assessed value of property (i.e., land and building). Property taxes generally cover a full calendar year, although bills are not issued until the spring of each year.

To illustrate, assume that Tantramar Management owns land and a building in the city of Regina. Tantramar's year end is December 31 and it makes adjusting entries annually. It receives its property tax bill of $6,000 for the calendar year on March 1, which is due to be paid on May 31.

In March, when Tantramar receives the property tax bill for the calendar year, two months of that year have passed. The company records the property tax expense for the months of January and February and the liability owed at that point as follows:

Mar. 1	Property Tax Expense ($6,000 × 2/12)	1,000	
	Property Tax Payable		1,000
	To record property tax expense for January and February and amount owing.		

A	=	L	+	OE
		+1,000		−1,000

Cash flows: no effect

On May 31, when Tantramar pays the property tax bill, the company records the payment of the liability recorded on March 1. It also records the expense incurred to date for the months of March, April, and May. As at May 31, five months have passed and should be recorded as property tax expense. The remaining seven months of the year are recorded as a prepayment, as shown in the following entry:

May 31	Property Tax Payable	1,000	
	Property Tax Expense ($6,000 × 3/12)	1,500	
	Prepaid Property Tax ($6,000 × 7/12)	3,500	
	Cash		6,000
	To record payment of property tax expense for March through May, and amount prepaid for June through December.		

A	=	L	+	OE
+3,500 −6,000		−1,000		−1,500

↓ Cash flows: −6,000

After the payment of the property tax, Tantramar has a zero balance in its liability account but still has a prepayment. Since Tantramar only makes adjusting entries annually, it would not adjust the prepaid property tax account until year end, December 31. At that time, it would make the following entry:

A	=	L	+	OE
−3,500				−3,500

Cash flows: no effect

Dec. 31	Property Tax Expense	3,500	
	Prepaid Property Tax		3,500
	To record property tax expense for June through December.		

There are other acceptable ways to record and adjust property taxes. Some companies would debit Property Tax Expense when the bill is recorded on March 1 and avoid a later adjusting entry. In addition, companies may prepare monthly or quarterly adjusting entries. Whatever way is used, at year end the companies would have the same ending balances. In this case, the accounts Prepaid Property Tax and Property Tax Payable should each have a zero balance and Property Tax Expense should have a balance of $6,000.

Current Maturities of Long-Term Debt

Companies often have a portion of long-term debt that will be due in the current year. That amount is considered a current liability. Assume that on January 1, 2011, Cudini Construction issues a $25,000, five-year note payable. Each January 1, starting on January 1, 2012, $5,000 of the note will be repaid. When financial statements are prepared on December 31, 2011, $5,000 should be reported on the balance sheet as a current liability and the remaining $20,000 of the note should be reported as a long-term liability.

It is not necessary to prepare an adjusting entry to recognize the current maturity of long-term debt. The proper statement classification of each liability account is recognized when the balance sheet is prepared. Forzani reports $7,501 thousand as the "current portion of long-term debt" in the current liabilities section of its balance sheet.

BEFORE YOU GO ON . . .

Review It

1. What is a determinable liability?
2. What are some examples of determinable current liabilities?
3. How is interest calculated on a note payable?
4. Why is sales tax not recorded as revenue to the company that collects it?

Do It

Prepare the journal entries to record the following transactions. Round any calculations to the nearest dollar.

1. Accrue interest on January 31 (the company's year end) for a $10,000, 30-month, 8% note payable issued on December 1. Interest is payable the first of each month, beginning January 1.
2. The cash register total for sales on April 2 is $280,500. This total includes sales taxes. The HST tax rate is 13%. Record the sales and sales taxes.
3. A property tax bill of $12,000 for the calendar year is received on May 1 and is due on June 30. Record the entry on May 1, assuming the company has a January 31 year end.

Action Plan

- The formula for interest is as follows: principal (face) value × annual interest rate × time.
- Record sales separately from sales taxes. To calculate sales, divide the total proceeds by 100% plus the sales tax rates. Then calculate HST by multiplying sales by the appropriate rate.
- Record the property tax expense and the property tax payable for amounts incurred (owed) to date.

Solution

Date	Account	Debit	Credit
Jan. 31	Interest Expense ($10,000 × 8% × 1/12)	67	
	Interest Payable		67
	To accrue interest on note payable.		
Apr. 2	Cash	282,500	
	Sales ($282,500 ÷ 113%)		250,000
	HST Payable ($250,000 × 13%)		32,500
	To record sales and sales taxes.		
May 1	Property Tax Expense ($12,000 × 3/12)	3,000	
	Property Tax Payable		3,000
	To record property tax for February, March, and April.		

Related exercise material: BE10–1, BE10–2, BE10–3, BE10–4, E10–1, E10–2, E10–3, and E10–4.

The Navigator

Uncertain Liabilities

In the previous section, we discussed current liabilities where there was a high degree of certainty with regard to whom is owed, when it is owed, and how much is owed. There was no uncertainty about the liability's existence, amount, or timing. In this section, we will discuss liabilities that have a lower degree of certainty but are still likely to occur. We will then discuss situations where it is unlikely that an obligation exists, or where the existence of a liability depends on the outcome of a future event.

Estimated Liabilities

STUDY OBJECTIVE 2

Account for estimated liabilities.

An **estimated liability** is a liability that is known to exist but whose amount and timing are uncertain. We know we owe someone, but are not necessarily sure how much and when. We may not even know whom we owe. There is a lower degree of certainty than in determinable liabilities, but as long as it is *likely* the company will have to settle the obligation, and the company can reasonably estimate the amount, the liability is recognized. Common estimated liabilities include product warranties, customer loyalty programs, and gift cards. We discuss these three examples in the following sections.

Alternative terminology Estimated liabilities are also known as *provisions*.

Product Warranties

Product warranties are promises made by the seller to a buyer to repair or replace the product if it is defective or does not perform as intended. Warranties (also known as guarantees) are usually issued by manufacturers. For a specified period of time after the item was sold, a manufacturer may promise to repair the item, replace it, or refund the buyer's money under certain conditions.

For example, Apple Computer Inc. offers a one-year warranty against "defects in materials and workmanship" on the sale of its iPod and iSight products. The company goes on to state that if a valid claim is received within the warranty period, it will either (1) repair the product at no charge, using new or refurbished replacement parts, (2) exchange the product with a product that is new or that has been manufactured from new or serviceable used parts and is at least functionally equivalent to the original product, or (3) refund the purchase price of the product. As a buyer, it is important to read all warranty contracts carefully because the promises they make can be quite different.

Warranties will lead to future costs for the manufacturer for the repair or replacement of defective units. At the time of the sale, it is not known which units will become defective, so it is not known in advance whom the company will have to pay. But the liability still exists even if the payee is unknown.

Also, the amount and the timing of the future warranty cost are not known, but these can be reasonably estimated. Based on their previous experience with a particular product, it is usually not that hard for companies such as Apple to estimate the future cost of servicing (honouring) the product's warranty. In addition, recording the estimated cost of product warranties as an expense and a liability in the period where the sale occurs also ensures that companies have recognized the full cost of the sale in the period the sale occurs. This is commonly known as matching expenses with revenues.

To illustrate the accounting for warranties, assume that Hermann Company sells 10,000 washers and dryers at an average price of $600 in the year ended December 31, 2011. The selling price includes a one-year warranty on parts. Based on past experience, it is expected that 500 units (5%) will be defective, and that warranty repair costs will average $100 per unit.

At December 31, it is necessary to accrue the estimated warranty costs for the 2011 sales. The calculation is as follows:

Number of units sold	10,000
Estimated rate of defective units	× 5%
Total estimated defective units	500
Average warranty repair cost	× $100
Estimated product warranty liability	$50,000

The adjusting entry is:

A	=	L	+	OE
		+50,000		−50,000

Cash flows: no effect

Dec. 31	Warranty Expense	50,000	
	Warranty Liability		50,000
	To accrue estimated warranty costs.		

In 2011, warranty contracts were honoured on 300 units at a total cost of $30,000. These costs are likely recorded when they are incurred, but for our illustration they are being recorded in one summary journal entry:

A	=	L	+	OE
−30,000		−30,000		

Cash flows: no effect

Dec. 31	Warranty Liability	30,000	
	Repair Parts Inventory (and/or Wages Payable)		30,000
	To record honouring of 300 warranty contracts on 2011 sales.		

At year end, a warranty expense of $50,000 is reported as an operating expense in the income statement. The estimated warranty liability of $20,000 ($50,000 – $30,000) is classified as a current liability on the balance sheet.

In 2012, all costs incurred to honour warranty contracts on 2011 sales should be debited to the Warranty Liability account, like what was shown above for the 2011 sales. The Warranty Liability account will be carried forward from year to year—increased by the current year's estimated expense and decreased by the actual warranty costs incurred. It is quite likely that the actual expenses will not exactly equal the estimated liability amount. Every year, as is done with accounts receivable and the allowance for doubtful accounts, the warranty liability should be reviewed and adjusted if necessary.

Customer Loyalty Programs

Alternative terminology Customer loyalty programs are also called *promotions* or *incentive programs*.

To attract or keep customers, many companies offer **customer loyalty programs** that result in future savings for the customers on the merchandise or services the company sells. These customer loyalty programs take varying forms. For example, the program may require customers to collect points. A common example of that is airline frequent flyer programs. Or the programs may involve cash discounts on future sales.

The most successful loyalty program in Canadian retail history is Canadian Tire "money" (CTM), first introduced in 1958. The "money" resembles real currency (although the bills are considerably smaller than Bank of Canada notes) and is issued with no expiry date. CTM is given out by the cashiers for purchases paid for by cash, debit card, or Canadian Tire Options MasterCard credit card. Customers can use CTM to buy anything at a Canadian Tire store. In fact, some privately owned businesses in Canada also accept CTM as payment since the owners of many of these businesses shop at Canadian Tire.

Loyalty programs such as frequent flyer programs or CTM are designed to increase sales and are important for many businesses. In recent years, there has been a lot of debate about whether the cost of such programs should be recorded as an expense or as a decrease in revenue. While there are a few exceptions, accountants have decided that when a loyalty program results in a reduced selling price, it should be accounted for as a decrease in revenue and not as an expense.

Loyalty programs, similar to product warranties, result in an estimated liability because at the time of the sale it is not known if or when customers will redeem the reward. However, as long as some redemptions are likely and can be reasonably estimated based on past experience, the decrease in revenue and a related liability should be recorded in the period when the reward was issued to ensure that liabilities are correctly recognized.

To illustrate, assume that Greenville Co-op has a rewards program where Greenville Co-op Gas Bar customers get a redemption reward of 3 cents per litre of gasoline that can be used in Greenville Co-op Food Stores on the purchase of groceries. On January 31, the gas bar sells 9,600 litres of gasoline. Greenville Co-op will record the following for the redemption rewards issued:

Jan. 31	Sales Discount for Redemption Rewards Issued (9,600 × \$0.03)	288	
	Redemption Rewards Liability		288
	To record redemption rewards issued on gasoline sales.		

A	=	L	+	OE
		+288		−288

Cash flows: no effect

The account Sales Discount for Redemption Rewards Issued is a contra sales account, and is deducted from sales to give net sales in the same way that sales returns and allowances are deducted from sales, as we learned in Chapter 5. The Redemption Rewards Liability is reported as a current liability on the balance sheet.

Helpful hint Reductions in revenue are recorded in the period the reward is issued, not when it is redeemed.

To illustrate what happens when the rewards are redeemed, assume that on February 1, customers redeem \$100 of the rewards in the Greenville Co-op Food Store when purchasing \$7,500 of groceries. Greenville Co-op makes the following entry that day (ignoring the cost of sales):

Feb. 1	Rewards Redemption Liability	100	
	Cash (\$7,500 − \$100)	7,400	
	Grocery Sales Revenue		7,500
	To record grocery sales and the redemption of rewards.		

A	=	L	+	OE
+7,400		−100		+7,500

↑ Cash flows: +7,400

Note that when the rewards are redeemed, the amount of cash collected is less than the sales revenue recognized. The liability account is reduced by the difference between the sales revenue and cash collected, which is the amount of the redemption. As with warranties, the liability account should be reviewed periodically and adjusted based on the company's experience with redemption rates.

Accounting for loyalty rewards programs and other promotional items has many additional complexities that we have not seen here. Further details on this topic will be left to an intermediate accounting course.

ACCOUNTING IN ACTION: ACROSS THE ORGANIZATION

These days it seems that almost every retailer offers some kind of customer loyalty program, through club memberships, discount cards, or points programs. Shoppers Drug Mart has taken the trend a step further by having its Optimum Points program benefit others as well as customers. Shoppers Optimum Points® Donation Program allows Optimum card holders to donate some or all of their points to one of many registered charitable organizations. The organizations can then use the points to purchase products and supplies they need for their day-to-day activities and ongoing fundraising events. A wide variety of charitable organizations, both national and provincial, have signed up to receive the points.

A company's marketing department is responsible for designing customer loyalty programs. Why would Shoppers' marketing department add the option of donating points to charity?

Gift Cards

Gift cards or gift certificates have become an increasingly popular source of revenue for many companies. In general, they are similar to unearned revenues in that the company receives cash in advance of providing the goods or the services. Thus, when gift cards are issued, an unearned revenue account (liability) is recorded. When the gift card is redeemed (used), the company will then record the sales or service revenue and reduce or debit the Unearned Revenue account.

The difficulty with gift cards is that it is unknown when and even if the card will be redeemed. Many companies find that the longer a gift card is outstanding, the less likely it is to be redeemed for merchandise. Similarly, companies may find that gift cards that have been used but have relatively small remaining balances are less likely to be redeemed than newer, high-balance gift cards.

The main accounting problem is: At what point should a company write off the gift card liability if it expects the gift card will never be redeemed? Recent changes to Canadian laws have prohibited expiry dates on gift cards. Theoretically, if the gift card has no expiration date, the company should indefinitely report the unused portion on the balance sheet as a liability.

But if it is unlikely that the company will have to settle a portion of the liability, then an obligation no longer exists. As with warranties and customer loyalty programs, a company with a gift card program will need to estimate the appropriate balance for the liability. Currently, accounting standards do not give clear guidance on this issue and thus we leave further discussion of this topic to a more advanced accounting course.

Lawsuits

In some circumstances, lawsuits result in an estimated liability. If it is likely that the company will lose the lawsuit, and if the amount can be reliably estimated, then the company must record a liability for the same reasons warranty liabilities are recorded. But lawsuits can involve a much higher degree of uncertainty than warranties. In that case, the accounting for a lawsuit is different than accounting for an estimated liability. This is covered in the next section on contingencies.

BEFORE YOU GO ON . . .

Review It

1. Explain the difference between determinable liabilities and estimated liabilities.
2. When should warranty liabilities and expenses be recorded?
3. Why is the estimated cost of loyalty programs debited to a contra revenue account rather than an expense account?
4. In what respect are gift cards similar to unearned revenues?

Do It

Hockey Gear Company sells hockey skates with a two-year warranty against defects. The company expects that of the units sold each year, 5% will be returned in the first year after they are sold and 2% will be returned in the second year. The average cost to repair or replace a defective unit under warranty is $50. The company reported the following sales and warranty cost information:

	Units Sold	Actual Warranty Costs Incurred
2010	10,000	$20,000
2011	15,000	45,000

Calculate the balance in the Warranty Expense and Warranty Liability accounts at the end of 2011.

Action Plan

- Calculate the warranty expense by multiplying the number of units sold by the percentage that is expected to be returned and by the average warranty cost.
- Record warranty expenses in the period of the sale.
- The warranty liability is increased by the expense in each period and decreased by the actual costs of repairs and replacements.

Solution

2010: Total defective units = 5% + 2% = 7%

10,000 × 7% = 700 × $50 = $35,000

Warranty Expense			Warranty Liability			
35,000		Actual	20,000	Estimate	35,000
				Bal. Dec. 31, 2010	15,000

2011: 15,000 × 7% = 1,050 × $50 = $52,500

Warranty Expense			Warranty Liability			
52,500		Actual	20,000	Estimate	35,000
				Bal. Dec. 31, 2010	15,000
		Actual	45,000	Estimate	52,500
				Bal. Dec. 31, 2010	22,500

Related exercise material: BE10–5, BE10–6, BE10–7, BE10–8, E10–6, E10–7, and E10–8.

The Navigator

Contingencies

STUDY OBJECTIVE 3

Account for contingencies.

Contingencies are events with uncertain outcomes. In these situations, it cannot be known with certainty if a gain (and a related asset) or loss (and a related liability) will result from the situation until one or more future events happen or do not happen. Although the topic of this chapter is liabilities, and contingent liabilities are far more common than contingent assets, we will discuss both contingent liabilities and contingent assets since there are some similarities in the accounting and disclosure requirements.

Contingent Liabilities

In the previous section, we have seen that liabilities are recorded even when estimations of the amount, timing, or even the payee are required. As long as it is considered *likely* that a present obligation exists, and the amount can be reliably estimated, the liability is recognized.

In other circumstances, there is a higher degree of uncertainty and one or more of the criteria for recognizing liabilities are not met. These circumstances include:

- a *possible* (but not likely) obligation exists but will be confirmed only by the occurrence or non-occurrence of an uncertain future event,
- a present obligation exists but it is not probable that the company will have to settle it, and
- a present obligation exists but the amount cannot be reliably measured.

Under International Financial Reporting Standards (IFRS), if any one of these circumstances exists, then it is called a **contingent liability**. Under IFRS, a company should not recognize a contingent liability in its balance sheet because it doesn't meet the definition of a liability. Contingent liabilities are disclosed only in the notes to the financial statements, unless the probability of occurrence is remote.

Under Canadian GAAP for Private Enterprises, contingent liabilities are viewed somewhat differently than under IFRS. Under this GAAP system a contingent liability is defined as a liability that is contingent on the occurrence or non-occurrence of some future event. The contingent liability would be recorded if **both** of the following conditions are met:

1. The contingency is likely (the chance of occurrence is high).
2. The amount of the contingency can be reasonably estimated.

Under IFRS, a liability would also be recorded if both those conditions existed, but such a liability would be considered an estimated liability, not a contingent liability. For example, in the previous section, we discussed how a lawsuit can be considered an estimated liability. Even though the existence of a liability is contingent on the outcome of the lawsuit, if it is likely the lawsuit will be lost, and the amount can be reliably estimated, it is considered an estimated liability.

Under IFRS, contingent liabilities are liabilities where there is too high a degree of uncertainty to record the liability. On the other hand, Canadian GAAP for Private Enterprises considers a liability to be a contingent liability as long as its ultimate existence depends on the outcome of a future event. Thus, a lawsuit would be considered a contingent liability under Canadian GAAP for Private Enterprises.

The differences between IFRS and Canadian GAAP for Private Enterprises are to a certain extent based on semantics because of the different definitions of contingent liabilities. But it is still important to understand the distinction, as private companies will have the choice to follow Canadian GAAP for Private Enterprises or IFRS, while public companies must follow IFRS. The IFRS rule of never recording contingent liabilities may sound less strict than Canadian GAAP for Private Enterprises where contingent liabilities are sometimes recorded. But in fact, IFRS is generally regarded as having a lower threshold for recognizing liabilities. Under IFRS, estimated liabilities are recognized for probable events, defined as being more likely than not. Under Canadian GAAP for Private Enterprises, only highly likely contingent liabilities are recognized.

Under Canadian GAAP for Private Enterprises, the existence of a contingent loss at the date of the financial statements should be disclosed in notes to the financial statements when:

- a contingent liability is likely but the amount of the loss cannot be reasonably estimated, or
- the existence of the contingent liability is not determinable.

Under Canadian GAAP for Private Enterprises, if a contingency is unlikely—the chance of occurrence is small—it should still be disclosed if the event could have a substantial negative effect on the company's financial position. Otherwise, it does not need to be disclosed. A loan guarantee for another company is an example of a contingency that should be disclosed even if the chance of having to pay the loan, because the other company defaulted on it, is small. Contingencies that can affect anyone who is operating a business, such as the general risk of a war, strike, or recession, are not reported in the notes to the financial statements.

Forzani's 2009 financial statements were prepared before Canadian public companies were required to use IFRS. At that time, Forzani followed rules similar to Canadian GAAP for Private Enterprises described above. It disclosed both guarantees and lawsuits in the notes to its financial statements. Here are two selected extracts from this note:

Illustration 10-1

Disclosure of contingent liabilities

THE FORZANI GROUP LTD.
Notes to the Consolidated Financial Statements
February 1, 2009

LE GROUPE FORZANI LTÉE | THE FORZANI GROUP LTD.

15. Contingencies and Guarantees

The Company has provided the following guarantees to third parties:

(a) The Company has provided guarantees to certain franchisees' banks pursuant to which it has agreed to buy back inventory from the franchisee in the event that the bank realizes on the related security... Historically, the Company has not had to repurchase significant inventory from franchisees pursuant to these guarantees. The Company has not recognized the guarantee in its financial statements.

(d) Claims and suits have been brought against the Company in the ordinary course of business. In the opinion of management, all such claims and suits are adequately covered by insurance, or if not so covered, the results are not expected to materially affect the Company's financial policies.

Contingent Assets

Like contingent liabilities, **contingent assets** arise from past events where the asset's existence will only be resolved when a future event occurs or does not occur. This event will confirm the existence of a future cash inflow or other economic benefits that will result in an asset. Examples of contingent assets include insurance claims or potential legal actions that could favour the company.

Contingent assets or gains are never recorded or accrued in the financial statements. They are disclosed in the notes only if it is likely that a gain will be realized. Under IFRS, if it is virtually certain that a gain will occur, the related asset is not considered a contingent asset. It is just considered to be an asset and is recognized in the financial statements as appropriate. Under Canadian GAAP for Private Enterprises, a contingent asset can only be recognized when the contingency is resolved and the asset is realized. Under both standards, it is not considered appropriate to disclose the existence of a contingent asset that in management's opinion is unlikely to occur.

ACCOUNTING IN ACTION: BUSINESS INSIGHT

There are many contingencies in the real world. Lawsuits are the most common type of contingency, followed by environmental contingencies. Environmental contingencies generally relate to liabilities that could be incurred in order to clean up environmental problems.

The Canadian National Railway Company discloses the following information in the notes to its financial statements: "A risk of environmental liability is inherent in railroad and related transportation operations..." The Company goes on to say, "The magnitude of such... liabilities and the costs of complying with future environmental laws and containing or remediating contamination cannot be reasonably estimated... There can thus be no assurance that liabilities or costs related to environmental matters will not be incurred in the future, or will not have a material adverse effect on the Company's financial position or results of operations in a particular quarter or fiscal year, or that the Company's liquidity will not be adversely impacted by such environmental liabilities or costs."

Environmental contingencies are generally considered to be harder to estimate than contingencies from lawsuits. What might be the reason for this difference?

BEFORE YOU GO ON . . .

Review It

1. Under IFRS, what is a contingent liability?
2. Under IFRS, when should a contingent liability be recorded? Disclosed?
3. Under Canadian GAAP for Private Enterprises, what is a contingent liability?
4. Under Canadian GAAP for Private Enterprises, when should a contingent liability be recorded? Disclosed?
5. When are contingent assets recorded? Disclosed?

Do It

A list of possible contingencies follows. Identify whether each of the following should be recorded, disclosed, or not reported:

1. A private company following Canadian GAAP risks being damaged by floods. The company is located on a flood plain but has never experienced any damage from flooding in the past.
2. The government may expropriate a private company's assets so that a new highway can be built. So far, there have been no discussions about how much the government might pay the company. Assume the company follows Canadian GAAP.
3. A public company is being sued for $1 million for unlawful termination of an employee.
4. A private company following Canadian GAAP has guaranteed other companies' loans but the guarantees are unlikely to result in any payments.
5. A reassessment of a public company's income tax will likely result in a refund.

Action Plan

- Remember that under IFRS, a contingent liability is a possible obligation or a present obligation where settlement is unlikely or the obligation cannot be measured. Contingent liabilities are never recorded; they are disclosed unless they are unlikely.
- Under Canadian GAAP for Private Enterprises, contingent liabilities are accrued when they are likely and estimable. Otherwise, they are only disclosed. They are not disclosed if they are unlikely.

- Remember that contingent assets are never recorded. They are only disclosed if they are likely.

Solution

1. No disclosure required.
2. Disclosure required.
3. If the company is likely to lose and the amount can be reasonably estimated, then this would be considered an estimated liability and it would be recorded; otherwise, just disclose.
4. Disclosure required.
5. Disclosure required.

The Navigator

Related exercise material: BE10–9, BE10–10, E10–9, and E10–10.

Payroll

STUDY OBJECTIVE 4

Determine payroll costs and record payroll transactions.

Payroll accounting involves more than just paying employee salaries and wages. In addition to paying salaries and wages, companies are required by law to have payroll records for each employee, to report and remit payroll deductions, and to respect provincial and federal laws on employee compensation. As mentioned in our feature story, there are up to 185 different pieces of legislation and regulations that employers have to consider when doing payroll. In this section, we will discuss some of the basic issues regarding payroll costs, journalizing payroll, and payroll records. In the appendix to this chapter, we explain calculating mandatory payroll deductions.

There are two types of payroll costs to a company: employee costs and employer costs. The first type, employee costs, involves the gross amount earned by employees. The second type, employer costs, involves amounts paid by the employer on behalf of the employee (employee benefits). We will explore employee and employer payroll costs in the following sections.

Employee Payroll Costs

Accounting for employee payroll costs involves calculating (1) gross pay, (2) payroll deductions, and (3) net pay.

Gross Pay

Gross pay, or earnings, is the total compensation earned by an employee. It consists of wages or salaries, plus any bonuses and commissions. The terms "salaries" and "wages" are often used interchangeably and the total amount of salaries or wages earned by the employee is called **gross pay**, or gross earnings.

Managerial, professional, administrative, and sales personnel are generally paid salaries. Salaries are usually based on a weekly, biweekly, monthly, or yearly rate. If the rate is a yearly one, it is pro-rated over the number of payroll periods (e.g., 26 or 52) that the company uses.

Part-time employees, store clerks, factory employees, and manual labourers are normally paid wages. Wages are based on a rate per hour or on piecework (an amount per unit of product). When wages are based on a rate per hour, total wages are determined by multiplying the hours worked by the hourly rate of pay.

In addition to the hourly pay rate, most companies are required by law to pay hourly workers for overtime work at the rate of at least one and one-half times the government-regulated minimum hourly wage. The number of hours that need to be worked before overtime becomes payable is based on a standard workweek. A 44-hour standard workweek is fairly common but this will vary by industry and occupation. Most employees in executive, managerial, and administrative positions do not earn overtime pay.

To illustrate gross pay for a wage earner, assume that Mark Jordan works for Academy Company as a shipping clerk. His authorized pay rate is $20 per hour. The calculation of Mark's gross pay (total wages) for the 48 hours shown on his time card for the weekly pay period ending June 20, 2009, is as follows:

Type of Pay	Hours	×	Rate	=	Gross Pay
Regular	44	×	$20	=	$ 880
Overtime	4	×	30	=	120
Total wages					$1,000

This calculation assumes that Mark receives one and one-half times his regular hourly rate ($20 × 1.5) for any hours worked in excess of 44 hours per week (overtime). Overtime rates can be as much as twice the regular rates.

Payroll Deductions

As anyone who has received a paycheque knows, gross pay is usually very different from the amount that is actually received. The difference is referred to as **payroll deductions**. Payroll deductions are also frequently called "withholdings" because these are the amounts that the employer withholds or holds back from the employee.

Payroll deductions may be mandatory or voluntary. Illustration 10-2 shows the types of payroll deductions that most companies usually make.

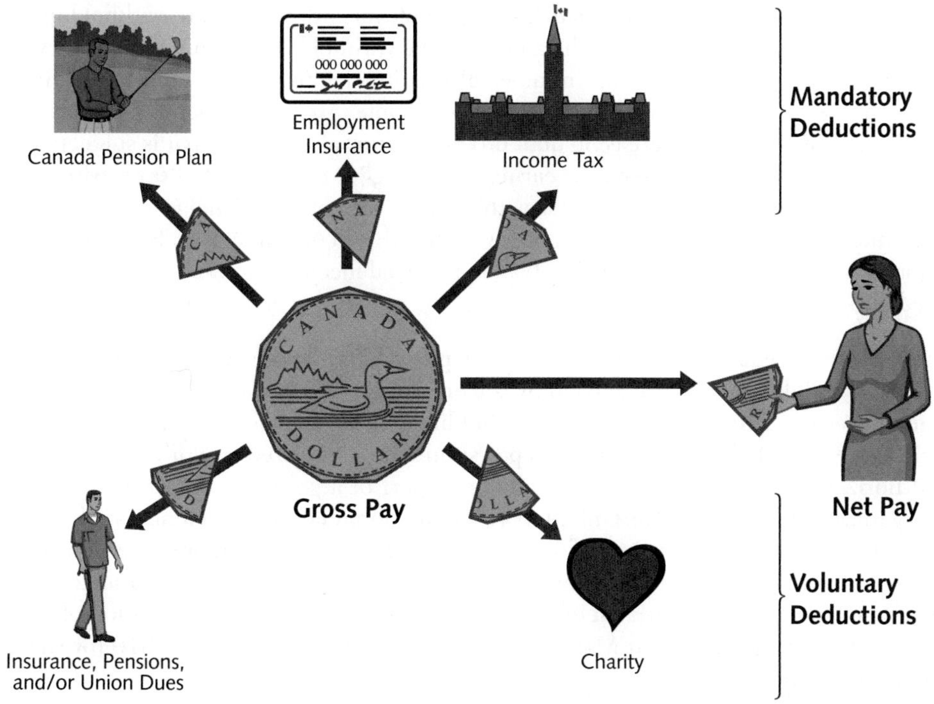

Illustration 10-2
Employee payroll deductions

Payroll deductions do not result in an expense for the employer. The employer is only a collection agent. The mandatory deductions are later paid to the government (for deductions such as Canada Pension Plan, Employment Insurance, and income tax). The voluntary deductions are later paid to some other agency (such as a union, an insurance company, or the United Way). The designated collection agency for the federal government is the Canada Revenue Agency (CRA), which collects money on behalf of the Receiver General of Canada, the cabinet minister responsible for accepting payments to the Government of Canada.

Mandatory Payroll Deductions. Mandatory deductions are required by law and include Canada Pension Plan contributions, Employment Insurance premiums, and personal income tax. We will discuss these three deductions in the following sections.

Canada Pension Plan. All employees between the ages of 18 and 70, except those employed in the province of Quebec, must contribute to the **Canada Pension Plan (CPP)**. Quebec has its own similar program, the Quebec Pension Plan (QPP). These mandatory plans give disability, retirement, and death benefits to qualifying Canadians.

Contribution rates are set by the federal government and are adjusted every January if there are increases in the cost of living. We will show how to calculate CPP contributions in Appendix 10A. For now, assume that Mark Jordan's CPP contribution for the weekly pay period ending June 20, 2009, is $46.17.

Employment Insurance. The *Employment Insurance Act* requires all Canadian workers who are not self-employed to pay **Employment Insurance (EI)** premiums. Employment Insurance is designed to give income protection (in the form of payments representing a portion of one's earnings) for a limited period of time to employees who are temporarily laid off, who are on parental leave, or who lose their jobs. Starting January 2010, if you are self employed you also may choose to pay EI to qualify for special benefits such as maternity or parental benefits. But this will not qualify you for employment insurance if you are not able to work.

Each year, the federal government determines the contribution rate and the maximum amount of premiums for the year. We will show how to calculate EI premiums in Appendix 10A. For now, assume that Mark Jordan's EI premium for the weekly pay period ending June 20, 2009, is $17.30.

Personal Income Tax. Under the *Income Tax Act*, employers are required to withhold income tax from employees for each pay period. The amount to be withheld is determined by three variables: (1) the employee's gross pay, (2) the number of credits claimed by the employee, and (3) the length of the pay period. The amount of provincial income taxes also depends on the province in which the employee works. There is no limit on the amount of gross pay that is subject to income tax withholdings. The higher the pay or earnings, the higher the amount of taxes withheld.

The calculation of personal income tax withholdings is complicated and is best done using payroll deduction tables supplied by the CRA. We will show this in Appendix 10A. For now, assume that Mark Jordan's federal income tax is $124.70 and provincial income tax is $67.25, for a total income tax owed of $191.95 on his gross pay of $1,000 for the weekly pay period ending June 20, 2009.

Voluntary Payroll Deductions. Unlike mandatory payroll deductions, which are required by law, voluntary payroll deductions are chosen by the employee.

Employees may choose to authorize withholdings for charitable, retirement, and other purposes. All voluntary deductions from gross pay should be authorized in writing by the employee. The authorization may be made individually or as part of a group plan. Deductions for charitable organizations, such as the United Way, or for financial arrangements, such as Canada Savings Bonds and the repayment of loans from company credit unions, are determined by each employee. In contrast, deductions for union dues, extended health insurance, life insurance, and pension plans are often determined on a group basis. In the calculation of net pay in the next section, we assume that Mark Jordan has voluntary deductions of $10 for the United Way and $5 for union dues.

Net Pay

The difference between an employee's gross pay, or total earnings, less any employee payroll deductions withheld from the earnings is known as **net pay**. This is the amount that the employer must pay to the employee.

Net pay is determined by subtracting payroll deductions from gross pay. For Mark Jordan, net pay for the weekly pay period ending June 20, 2009, is $729.58, as shown in Illustration 10-3:

Illustration 10-3
Employee payroll deductions

Gross pay		$1,000.00
Payroll deductions:		
CPP	$ 46.17	
EI	17.30	
Income tax (federal and provincial)	191.95	
United Way	10.00	
Union dues	5.00	270.42
Net pay		$ 729.58

Before we learn how to record employee payroll costs and deductions, we will turn our attention to *employer* payroll costs. After this discussion, we will record the total employee and employer payroll costs for Academy Company, where Mark Jordan works.

Employer Payroll Costs

Employer payroll costs are amounts that the federal and provincial governments require employers to pay. The federal government requires CPP and EI contributions from employers. The provincial governments require employers to fund a workplace health, safety, and compensation plan. These contributions, plus such items as paid vacations and pensions, are referred to as **employee benefits**. Employer payroll costs are not debited to the Salaries and Wages Expense account, but rather to a separate Employee Benefits Expense account.

Canada Pension Plan

Employers must also contribute to the CPP. For each dollar withheld from the employee's gross pay, the employer must contribute an equal amount. The CPP Payable account is credited for both the employees' and employer's CPP contributions.

Employment Insurance

Employers are required to contribute 1.4 times an employee's EI premiums. The EI Payable account is credited for both the employees' and employer's EI premiums.

Workplace Health, Safety, and Compensation

Each provincial workplace health, safety, and compensation plan gives benefits to workers who are injured or disabled on the job. The cost of this program is paid entirely by the employer; employees do not make contributions to these plans. Employers are assessed a rate—usually between 0.25% and 10% of their gross payroll—based on the risk of injury to employees in their industry and past experience.

Helpful hint CPP contributions and EI premiums are paid by both the employer and the employee. Workers' compensation premiums are paid entirely by the employer.

Additional Employee Benefits

In addition to the three employer payroll costs described above, employers have other employee benefit costs. Two of the most important are paid absences and post-employment benefits. We will describe these briefly here, but leave further details to an intermediate accounting course.

Paid Absences. Employees have the right to receive compensation for absences under certain conditions. The compensation may be for paid vacations, sick pay benefits, and paid statutory holidays. A liability should be estimated and accrued for future paid absences. Ordinarily, vacation pay is the only paid absence that is accrued. Other types of paid absences are disclosed only in notes to the statements.

Post-Employment Benefits. Post-employment benefits are payments by employers to retired or terminated employees. These payments are for (1) pensions, and (2) supplemental health care, dental care, and life insurance. Employers must use the accrual basis in accounting for post-employment benefits. It is important to match the cost of these benefits with the periods where the employer benefits from the services of the employee.

Recording the Payroll

Recording the payroll involves maintaining payroll records, recording payroll expenses and liabilities, paying the payroll, and filing and remitting payroll deductions.

Payroll Records

A separate record of an employee's gross pay, payroll deductions, and net pay for the calendar year is kept for each employee and updated after each pay period. It is called the **employee earnings record** and its cumulative payroll data are used by the employer to (1) determine when an employee has reached the maximum earnings subject to CPP and EI premiums, (2) file information returns with the CRA (as explained later in this section), and (3) give each employee a statement of gross pay and withholdings for the year.

An extract from Mark Jordan's employee earnings record for the month of June is shown in Illustration 10-4. This record includes the pay details shown in Illustration10-3 for the week ending June 20, 2009, highlighted in red.

Illustration 10-4

Employee earnings record

ACADEMY COMPANY
Employee Earnings Record
Year Ending December 31, 2009

Name	Mark Jordan	Address	162 Bowood Avenue
Social Insurance Number	113-114-496		Toronto
Date of Birth	December 24, 1985		Ontario, M4N 1Y6
Date Employed	September 1, 2007	Telephone	416-486-0669
Date Employment Ended		E-mail	jordan@sympatico.ca
Job Title	Shipping Clerk	Claim Code	1

		Gross Pay				Deductions						Payment	
2009 Period Ending	Total Hours	Regular	Overtime	Total	Cumulative	CPP	EI	Income Tax	United Way	Union Dues	Total	Net Amount	Cheque #
June 6	46	880.00	60.00	940.00	19,940.00	43.20	16.26	172.30	10.00	5.00	246.76	693.24	974
13	47	880.00	90.00	970.00	20,910.00	44.68	16.78	182.25	10.00	5.00	258.71	711.29	1028
20	48	880.00	120.00	1,000.00	21,910.00	46.17	17.30	191.95	10.00	5.00	270.42	729.58	1077
27	46	880.00	60.00	940.00	22,850.00	43.20	16.26	172.30	10.00	5.00	246.76	693.24	1133
June Total		3,520.00	330.00	3,850.00		177.25	66.60	718.80	40.00	20.00	1,022.65	2,827.35	

In addition to employee earnings records, many companies find it useful to prepare a **payroll register**. This record accumulates the gross pay, deductions, and net pay per employee for each pay period and becomes the documentation for preparing paycheques for each employee. Academy Company's payroll register for the week ended June 20, 2009, is presented in Illustration 10-5. It shows the data for Mark Jordan in the wages section, highlighted in red. In this example, Academy Company's total weekly payroll is $34,420, as shown in the gross pay column.

Illustration 10-5

Payroll register

ACADEMY COMPANY
Payroll Register
Week Ending June 20, 2009

		Gross Pay			Deductions						Payment	
Employee	Total Hours	Regular	Overtime	Gross	CPP	EI	Income Tax	United Way	Union Dues	Total	Net Pay	Cheque #
Office Salaries												
Aung, Ng	44	1,276.00		1,276.00	59.83	22.07	276.78	15.00		373.68	902.32	998
Canton, Mathew	44	1,298.00		1,298.00	60.92	22.46	283.89	20.00		387.27	910.73	999
Mueller, William	44	1,166.00		1,166.00	54.39	20.17	241.80	11.00		327.36	838.64	1024
Subtotal		10,400.00		10,400.00	452.40	179.92	2,231.21	180.00		3,043.53	7,356.47	
Wages												
Caron, Réjean	44	880.00	60.00	940.00	43.20	16.26	172.30	10.00	5.00	246.76	693.24	1025
Jordan, Mark	48	880.00	120.00	1,000.00	46.17	17.30	191.95	10.00	5.00	270.42	729.58	1077
Milroy, Lee	47	880.00	90.00	970.00	44.68	16.78	182.25	10.00	5.00	258.71	711.29	1078
Subtotal		22,000.00	2,020.00	24,020.00	1,044.88	415.55	4,491.65	300.00	150.00	6,402.08	17,617.92	
Total		32,400.00	2,020.00	34,420.00	1,497.28	595.47	6,722.86	480.00	150.00	9,445.61	24,974.39	

Note that this record is a listing of each employee's payroll data for the June 20, 2009, pay period. In some companies, the payroll register is a special journal. Postings are made directly to ledger accounts. In other companies, the payroll register is a supplementary record that gives the data for a general journal entry and later posting to the ledger accounts. At Academy Company, the second procedure is used.

Recording Payroll Expenses and Liabilities

Payroll expenses are equal to the employees' gross salaries and wages plus the employer's payroll costs. Typically, as shown in the following entry, employee payroll costs and employer's payroll costs are recorded in separate journal entries.

Employee Payroll Costs. A journal entry is made to record the employee portion of the payroll. For the week ending June 20, the entry for Academy Company, using total amounts from the company's payroll register for the period, as shown in Illustration 10-5, is as follows:

June 20	Salaries Expense	10,400.00	
	Wages Expense	24,020.00	
	CPP Payable		1,497.28
	EI Payable		595.47
	Income Tax Payable		6,722.86
	United Way Payable		480.00
	Union Dues Payable		150.00
	Salaries and Wages Payable		24,974.39
	To record payroll for week ending June 20.		

A	=	L	+	OE
		+1,497.28		−10,400.00
		+595.47		−24,020.00
		+6,722.86		
		+480.00		
		+150.00		
		+24,974.39		

Cash flows: no effect

The above journal entry records the gross pay of $34,420 in Academy Company's Salaries Expense and Wages Expense account. Separate expense accounts are used for gross pay because office workers are on salary and other employees are paid an hourly rate. The net pay of $24,974.39 that is owed to employees is recorded in the Salaries and Wages Payable account. This is equal to the sum of the individual cheques that the employees will receive when the payroll is paid. Academy Company uses separate liabilities accounts for the amounts that it owes for its employee payroll deductions to the government for CPP, EI, and income tax, and amounts owed to third parties like United Way and for union dues.

Employer Payroll Costs. Employer payroll costs are usually recorded when the payroll is journalized. The entire amount of gross pay is subject to four of the employer payroll costs mentioned earlier: CPP, EI, workers' compensation, and vacation pay. For the June 20 payroll, Academy Company's CPP is $1,497.28 ($1,497.28 × 1). Its EI premium is $833.66 ($595.47 × 1.4).

Assume that Academy Company is also assessed for workers' compensation at a rate of 1%. Its expense for the week would therefore be $344.20 [($10,400 + $24,020) × 1%]. For vacation pay, assume that Academy Company employees accrue vacation days at an average rate of 4% of the gross payroll (equivalent to two weeks of vacation). The accrual for vacation benefits in one pay period—one week—is therefore $1,376.80 [($10,400 + $24,020) × 4%].

Some provinces, including the Province of Ontario, require an additional employer payroll cost—an employer health tax to help fund health care. The maximum health tax in the Province of Ontario is 1.95% of payroll, but the tax rate varies by the amount of payroll, and the first $400,000 of remuneration is exempt from this tax. Academy's payroll for the year has not yet reached this level so it is exempt from this health tax.

Accordingly, the entry to record the employer payroll costs or employee benefits associated with the June 20 payroll is as follows:

June 20	Employee Benefits Expense	4,051.94	
	CPP Payable		1,497.28
	EI Payable		833.66
	Workers' Compensation Payable		344.20
	Vacation Pay Payable		1,376.80
	To record employer payroll costs on June 20 payroll.		

A	=	L	+	OE
		+1,497.28		−4,051.94
		+ 833.66		
		+ 344.20		
		+ 1,376.80		

Cash flows: no effect

Employer payroll costs are debited to a separate expense account, normally called Employee Benefits Expense, so the employer can keep track of these costs. It is combined with Salaries and Wages Expense on the income statement. The liability accounts are classified as current liabilities since they will be paid within the next year.

Recording Payment of the Payroll

Payment of the payroll by cheque or electronic funds transfer (EFT) is made from either the employer's regular bank account or a payroll bank account. Each paycheque or EFT is usually accompanied by a statement of earnings document. This shows the employee's gross pay, payroll deductions, and net pay for the period and for the year to date.

After the payroll has been paid, the cheque numbers are entered in the payroll register. The entry to record payment of the payroll for Academy Company follows:

A	=	L	+	OE
−24,974.39		−24,974.39		

⬇ Cash flows: −24,974.39

June 20	Salaries and Wages Payable	24,974.39	
	Cash		24,974.39
	To record payment of payroll.		

Note that Academy Company is only recording payments to its employees in this entry and not its payroll deductions. Employee and employer deductions will be remitted to government authorities or other third parties when they are due later in the month.

Many companies use a separate bank account for payroll. Only the total amount of each period's payroll is transferred, or deposited, into that account before it is distributed. This helps the company determine if there are any unclaimed amounts.

When companies report and remit their payroll deductions, they combine withholdings of CPP, EI, and income tax. Generally, the withholdings must be reported and remitted monthly on a Statement of Account for Current Source Deductions (known by the CRA as the PD7A remittance form), and no later than the 15th day of the month following the month's pay period. Depending on the size of the payroll deductions, however, the employer's payment deadline could be different. For example, large employers must remit more often than once a month, and small employers with perfect payroll deduction remittance records can remit quarterly.

Workplace health, safety, and compensation costs are remitted quarterly to the provincial workers' compensation commission or board. Remittances can be made by mail or through deposits at any Canadian financial institution. When payroll deductions are remitted, payroll liability accounts are debited and Cash is credited.

The entry to record the remittance of payroll deductions by Academy Company in the following month is as follows:

A	=	L	+	OE
−12,120.75		−2,994.56		
		−1,429.13		
		−6,722.86		
		−480.00		
		−150.00		
		−344.20		

⬇ Cash flows: −12,120.75

July 13	CPP Payable ($1,497.28 + $ 1,497.28)	2,994.56	
	EI Payable ($595.47 + $833.66)	1,429.13	
	Income Tax Payable	6,722.86	
	United Way Payable	480.00	
	Union Dues Payable	150.00	
	Workers' Compensation Payable	344.20	
	Cash		12,120.75
	To record payment of payroll deductions for June 20 payroll.		

Note that the vacation pay liability recorded on June 20 is not debited or "paid" until the employees actually take their vacation.

Other payroll information returns or forms must be filed by the employer with the government by the last day of February each year. In addition, as noted previously, employers must give employees a Statement of Remuneration Paid (called a T4 slip by the CRA) by the same date.

ACCOUNTING IN ACTION: ALL ABOUT YOU

Employers are required by law each month to remit to the CRA mandatory payroll deductions as well as the employer's share of CPP and EI. Failure to do so can lead to interest and stiff penalties.

What happens if you are self-employed and providing consulting services to a company? If you are self employed, you are required to pay CPP equal to both the employee's and employer's share, and you are also responsible for paying income tax. Starting January 2010, if you are self-employed you can choose to pay EI to qualify for special benefits such as maternity or parental benefits. But this will not qualify you for employment insurance if you are not able to work. If you choose to pay EI, you will not be required to pay the employers' portion of the EI premium.

It may seem beneficial to some companies to hire consultants and avoid paying the employer's share of CPP and EI as well as other benefits. However, the CRA has strict guidelines as to whether an individual is considered an employee or a self-employed consultant. If a company inappropriately treats an individual as self-employed and fails to deduct CPP and EI, the company will be required to pay both the employer's and employee's share of CPP and EI as well as penalties and interest.

If you are providing services to a company, what are the advantages and disadvantages of being a self-employed consultant versus an employee of the company?

BEFORE YOU GO ON . . .

Review It

1. What is the difference between gross pay and net pay?
2. What are the mandatory payroll deductions?
3. What is the difference between employee payroll deductions and employer payroll costs?

Do It

Prepare the journal entries to record the following transactions. Round any calculations to the nearest dollar.

1. A company's gross wages amount to $10,000 for the week ended July 11. The following amounts are deducted from the employees' wages: CPP of $495; EI of $173; income tax of $3,965; and health insurance of $950. Assume employees are paid in cash on July 11.
2. The company accrues employer's payroll costs on the same day as it records payroll. Assume vacation days are accrued at an average rate of 4% of the gross payroll and that the health insurance is 100% funded by the employees.
3. Record the payment of the mandatory payroll deductions from the July 11 payroll on August 15.

Action Plan

- Record both the employees' portion of the payroll and the benefits owed by the employer.
- Employee deductions are not an expense to the employer.
- The vacation pay liability is not "paid" until the employees actually take their vacation.

Solution

July 11	Wages Expense	10,000	
	CPP Payable		495
	EI Payable		173
	Income Tax Payable		3,965
	Health Insurance Payable		950
	Cash		4,417
	To record payment of wages for week ending July 11.		

July	11	Employee Benefits Expense	1,137	
		CPP Payable		495
		EI Payable ($173 × 1.4)		242
		Vacation Pay Payable ($10,000 × 4%)		400
		To record employer's payroll costs on July 11 payroll.		
Aug.	15	CPP Payable ($495 + $495)	990	
		EI Payable ($173 + $242)	415	
		Income Tax Payable	3,965	
		Cash		5,370
		To record payment of mandatory payroll deductions.		

The Navigator

Related exercise material: BE10–11, BE10–12, BE10–13, E10–11, and E10–12.

Financial Statement Presentation

STUDY OBJECTIVE 5

Prepare the current liabilities section of the balance sheet.

Under Canadian GAAP, current liabilities are the first category reported in the liabilities section of the balance sheet. Each of the main types of current liabilities is listed separately. In addition, the terms of operating lines of credit and notes payable and other information about the individual items are disclosed in the notes to the financial statements.

Current liabilities are usually listed in order of liquidity, by maturity date. Sometimes it is difficult to determine which specific obligations should be listed in which order. A more common method of presenting current liabilities is to list them by order of size, with the largest ones first. Many companies show bank loans, notes payable, and accounts payable first, regardless of the amounts.

As discussed in Chapter 4, some companies reporting under IFRS may choose to order their current liability category on the lower section of the balance sheet, in order of reverse liquidity. Or they may choose to continue with the traditional placement as the first liability category on the balance sheet, in order of liquidity.

The following is an excerpt from Tim Hortons' balance sheet:

Illustration 10-6

Presentation of current liabilities

TIM HORTONS INC.
Balance Sheet (partial)
March 29, 2009
(in thousands)

Current assets	$392,002
Current liabilities	
Accounts payable	$111,803
Accrued expenses	53,619
Gift certificate obligations	10,685
Cash card obligations	35,144
Advertising fund restricted liabilities	46,293
Current portion of long-term obligations	6,753
Total current liabilities	$264,297

Tim Hortons also discloses information about contingencies in the notes to its financial statements, as follows:

Illustration 10-7
Disclosure of contingent liabilities

TIM HORTONS INC.
Notes to Consolidated Financial Statements (partial)
March 29, 2009

NOTE 7 COMMITMENTS AND CONTINGENCIES

The Company has guaranteed certain lease and debt payments, primarily related to franchisees, amounting to $0.7 million. In the event of default by a franchise owner, the Company generally retains the right to acquire possession of the related restaurants. The Company is also the guarantor on $11.5 million in letters of credit and surety bonds with various parties; however, management does not expect any material loss to result from these instruments because management does not believe performance will be required. The length of the lease, loan and other arrangements guaranteed by the Company or for which the Company is contingently liable varies, but generally does not exceed seven years. ...

On June 12, 2008, a claim was filed against the Company and certain of its affiliates in the Ontario Superior Court of Justice ("Court") by two of its franchisees, Fairview Donut Inc. and Brule Foods Ltd., alleging, generally, that the Company's Always Fresh baking system and expansion of lunch offerings have led to lower franchisee profitability. The claim, which seeks class action certification on behalf of Canadian franchisees, asserts damages of approximately $1.95 billion. The Company believes the claim is frivolous and completely without merit, and the Company intends to vigorously defend the action. However, there can be no assurance that the outcome of the claim will be favourable to the Company or that it will not have a material adverse impact on the Company's financial position or liquidity in the event that the determinations by the Court and/or appellate court are not in accordance with the Company's evaluation of this claim. Neither the probability of this claim's success nor the ultimate amount payable, if any, are determinable at this time, and, coupled with the Company's position that this claim is without merit, the Company has not recorded any provisions in the Condensed Consolidated Financial Statements related to this claim. ...

Companies must carefully monitor the relationship of current liabilities to current assets. This relationship is critical in evaluating a company's short-term ability to pay debt. There is usually concern when a company has more current liabilities than current assets, because it may not be able to make its payments when they become due.

In Tim Hortons' case, it has a positive current ratio. You will recall from Chapter 4 that the current ratio is calculated by dividing current assets by current liabilities. Tim Hortons' current ratio is 1.48:1 ($392,002 ÷ $264,297), which indicates that Tim Hortons has enough current assets to cover its current liabilities. In addition, Tim Hortons discloses in the notes to its financial statements that it has overdraft protection of $15 million and a $300-million operating line of credit that it can draw on for additional liquidity requirements.

Recall also that the current ratio should never be interpreted without also looking at the receivables and inventory turnover ratios to ensure that all of the current assets are indeed liquid. It is also important to look at the acid-test ratio. If we wanted to do a more complete analysis of Tim Hortons' liquidity, we would need additional information.

BEFORE YOU GO ON . . .

Review It

1. Describe the reporting and disclosure requirements for current liabilities.
2. What current liabilities does The Forzani Group report and in what order? The answer to this question is at the end of the chapter.

Related exercise material: BE10–14, BE10–15, E10–5, E10-13, and E10–14.

The Navigator

APPENDIX 10A ▶ PAYROLL DEDUCTIONS

STUDY OBJECTIVE 6

Calculate mandatory payroll deductions.

Mandatory Payroll Deductions

As discussed in the chapter, payroll deductions may be mandatory or voluntary. Mandatory deductions are required by law and include Canada Pension Plan contributions, Employment Insurance premiums, and income tax. We discuss how to calculate these in the following sections.

Canada Pension Plan (CPP)

CPP contributions are based on a maximum ceiling or limit (called the maximum pensionable earnings) less a basic yearly exemption, and on the contribution rate set each year by the federal government. As of January 1, 2009, the following amounts were in effect:

Maximum pensionable earnings	$46,300
Basic yearly exemption	$3,500
CPP contribution rate	4.95%
Maximum annual employee CPP contribution	$2,118.60

Pensionable earnings are gross earnings less the basic yearly exemption.

Illustration 10A-1 shows the formulas and calculations used to determine Mark Jordan's CPP contribution on his gross pay of $1,000 for the weekly pay period ending June 20, 2009.

Illustration 10A-1 ➜

Formula for CPP contributions

Step 1	Basic Yearly Exemption	÷	Number of Pay Periods in a Year	=	Basic Pay-Period Exemption
	$3,500	÷	52 weeks in a year	=	$67.30 per week
Step 2	Employee's Gross Pay	−	Basic Pay-Period Exemption	=	Employee's Pensionable Earnings
	$1,000.00	−	$67.30	=	$932.70
Step 3	Employee's Pensionable Earnings	×	CPP Contribution Rate	=	Employee's CPP Contribution
	$932.70	×	4.95%	=	$46.17

Note that the basic pay-period exemption of $67.30 is a per-week exemption and is used in this case because Academy Company pays its employees weekly. If a company pays its employees monthly, the basic pay-period exemption would be $291.67 ($3,500 ÷ 12).

An employer stops deducting CPP contributions if and when the employee's earnings are greater than the maximum pensionable earnings. In this way, the employee's CPP contributions will not be greater than the maximum annual CPP contribution. Self-employed individuals pay both the employee and employer share of CPP.

Employment Insurance (EI)

EI calculations are based on a maximum earnings ceiling (called the maximum annual insurable earnings) and the contribution rate set by the federal government each year. Different from CPP, there is no basic yearly exemption. For 2009, the following amounts were in effect:

Maximum insurable earnings	$42,300
EI contribution rate	1.73%
Maximum annual employee EI premium	$731.79

In most cases, **insurable earnings** are gross earnings.

The required EI premium is calculated by multiplying the employee's insurable earnings by the EI contribution rate. Illustration 10A-2 shows the formula and calculations to determine Mark Jordan's EI premium on his gross pay of $1,000 for the pay period ending June 20, 2009.

Illustration 10A-2
Formula for EI premiums

Employee's Insurable Earnings	×	EI Contribution Rate	=	Employee's EI Premium
$1,000	×	1.73%	=	$17.30

An employer stops deducting EI premiums if and when the employee's earnings are greater than the maximum insurable earnings. In this way, the employee's EI premiums will not be greater than the maximum annual EI premium. Self-employed individuals who have chosen to pay EI pay only the employee's share of EI.

Personal Income Tax

Income tax deductions are based on income tax rates set by the federal and provincial governments. The federal government uses a progressive tax scheme when calculating income taxes. Basically, this means that the higher the pay or earnings, the higher the income tax percentage, and thus the higher the amount of taxes withheld. For example, effective April 1, 2009, the federal tax rates were:

- 15.5% **on the first** $41,200 of taxable income, plus
- 22% **on the next** $41,199 of taxable income (on the portion of taxable income between $41,200 and $82,399), plus
- 26% **on the next** $43,865 of taxable income (on the portion of taxable income between $82,399 and $126,264), plus
- 29% of taxable income **over** $126,264.

Taxable income is determined by the employee's gross pay and the amount of personal tax credits claimed by the employee. **Personal tax credits** are amounts deducted from an individual's income taxes and determine the amount of income taxes to be withheld. To indicate to the Canada Revenue Agency (CRA) which credits he or she wants to claim, the employee must complete a Personal Tax Credits Return (known as a TD1 form). In 2009, all individuals were entitled to a minimum personal credit (called the basic personal credit) of $10,375.

In addition, provincial income taxes must be calculated. All provinces, except Alberta, also use a progressive tax scheme. Each province has its own specific tax rates and calculations.

As you can see, the calculation of personal income tax deductions is very complicated. Consequently it is best done using one of the many payroll accounting programs that are available or by using the payroll deduction tools provided by the CRA. These tools include: (1) Payroll Deduction Tables, (2) Tables on Diskette, and (3) the Payroll Deductions Online Calculator. We will illustrate how to use the payroll deduction tables.

Using Payroll Deduction Tables

Payroll deduction tables are prepared by the CRA and can be easily downloaded from the CRA website at <http://www.cra-arc.gc.ca/tx/bsnss/tpcs/pyrll/menu-eng.html>. There are separate payroll deduction tables for determining federal tax deductions, provincial tax deductions, Canada Pension Plan contributions, and Employment Insurance premiums.

These tables are updated at least once a year on January 1 to reflect the new rates for that year. Income tax tables are also reissued during the year if the federal or provincial governments make changes to income tax rates during the year. It is important to make sure you have the tables that are in effect during the payroll period for which you are calculating deductions.

There are separate sections of the federal and provincial income tax and the CPP tables for weekly, biweekly, semi-monthly, and monthly pay periods. Thus, when determining these amounts, it is important to make sure you are using the table prepared for the company's pay period. The Academy Company would use the weekly tables.

Illustration 10A-3 Excerpts from CPP, EI, and Income Tax Deduction Tables prepared by the Canada Revenue Agency, effective April 1, 2009

Reproduced with permission of the Minister of Public Works and Government Services Canada, 2009.

Canada Pension Plan Contributions / **Cotisations au Régime de pensions du Canada**

Weekly (52 pay periods a year) / Hebdomadaire (52 périodes de paie par année)

Pay Rémunération From - De	To - À	CPP RPC	Pay Rémunération From - De	To - À	CPP RPC	Pay Rémunération From - De	To - À	CPP RPC	Pay Rémunération From - De	To - À	CPP RPC
910.44	920.43	41.98	1630.44	1640.43	77.62	2350.44	2360.43	113.26	3070.44	3080.43	148.90
920.44	930.43	42.48	1640.44	1650.43	78.12	2360.44	2370.43	113.76	3080.44	3090.43	149.40
930.44	940.43	42.97	1650.44	1660.43	78.61	2370.44	2380.43	114.25	3090.44	3100.43	149.89
940.44	950.43	43.47	1660.44	1670.43	79.11	2380.44	2390.43	114.75	3100.44	3110.43	150.39
950.44	960.43	43.96	1670.44	1680.43	79.60	2390.44	2400.43	115.24	3110.44	3120.43	150.88
960.44	970.43	44.46	1680.44	1690.43	80.10	2400.44	2410.43	115.74	3120.44	3130.43	151.38
970.44	980.43	44.95	1690.44	1700.43	80.59	2410.44	2420.43	116.23	3130.44	3140.43	151.87
980.44	990.43	45.45	1700.44	1710.43	81.09	2420.44	2430.43	116.73	3140.44	3150.43	152.37
990.44	1000.43	45.94	1710.44	1720.43	81.58	2430.44	2440.43	117.22	3150.44	3160.43	152.86
1000.44	1010.43	46.44	1720.44	1730.43	82.08	2440.44	2450.43	117.72	3160.44	3170.43	153.36
1010.44	1020.43	46.93	1730.44	1740.43	82.57	2450.44	2460.43	118.21	3170.44	3180.43	153.85
1020.44	1030.43	47.43	1740.44	1750.43	83.07	2460.44	2470.43	118.71	3180.44	3190.43	154.35
1030.44	1040.43	47.92	1750.44	1760.43	83.56	2470.44	2480.43	119.20	3190.44	3200.43	154.84
1040.44	1050.43	48.42	1760.44	1770.43	84.06	2480.44	2490.43	119.70	3200.44	3210.43	155.34
1050.44	1060.43	48.91	1770.44	1780.43	84.55	2490.44	2500.43	120.19	3210.44	3220.43	155.83
1060.44	1070.43	49.41	1780.44	1790.43	85.05	2500.44	2510.43	120.69	3220.44	3230.43	156.33
1070.44	1080.43	49.90	1790.44	1800.43	85.54	2510.44	2520.43	121.18	3230.44	3240.43	156.82
1080.44	1090.43	50.40	1800.44	1810.43	86.04	2520.44	2530.43	121.68	3240.44	3250.43	157.32

Employment Insurance Premiums / Cotisations à l'assurance-emploi

Insurable Earnings Rémunération assurable From - De	To - À	EI premium Cotisation d'AE	Insurable Earnings Rémunération assurable From - De	To - À	EI premium Cotisation d'AE	Insurable Earnings Rémunération assurable From - De	To - À	EI premium Cotisation d'AE	Insurable Earnings Rémunération assurable From - De	To - À	EI premium Cotisation d'AE
999.14	999.71	17.29	1040.76	1041.32	18.01	1082.37	1082.94	18.73	1123.99	1124.56	19.45
999.72	1000.28	17.30	1041.33	1041.90	18.02	1082.95	1083.52	18.74	1124.57	1125.14	19.46
1000.29	1000.86	17.31	1041.91	1042.48	18.03	1083.53	1084.10	18.75	1125.15	1125.72	19.47
1000.87	1001.44	17.32	1042.49	1043.06	18.04	1084.11	1084.68	18.76	1125.73	1126.30	19.48
1001.45	1002.02	17.33	1043.07	1043.64	18.05	1084.69	1085.26	18.77	1126.31	1126.87	19.49
1002.03	1002.60	17.34	1043.65	1044.21	18.06	1085.27	1085.83	18.78	1126.88	1127.45	19.50
1002.61	1003.17	17.35	1044.22	1044.79	18.07	1085.84	1086.41	18.79	1127.46	1128.03	19.51
1003.18	1003.75	17.36	1044.80	1045.37	18.08	1086.42	1086.99	18.80	1128.04	1128.61	19.52
1003.76	1004.33	17.37	1045.38	1045.95	18.09	1087.00	1087.57	18.81	1128.62	1129.19	19.53
1004.34	1004.91	17.38	1045.96	1046.53	18.10	1087.58	1088.15	18.82	1129.20	1129.76	19.54
1004.92	1005.49	17.39	1046.54	1047.10	18.11	1088.16	1088.72	18.83	1129.77	1130.34	19.55
1005.50	1006.06	17.40	1047.11	1047.68	18.12	1088.73	1089.30	18.84	1130.35	1130.92	19.56
1006.07	1006.64	17.41	1047.69	1048.26	18.13	1089.31	1089.88	18.85	1130.93	1131.50	19.57
1006.65	1007.22	17.42	1048.27	1048.84	18.14	1089.89	1090.46	18.86	1131.51	1132.08	19.58
1007.23	1007.80	17.43	1048.85	1049.42	18.15	1090.47	1091.04	18.87	1132.09	1132.65	19.59
1007.81	1008.38	17.44	1049.43	1049.99	18.16	1091.05	1091.61	18.88	1132.66	1133.23	19.60
1008.39	1008.95	17.45	1050.00	1050.57	18.17	1091.62	1092.19	18.89	1133.24	1133.81	19.61
1008.96	1009.53	17.46	1050.58	1051.15	18.18	1092.20	1092.77	18.90	1133.82	1134.39	19.62

Federal tax deductions
Effective April 1, 2009
Weekly (52 pay periods a year)
Also look up the tax deductions in the provincial table

Retenues d'impôt fédéral
En vigueur le 1er avril 2009
Hebdomadaire (52 périodes de paie par année)
Cherchez aussi les retenues d'impôt dans la table provinciale

Pay Rémunération		Federal claim codes/Codes de demande fédéraux										
		0	1	2	3	4	5	6	7	8	9	10
From De	Less than Moins de	Deduct from each pay / Retenez sur chaque paie										
920	928	136.60	106.65	103.80	98.10	92.45	86.75	81.05	75.35	69.70	64.00	58.30
928	936	138.35	108.40	105.55	99.90	94.20	88.50	82.80	77.15	71.45	65.75	60.05
936	944	140.10	110.20	107.35	101.65	95.95	90.25	84.60	78.90	73.20	67.50	61.80
944	952	141.85	111.95	109.10	103.40	97.70	92.05	86.35	80.65	74.95	69.25	63.60
952	960	143.60	113.70	110.85	105.15	99.50	93.80	88.10	82.40	76.70	71.05	65.35
960	968	145.40	115.45	112.60	106.90	101.25	95.55	89.85	84.15	78.50	72.80	67.10
968	976	147.15	117.20	114.35	108.70	103.00	97.30	91.60	85.95	80.25	74.55	68.85
976	984	148.90	119.00	116.15	110.45	104.75	99.05	93.40	87.70	82.00	76.30	70.60
984	992	150.65	120.75	117.90	112.20	106.50	100.85	95.15	89.45	83.75	78.05	72.40
992	1000	152.40	122.50	119.65	113.95	108.30	102.60	96.90	91.20	85.50	79.85	74.15
1000	1012	154.60	124.70	121.85	116.15	110.50	104.80	99.10	93.40	87.70	82.05	76.35
1012	1024	157.25	127.35	124.50	118.80	113.10	107.45	101.75	96.05	90.35	84.65	79.00
1024	1036	159.90	130.00	127.15	121.45	115.75	110.05	104.40	98.70	93.00	87.30	81.60
1036	1048	162.55	132.60	129.75	124.10	118.40	112.70	107.00	101.35	95.65	89.95	84.25
1048	1060	165.20	135.25	132.40	126.70	121.05	115.35	109.65	103.95	98.30	92.60	86.90
1060	1072	167.80	137.90	135.05	129.35	123.70	118.00	112.30	106.60	100.90	95.25	89.55
1072	1084	170.45	140.55	137.70	132.00	126.30	120.65	114.95	109.25	103.55	97.85	92.20
1084	1096	173.10	143.20	140.35	134.65	128.95	123.25	117.60	111.90	106.20	100.50	94.80
1096	1108	175.75	145.80	142.95	137.30	131.60	125.90	120.20	114.55	108.85	103.15	97.45
1108	1120	178.40	148.45	145.60	139.90	134.25	128.55	122.85	117.15	111.50	105.80	100.10
1120	1132	181.00	151.10	148.25	142.55	136.90	131.20	125.50	119.80	114.10	108.45	102.75
1132	1144	183.65	153.75	150.90	145.20	139.50	133.85	128.15	122.45	116.75	111.05	105.40
1144	1156	186.30	156.40	153.55	147.85	142.15	136.45	130.80	125.10	119.40	113.70	108.00
1156	1168	188.95	159.00	156.15	150.50	144.80	139.10	133.40	127.75	122.05	116.35	110.65
1168	1180	191.60	161.65	158.80	153.10	147.45	141.75	136.05	130.35	124.70	119.00	113.30

Ontario provincial tax deductions
Effective April 1, 2009
Weekly (52 pay periods a year)
Also look up the tax deductions in the federal table

Retenues d'impôt provincial de l'Ontario
En vigueur le 1er avril 2009
Hebdomadaire (52 périodes de paie par année)
Cherchez aussi les retenues d'impôt dans la table fédérale

Pay / Rémunération		Provincial claim codes/Codes de demande provinciaux										
		0	1	2	3	4	5	6	7	8	9	10
From / De	Less than / Moins de	Deduct from each pay / Retenez sur chaque paie										
938	946	72.45	62.10	61.00	58.80	56.55	54.35	52.10	49.90	47.65	45.45	43.20
946	954	73.20	62.85	61.75	59.50	57.30	55.05	52.85	50.60	48.40	46.15	43.95
954	962	73.90	63.60	62.45	60.25	58.00	55.80	53.55	51.35	49.10	46.90	44.65
962	970	74.65	64.30	63.20	61.00	58.75	56.55	54.30	52.10	49.85	47.60	45.40
970	978	75.40	65.05	63.95	61.70	59.50	57.25	55.05	52.80	50.60	48.35	46.15
978	986	76.10	65.80	64.65	62.45	60.20	58.00	55.75	53.55	51.30	49.10	46.85
986	994	76.85	66.50	65.40	63.15	60.95	58.70	56.50	54.25	52.05	49.80	47.60
994	1002	77.60	67.25	66.15	63.90	61.70	59.45	57.25	55.00	52.80	50.55	48.35
1002	1010	78.30	68.00	66.85	64.65	62.40	60.20	57.95	55.75	53.50	51.30	49.05
1010	1018	79.05	68.70	67.60	65.35	63.15	60.90	58.70	56.45	54.25	52.00	49.80
1018	1030	79.95	69.60	68.50	66.30	64.05	61.85	59.60	57.40	55.15	52.95	50.70
1030	1042	81.05	70.70	69.60	67.40	65.15	62.95	60.70	58.50	56.25	54.05	51.80
1042	1054	82.15	71.80	70.70	68.50	66.25	64.05	61.80	59.60	57.35	55.15	52.90
1054	1066	83.25	72.90	71.80	69.60	67.35	65.15	62.90	60.70	58.45	56.25	54.00
1066	1078	84.35	74.00	72.90	70.70	68.45	66.25	64.00	61.75	59.55	57.30	55.10
1078	1090	85.45	75.10	74.00	71.80	69.55	67.30	65.10	62.85	60.65	58.40	56.20
1090	1102	86.55	76.20	75.10	72.85	70.65	68.40	66.20	63.95	61.75	59.50	57.30
1102	1114	87.65	77.30	76.20	73.95	71.75	69.50	67.30	65.05	62.85	60.60	58.40
1114	1126	88.75	78.40	77.30	75.05	72.85	70.60	68.40	66.15	63.95	61.70	59.50
1126	1138	89.85	79.50	78.40	76.15	73.95	71.70	69.50	67.25	65.05	62.80	60.60

Illustration 10A-3 shows excerpts from the CPP, EI, and federal and Ontario income tax tables effective April 1, 2009. You can use these tables to determine the appropriate deductions for Mark Jordan's gross pay of $1,000 during the pay period ended June 20, 2009.

In the CPP table, under the Pay column, find $1,000. The CPP deduction for the pay range $990.44 to $1,000.43 is $45.94. Earlier in the appendix we showed how to calculate Mark Jordan's CPP and determined it was $46.17. Why the difference? The amount shown in the table is calculated using the mid-point in the range. As the mid-point is not equal to $1,000, there is a difference between the two amounts. Both ways of determining the CPP contribution are correct—the table is just slightly less precise than the calculation. The Academy Company could have used either amount.

In the EI table, under the Insurable Earnings column, find $1,000. The EI deduction in the pay range $999.72 to $1,000.28 is $17.30. This is exactly the same amount we calculated earlier in the appendix because Mark Jordan's pay of $1,000 is the mid-point of this range. As with CPP, companies can either calculate the EI as shown earlier, or use the tables. Both amounts are correct—the table is just slightly less precise than the calculation.

In the Federal Tax Deduction table, first find $1,000 in the Pay column. Now follow across the table to the Federal Claim Code 1 column. The federal tax deduction in the "from" $1,000 to "less than" $1,012 range, claim code 1, is $124.70. The same process is used in the Ontario Tax Deduction table. In the "from" $994 to "less than" $1,002 range, Provincial claim code 1, the provincial tax deduction is $67.25. These amounts agree with the amounts given for Mark Jordan's income tax deduction earlier in the chapter.

Claim code 1 is used for individuals who qualify for only the basic personal credit on the TD1 form discussed earlier in the appendix. You will notice on the Federal and Provincial Tax Deduction tables that the higher the claim code, the lower the income tax deduction. These claim codes can be used for employees who will have more personal tax credits. We have assumed that Mark Jordan will qualify for only the basic personal credit.

As mentioned earlier, employers may also use the Tables on Diskette or the Payroll Deductions Online Calculator to determine payroll deductions. All three methods will provide correct deductions as long as the correct dates, gross pay, pay period, and claim codes are used.

BEFORE YOU GO ON . . .

Do It

Highland Company pays salaries on a weekly basis. The payroll for the week ended May 29, 2009, includes three employees as follows:

Employee Name	Weekly Earnings	Claim Code
Hudson, James	$ 975	4
Randell, Findley	$ 975	2
Jaegeun, Kim	$1,125	1

Determine the appropriate mandatory payroll deductions and net pay for each employee. Calculate the CPP and EI deductions using the formula provided in Appendix 10A. Use the tables in Illustration 10A-3 to determine federal and provincial income taxes.

Action Plan

- The CPP basic pay-period deduction is the annual basic deduction divided by number of pay periods in a year.
- CPP deductions are equal to an employee's pensionable earnings times the CPP contribution rate.
- EI premiums are equal to an employee's insurable earnings times the EI premium rate.
- The federal tax deduction is the amount in the correct Pay range and Claim Code column on the Federal Tax Deduction Table.
- The provincial tax deduction is the amount in the correct Pay range and Claim Code column on the Provincial Tax Deduction Table.

Solution

		Deductions					
Employee	Gross Pay	CPP	EI	Federal Income Tax	Provincial Income Tax	Total	Net Pay
Hudson, James	$ 975.00	44.93[1]	16.87[3]	103.00	59.50	224.30	750.70
Randell, Findley	975.00	44.93	16.87	114.35	63.95	240.10	734.90
Jaegeun, Kim	1,125.00	52.36[2]	19.46[4]	151.10	78.40	301.32	823.68

Calculations:

Note: CPP basic pay period deduction = $3,500 ÷ 52 = $67.30

[1] ($975.00 – $67.30) × 4.95% = $44.93

[2] ($1,125.00 – $67.30) × 4.95% = $52.36

[3] $975.00 × 1.73% = $16.87

[4] $1,125.00 × 1.73% = $19.46

The Navigator

Related exercise material: *BE10–16, *BE10–17, *BE10–18, *E10–15, and *E10–16.

Demonstration Problem

Benoit Company has the following selected transactions:

Feb. 1 Signed a $50,000, six-month, 7% note payable to the CIBC, receiving $50,000 in cash. Interest is payable at maturity.
10 Cash register receipts totalled $37,565, plus 13% HST.
28 The payroll for the month is salaries of $50,000. CPP contributions and EI premiums withheld are $2,475 and $865, respectively. A total of $15,000 in income taxes is withheld. The salaries are paid on March 1.

The following adjustment data are noted at the end of the month:

1. Interest expense should be accrued on the note.
2. Employer payroll costs are recorded. In addition to mandatory costs, the company also pays $800 a month for a dental plan for all its employees.
3. Some sales were made under warranty. Of the units sold under warranty this month, 350 are expected to become defective. Repair costs are estimated to be $40 per defective unit.

Instructions

(a) Record the February transactions. Round your calculations to the nearest dollar.
(b) Record the adjusting entries at February 28.

WILEY PLUS
Demonstration Problems

Solution to Demonstration Problem

(a)

Feb. 1	Cash	50,000	
	Notes Payable		50,000
	Issued six-month, 7% note to CIBC.		
10	Cash	42,448	
	Sales		37,565
	HST Payable ($37,565 × 13%)		4,883
	To record sales and sales tax payable.		
28	Salaries Expense	50,000	
	Income Taxes Payable		15,000
	CPP Payable		2,475
	EI Payable		865
	Salaries Payable		31,660
	To record February salaries.		

(b)

Feb. 28	Interest Expense ($50,000 × 7% × $^1/_{12}$)	292	
	Interest Payable		292
	To record accrued interest for February.		
28	Employee Benefits Expense	4,486	
	CPP Payable ($2,475 × 1)		2,475
	EI Payable ($865 × 1.4)		1,211
	Dental Plan Payable		800
	To record employee benefit costs for February.		
28	Warranty Expense (350 × $40)	14,000	
	Warranty Liability		14,000
	To record estimated product warranty liability.		

Action Plan

- Remember that interest rates are annual rates and must be adjusted for periods of time less than one year.
- Remember that sales taxes collected must be sent to the government and are not part of sales revenue.
- Remember that employee deductions for CPP, EI, and income tax reduce the salaries payable.
- Employer contributions to CPP, EI, and the dental plan create an additional expense.
- Warranty costs are expensed in the period when the sales occur.

The Navigator

Summary of Study Objectives

1. ***Account for determinable or certain current liabilities.*** Liabilities are present obligations arising from past events, to make future payments of assets or services. Determinable liabilities have certainty about their existence, amount, and timing—in other words, they have a known amount, payee, and due date. Examples of determinable current liabilities include operating lines of credit, notes payable, accounts payable, sales taxes, unearned revenue, current maturities of long-term debt, and accrued liabilities such as property taxes, payroll, and interest.

2. ***Account for estimated liabilities.*** Estimated liabilities exist, but their amount or timing is uncertain. As long as it is *likely* the company will have to settle the obligation, and the company can reasonably estimate the amount, the liability is recognized. Product warranties, customer loyalty programs, and gift cards result in liabilities that must be estimated. They are recorded either as an expense (for warranties) or as a decrease in revenue (for customer loyalty programs) and a liability in the period when the sales occur. These liabilities are reduced when repairs under warranty or redemptions occur. Gift cards are similar to unearned revenues and result in a liability until the gift card is redeemed. As some cards are never redeemed, it is necessary to make adjustments to the liability.

3. ***Account for contingencies.*** A contingency depends on a future event to confirm its existence (and possibly the amount and timing). Under IFRS, a contingent liability is a possible obligation or a present obligation where settlement is unlikely or the obligation cannot be measured. Contingent liabilities are never recorded; they are disclosed unless they are unlikely. Under Canadian GAAP for Private Enterprises, contingent liabilities are accrued when they are likely and estimable. Otherwise, they are only disclosed. They are not disclosed if they are unlikely. Contingent assets are not recorded. They are only disclosed if they are likely.

4. ***Determine payroll costs and record payroll transactions.*** Payroll costs consist of employee and employer payroll costs. In recording employee costs, Salaries and Wages Expense is debited for the gross pay, individual liability accounts are credited for payroll deductions, and Salaries and Wages Payable is credited for net pay. In recording employer payroll costs, Employee Benefits Expense is debited for the employer's share of CPP, EI, workers' compensation, vacation pay, and any other deductions or benefits provided. Each benefit is credited to its specific current liability account.

5. ***Prepare the current liabilities section of the balance sheet.*** The nature and amount of each current liability and contingency should be reported in the balance sheet or in the notes accompanying the financial statements. Under Canadian GAAP, current liabilities are reported first and in order of liquidity. Under IFRS, there is the option to report current liabilities on the lower section of the balance sheet and in reverse order of liquidity.

6. ***Calculate mandatory payroll deductions (Appendix 10A).*** Mandatory payroll deductions include CPP, EI, and income taxes. CPP is calculated by multiplying pensionable earnings (gross pay minus the pay period exemption) by the CPP contribution rate. EI is calculated by multiplying insurable earnings by the EI contribution rate. Federal and provincial income taxes are calculated using a progressive tax scheme and are based on taxable earnings and personal tax credits. The calculations are very complex and it is best to use one of the CRA income tax calculation tools such as payroll deduction tables.

The Navigator

Glossary

WILEY PLUS Glossary
Key Term Matching Activity

Canada Pension Plan (CPP) A mandatory federal plan that gives disability, retirement, and death benefits to qualifying Canadians. (p. 571)

Collateral Property pledged as security for a loan. (p. 559)

Contingency Events with uncertain outcomes. (p. 567)

Contingent asset A possible asset that arises from past events and whose existence will be resolved only when a future event occurs or does not occur. (p. 568)

Contingent liability A possible obligation whose existence will be confirmed only by the occurrence or non-occurrence of a future event or a present obligation where it is not likely it will have to be settled or the amount cannot be reasonably determined. (p. 567)

Customer loyalty programs Programs that result in future savings for the customers on the merchandise or services the company sells. (p. 564)

Determinable liability A liability whose existence, amount, and timing are known with certainty. (p. 558)

Employee benefits Payments made by an employer, in addition to wages and salaries, to give pension, insurance, medical, or other benefits to its employees. (p. 573)

Employee earnings record A separate record of an employee's gross pay, payroll deductions, and net pay for the calendar year. (p. 574)

Employment Insurance (EI) A federal mandatory insurance program designed to give income protection for a limited period of time to employees who are temporarily laid off, who are on parental leave, or who lose their jobs. (p. 572)

Estimated liability A liability that is known to exist but whose amount or timing is uncertain. (p. 563)

Gross pay Total compensation earned by an employee. Also known as gross earnings. (p. 570)

Insurable earnings Gross earnings used to calculate EI deductions. There is a maximum amount of insurable earnings set each year by the government. (p. 581)

Net pay Gross pay less payroll deductions. (p. 572)

Notes payable Obligations in the form of written promissory notes. (p. 559)

Operating line of credit Pre-authorized approval to borrow money at a bank when it is needed, up to a preset limit. (p. 559)

Payroll deductions Deductions from gross pay to determine the amount of a paycheque. (p. 571)

Payroll register A record that accumulates the gross pay, deductions, and net pay per employee for each pay period and becomes the documentation for preparing a paycheque for each employee. (p. 574)

Pensionable earnings Gross earnings less the basic yearly exemption. There is a maximum amount of pensionable earnings set each year by the government. (p. 580)

Personal tax credits Amounts deducted from an individual's income taxes that determine the amount of income taxes to be withheld. (p. 581)

Prime rate The interest rate banks charge their best customers. (p. 559)

Product warranties Promises made by the seller to a buyer to repair or replace a product if it is defective or does not perform as intended. (p. 563)

Trade payables Accounts and notes payable that result from purchase transactions with suppliers. (p. 559)

Note: All questions, exercises, and problems below with an asterisk (*) relate to material in Appendix 10A

Self-Study Questions

WILEY PLUS Quizzes

Answers are at the end of the chapter.

(SO 1) AP 1. Gilbert Company borrows $88,500 on July 1, 2011, from the Bank of Nova Scotia by signing an eight-month, 6% note. Interest is payable at maturity. What is the accrued interest at December 31, 2011?
(a) $5,310
(b) $3,540
(c) $3,982
(d) $2,655

(SO 1) AP 2. RedEarth Company, located in Ontario, has $5,007 of sales, which included 13% HST. What is the amount (rounded to the nearest dollar) that should be credited to HST Payable?
(a) $651
(b) $354
(c) $576
(d) $401

(SO 1) AP 3. On March 1, Swift Current Company receives its property tax assessment of $13,200 for the 2011 calendar year. The property tax bill is due May 1. If Swift Current prepares quarterly financial statements, how much property tax expense should the company report for the quarter ended March 31, 2011?
(a) $3,300
(b) $4,400
(c) $1,100
(d) $13,200

4. Big Al's Appliance Store offers a two-year warranty on all appliances sold. The company estimates that 5% of all appliances sold need to be serviced at an average cost of $100 each. At December 31, 2010, the Warranty Liability account had a balance of $20,000. During 2011, the store spends $14,500 repairing 145 appliances. An additional 4,500 appliances are sold in 2011. On the 2011 income statement, warranty expense will be: (SO 2) AP
(a) $28,000.
(b) $22,500.
(c) $14,500.
(d) $20,000.

5. Friendly Department Store has a customer loyalty program in which customers receive points when they make a purchase. The points can be redeemed on future purchases. The value of the points issued should be recorded as: (SO 2) K
(a) a contra revenue when the points are issued.
(b) an expense when the points are issued.
(c) a contra revenue when the points are redeemed.
(d) an expense when the points are redeemed.

(SO 3) K 6. Under IFRS, a contingent liability is defined as:
   (a) a *possible* obligation whose existence will be confirmed only by the occurrence or non-occurrence of uncertain future events.
   (b) a present obligation that is not recognized because it is not probable the company will have to settle the obligation.
   (c) a present obligation that is not recognized because the amount of the obligation cannot be reliably measured.
   (d) any of the above.

(SO 3) K 7. Under Canadian GAAP for Private Enterprises, if a contingent asset is reasonably estimable and it is likely that the contingency will occur, the contingent asset should:
   (a) be accrued in the accounts.
   (b) be disclosed in the notes accompanying the financial statements.
   (c) not be recorded or disclosed until the contingency actually happens.
   (d) be collected immediately.

(SO 4) AP 8. In a recent pay period, Blue Company employees have gross salaries of $17,250. Total deductions are: CPP $866, EI $298, and income taxes $4,312. What is Blue Company's total payroll expense for this pay period? Ignore vacation benefits and workers' compensation.
   (a) $17,250
   (b) $18,533
   (c) $11,774
   (d) $18,414

9. Under IFRS, current liabilities: (SO 5) K
   (a) must be presented in reverse order of liquidity.
   (b) must be presented after long-term liabilities in the balance sheet.
   (c) are combined with long-term liabilities.
   (d) may be presented before or after long-term liabilities in the balance sheet.

*10. During the first week of May 2009, Emily Marquette worked 42 hours at an hourly wage of $25 per hour for an employer in Ontario. Using the payroll deduction tables in Appendix 10A, what was her net pay, assuming her only personal tax credit is the basic personal amount? (SO 4, 6) A
   (a) $1,050.00
   (b) $776.36
   (c) $842.95
   (d) $736.06

The Navigator

Questions

(SO 1) K 1. Why is a present commitment to purchase an asset in the future not recorded as a liability?

(SO 1) K 2. How is a note payable similar to, and different from, (a) an account payable, and (b) an operating line of credit?

(SO 1) K 3. What is the difference between an operating line of credit and a bank overdraft?

(SO 1) C 4. Your roommate says, "Sales taxes are reported as revenues in the income statement." Do you agree? Explain.

(SO 1) C 5. Explain how property taxes should be recorded when the bill arrives sometime in the spring but covers the entire calendar year.

(SO 1) C 6. Laurel Hyatt believes that if a company has a long-term liability, the entire amount should be classified as long-term liabilities. Is Laurel correct? Explain.

(SO 2) C 7. The accountant for Amiable Appliances feels that warranty expense should not be recorded unless an appliance is returned for repair. "Otherwise, how do you know if the appliance will be returned, and if so, how much it will cost to fix?" he says. Do you agree? Explain.

8. Explain what happens if the estimated warranty liability does not agree with the actual warranty costs incurred. (SO 2) C

9. A restaurant recently started a customer loyalty program. For all bills in excess of $100, the customer receives a 2-for-1 voucher for an appetizer for future meals. How should the restaurant account for the vouchers? (SO 2) C

10. Why is the cost of product warranties recorded as an expense but the cost of rewards issued in a customer loyalty program is recorded as a decrease in revenue? (SO 2) C

11. In what respects are gift cards similar to unearned revenues and why are they classified as a liability? How is a gift card different than an airline's unearned passenger revenue for flights paid in advance? (SO 2) C

12. What are the differences between determinable, estimated, and contingent liabilities? (SO 1, 2, 3

13. What are the differences between the definitions of a contingent liability under IFRS and under Canadian GAAP for Private Enterprises? (SO 3) C

(SO 3) C 14. Under what circumstances is a contingent liability recorded in the accounts? Under what circumstances is a contingent liability disclosed only in the notes to the financial statements?

(SO 3) C 15. What is a debt guarantee? Why is a debt guarantee an example of a contingent liability?

(SO 3) C 16. What is the difference between a contingent liability and a contingent asset? Give an example of each.

(SO 3) C 17. What is the accounting treatment for (a) contingent liabilities and (b) contingent assets? Why is it not the same?

(SO 4) C 18. What is the difference between salaries and wages?

(SO 4) C 19. What is the difference between gross pay and net pay? Which amount (gross or net) should a company record as salaries and wages expense?

(SO 4) C 20. Explain the different types of employee and employer payroll deductions, and give examples of each.

(SO 4) K 21. What are an employee earnings record and a payroll register?

22. To whom, and how often, are payroll deductions remitted? (SO 4) C

23. What are some additional employee benefits paid by employers? How are they accounted for? (SO 4) K

24. In what order should current liabilities be listed on the balance sheet? (SO 5) K

25. How is an operating line of credit reported or disclosed in the financial statements? (SO 5) K

26. Where in the financial statements should a company report employee payroll deductions? Employer payroll costs? (SO 5) K

27. How can a company determine if its current liabilities are too high? (SO 5) K

*28. Explain how CPP and EI are each calculated. (SO 6) K

*29. How is the amount deducted from an employee's wages for income tax determined? (SO 6) K

Brief Exercises

BE10–1 Bourque Company borrows $60,000 from First Bank on July 1, 2010, signing a nine-month, 6% note payable. Interest is payable the first of each month, starting August 1. Prepare journal entries for Bourque Company to record: (a) the receipt of the proceeds of the note on July 1, 2010; (b) the first interest payment on August 1, 2010; (c) the accrual of interest at Bourque's year end, December 31, 2010; and (d) the payment of the note at maturity, April 1, 2011.

Record note payable. (SO 1) AP

BE10–2 Auto Supply Company reports cash sales of $11,526 on March 16. All sales are subject to 13% HST. Record the sales assuming the sales amount of $11,526 (a) does not include the HST, and (b) does include the HST.

Calculate and record HST. (SO 1) AP

BE10–3 Summertime Productions Company in Prince Edward Island reports cash sales of $8,200 on July 23. All sales are subject to 5% GST and 10% PST. Calculate the (a) sales taxes collected, (b) total amount collected, and (c) combined sales tax rate in effect in Prince Edward Island.

Calculate PST and GST. (SO 1) AP

BE10–4 Dresner Company has a December 31 fiscal year end. It receives a $7,620 property tax bill for the 2011 calendar year on February 28, 2011. The bill is payable on May 31. Prepare entries for February 28, May 31, and December 31, assuming the company adjusts its accounts annually.

Record property tax. (SO 1) AP

BE10–5 On December 1, Ng Company introduces a new product that includes a two-year warranty on parts. In December, 1,000 units are sold. Management believes that 6% of the units will be defective and that the average warranty cost will be $70 per unit. (a) Prepare the adjusting entry at December 31 to accrue the estimated warranty cost. (b) The following year, the cost of defective parts replaced under the warranty was $3,800. Prepare an entry to record the replacement of the parts.

Record warranty. (SO 2) AP

Record loyalty rewards issued and redeemed.
(SO 2) AP

BE10–6 One-Stop Department Store has a loyalty program where customers are given One-Stop "Money" for cash or debit card purchases. The amount they receive is equal to 2% of the pre-tax sales total. Customers can use the One-Stop Money to pay for part or all of their next purchase at One-Stop Department Store. On July 3, 2011, Judy Wishloff purchases merchandise for $150. She uses $20 of One-Stop Money that she has from earlier purchases, and pays for the rest of the purchase with cash. What entry or entries will One-Stop Department Store record for this transaction? Ignore taxes.

Record estimated liability for cash rebate program.
(SO 2) AP

BE10–7 In September, Mega-Big Motion Picture Company sells 100,000 copies of a recently released DVD of a popular movie. Each DVD contains a $4 rebate if the consumer sends in proof of purchase with the completed rebate form. Mega-Big estimates that 15% of the purchasers will claim the rebate. Prepare an adjusting entry at September 30 to accrue the estimated rebate liability. Assume in October that 2,000 rebate forms are received and processed. Prepare one journal entry to record processing the rebate forms.

Record gift cards issued and redeemed.
(SO 2) AP

BE10–8 Rikard's Menswear sells $4,200 of gift cards for cash in December 2010. Rikard's has a December 31 fiscal year end and uses a perpetual inventory system. In January 2011, $2,950 of the gift cards are redeemed for merchandise, with a cost of $1,325. Prepare journal entries for Rikard's for December 2010 and January 2011.

Account for contingencies.
(SO 3) C

BE10–9 For each of the following independent situations, indicate whether it should be (1) recorded, (2) disclosed, or (3) neither recorded nor disclosed. Explain your reasoning and indicate if the accounting treatment would be the same or different under IFRS and Canadian GAAP for Private Enterprises.

(a) A customer has sued a company for $1 million. Currently the company is unable to determine if it will win or lose the lawsuit.
(b) A customer has sued a company for $1 million. The company will likely lose the lawsuit.
(c) A company has appealed an income tax assessment by the CRA. If the company's appeal is successful, it will recover $100,000 of income tax. The company's accountant has advised management that the company has a good chance of winning the appeal.
(d) A company has guaranteed a $300,000 loan for one of its key suppliers. The supplier has a good credit rating and is not expected to default on the loan.

Discuss contingent liability.
(SO 3) AP

BE10–10 Athabasca Toil & Oil Company, a public company, is a defendant in a lawsuit for improper discharge of pollutants and waste into the Athabasca River. Athabasca's lawyers have advised that the company will likely lose this lawsuit and that it could settle out of court for $50,000. How should Athabasca record this current liability? What are the arguments for and against recording this contingent liability?

Calculate gross, net pay, and employer costs.
(SO 4) AP

BE10–11 Becky Sherrick's regular hourly wage rate is $16, and she receives an hourly rate of $24 for work over 40 hours per week. In the pay period ended January 5, Becky worked 43 hours. Becky's CPP deductions total $31.91, EI deductions total $12.32, and her income tax withholdings are $104.65. (a) Calculate Becky's gross and net pay for the pay period. (b) What are Becky's employer's costs for CPP, EI, and income tax?

Record payroll.
(SO 4) AP

BE10–12 Data for Becky Sherrick are given in BE10–11. Prepare the journal entries to record Becky's pay for the period, including employer costs, assuming she was paid on January 5.

Record payroll.
(SO 4) AP

BE10–13 Bri Company's gross pay for the week ended August 22 totalled $70,000, from which $3,330 was deducted for CPP, $1,211 for EI, and $19,360 for income tax. Prepare the entries to record (a) the employee payroll costs, assuming salaries were paid August 22, and (b) the employer payroll costs, assuming these will not be paid until September.

BE10–14 Identify which of the following items should be classified as a current liability. For those that are not current liabilities, identify where they should be classified.

Identify current liabilities. (SO 1, 2, 3, 4, 5) K

1. A product warranty
2. Cash received in advance for airline tickets
3. HST collected on sales
4. Bank indebtedness
5. Interest owing on an overdue account payable
6. Interest due on an overdue account receivable
7. A lawsuit pending against a company. The company is not sure of the likely outcome.
8. Amounts withheld from the employees' weekly pay
9. Prepaid property tax
10. A $75,000 mortgage payable, of which $5,000 is due in the next year

BE10–15 Suncor Energy Inc. reported the following current assets and current liabilities (in millions) at December 31, 2008:

Prepare current liabilities section and calculate ratios. (SO 5) AP

Accounts payable and accrued liabilities	$3,229
Accounts receivable	1,580
Cash	660
Income taxes payable	192
Income taxes recoverable	88
Inventories	909
Sales taxes payable	97
Short-term debt	11

(a) Prepare the current liabilities section of the balance sheet.
(b) Calculate the current and the acid-test ratios.

***BE10–16** Cecilia Hernandez earned $55,200 in 2009 and was paid on a monthly basis. She worked for HillSide Tours for all of 2009. What were her CPP and EI deductions in (a) January 2009 and (b) December 2009?

Calculate CPP and EI deductions. (SO 6) AP

***BE10–17** In 2009, Viktor Petska was paid a gross salary of $1,090 on a weekly basis. For the week ended May 8, 2009: (a) calculate his CPP and EI deductions and (b) use the excerpts in Illustration 10A-3 to determine his income tax deductions assuming his TD1 claim code is 1.

Calculate payroll deductions. (SO 6) AP

***BE10–18** Augustus Jackson earns $720 for a 40-hour week and is paid time and a half for hours above 40. During the week ended April 24, 2009, he worked 50 hours. (a) Calculate his gross pay for the week. (b) Calculate his CPP and EI deductions. (c) Use the excerpts in Illustration 10A-3 to determine his income tax deductions assuming his TD1 claim code is 3. (d) Calculate his net pay.

Calculate gross pay, payroll deductions, and net pay. (SO 4, 6) AP

Exercises

E10–1 Briffet Construction borrows $200,000 from TD Bank on October 1, 2010. It signs a 10-month, 6% note payable. Interest is payable the first of each month, starting November 1.

Record note payable and note receivable; interest paid monthly. (SO 1) AP

Instructions

(a) Record for Briffet Construction (1) the transaction on October 1, 2010; (2) the first interest payment on November 1, 2010; and (3) the payment of the note on August 1, 2011.
(b) Record for TD Bank (1) the transaction on October 1, 2010; (2) the first interest receipt on November 1, 2010; and (3) the collection of the note on August 1, 2011.

Record note payable and note receivable; interest paid at maturity.
(SO 1) AP

E10–2 On March 1, 2011, Tundra Trees Company purchased equipment from Edworthy Equipment Dealership for $20,000, terms n/30. On March 31, Tundra was unable to pay its account. Edworthy agreed to accept a seven-month, 8% note payable to settle the account. Interest is due at maturity. Tundra Trees has a July 31 fiscal year end. Edworthy has a May 31 fiscal year end. Both companies adjust their accounts annually. Tundra honours the note at maturity.

Instructions

(a) For Tundra Trees, record: (1) the transactions on March 1 and March 31, 2011; (2) the adjusting entry on July 31, 2011; and (3) the payment of the note on October 31, 2011.
(b) For Edworthy Equipment, record: (1) the transactions on March 1 and March 31, 2011 (assume the equipment had cost Edworthy $12,000); (2) the adjusting entry on May 31, 2011; and (3) the collection of the note on October 31, 2011.

Record sales taxes.
(SO 1) AP

E10–3 In providing accounting services to small businesses, you encounter the following independent situations:

1. Sainsbury Company rang up $26,500 of sales, plus HST of 13%, on its cash register on April 10.
2. Hockenstein Company prices its merchandise with sales taxes included. Its register total for April 15 is $33,674, which includes 13% HST.
3. Montgomery Company rang up $30,000 of sales, before sales taxes, on its cash register on April 21. The company charges 5% GST and 10% PST on all sales. PST is charged on sales plus GST.

Instructions

Record the sales transactions and related taxes for each client.

Record unearned subscription revenue.
(SO 1) AP

E10–4 Westwood Company publishes a monthly skateboard magazine, *Adventure Time*. Subscriptions to the magazine cost $48 per year. In October 2010, Westwood sells 6,000 subscriptions, which begin with the November issue. Westwood prepares financial statements quarterly and recognizes subscription revenue earned at the end of each quarter. Westwood's year end is December 31.

Instructions

(a) Prepare the entry in October for the receipt of the subscriptions.
(b) Prepare the adjusting entry at December 31, 2010, to record subscription revenue earned by the end of December.
(c) Prepare the adjusting entry at March 31, 2011, to record subscription revenue earned in the first quarter of 2011.

Record property tax; determine financial statement impact.
(SO 1, 5) AP

E10–5 Seaboard Company receives its annual property tax bill of $18,660 for the 2011 calendar year on May 31, 2011, and it is payable on July 31, 2011. Seaboard has a December 31 fiscal year end.

Instructions

(a) Prepare the journal entries for Seaboard on May 31, July 31, and December 31, 2011, assuming that the company makes monthly adjusting entries. (Assume property tax expense in 2010 was $1,475 per month.)
(b) What is recorded on Seaboard's December 31, 2011, balance sheet and income statement for the year ended December 31, 2011, in regard to property taxes?

Record warranty costs.
(SO 2) AP

E10–6 Sinclair Company sells popcorn makers under a 90-day warranty for defective merchandise. Based on past experience, Sinclair estimates that 3% of the units sold will become defective in the warranty period. Management estimates that the average cost of replacing or repairing a defective unit is $15. The units sold and actual units defective in the last two months of 2011 are as follows:

Month	Units Sold	Units Defective
November	45,000	450
December	48,000	930
	93,000	1,380

Instructions

(a) Calculate the estimated warranty liability at December 31 for the units sold in November and December.

(b) Prepare the journal entries to record (1) the estimated liability for warranties, and (2) the costs incurred in honouring the 1,380 warranty claims as at December 31 (assume an actual cost of $20,700).

E10–7 The CopyCat Company manufactures and sells photocopiers, with a two-year service warranty. The company estimates that on average it will make 10 service calls a year for each unit sold over the two-year warranty period, at an average cost of $60 per service call.

Calculate warranty costs for multiple years.
(SO 2) AP

The company reports the following sales and service call information:

	2009	2010	2011
Sales (units)	2,000	2,200	2,400
Actual service calls	20,000	40,000	50,000

Instructions

(a) Calculate the warranty expense for each year.

(b) Calculate the warranty liability at the end of each year.

E10–8 Steig's Sports Store has a customer loyalty program in which it issues points to customers for every cash purchase that can be applied to future purchases. For every dollar spent, a customer receives five points. Each point is worth one cent. There is no expiry date on the points. Steig's estimates that 15% of the points issued will eventually be redeemed. Steig's has a December 31 year end.

Calculate customer loyalty program liability.
(SO 2) AP

The program was started in 2010. During 2010, 600,000 points were issued. In 2011, 800,000 points were issued. Redemptions total 50,000 points in 2010 and 80,000 in 2011.

Instructions

(a) What amount should be recorded as contra revenue (sales discounts for redemption rewards issued) in 2010? In 2011?

(b) What was the value of the points redeemed in 2010? In 2011?

(c) What is the redemption rewards liability that should be reported at December 31, 2010? At December 31, 2011?

(d) When the points are redeemed, how is this accounted for? What is the impact of the point redemptions on profit?

E10–9 A list of possible liabilities follows:

Identify type of liability.
(SO 1, 2, 3) C

1. An automobile company recalled a particular car model because of a possible problem with the brakes. The company will pay to replace the brakes.
2. A large retail store has a policy of refunding purchases to dissatisfied customers under a widely advertised "money-back, no questions asked" guarantee.
3. A manufacturer offers a three-year warranty at the time of sale.
4. To promote sales, a company offers prizes (e.g., a chance to win a trip) in return for a specific type of bottle cap.
5. A local community has filed suit against a chemical company for contamination of drinking water. The community is demanding compensation, and the amount is uncertain. The company is vigorously defending itself.

Instructions

(a) State whether you believe each of the above liabilities is determinable, estimable, or contingent, and explain why.
(b) If you identify the liability as contingent in part (a), state what factors should be considered in determining if it should be recorded, disclosed, or neither recorded nor disclosed in the financial statements.

Analyze contingent liability.
(SO 3) AP

E10–10 Sleep-a-Bye Baby Company, a public company, is the defendant in a lawsuit alleging that its portable baby cribs are unsafe. The company has offered to replace the cribs free of charge for any concerned parent. Nonetheless, it has been sued for damages and distress amounting to $1.5 million. The company plans to vigorously defend its product safety record in court.

Instructions

(a) What should the company record or report in its financial statements for this situation? Explain why.
(b) What if Sleep-a-Bye Baby Company's lawyers advise that it is likely the company will have to pay damages of $100,000? Does this change what should be recorded or reported in the financial statements? Explain.
(c) How would your answers to (a) and (b) change if Sleep-a-Bye Baby Company were a private company that had chosen to follow Canadian GAAP?

Record payroll.
(SO 4) AP

E10–11 Hidden Dragon Restaurant's gross payroll for August is $41,500. The company deducted $1,860 for CPP, $718 for EI, and $8,025 for income taxes from the employees' cheques. Employees are paid monthly at the end of each month.

Instructions

(a) Prepare a journal entry for Hidden Dragon on August 31 to record the payment of the August payroll to employees.
(b) Prepare a journal entry on August 31 to accrue Hidden Dragon's employer payroll costs. Assume that Hidden Dragon is assessed workers' compensation premiums at a rate of 1% per month and accrues for vacation pay at a rate of 4% per month.
(c) On September 15, Hidden Dragon pays the government the correct amounts for August's payroll. Prepare a journal entry to record this remittance.

Calculate gross pay, prepare payroll register, and record payroll.
(SO 4) AP

E10–12 Ahmad Company has the following data for the weekly payroll ending May 31:

	Hours Worked						Hourly	CPP	Income Tax	Health
Employee	M	Tu	W	Th	F	S	Rate	Deduction	Withheld	Insurance
A. Kassam	8	8	9	8	10	3	$11	$23.35	$81	$10
H. Faas	8	8	8	8	8	2	13	24.34	87	15
G. Labute	9	10	8	10	8	0	14	29.59	107	15

Employees are paid 1.5 times the regular hourly rate for all hours worked over 40 hours per week. Ahmad Company must make payments to the workers' compensation plan equal to 2% of the gross payroll. In addition, Ahmad matches the employees' health insurance contributions and accrues vacation pay at a rate of 4%.

Instructions

(a) Prepare the payroll register for the weekly payroll. Calculate each employee's EI deduction at a rate of 1.73% of gross pay.
(b) Record the payroll and Ahmad Company's employee benefits.

Determine financial statement impact of transactions.
(SO 1, 2, 3, 4) AP

E10–13 Here is a list of transactions:

1. Purchased inventory (perpetual system) on account.

2. Extended the payment terms of the account payable in item 1 above by issuing a nine-month, 5% note payable.
3. Recorded accrued interest on the note payable from item 2 above.
4. Recorded cash sales of $8,000, plus HST of 13%.
5. Recorded wage expense of $35,000. Paid employees $25,000; the difference was for various payroll deductions withheld.
6. Recorded employer's share of employee benefits.
7. Accrued property taxes payable when bill received.
8. Disclosed a contingent liability on a lawsuit whose outcome the company cannot determine.
9. Recorded the estimated liability for product warranties outstanding.
10. Paid product warranty claims that were accrued in item 9 above.

Instructions

Set up a table using the format shown below. Indicate the effect ("+" for increase, "–" for decrease, and "NE" for no effect) of each of the above transactions on the financial statement categories indicated. The first one has been done for you as an example.

	Assets	Liabilities	Owner's Equity	Revenues	Expenses	Profit
1.	+	+	NE	NE	NE	NE

E10–14 Larkin Company has the following liability accounts at August 31, 2011, after posting adjusting entries:

Prepare current liabilities section of balance sheet. Calculate current and acid-test ratios.
(SO 5) AP

Accounts payable	$ 72,000
Bank indebtedness	50,000
CPP payable	6,000
Customer loyalty liability	4,000
EI payable	3,000
HST payable	12,000
Income tax payable	28,000
Interest payable	8,000
Mortgage payable	120,000
Note payable	80,000
Property taxes payable	8,000
Unearned revenue	24,000
Warranty liability	18,000
Workers' compensation payable	1,000

Additional information:

1. Bank indebtedness is from an operating line of credit that is due on demand.
2. On August 31, 2011, the unused operating line of credit is $25,000.
3. Customer loyalty and warranty costs are expected to be incurred within one year.
4. Of the mortgage, $10,000 is due each year.
5. The note payable matures in three years.
6. On August 31, 2011, the company had current assets composed of accounts receivable of $145,000; inventory of $220,000; and prepaid assets of $10,000.

Instructions

(a) Prepare the current liabilities section of the balance sheet.
(b) Calculate Larkin's current ratio and acid-test ratio.
(c) Explain why the company did not report any cash as part of its current assets.

***E10–15** Kate Gough's regular hourly wage rate is $20.50, and she receives a wage of 1.5 times the regular hourly rate for work over 40 hours per week. In a September weekly pay period, Kate worked 44 hours. Kate lives in Ontario and has a claim code of 1 for tax deductions.

Calculate gross pay and payroll deductions; record payroll.
(SO 4, 6) AP

Instructions

(a) Calculate Kate's gross pay and her payroll deductions. Use Illustration 10A-3 to determine her income tax deductions.
(b) Record Kate's salary on September 16, assuming it was also paid on this date.
(c) Record the employer's related payroll costs on September 16, assuming they were not paid on this date.

Calculate gross pay and payroll deductions.
(SO 6) AP

*E10–16 In 2009, Donald Green worked for the Green Red Company and earned a gross salary of $48,000 for the year ($4,000 per month). He is paid once a month at the end of each month.

Instructions

Calculate Donald's CPP and EI deductions for the following:

(a) September 2009
(b) October 2009
(c) November 2009
(d) December 2009
(e) In total for 2009

Problems: Set A

Identify liabilities.
(SO 1, 2, 3, 4, 5) AP

P10–1A The following transactions occurred in Wendell Company in the year ended December 31:

1. Wendell purchased goods for $120,000 on December 23, terms n/30, FOB shipping point. The goods were shipped on December 27.
2. Weekly salaries of $60,000 are paid every Friday for a five-day (Monday to Friday) workweek. This year, December 31 is a Wednesday. Payroll deductions include income tax withholdings of $18,000, and CPP of $3,000, and EI of $1,000.
3. Wendell is the defendant in a $500,000 negligence suit. Wendell's lawyers estimate that Wendell may suffer a $95,000 loss if it loses the suit. In the lawyers' opinion, the likelihood of success in the case cannot be determined at this time.
4. Wendell issued a $500,000, five-year, 6% note payable on July 1. The note requires payment of the principal in instalments of $100,000 each June 30 for the next five years. Interest is due monthly on the first of each month.
5. The company received $25,000 from customers in December for services to be performed in January.
6. Wendell issued a mail-in purchase rebate on one of its specialty inventory items sold between September 1 and November 30. Each item was sold for $45 and had a $4 rebate attached to it. A total of 4,500 items were sold in that period. Wendell estimates that 25% of the customers will request a rebate. By December 31, Wendell had issued $3,900 in rebates.
7. The company has a $100,000 operating line of credit. No money is owed on this line of credit to date.

Instructions

Identify which transactions above should be presented in the current liabilities section and which in the long-term liabilities section of Wendell's balance sheet on December 31. Identify the account title(s) and amount(s) for each reported liability.

Taking It Further

Indicate any information that should be disclosed in the notes to Wendell's financial statements.

Record note transactions; show financial statement presentation.
(SO 1, 5) AP

P10–2A The current liabilities section of the December 31, 2010, balance sheet of Learnstream Company included notes payable of $14,000 and interest payable of $490. The note payable was issued to Tanner Company on June 30, 2010. Interest of 7% is payable at maturity, March 31, 2011.

The following selected transactions occurred in the year ended December 31, 2011:

Jan.	12	Purchased merchandise on account from McCoy Company for $20,000, terms n/30. Learnstream uses a perpetual inventory system.
	31	Issued a $20,000, three-month, 5% note to McCoy Company in payment of an account. Interest is payable monthly.
Feb.	28	Paid interest on the McCoy note (see January 31 transaction).
Mar.	31	Paid the Tanner note, plus interest.
	31	Paid interest on the McCoy note (see January 31 transaction).
Apr.	30	Paid the McCoy note, plus one month's interest (see January 31 transaction).
Aug.	1	Purchased equipment from Scottie Equipment by paying $11,000 cash and signing a $30,000, 10-month, 6% note. Interest is payable at maturity.
Oct.	30	Borrowed $100,000 cash from the First Interprovincial Bank by signing a 10-year, 5% note payable. Interest is payable quarterly on December 31, March 31, June 30, and September 30. Of the principal, $10,000 must be paid each September 30.
Dec.	31	Paid interest on the First Interprovincial Bank note (see September 30 transaction).

Instructions

(a) Record the transactions and any adjustments required at December 31.
(b) Show the balance sheet presentation of notes payable and interest payable at December 31.
(c) Show the income statement presentation of interest expense for the year.

Taking It Further

Why is it important to correctly classify notes payable as either current or non-current in the balance sheet?

Record current liability transactions; prepare current liabilities section.
(SO 1, 2, 4, 5) AP

P10–3A On January 1, 2011, Shumway Software Company's general ledger contained these liability accounts:

Accounts payable	$42,500
Customer loyalty program liability	4,500
CPP payable	1,340
EI payable	702
HST payable	11,400
Income tax payable	2,915
Unearned service revenue	15,000
Vacation pay payable	7,680

In January, the following selected transactions occurred:

Jan.	2	Issued a $50,000, four-month, 7% note. Interest is payable at maturity.
	5	Sold merchandise for $8,800 cash, plus 13% HST. The cost of this sale was $4,600. Shumway Software uses a perpetual inventory system.
	12	Provided services for customers who had made advance payments of $8,500. Assume HST is not charged for these services.
	14	Paid the Receiver General (federal government) for sales taxes collected in December 2010.
	15	Paid the Receiver General for amounts owing from the December payroll for CPP, EI, and income tax.
	17	Paid $20,000 to creditors on account.
	20	Sold 500 units of a new product on account for $55 per unit, plus 13% HST. This new product has a one-year warranty. It is estimated that 9% of the units sold will be returned for repair at an average cost of $10 per unit. The cost of this sale was $25 per unit.

29 Provided $2,300 of services for customers in exchange for customer loyalty rewards redeemed in the month. Assume that HST of 13% is included in $2,300.
31 Recorded and paid the monthly payroll. Gross salaries were $16,000. Amounts withheld included CPP of $720, EI of $277, and income tax of $3,215.

Instructions

(a) Record the transactions.
(b) Record adjusting entries for the following:
1. Interest on the note payable
2. The estimated warranty liability
3. Employee benefits for CPP, EI, and vacation pay (accrued at a rate of 4%)
4. Estimated property taxes totalling $7,560 in 2011
(c) Prepare the current liabilities section of the balance sheet at January 31.

Taking It Further

Explain when the company should reduce its vacation pay liability.

Record warranty transactions.
(SO 2) AP

P10–4A On January 1, 2009, Hopewell Company began a warranty program to stimulate sales. It is estimated that 5% of the units sold will be returned for repair at an estimated cost of $30 per unit. Sales and warranty figures for the three years ended December 31 are as follows:

	2009	2010	2011
Sales (units)	1,500	1,700	1,800
Sales price per unit	$150	$120	$125
Units returned for repair under warranty	75	90	105
Actual warranty costs	$2,250	$2,400	$2,640

Instructions

(a) Calculate the warranty expense for each year and warranty liability at the end of each year.
(b) Record the warranty transactions for each year. Credit Repair Parts Inventory for the actual warranty costs.
(c) To date, what percentage of the units sold have been returned for repair under warranty? What has been the average actual warranty cost per unit for the three year period?

Taking It Further

Assume that at December 31, 2011, management reassesses its original estimates and decides that it is more likely that the company will have to service 7% of the units sold in 2011. Management also determines that the average actual cost per unit incurred to date (as calculated in (c) above), is more reasonable than its original estimate. What should be the balance in the warranty liability account at December 31, 2011?

Record customer loyalty program and gift card transactions; determine impact on financial statements.
(SO 2) AP

P10–5A Save-Always Stores started a customer loyalty program at the beginning of 2010 in which customers making cash purchases of gasoline at Save-Always Gas Bars are issued rewards in the form of grocery coupons. For each litre of gasoline purchased, the customer gets a grocery coupon for 3.5 cents that can be redeemed in Save-Always Food Stores. The coupons have no expiry date. Save-Always Stores began selling gift cards in 2011 that do not have expiry dates.

The following are selected transactions in 2010 and 2011:

1. In 2010, the Gas Bars sold 3.5 million litres of gasoline, issuing grocery coupons for these sales.
2. In 2010, customers redeemed $45,000 of the grocery coupons in the Food Stores while purchasing $1.8 million of groceries, paying the balance in cash.
3. In 2011, the Gas Bars sold 4.25 million litres of gasoline, issuing grocery coupons for these sales.
4. In 2011, customers redeemed $52,500 of the grocery coupons in the Food Stores while purchasing $2,230,000 of groceries, paying for the balance in cash.

5. In 2011, customers purchased $75,000 of gift cards, and $45,400 of the cards were redeemed by the end of the year.

Instructions

(a) Indicate if the following items will increase, decrease, or have no effect on each of revenues, expenses, and profit:
   1. Issuing grocery coupons
   2. Redeeming grocery coupons
   3. Issuing gift cards
   4. Redeeming gift cards

(b) Record the above transactions.

(c) What balances will be included in current liabilities at December 31, 2010 and 2011, regarding the customer loyalty program and gift cards?

Taking It Further

What factors should management consider in determining if current liabilities are correctly valued at December 31, 2011?

Discuss reporting of contingent liabilities and assets.
(SO 3, 5) AP

P10–6A Mega Company, a public company, is preparing its financial statements for the year ended December 31, 2011. It is now January 31, 2012, and the following situations are being reviewed to determine the appropriate accounting treatment:

1. Mega Company is being sued for a possible malfunction of one of its products. In July 2011, a customer suffered a serious injury while operating the product. The company is vigorously defending itself as it is clear the customer was intoxicated when using the product.
2. In a separate lawsuit, Mega is being sued by an employee who was injured on the job in February 2011. It is likely that the company will lose this lawsuit, but a reasonable estimate cannot be made of the amount of the obligation.
3. Since June 2009, Mega has guaranteed a bank loan for one of its main suppliers. In September 2011, the supplier started experiencing financial difficulties, which have continued. On December 16, 2011, the bank called Mega Company to confirm that if the supplier is unable repay the loan in January 2012, the bank will be seeking payment from Mega Company under the guarantee.
4. On January 7, 2012, a potential customer injured himself when he slipped on the floor in the foyer of Mega Company's office building. Mega Company did not have appropriate floor mats in place and melting snow from the customer's boots made the floor very dangerous. Mega has negotiated a potential settlement with the individual's lawyer.
5. If Mega loses the lawsuit mentioned in part 2 above, then its insurance company will likely pay it a portion of the damages.

Instructions

For each of the above situations, recommend whether Mega Company should (a) make an accrual in its December 31, 2011, financial statements; (b) disclose the situation in the notes to the financial statements; or (c) not report it. Provide a rationale for your recommendations.

Taking It Further

What are the differences between accounting for contingencies under IFRS versus Canadian GAAP for Private Enterprises?

Discuss reporting of contingent liability and asset.
(SO 3, 5) AP

P10–7A Atom Construction Company is in the second year of a three-year construction schedule to build a nuclear plant for the Province of Ontario. The province has agreed to pay the company a bonus if the plant is completed on time and on budget. Atom Construction Company has never missed a deadline and also has a history of completing projects on budget.

Instructions

(a) What should the Province of Ontario record or disclose in its financial statements in this situation? Explain why.
(b) What should Atom Construction Company record or disclose in its financial statements in this situation? Explain why.

Taking It Further

Why are there differences in how contingent liabilities and contingent assets are accounted for?

Prepare payroll register and record payroll.
(SO 4) AP

P10–8A Sure Value Hardware has four employees who are paid on an hourly basis, plus time-and-a-half for hours worked in excess of 40 hours a week. Payroll data for the week ended March 14, 2011, follow:

Employee	Total Hours	Hourly Rate	CPP	EI	Income Tax	United Way
I. Dahl	37.5	$16.00	$26.37	$10.38	$ 89.70	$ 7.50
F. Gualtieri	42	15.00	28.60	11.16	99.35	8.00
G. Ho	44	14.50	30.68	11.54	108.00	5.00
A. Israeli	46	14.50	32.83	12.29	122.75	10.00

The first three employees are sales clerks (store wages expense) and the other employee does administrative duties (office wages expense).

Instructions

(a) Prepare a payroll register for the weekly payroll.
(b) Record the payroll on March 14 and the accrual of employee benefits expense.
(c) Record the payment of the payroll on March 14.
(d) Record the payment of employee benefits on April 15.

Taking It Further

Does the owner of a proprietorship need to deduct CPP, EI, and income taxes on his or her drawings?

Record and post payroll transactions.
(SO 4) AP

P10–9A The following payroll liability accounts are included in the ledger of Drumheller Company on January 1, 2011:

Canada Pension Plan payable	$ 5,454
Canada Savings Bonds payable	2,500
Disability insurance payable	1,050
Employment Insurance payable	3,050
Income tax payable	16,800
Union dues payable	1,250
Vacation pay payable	6,450
Workers' compensation payable	5,263

In January, the following transactions occurred:

Jan. 8 Sent a cheque to the insurance company for the disability insurance.
10 Sent a cheque for $1,250 to the union treasurer for union dues.
11 Purchased Canada Savings Bonds for employees by writing a cheque for $2,500.
12 Issued a cheque to the Receiver General for the amounts due for CPP, EI, and income tax.
20 Paid the amount due to the workers' compensation plan.
31 Completed the monthly payroll register, which shows office salaries $24,600; store wages $38,700; CPP withheld $2,845; EI withheld $1,095; income tax withheld $15,620; union dues withheld $950; Canada Savings Bond deductions $1,200; and long-term disability insurance premiums $1,100.

31 Prepared payroll cheques for the net pay and distributed the cheques to the employees.

At January 31, the company also made the following adjusting entries for employee benefits:

1. The employer's share of CPP and EI
2. Workers' compensation plan at 5% of gross pay
3. Vacation pay at 4% of gross pay

Instructions

(a) Enter the beginning balances in general ledger accounts.
(b) Journalize and post the January transactions and adjustments.

Taking It Further

What is the purpose of an employee's earning record?

Prepare current liabilities section; calculate and comment on ratios.
(SO 5) AP

P10–10A Kangaroo Media Inc. reports the following current assets and current liabilities at December 31, 2008 (in thousands):

Accounts payable and accrued liabilities	$1,993
Accounts receivable	897
Cash and cash equivalents	9,266
Short-term investments	160
Current portion of long-term debt	3,199
Deferred revenues	211
Inventories	128
Prepaid expenses	128

Instructions

(a) Prepare the current liabilities section of the balance sheet.
(b) Calculate the current and acid-test ratios.
(c) At December 31, 2007, Kangaroo Media Inc. had current assets of $27,177 thousand, cash plus short-term investments plus accounts receivable of $25,662 thousand, and current liabilities of $6,813 thousand. Did the current and acid-test ratios improve or weaken in 2008?

Taking It Further

What other factors should be considered in assessing Kangaroo Media's solvency?

Calculate payroll deductions.
(SO 6) AP

***P10–11A** Western Electric Company pays its support staff weekly and its electricians on a semi-monthly basis. The following support staff payroll information is available for the week ended June 5, 2009:

Employee Name	Weekly Earnings	Claim Code
Chris Tam	$ 945	2
Terry Ng	1,135	4
Olga Stavtech	1,135	1
Alana Mandell	1,067	1

The electricians' salaries are based on their experience in the field, as well as the number of years they have worked for the company. All three electricians have been with the company more than two years. The annual salaries of these employees are as follows:

Employee Name	Annual Salary for 2009
Sam Goodspeed	$40,840
Marino Giancarlo	60,760
Hillary Radley	70,480

Instructions

(a) Determine the mandatory payroll deductions and net pay for each of the support staff. Calculate the CPP and EI deductions using the formula provided in Appendix 10A. Use the tables in Illustration 10A-3 to determine federal and provincial income taxes.

(b) Calculate the CPP and EI deductions for each of the electricians for their June 15, 2009, semi-monthly payroll.

(c) In which semi-monthly pay period will each of the electricians reach their maximum CPP and EI payments for 2009?

Taking It Further

Why are there separate payroll deduction tables for determining weekly, semi-monthly, and monthly income tax deductions?

Problems: Set B

Identify liabilities.
(SO 1, 2, 3, 4, 5) AP

P10–1B The following transactions occurred in Iqaluit Company in the year ended April 30:

1. Iqaluit purchased goods for $12,000 on April 29, terms n/30, FOB destination. The goods arrived on May 3.
2. Weekly salaries of $90,000 are paid every Friday for a five-day (Monday to Friday) work-week. This year, April 30 is a Thursday. Payroll deductions include income tax withholdings of $27,000, and CPP of $4,500, and EI of $1,500.
3. Property taxes of $40,000 were assessed on March 1 for the calendar year. They are payable on May 1.
4. The company purchased equipment for $35,000 on April 1. It issued a six-month, 5% note in payment. Interest is payable monthly on the first of each month.
5. Iqaluit offered a two-year warranty on one of its new products. It estimated it would cost $45 to honour each warranty and that 5% of the units sold would be returned for replacement within the warranty period. By April 30, 10,000 units of the product had been sold and customers had returned 100 units under the warranty.
6. The company has a $225,000, 20-year mortgage payable; $9,250 of the principal must be paid within the next year.
7. Iqaluit was named in a $1-million lawsuit alleging negligence for an oil spill that leaked into the neighbouring company's water system. Iqaluit's lawyers estimate that the company will likely lose the suit and expect the company will have to pay $250,000 in restoration costs.

Instructions

Identify which transactions above should be presented in the current liabilities section and which in the long-term liabilities section of Iqaluit's balance sheet on April 30. Identify the account title(s) and amount(s) for each reported liability.

Taking It Further

Indicate any information that should be disclosed in the notes to Iqaluit's financial statements.

Record note transactions; show financial statement presentation.
(SO 1, 5) AP

P10–2B MileHi Mountain Bikes markets mountain-bike tours to clients vacationing in various locations in the mountains of British Columbia. The current liabilities section of the October 31, 2010, balance sheet included notes payable of $15,000 and interest payable of $375 related to a six-month, 6% note payable to Eifert Company on December 1, 2010.

During the year ended October 31, 2011, MileHi had the following transactions related to notes payable:

<u>2010</u>
Dec. 1 Paid the $15,000 Eifert note, plus interest.

2011

Apr. 1 Issued a $75,000, nine-month, 7% note to Mountain Real Estate for the purchase of additional mountain property on which to build bike trails. Interest is payable quarterly on July 1, September 1, and at maturity on December 1.

30 Purchased Mongoose bikes to use as rentals for $8,000, terms n/30.

May 31 Issued Mongoose an $8,000, three-month, 8% note payable in settlement of its account (see April 30 transaction). Interest is payable at maturity.

July 1 Paid interest on the Mountain Real Estate note (see April 1 transaction).

Aug. 31 Paid the Mongoose note, plus interest (see May 31 transaction).

Oct. 1 Paid interest on the Mountain Real Estate note (see April 1 transaction).

1 Borrowed $90,000 cash from Western Bank by issuing a five-year, 6% note. Interest is payable monthly on the first of the month. Principal payments of $18,000 must be made on the anniversary of the note each year.

Instructions

(a) Record the transactions and any adjustments required at October 31, 2011.

(b) Show the balance sheet presentation of notes payable and interest payable at October 31, 2011.

(c) Show the income statement presentation of interest expense for the year.

Taking It Further

Why is it important to correctly classify notes payable as either current or non-current in the balance sheet?

Record current liability transactions; prepare current liabilities section.

(SO 1, 2, 4, 5) AP

P10–3B On January 1, 2011, Zaur Company's general ledger had these liability accounts:

Accounts payable	$52,000
Customer loyalty program liability	2,150
CPP payable	1,905
EI payable	850
HST payable	11,390
Income tax payable	4,640
Unearned service revenue	16,000
Vacation pay liability	9,120
Warranty liability	5,750

In January, the following selected transactions occurred:

Jan. 5 Sold merchandise for $15,800 cash, plus 13% HST. Zaur uses a periodic inventory system.

12 Provided services for customers who had previously made advance payments of $7,000.

14 Paid the Receiver General (federal government) sales taxes collected in December 2010.

15 Paid the Receiver General for amounts owing from the December payroll for CPP, EI, and income tax.

16 Borrowed $18,000 from HSBC Bank on a three-month, 6% note. Interest is payable monthly on the 15th day of the month.

17 Paid $32,000 to creditors on account.

20 Sold 500 units of a new product on account for $60 per unit, plus 13% HST. The cost of the product sold is $25 per unit. This new product has a two-year warranty. It is expected that 6% of the units sold will be returned for repair at an average cost of $10 per unit.

30 Customers redeemed $1,750 of loyalty points in exchange for services. Assume that HST of 13% is included in this amount.

31 Issued 50,000 loyalty points worth $1 each. Based on past experience, 10% of these coupons are expected to be redeemed.

31 Determined that the company had used $875 of parts inventory in January to honour warranty contracts.
31 Recorded and paid the monthly payroll. Gross salaries were $22,500. Amounts withheld include CPP of $1,027, EI of $289, and income tax of $5,135.

Instructions

(a) Record the transactions.
(b) Record adjusting entries for the following:
1. Interest on the note payable for half a month
2. The estimated warranty liability
3. Employee benefits, which include CPP, EI, and vacation pay that is accrued at a rate of 4%
(c) Prepare the current liabilities section of the balance sheet at January 31.

Taking It Further

Explain when the company should reduce its vacation pay liability.

Record warranty transactions.
(SO 2) AP

P10–4B On January 1, 2009, Logue Company began a warranty program to stimulate sales. It is estimated that 5% of the units sold will be returned for repair at an estimated cost of $25 per unit. Sales and warranty figures for the three years ended December 31 are as follows:

	2009	2010	2011
Sales (units)	1,200	1,320	1,420
Sales price per unit	$100	$105	$110
Units returned for repair under warranty	60	70	80
Actual warranty costs	$1,275	$1,600	$1,960

Instructions

(a) Calculate the warranty expense for each year and warranty liability at the end of each year.
(b) Record the warranty transactions for each year. Credit Repair Parts Inventory for the actual warranty costs.
(c) To date, what percentage of the units sold have been returned for repair under warranty? What has been the average actual warranty cost per unit for the three year period?

Taking It Further

Suppose at December 31, 2011, management reassesses its original estimates and decides that it is more likely that the company will have to service 7% of the units sold in 2011. Management also determines that the original estimate of the cost per unit is the appropriate cost to use for future repair work. What should be the balance in the warranty liability account at December 31, 2011?

Record customer loyalty program and gift card transactions; determine impact on financial statements.
(SO 2) AP

P10–5B Caribou County Service Station started a customer loyalty program at the beginning of 2010 in which customers making cash purchases of gasoline at the gas bar are issued rewards in the form of coupons. For each litre of gasoline purchased, the customer gets a coupon for 2.5 cents that can be redeemed in the service department toward such things as oil changes or repairs. The coupons have no expiry date. Caribou County Service Station began selling gift cards in 2011 that do not have expiry dates.

The following are selected transactions in 2010 and 2011:

1. In 2010, the gas bar sold 750,000 litres of gasoline, issuing coupons for these sales.
2. In 2010, customers redeemed $5,950 of the coupons in the service department while purchasing $23,800 of repair services for their vehicles, paying the balance in cash.
3. In 2011, the gas bar sold 810,000 litres of gasoline, issuing coupons for these sales.
4. In 2011, customers redeemed $9,500 of the coupons in the service department while purchasing $30,230 of repair services for their vehicles, paying for the balance in cash.
5. In 2011, customers purchased $3,950 of gift cards, and $1,500 of the cards were redeemed by the end of the year.

Instructions

(a) Indicate if the following items will increase, decrease, or have no effect on each of revenues, expenses, and profit:

1. Issuing coupons
2. Redeeming coupons
3. Issuing gift cards
4. Redeeming gift cards

(b) Record the above transactions.
(c) What balances will be included in current liabilities at December 31, 2010 and 2011, regarding the customer loyalty program and gift cards?

Taking It Further

What factors should management consider in determining if current liabilities are correctly valued at December 31, 2011?

Discuss reporting of contingent liabilities and assets.
(SO 3, 5) AP

P10–6B Big Fork Company, a private company that follows Canadian GAAP, is preparing its financial statements for the year ended December 31, 2011. It is now February 15, 2012, and the following situations are being reviewed to determine the appropriate accounting treatment:

1. Since 2004, Big Fork has guaranteed a bank loan for one of its main customers, Little Fork. Little Fork has always made all of its payments in a timely fashion.
2. The company is being sued for a possible malfunction of one of its products. In March 2011, a customer suffered a serious injury while operating the product. The company is defending itself but it is clear that there was an error in the published operations manual for the product. It is likely that the company will lose this lawsuit, but a reasonable estimate cannot be made of the amount of the obligation.
3. Big Fork is being sued by an employee for wrongful dismissal and defamation of character. The employee was fired on August 2, 2011. The company is vigorously defending itself because the employee had a long and documented history of poor performance and being intoxicated at work.
4. If Big Fork loses the lawsuit mentioned in part 2 above, then its insurance company will likely pay it for a portion of the damages.
5. On January 7, 2012, a sales representative from one of the company's suppliers injured herself on a visit to Big Fork's offices. She tripped over equipment that had not been properly stored and will be unable to work for several months as a result of her injuries. A claim against Big Fork has been filed by the sales representative's insurance company.

Instructions

For each of the above situations, recommend whether Big Fork Company should (a) make an accrual in its December 31, 2011, financial statements; (b) disclose the situation in the notes to the financial statements; or (c) not report it. Provide a rationale for your recommendations.

Taking It Further

What are the differences between accounting for contingencies under IFRS versus Canadian GAAP for Private Enterprises?

Discuss reporting of contingent asset.
(SO 3, 5) AP

P10–7B On March 4, a fire destroyed the chemistry building on the College of Learning's campus. The college, a private institution, has filed a claim with its insurance company. At March 31, the college's year end, the claim has not been settled.

Instructions

Under each of the following independent assumptions, explain what the college should record or disclose in its March 31 financial statements:

(a) The insurance claim is likely to be successful.
(b) The insurance claim is unlikely to be successful because the insurance company believes the fire is suspicious.
(c) The college receives written confirmation from the insurance company that the claim will be paid in full, but it will not happen before the financial statements are issued.

Taking It Further

Why are there differences in how contingent liabilities and contingent assets are accounted for?

Prepare payroll register and record payroll.
(SO 4) AP

P10–8B Scoot Scooters has four employees who are paid on an hourly basis, plus time-and-a-half for hours in excess of 40 hours a week. Payroll data for the week ended February 15, 2011, follow:

Employee	Total Hours	Hourly Rate	CPP	EI	Income Tax	United Way
P. Kilchyk	40	$12.75	$21.91	$ 8.82	$66.20	$5.00
B. Quon	42	14.00	26.47	10.41	81.95	7.25
C. Pospisil	40	15.25	26.86	10.55	83.55	5.50
B. Verwey	44	13.50	27.41	10.74	85.10	8.25

Instructions

(a) Prepare a payroll register for the weekly payroll.
(b) Record the payroll on February 15 and the accrual of employee benefits expense.
(c) Record the payment of the payroll on February 15.
(d) Record the payment of the employee benefits on March 15.

Taking It Further

Does the owner of a proprietorship have to deduct CPP, EI, and income taxes from his or her own drawings?

Record and post payroll transactions.
(SO 4) AP

P10–9B The following payroll liability accounts are included in the ledger of Amora Company on January 1, 2011:

Canada Pension Plan payable	$ 8,878
Canada Savings Bonds payable	2,420
Employment Insurance payable	3,723
Income tax payable	22,500
Union dues payable	1,200
United Way donations payable	750
Vacation pay payable	10,704
Workers' compensation payable	5,676

In January, the following transactions occurred:

Jan. 7 Issued a cheque to United Way.
10 Sent a cheque to the union treasurer for union dues.
12 Issued a cheque to the Receiver General for the amounts due for CPP, EI, and income tax.
17 Purchased Canada Savings Bonds for employees by writing a cheque for $2,420.
20 Paid the workers' compensation plan.
31 Prepared the monthly payroll register, which showed office salaries $41,200; store wages $50,300; CPP withheld $4,168; EI withheld $1,583; income tax withheld $21,700; union dues withheld $1,250; United Way contributions $750; and Canada Savings Bonds deductions $1,210.
31 Prepared payroll cheques for the net pay and distributed them to employees.

At January 31, the company also made the following adjusting entries for employee benefits:

1. The employer's share of CPP and EI
2. Workers' compensation plan at 7% of gross pay
3. Vacation pay at 4% of gross pay

Instructions

(a) Enter the beginning balances in general ledger accounts.
(b) Record and post the January transactions and adjustments.

Taking It Further

What type of information does an employer keep track of for each employee?

P10–10B Shoppers Drug Mart Corporation reports the following current assets and current liabilities at January 3, 2009 (in thousands of dollars):

Prepare current liabilities section; calculate and comment on ratios.
(SO 5) AP

Accounts payable and accrued liabilities	$1,018,505
Accounts receivable	448,476
Bank indebtedness	240,844
Cash	36,567
Commercial paper	339,957
Dividends payable	46,709
Future income tax asset	83,279
Income taxes recoverable	8,835
Inventory	1,743,253
Prepaid expense and deposits	64,054
Short-term debt	197,845

Instructions

(a) Prepare the current liabilities section of the balance sheet.
(b) Calculate the current and the acid-test ratio.
(c) On December 29, 2007, Shoppers had current assets of $2,150,137 thousand, cash plus short-term investments plus accounts receivable of $399,894 thousand, and current liabilities of $2,158,320 thousand. Did the current and acid-test ratios improve or weaken in 2008?

Taking It Further

What other factors should be considered in assessing Shoppers Drug Mart's liquidity?

***P10–11B** Slovak Plumbing Company pays its support staff weekly and its plumbers on a semi-monthly basis. The following support staff payroll information is available for the week ended May 8, 2009:

Calculate payroll deductions.
(SO 6) AP

Employee Name	Weekly Earnings	Claim Code
Dan Quinn	$ 995	1
Karol Holub	1,030	3
Al Lowhorn	1,074	1
Irina Kostra	940	4

The plumbers' salaries are based on their experience in the field, as well as the number of years they have worked for the company. All three plumbers have been with the company more than two years. The annual salary of these employees is as follows:

Employee Name	Annual Salary for 2009
Branislav Dolina	$75,760
Henrietta Koleno	64,980
Aida Krneta	41,180

Instructions

(a) Determine the mandatory payroll deductions and net pay for each of the support staff. Calculate the CPP and EI deductions using the formula provided in Appendix 10A. Use the tables in Illustration 10A-3 to determine federal and provincial income taxes.
(b) Calculate the CPP and EI deductions for each of the plumbers for their May 15, 2009, semi-monthly payroll.
(c) In which semi-monthly pay period will each of the plumbers reach their maximum CPP and EI payments for 2009?

Taking It Further

Why are there separate payroll deduction tables for determining income tax deductions for weekly, semi-monthly, and monthly pay periods?

Continuing Cookie Chronicle

(*Note:* This is a continuation of the Cookie Chronicle from Chapters 1 through 9.)

Recall that Cookie Creations borrowed $2,000 on November 16, 2010, from Natalie's grandmother. Interest on the note is 3% per year and the note plus interest was to be repaid in 12 months.

Natalie is considering paying back her grandmother before the note becomes due in November 2011.

Instructions

(a) Calculate the total interest expense recorded in 2010. Calculate total interest expense to be incurred in 2011 if the loan is repaid on its due date.
(b) If Natalie's grandmother's loan were to be repaid at the end of August 2011, calculate Cookie Creations' cash savings.
(c) Identify to Natalie some of the advantages and disadvantages of repaying the loan before it becomes due.
(d) Prepare the journal entry to record the loan repayment at the end of August 2011. Recall that a monthly adjusting journal entry was prepared for the months of November 2010 (half month), December 2010, and January 2011.

Cumulative Coverage—Chapters 3 to 10

The unadjusted trial balance of LeBrun Company at its year end, July 31, 2011, is as follows:

LEBRUN COMPANY
Trial Balance
July 31, 2011

	Debit	Credit
Cash	$ 17,400	
Petty cash	200	
Accounts receivable	38,500	
Allowance for doubtful accounts		$ 2,000
Note receivable (due December 31, 2011)	10,000	
Merchandise inventory	40,900	
Prepaid expenses	16,000	
Land	50,000	
Building	155,000	
Accumulated depreciation—building		10,800
Equipment	25,000	
Accumulated depreciation—equipment		12,200
Patent	75,000	
Accumulated amortization—patent		15,000
Accounts payable		78,900
Mortgage payable (due August 1, 2026)		124,200
S. LeBrun, capital		127,690
S. LeBrun, drawings	54,000	
Sales		750,000
Cost of goods sold	450,000	
Operating expenses	181,220	
Interest revenue		400
Interest expense	7,970	
Totals	$1,121,190	$1,121,190

Adjustment data:

1. The July 31 bank statement reported debit memos for service charges of $45 and a $650 NSF (not sufficient funds) cheque that had been received from a customer for the purchase of merchandise in July.
2. Estimated uncollectible accounts receivable at July 31 are 10% of gross accounts receivable.
3. The note receivable bears interest of 8% and was issued on December 31, 2010. Interest is payable the first of each month.
4. A physical count of inventory determined that $39,200 of inventory was actually on hand.
5. Prepaid expenses of $5,500 expired in the year (use the account Operating Expenses).
6. Depreciation is calculated on the long-lived assets using the following methods and useful lives:

    Building: straight-line, 25 years, $15,000 residual value
    Equipment: double diminishing-balance, five years, $2,500 residual value
    Patent: straight-line, five years, no residual value

7. The 7% mortgage payable was issued on August 1, 2001. Interest is paid monthly at the beginning of each month for the previous month's interest. Of the mortgage principal, $1,680 is currently due.
8. Accrued liabilities for salaries at July 31 are $1,975.

Instructions

(a) Prepare the adjusting journal entries required at July 31. (Round your calculations to the nearest dollar.)
(b) Prepare an adjusted trial balance at July 31.
(c) Prepare a multiple-step income statement and statement of owner's equity for the year, and a balance sheet at July 31.

BROADENING YOUR PERSPECTIVE

Financial Reporting and Analysis

Financial Reporting Problem

BYP10–1 Refer to the financial statements of The Forzani Group Ltd. and the Notes to Consolidated Financial Statements in Appendix A.

Instructions

Answer the following questions about the company's current and contingent liabilities:

(a) What were Forzani's total current liabilities at February 1, 2009? What was the increase (decrease) in total current liabilities from the previous year?
(b) Which specific current liabilities did Forzani present on the February 1, 2009, balance sheet?
(c) Calculate Forzani's current ratio, acid-test ratio, receivables, and inventory turnover ratios, and operating cycle for 2009 and 2008. For 2008, beginning accounts receivable was $65,543 thousand and beginning inventory was $302,207 thousand. Comment on Forzani's overall liquidity.
(d) Does Forzani report any contingent liabilities? If so, where are they disclosed? Explain the nature, amount, and significance of Forzani's principal types of contingent liabilities, if any.

Interpreting Financial Statements

BYP10–2 Saputo Inc. reported the following information about contingencies in the notes to its March 31, 2009, financial statements:

SAPUTO INC.
Notes to the Consolidated Financial Statements
March 31,2009

NOTE 18 COMMITMENTS AND CONTINGENCIES

The Company guarantees to certain lessors a portion of the residual value of certain leased assets with respect to operations which mature until 2014. If the market value of leased assets, at the end of the respective operating lease term, is inferior to the guaranteed residual value, the Company is obligated to indemnify the lessor, specific to certain conditions, for the shortfall up to a maximum value. The Company believes that the potential indemnification will not have a significant effect on the consolidated financial statements.

Claims

The Company is defendant to certain claims arising from the normal course of its business. The Company is also defendant in certain claims and/or assessments from tax authorities in various jurisdictions. The Company believes that the final resolution of these claims and/or assessments will not have a material adverse effect on its earnings or financial position.

INDEMNIFICATIONS

The Company from time to time offers indemnifications to third parties in the normal course of its business, in connection with business or asset acquisitions or dispositions. These indemnification provisions may be in connection with breach of representations and warranties and for future claims for certain liabilities, including liabilities related to tax and environmental matters. The terms of these indemnification provisions vary in duration. At March 31, 2009, given that the nature and amount of such indemnifications depend on future events, the Company is unable to reasonably estimate its maximum potential liability under these agreements. The Company has not made any significant indemnification payments in the past, and as at March 31, 2009 and 2008, the Company has not recorded a liability associated with these indemnifications.

Instructions

(a) Why would Saputo Inc. disclose information about these legal disputes in the notes to the financial statements instead of accruing an amount for these as liabilities in its accounting records?
(b) Where should Saputo Inc. record the legal costs incurred to date (i.e., the costs before going to trial) on the disputes (claims)?
(c) In the first paragraph above, Saputo Inc. provides an explanation of an obligation it has with respect to certain leased assets. What factors might cause the market value of the leased assets to decline significantly?

Critical Thinking

Collaborative Learning Activity

Note to instructor: Additional instructions and material for this group activity can be found on the Instructor Resource Site.

WILEY PLUS Working in Groups

BYP10–3 In this group activity, you will work in pairs to review the accounting for notes payable and its relationship to the accounting for notes receivable (Chapter 8).

On September 1, 2011, a borrower signs a 6-month, 5.5% note payable in exchange for $10,000 cash. Interest is payable at maturity. Both the borrower and lender have a December 31 year end and adjustments are made only annually.

Instructions

(a) In your pair, decide who will play the roles of lender and borrower.
(b) Based on your role, record the journal entries for:
 1. issue of the note
 2. year-end adjustments
 3. maturity of the note
(c) Compare your answer to that of your partner. If they are different, explain how you decided on your journal entries.
(d) You may be asked by your instructor to write a short quiz on this topic.

Communication Activity

WileyPLUS Writing Handbook

BYP10–4 The Show Time movie theatre sells thousands of gift certificates every year. The certificates can be redeemed at any time since they have no expiry date. Some of them may never be redeemed (because they are lost or forgotten, for example). The owner of the theatre has raised some questions about the accounting for these gift certificates.

Instructions

Write a memo to answer the following questions from the owner:

(a) Why is a liability recorded when these certificates are sold? After all, they bring customers into the theatre, where they spend money on snacks and drinks. Why should something that helps generate additional revenue be treated as a liability?
(b) How should the gift certificates that are never redeemed be treated? At some point in the future, can the liability related to them be eliminated? If so, what type of journal entry would be made?

Ethics Case

WileyPLUS Ethics in Accounting

BYP10–5 Nice Nuke Corporation, which owns and operates a nuclear plant, recently received notice from the provincial government that it has to find a new disposal site for its radioactive waste. The company was also told that it is responsible for the environmental cleanup of the old site. The vice-president of engineering and the vice-president of finance meet to discuss the situation. The engineer says that it could take many years to clean up the site and that the cost could be considerable—a minimum of $50 million and perhaps as much as $100 million.

The vice-president of finance says that there is no way that the company can afford to record this liability. He says he is not even sure that he wants to disclose the potential liability, because of how this could affect the company's share price.

Instructions

(a) Who are the stakeholders in this situation?
(b) What are the alternative reporting options that the company can use?
(c) What is the likely impact of each alternative on the company's financial position?
(d) Is there anything unethical in what the vice-president of finance suggests doing about this potential liability?
(e) What do you recommend the company do?

"All About You" Activity

BYP10–6 In the "All About You" feature, you learned who is responsible for remitting income tax, CPP, and EI to the CRA if you are an employee or self-employed. You also learned that the CRA has strict guidelines as to whether someone is self-employed or an employee.

Assume that as a new graduate you are accepting a position where you will be providing consulting services to a company. You have agreed to provide the services for $3,000 a month. The company's manager of human resources suggests that you may want to be considered self-employed rather than an employee of the company. Before you make your decision, you need to better understand the CRA's guidelines and the financial implications.

(a) Go to Canada Revenue Agency's website www.cra-arc.gc.ca and search for document RC4110 "Employee or Self-Employed?". What are the factors that should be considered when determining if a worker is an employee or self-employed?

(b) Assume you are an employee and you are paid monthly and that the following is deducted from your gross earnings:

CPP	$134.06
EI	51.90
Income tax	429.84

What is the amount of cash you will receive each month? What is the total amount of cash you will receive in a year?

(c) Based on the information in (b), what is the total CPP you will pay in a year? What is the total EI you will pay in a year?

(d) Assume you are self-employed, and you have chosen to pay EI. What is the amount of cash you will receive each month? What is the total CPP you will have to pay in a year? What is the total EI you will have to pay in a year?

(e) Assuming that you will pay the same amount of income tax as you would if you were an employee, calculate the amount of cash you will receive if you are self-employed.

(f) Based on your answers to (c) and (e), do you want to be self-employed or an employee of the company? Explain.

(g) If you had the opportunity to provide consulting services to another company in your spare time, would your answer in (f) be different? Explain.

ANSWERS TO CHAPTER QUESTIONS

Answers to Accounting in Action Insight Questions

Across the Organization Insight, p. 565

Q: A company's marketing department is responsible for designing customer loyalty programs. Why would Shoppers' marketing department add the option of donating points to charity?

A: Most customer loyalty programs were designed under the assumption that customers are motivated by cost savings. Shoppers realized that some customers have enough disposable income that cost saving is not a motivation. But many of these customers are motivated by the desire to help others. Thus the option to donate points has the potential to appeal to a wider base of customers and increase the program's success.

Business Insight, p. 569

Q: Environmental contingencies are generally considered to be harder to estimate than contingencies from lawsuits. What might be the reason for this difference?

A: The requirement to account for environmental contingencies is relatively new compared with the requirement to account for contingencies from lawsuits. Although it is difficult to predict whether the company will win or lose a lawsuit and what type of settlement may be involved, there is a vast history of case law that can be used to help a company form an opinion. Environmental regulations, in contrast, are still evolving and there is often no system (e.g., regulatory compliance audits or environmental site assessment data) that would help a company estimate the possible cost, or even the existence, of environmental contingencies for many years.

All About You Insight, p. 577

Q: If you are providing services to a company, what are the advantages and disadvantages of being a self-employed consultant versus an employee of the company?

A: As a self-employed individual, your monthly cash received from the company would be higher as no CPP, EI, and income tax will be deducted. On the other hand, you will have to make quarterly instalment payments of CPP, EI (if you choose to pay it) and income taxes. If you are self-employed, you may be able to deduct certain expenses to reduce your income tax.

However, some individuals may not manage their cash properly and may be unable to make the remittances when required. In addition, you will have to pay twice as much for CPP and you will not qualify for EI benefits. If you are self-employed, you would not qualify for other benefits offered to employees by the company either.

Answer to Forzani Review It Question 2, p. 579

The Forzani Group reports only three current liabilities: (1) current indebtedness under its revolving credit facility, (2) accounts payable and accrued liabilities, and (3) the current portion of long-term debt. The three liabilities may be listed in order of maturity, but we don't have enough information to determine this.

Answers to Self-Study Questions

1. d 2. c 3. a 4. b 5. a 6. d 7. b 8. b 9. d *10. b

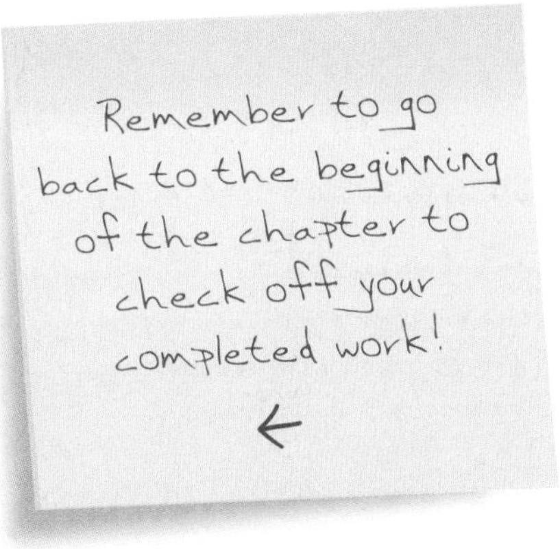
Remember to go
back to the beginning
of the chapter to
check off your
completed work!
←

APPENDIX A ▸ SPECIMEN FINANCIAL STATEMENTS

The Forzani Group Ltd.

In this appendix we illustrate current financial reporting with a comprehensive set of corporate financial statements that are prepared in accordance with generally accepted accounting principles. We are grateful for permission to use the actual financial statements of The Forzani Group Ltd.—Canada's largest sporting goods retailer.

Forzani's financial statement package features a balance sheet, statement of operations (or income statement as we know it), statements of retained earnings,comprehensive earnings and accumulated other comprehensive earnings (loss), cash flow statement, and notes to the financial statements. The financial statements are preceded by two reports: a statement of management's responsibilities for financial reporting and the auditors' report.

We encourage students to use these financial statements in conjunction with relevant material in the textbook. As well, these statements can be used to solve the Review It questions in the Before You Go On section within the chapter and the Financial Reporting Problem in the Broadening Your Perspective section of the end-of-chapter material.

Annual reports, including the financial statements, are reviewed in detail on the companion website to this textbook.

Management's Responsibilities For Financial Reporting

The Annual Report, including the consolidated financial statements, is the responsibility of the management of the Company. The consolidated financial statements were prepared by management in accordance with generally accepted accounting principles. The significant accounting policies used are described in Note 2 to the consolidated financial statements. The integrity of the information presented in the financial statements, including estimates and judgments relating to matters not concluded by year-end, is the responsibility of management. Financial information presented elsewhere in this Annual Report has been prepared by management and is consistent with the information in the consolidated financial statements.

Management is responsible for the development and maintenance of systems of internal accounting and administrative controls. Such systems are designed to provide reasonable assurance that the financial information is accurate, relevant and reliable, and that the Company's assets are appropriately accounted for and adequately safeguarded (refer also to page 55 under "internal control over financial reporting"). The Board of Directors is responsible for ensuring that management fulfils its responsibilities for final approval of the annual consolidated financial statements. The Board appoints an Audit Committee consisting of three directors, none of whom is an officer or employee of the Company or its subsidiaries. The Audit Committee meets at least four times each year to discharge its responsibilities under a written mandate from the Board of Directors. The Audit Committee meets with management and with the independent auditors to satisfy itself that they are properly discharging their responsibilities, reviews the consolidated financial statements and the Auditors' Report, and examines other auditing, accounting and financial reporting matters. The consolidated financial statements have been reviewed by the Audit Committee and approved by the Board of Directors of The Forzani Group Ltd. The consolidated financial statements have been examined by the shareholders' auditors, Ernst & Young, LLP, Chartered Accountants. The Auditors' Report outlines the nature of their examination and their opinion on the consolidated financial statements of the Company. The independent auditors have full and unrestricted access to the Audit Committee, with and without management present.

Robert Sartor
Chief Executive Officer

Micheal R. Lambert, CA
Chief Financial Officer

Auditor's Report

To the Shareholders of
The Forzani Group Ltd.

We have audited the consolidated balance sheets of The Forzani Group Ltd. as at February 1, 2009 and February 3, 2008 and the consolidated statements of operations, retained earnings, comprehensive earnings, accumulated other comprehensive earnings (loss) and cash flows for the 52 week period ended February 1, 2009 and the 53 week period ended February 3, 2008. These financial statements are the responsibility of the Company's management. Our responsibility is to express an opinion on these financial statements based on our audits.

We conducted our audits in accordance with Canadian generally accepted auditing standards. Those standards require that we plan and perform an audit to obtain reasonable assurance whether the financial statements are free of material misstatement. An audit includes examining, on a test basis, evidence supporting the amounts and disclosures in the financial statements. An audit also includes assessing the accounting principles used and significant estimates made by management, as well as evaluating the overall financial statement presentation.

In our opinion, these consolidated financial statements present fairly, in all material respects, the financial position of the Company as at February 1, 2009 and February 3, 2008 and the results of its operations and its cash flows for the 52 week period ended February 1, 2009 and the 53 week period ended February 3, 2008 in accordance with Canadian generally accepted accounting principles.

Ernst & Young LLP

Calgary, Canada
April 7, 2009

Ernst & Young LLP
Chartered Accountants

The Forzani Group Ltd.
Consolidated Balance Sheets
(in thousands)

As at		February 1, 2009		February 3, 2008
ASSETS				
Current				
Cash	$	3,474	$	47,484
Accounts receivable		84,455		75,506
Inventory (Note 3)		291,497		319,445
Prepaid expenses (Note 4)		2,827		14,501
		382,253		456,936
Capital assets (Note 5)		196,765		188,621
Goodwill and other intangibles (Note 6)		91,481		89,335
Other assets (Note 7)		9,280		3,863
Future income tax asset (Note 12)		9,681		16,209
	$	689,460	$	754,964
LIABILITIES				
Current				
Indebtedness under revolving credit facility (Note 8)	$	17,130	$	-
Accounts payable and accrued liabilities		277,820		279,910
Current portion of long-term debt (Note 8)		7,501		51,863
		302,451		331,773
Long-term debt (Note 8)		126		6,586
Deferred lease inducements		47,811		55,089
Deferred rent liability		5,893		6,033
		356,281		399,481
SHAREHOLDERS' EQUITY				
Share capital (Note 11)		147,161		157,105
Contributed surplus		6,401		7,210
Accumulated other comprehensive earnings (loss)		863		(8)
Retained earnings		178,754		191,176
		333,179		355,483
	$	689,460	$	754,964

See accompanying notes to the consolidated financial statements
Approved on behalf of the Board:

Roman Doroniuk, CA

John M. Forzani

The Forzani Group Ltd.

Consolidated Statements of Operations
(in thousands, except per share data)

	For the 52 weeks ended February 1, 2009	For the 53 weeks ended February 3, 2008
Revenue		
Retail	$ 994,043	$ 969,256
Wholesale	352,715	361,753
	1,346,758	1,331,009
Cost of sales	863,239	852,608
Gross margin	483,519	478,401
Operating and administrative expenses		
Store operating	277,089	251,630
General and administrative	109,328	103,801
	386,417	355,431
Operating earnings before undernoted items	97,102	122,970
Amortization of capital assets	47,613	44,468
Interest	5,175	5,797
Loss on sale of investment (Note 21)	-	864
	52,788	51,129
Earnings before income taxes	44,314	71,841
Income tax expense (recovery) (Note 12)		
Current	6,273	27,439
Future	8,716	(3,049)
	14,989	24,390
Net earnings	$ 29,325	$ 47,451
Earnings per share (Note 11(c))	$ 0.94	$ 1.40
Diluted earnings per share (Note 11(c))	$ 0.93	$ 1.39

See accompanying notes to the consolidated financial statements

The Forzani Group Ltd.

Consolidated Statements of Retained Earnings, Comprehensive Earnings and Accumulated Other Comprehensive Earnings (Loss)
(in thousands)

Consolidated Statements of Retained Earnings	For the 52 weeks ended February 1, 2009	For the 53 weeks ended February 3, 2008
Retained earnings, beginning of period	$ 191,176	$ 171,095
Adjustment arising from adoption of new accounting policy (Note 2)	(1,357)	-
Adjusted Retained earnings, beginning of period	$ 189,819	$ 171,095
Net earnings	29,325	47,451
Dividends paid (Note 11(f))	(9,327)	(2,472)
Adjustment arising from shares purchased under a normal course issuer bid (Note 11(e))	(31,063)	(24,898)
Retained earnings, end of period	$ 178,754	$ 191,176

Consolidated Statements of Comprehensive Earnings		
Net earnings	$ 29,325	$ 47,451
Other comprehensive earnings (loss):		
Unrealized foreign currency gains and (losses) on cash flow hedges	1,340	(138)
Tax impact	(469)	51
Other comprehensive earnings (loss)	871	(87)
Comprehensive earnings	$ 30,196	$ 47,364

Consolidated Statements of Accumulated Other Comprehensive Earnings (Loss) ("AOCE")		
Accumulated other comprehensive earnings (loss), beginning of period	$ (8)	$ -
Transitional adjustment upon adoption of new financial instruments standard	-	79
Accumulated other comprehensive earnings (loss), beginning of period, as restated	(8)	79
Other comprehensive earnings (loss)	871	(87)
Accumulated other comprehensive earnings (loss), end of period	$ 863	$ (8)

See accompanying notes to the consolidated financial statements

The Forzani Group Ltd.

Consolidated Statements of Cash Flows
(in thousands)

	For the 52 weeks ended February 1, 2009	For the 53 weeks ended February 3, 2008
Cash provided by (used in) operating activities		
Net earnings	$ 29,325	$ 47,451
Items not involving cash:		
Amortization of capital assets	47,613	44,468
Amortization of deferred finance charges	377	738
Amortization of deferred lease inducements	(11,500)	(11,109)
Rent expense (Note 9)	152	524
Stock-based compensation (Note 11(d))	(174)	2,756
Future income tax expense (recovery)	8,716	(3,049)
Loss on sale of investment (Note 21)	-	864
Unrealized loss on ineffective hedges	321	44
	74,830	82,687
Changes in non-cash elements of working capital related to operating activities (Note 9)	20,913	23,737
	95,743	106,424
Cash provided by (used in) financing activities		
Net proceeds from issuance of share capital (Note 11(b))	2,384	13,273
Share repurchase via normal course issuer bid (Note 11(e))	(44,027)	(33,331)
Long-term debt	(51,199)	(19,198)
Revolving credit facility	17,130	-
Lease inducements received	4,221	7,648
Dividends paid (Note 11(f))	(9,327)	(2,472)
	(80,818)	(34,080)
Changes in non-cash elements of financing activities (Note 9)	(1,121)	(1,698)
	(81,939)	(35,778)
Cash provided by (used in) investing activities		
Capital assets	(52,139)	(40,660)
Other assets	(2,998)	2,151
Acquisition of wholly-owned subsidiaries (Note 17)	-	(8,774)
	(55,137)	(47,283)
Changes in non-cash elements of investing activities (Note 9)	(2,677)	1,363
	(57,814)	(45,920)
Increase (decrease) in cash	(44,010)	24,726
Net cash position, opening	47,484	22,758
Net cash position, closing	$ 3,474	$ 47,484

See accompanying notes to the consolidated financial statements

The Forzani Group Ltd.

Notes to Consolidated Financial Statements (tabular amounts in thousands)

1. Nature of Operations

The Forzani Group Ltd. ("FGL" or "the Company") is Canada's largest national retailer of sporting goods, offering a comprehensive assortment of brand-name and private-brand products, operating stores from coast to coast, under the following corporate and franchise banners: Sport Chek, Coast Mountain Sports, Sport Mart, National Sports, Athletes World, Sports Experts, Intersport, Econosports, Atmosphere, RnR, Tech Shop, Pegasus, Nevada Bob's Golf, Hockey Experts, S3 and The Fitness Source.

2. Significant Accounting Policies

The preparation of the financial statements in conformity with Canadian generally accepted accounting principles ("GAAP") requires management to make estimates and assumptions that affect the reported amounts of assets and liabilities and disclosures of contingent assets and liabilities at the date of the consolidated financial statements and the reported amounts of revenue and expenses during the reporting period. Actual results could differ materially from these estimates. Estimates are used when accounting for items such as employee benefits, product warranties, inventory provisions, amortization and assessment for impairment, uncollectible receivables and the liability for the Company's loyalty program. The financial statements have, in management's opinion, been prepared within reasonable limits of materiality and within the framework of the accounting policies summarized below:

(a) Organization

The consolidated financial statements include the accounts of The Forzani Group Ltd. and its subsidiaries, all of which are wholly owned.

(b) Inventory valuation

Inventory is valued at the lower of laid-down cost and net realizable value. Laid-down cost is determined using the weighted average cost method and includes invoice cost, duties, freight, and distribution costs. Net realizable value is defined as the expected selling price.

Volume rebates and other supplier discounts are included in income when earned. Volume rebates are accounted for as a reduction of the cost of the related inventory and are "earned" when the inventory is sold. All other rebates and discounts are "earned" when the related expense is incurred.

(c) Capital assets

Capital assets are recorded at cost and are amortized using the following methods and rates:

Asset	Basis	Rate
Building	Declining balance	4%
Building and leased land	Straight-line	Lesser of the term of the lease or estimated useful life, not exceeding 20 years
Furniture, fixtures, equipment, software and automotive	Straight-line	3-8 years
Leasehold improvements	Straight-line	Lesser of the term of the lease and estimated useful life, not exceeding 10 years

The carrying value of long-lived assets is reviewed at least annually or whenever events indicate a potential impairment has occurred. An impairment loss is recorded if and when a long-lived asset's carrying value exceeds the sum of the undiscounted cash flows expected from its use and eventual disposition. The impairment loss is measured as the amount by which the carrying value exceeds its fair value.

(d) Variable interest entities

Variable interest entities ("VIE") are consolidated by the Company if and when the Company is the primary beneficiary of the VIE, as described in Canadian Institute of Chartered Accountants ("CICA") Accounting Guideline 15, *Consolidation of Variable Interest Entities.*

(e) Goodwill and other intangibles

Goodwill represents the excess of the purchase price of entities acquired over the fair market value of the identifiable net assets acquired.

Goodwill and other intangible assets with indefinite lives are not amortized, but tested for impairment at year end or more frequently if events or changes in circumstances indicate the asset might be impaired and, if required, asset values reduced accordingly. The method used to assess impairment is a review of the fair value of the asset based on expected present value of future cash flows.

Non-competition agreement costs are amortized, on a straight-line basis, over the life of the agreements, not exceeding five years.

(f) Other assets

Other assets include system and interactive development costs, long-term receivables and other deferred charges.

System development costs relate to the implementation of computer software. Upon activation, costs are amortized over the estimated useful lives of the systems (3 – 8 years).

Long-term receivables are carried at cost less a valuation allowance, if applicable.

(g) Deferred lease inducements and property leases

Deferred lease inducements represent cash and non-cash benefits that the Company has received from landlords pursuant to store lease agreements. These lease inducements are amortized against rent expense over the term of the lease.

The Company capitalizes any rent expense during a related fixturing period as a cost of leasehold improvements. Such expense is recognized on a straight-line basis over the life of the lease.

(h) Revenue recognition

Revenue includes sales to customers through corporate stores operated by the Company and sales to, and service fees from, franchise stores and others. Sales to customers through corporate stores operated by the Company are recognized at the point of sale, net of an estimated allowance for sales returns. Sales of merchandise to franchise stores and others are recognized at the time of shipment. Royalties and administration fees are recognized when earned, in accordance with the terms of the franchise/license agreements.

(i) Store opening expenses

Operating costs incurred prior to the opening of new stores, other than rent incurred during the fixturing period, are expensed as incurred.

(j) Fiscal year

The Company's fiscal year follows a retail calendar. The fiscal years for the consolidated financial statements presented are the 52-week period ended February 1, 2009 and the 53-week period ended February 3, 2008.

(k) Foreign currency translation

Foreign currency accounts are translated to Canadian dollars. At the transaction date, each asset, liability, revenue or expense is translated into Canadian dollars using the exchange rate in effect at that date. At the year-end date, monetary assets and liabilities are translated into Canadian dollars using the exchange rate in effect at that date, and the resulting foreign exchange gains and losses are included in income.

(l) Stock-based compensation

The Company accounts for stock-based compensation using the fair value method. The fair value of the options granted are estimated at the date of grant using the Black-Scholes valuation model and recognized as an expense over the option-vesting period.

(m) Income taxes

The Company follows the liability method under which future income tax assets and liabilities are determined based on differences between the financial reporting and tax basis of assets and liabilities, measured using tax rates substantively enacted at the balance sheet dates.

Changes in tax rates are reflected in the consolidated statements of operations in the period in which they are substantively enacted.

(n) Asset retirement obligations

The Company recognizes asset retirement obligations in the period in which a reasonable estimate of the fair value can be determined. The liability is measured at fair value and is adjusted to its present value in subsequent periods through accretion expense. The associated asset retirement costs are capitalized as part of the carrying value of the related asset and amortized over its useful life.

(o) Financial Instruments - Recognition and Measurement – CICA Section 3855

Section 3855 establishes standards for recognizing and measuring financial assets, financial liabilities, and non-financial derivatives. It requires that financial assets and financial liabilities, including derivatives, be recognized on the consolidated balance sheet when the Company becomes a party to the contractual provisions of the financial instrument or non-financial derivative contract. It also requires that all financial assets and liabilities are to be classified as either a) Held for Trading, b) Available for Sale, c) Held to Maturity, d) Loans/Receivables, or e) Other Financial Liabilities, depending on the Company's stated intention and/or historical practice. Under this standard, all financial instruments are required to be measured at fair value (or amortized cost) upon initial recognition, except for certain related party transactions. Treatment of the fair value of each financial instrument is determined by its classification.

In accordance with the standard, the Company's financial assets and liabilities are generally classified as follows:

Asset/Liability	Category	Measurement
Assets		
Cash	Held for trading	Fair value
Accounts receivable	Loans/Receivables	Amortized cost
Long-term receivables	Loans/Receivables	Amortized cost
Liabilities		
Indebtedness under revolving credit facility	Other financial liabilities	Amortized cost
Accounts payable and accrued liabilities	Other financial liabilities	Amortized cost
Long-term debt	Other financial liabilities	Amortized cost

Foreign currency options and forward exchange contracts, which are included in accounts receivable, have been classified as held for trading and measured at fair value. Fair value is determined by reference to published price quotations.

New Accounting Policies

Effective February 4, 2008 the Company adopted the following accounting standards issued by the CICA:

Capital Disclosures – CICA Section 1535

The standard establishes disclosure requirements about an entity's capital and how it is managed. The new standard requires disclosure of an entity's objectives, policies and processes for managing capital, quantitative data about what an entity regards as capital and whether the entity has complied with any externally imposed capital requirements and the consequences of any non-compliance. Additional disclosure required as a result of the adoption of this standard is contained in Note 10.

Financial Instruments - Disclosures (CICA Section 3862) and Financial Instruments – Presentation (CICA Section 3863)

The standards replace Section 3861, *Financial Instruments - Disclosure and Presentation*, revising and enhancing disclosure requirements while carrying forward, substantially unchanged, its presentation requirements. These new sections place increased emphasis on disclosure about the nature and extent of risks arising from financial instruments and how the entity manages those risks. Additional disclosure required as a result of the adoption of this standard is contained in Note 16.

Inventory - CICA Section 3031

The standard introduces significant changes to the measurement and disclosure of inventories, including the allocation of overhead based on normal capacity, the use of the specific cost method for inventories that are not ordinarily interchangeable for goods and services produced for specific purposes, and the reversal of previous write-downs to net realizable value when there is a subsequent increase in the value of inventories. Inventory policies, carrying amounts, amounts recognized as an expense, write-downs and the reversals of write-downs are required to be disclosed.

Under the prior guidance, the Company included storage costs in the cost of inventory. This is no longer permitted, resulting in a $1,357,000 adjustment to opening inventory for the year and a corresponding adjustment to opening retained earnings. Prior periods have not been restated.

Future Accounting Pronouncements

The following are new standards that have been issued by the CICA that are not yet effective but may impact the Company:

Goodwill and Intangible Assets

In November 2007, the CICA issued Section 3064, *Goodwill and Intangible Assets* ("Section 3064"). Section 3064, which replaces Section 3062, *Goodwill and Intangible Assets*, and Section 3450, *Research and Development Costs*, establishes standards for the recognition, measurement and disclosure of goodwill and intangible assets. This standard is effective for the Company for interim and annual consolidated financial statements relating to fiscal years beginning on or after October 1, 2008. The Company is currently assessing the impact that this section will have on its financial position and results of operations. Any adjustment required will be recorded through opening retained earnings in the first quarter of the Company's fiscal 2010 year.

Business Combinations and Consolidated Financial Statements – CICA Section 1582 and 1601

As of January 30, 2011, the Company will be required to adopt new CICA standards with respect to business combinations and consolidated financial statements. The new CICA Section 1582 will replace CICA Section 1581 and is meant to align the accounting for business combinations under Canadian GAAP with the requirements of International Financial Reporting Standards. Likewise, CICA Section 1601 will replace CICA Section 1600 with respect to consolidated financial statements.

Under sections 1582 and 1601 the definition of a business is expanded and is described as an integrated set of activities and assets that are capable of being managed to provide a return to investors or economic benefits to owners, members or participants. In addition, acquisition costs are not part of the purchase consideration and are to be expensed when incurred. With the adoption of these standards, the Company expects that all acquisition related costs will be expensed through the statement of operations. These standards will be applied on a prospective basis.

International Financial Reporting Standards ("IFRS")

In February 2008, the CICA announced that GAAP for publicly accountable enterprises will be replaced by IFRS for fiscal years beginning on or after January 1, 2011. Companies will be required to provide IFRS comparative information for the previous fiscal year. Accordingly, the conversion from GAAP to IFRS will be applicable to the Company's reporting for the first quarter of fiscal 2012 for which the current and comparative information will be prepared under IFRS.

The Company is in the process of completing the scoping and assessment phase of the transition. This phase identified a number of topics possibly impacting either the Company's financial results and/or the Company's effort necessary to changeover to IFRS. This phase is ongoing, as the Company will continue to assess future International Accounting Standards Board ("IASB") pronouncements for transitional impacts.

The Company has started the key elements phase of implementation which includes the identification, evaluation and selection of accounting policies necessary for the Company to transition to IFRS. Consideration of impacts on operational elements such as information technology and internal control over financial reporting are integral to this process.

Although the Company's impact assessment activities are underway and progressing according to plan, continued progress is necessary before the Company can prudently increase the specificity of the disclosure of pre- and post-IFRS changeover accounting policy differences.

3. Inventory

Included within cost of sales for the period ended February 1, 2009, are normal course charges to inventory made throughout the year, of $12,265,000 (2008 – $12,514,000). These charges include the disposal of obsolete and damaged product, inventory shrinkage and permanent markdowns to net realizable values.

4. Prepaid Expenses

	2009	2008
Prepaid rent	$ -	$ 10,200
Advertising	1,348	1,720
Service contracts	785	773
Other	694	1,808
	$ 2,827	$ 14,501

5. Capital Assets

	2009			2008		
	Cost	Accumulated Amortization	Net Book Value	Cost	Accumulated Amortization	Net Book Value
Land	$ 3,173	$ -	$ 3,173	$ 3,173	$ -	$ 3,173
Buildings	20,928	5,382	15,546	20,928	4,680	16,248
Building on leased land	4,583	3,114	1,469	4,583	2,852	1,731
Furniture, fixtures, equipment, software and automotive	243,564	173,611	69,953	217,365	149,386	67,979
Leasehold improvements	260,030	167,435	92,595	239,439	146,003	93,436
Construction in progress	14,029	-	14,029	6,054	-	6,054
	$ 546,307	$ 349,542	$ 196,765	$ 491,542	$ 302,921	$ 188,621

6. Goodwill and Other Intangibles

	2009			2008		
	Cost	Accumulated Amortization	Net Book Value	Cost	Accumulated Amortization	Net Book Value
Goodwill	$ 61,162	$ 1,178	$ 59,984	$ 61,162	$ 1,178	$ 59,984
Trademarks/Trade names	32,359	934	31,425	30,140	934	29,206
Non-competition agreements	4,000	3,928	72	4,000	3,855	145
	$ 97,521	$ 6,040	$ 91,481	$ 95,302	$ 5,967	$ 89,335

7. Other Assets

	2009			2008		
	Cost	Accumulated Amortization	Net Book Value	Cost	Accumulated Amortization	Net Book Value
Interactive development	$ 2,649	$ 2,649	$ -	$ 2,649	$ 2,649	$ -
System development	1,641	1,641	-	1,641	1,641	-
Other deferred charges	6,967	3,153	3,814	4,176	2,094	2,082
	$ 11,257	$ 7,443	$ 3,814	$ 8,466	$ 6,384	$ 2,082

	2009	2008
Depreciable other assets net book value (see above)	$ 3,814	$ 2,082
Deferred advertising charges	2,566	-
Long-term receivables (at interest rates of prime plus 1% and expiring between September 2010 and July 2011)	2,900	1,781
	$ 9,280	$ 3,863

8. Long Term Debt

	2009	2008
G.E. term loan	$ -	$ 49,744
Mortgage with monthly payments of $58,000 and an interest rate of 6.2% compounded semi-annually, secured by land and building, expiring October 2009.	5,458	5,782
Vendor take-back, unsecured with implied interest rate of 4.8% and payments due March 2009	2,043	2,792
Asset retirement obligation	126	113
Other	-	18
	7,627	58,449
Less current portion	7,501	51,863
	$ 126	$ 6,586

Principal payments on the above, due in the next five years, are as follows:

2010	$ 7,501
2011	$ -
2012	$ -
2013	$ -
2014	$ -

Effective June 11, 2008, the Company renewed its credit agreement with GE Canada Finance Holding Company. The renewed agreement increased the $235 million credit facility, which was comprised of a $185 million revolving loan and a $50 million term loan, to a $250 million facility, comprised entirely of a revolving loan and having a June 11, 2013 expiry date. Under the terms of the credit agreement, the interest rate payable on the revolving loan is based on the Company's financial performance as determined by its interest coverage ratio. As at February 1, 2009, the interest rate paid was bank prime less 0.45%. The facility is collateralized by general security agreements against all existing and future acquired assets of the Company. As at February 1, 2009, the Company is in compliance with its financial covenant.

Based on estimated interest rates currently available to the Company for mortgages with similar terms and maturities, the fair value of the mortgage at February 1, 2009 amounted to approximately $6,119,000 (2008 - $5,274,000). Interest costs incurred for the 52-week period ended February 1, 2009 on long-term debt amounted to $851,000 (2008 - $3,178,000). The fair value of the other long-term debt components above approximates book value given their short terms to maturity and floating interest rates.

9. Supplementary Cash Flow Information

	For the 52 weeks ended February 1, 2009	For the 53 weeks ended February 3, 2008
Rent expense		
Straight-line rent expense	$ (140)	$ 228
Non-cash free rent	292	296
	$ 152	$ 524
Change in non-cash elements of working capital related to operating activities		
Accounts receivable	$ (11,137)	$ (9,963)
Inventory	21,753	13,772
Prepaid expenses	11,674	(11,813)
Financial Instruments	764	-
Accounts payable and accrued liabilities	(2,141)	31,741
	$ 20,913	$ 23,737
Change in non-cash elements of financing activities		
Lease inducements	$ (907)	$ (1,115)
Long-term debt	-	(568)
Change in fair value of cash flow hedge	871	-
Net financial assets	(1,085)	(15)
	$ (1,121)	$ (1,698)
Change in non-cash elements of investing activities		
Capital assets	$ 668	$ 795
Other assets	(3,345)	568
	$ (2,677)	$ 1,363
Net cash interest paid	$ 4,648	$ 5,017
Net cash taxes paid	$ 26,109	$ 29,509

10. Capital Disclosures

The Company's objectives in managing capital are to ensure sufficient liquidity to pursue its strategy of organic growth combined with strategic acquisitions and to deploy capital to provide an appropriate return on investment to its shareholders. The Company's overall strategy remains unchanged from the prior year. The capital structure of the Company consists of cash, short and long-term debt and shareholders' equity comprised of retained earnings and share capital. The Company manages its capital structure and makes adjustments to it in light of economic conditions and the risk characteristics of the underlying assets. The Company's primary uses of capital are to finance non-cash working capital requirements, capital expenditures and acquisitions, which are currently funded from its internally-generated cash flows. The Company is in compliance with all externally imposed capital requirements, including its debt covenant.

11. Share Capital

(a) *Authorized*

An unlimited number of Class A shares (no par value)

An unlimited number of Preferred shares, issuable in series

(b) *Issued*

Class A shares	Number	Consideration
Balance, January 28, 2007	33,696	$ 148,424
Shares issued upon employees exercising stock options	1,077	13,273
Stock-based compensation related to options exercised	-	3,841
Shares repurchased via normal course issuer bid	(1,803)	(8,433)
Balance, February 3, 2008	32,970	157,105
Shares issued upon employees exercising stock options	192	2,384
Stock-based compensation related to options exercised	-	636
Shares repurchased via normal course issuer bid	(2,694)	(12,964)
Balance, February 1, 2009	**30,468**	**$ 147,161**

(c) *Earnings Per Share*

	2009	2008
Basic	$ 0.94	$ 1.40
Diluted	$ 0.93	$ 1.39

The Company uses the treasury stock method to calculate diluted earnings per share. Under the treasury stock method, the numerator remains unchanged from the basic earnings per share calculation, as the assumed exercise of the Company's stock options does not result in an adjustment to earnings. Diluted calculations assume that options under the stock option plan have been exercised at the later of the beginning of the year or date of issuance, and that the funds derived therefrom would have been used to repurchase shares at the average market value of the Company's stock, 2009 – $13.11 (2008 - $19.91). Anti-dilutive options, 2009 – 1,264,000 (2008 – 26,000) are excluded from the effect of dilutive securities. The reconciliation of the denominator in calculating diluted earnings per share is as follows:

	2009	2008
Weighted average number of Class A shares outstanding (basic)	31,298	33,787
Effect of dilutive options	67	370
Weighted average number of common shares outstanding (diluted)	31,365	34,157

(d) Stock Option and Unit Plans

The Company has granted stock options to directors, officers and employees to purchase Class A shares at prices between $7.70 and $23.00 per share. These options expire on dates between February 2009 and June 2013.

The Company has three stock option plans. The first plan has the following general terms: options vest over a period ranging from 2 to 5 years and the maximum term of the options granted is 5 years. During the year, no options (2008 – Nil) were issued under this plan. The related stock-based compensation expense was $25,000 (2008 - $323,000).

The second plan has the following general terms: options vest over a period ranging from 2 to 5 years dependent on the Company achieving certain performance targets (in 2007 these targets were met thereby causing the options to become fully vested by the first quarter of fiscal 2008), and the maximum term of the options granted is 5 years. During the year, 120,000 (2008 – 200,000 options) were issued under this plan. The related stock-based compensation expense of $383,000 was recognized immediately (2008 - $1,886,000) as the Company met the targets in fiscal 2007.

The third plan, which forms part of a Long Term Incentive Plan ("LTIP"), has the following general terms: option grants are made annually and options vest over 3 years with a maximum term of 5 years. Under the terms of the plan, options issued carry a tandem share appreciation right ("TSAR") which allows holders to exercise vested options in either the traditional fashion, where shares are issued from treasury, or surrender their option in exchange for an amount of cash equaling the difference between the market price for a common share on the date of surrender and the strike price of the option. The final details of this plan were approved by the Company in the third quarter of fiscal 2008. During the year, as a result of the TSAR exercise history being predominantly for cash, the Company deemed the plan to be cash-settled and accounted for it as a liability-classified award with TSARs measured at their fair value on the date of issuance, and re-measured at each reporting period, until settlement. During the year ended February 1, 2009, 309,590 options (2008 – 388,710) were issued under this plan and a credit of $582,000 to stock-based compensation expense was recognized (2008 - $547,000 expensed).

The total number of shares authorized for option grants under all option plans is 3,406,622.

During the 52-weeks ended February 1, 2009, the following options were granted:

Options issued	Weighted average fair value per option	Weighted average risk-free rate	Weighted average expected option life	Weighted average expected volatility	Weighted average expected dividend yield
429,590	$2.99	2.93%	3.00	27.41%	2.01%

A summary of the status of the Company's stock option plans as of February 1, 2009 and February 3, 2008, and any changes during the period ending on those dates is presented below:

	2009		2008	
Stock Options	Options	Weighted Average Exercise Price	Options	Weighted Average Exercise Price
Outstanding, beginning of year	1,658	$15.04	2,157	$12.85
Granted	430	$15.85	589	$18.08
Exercised	(204)	$12.39	(1,077)	$12.33
Forfeited	(189)	$14.93	(11)	$13.32
Outstanding, end of year	1,695	$15.56	1,658	$15.04
Options exercisable at year end	1,174		1,254	

The following table summarizes information about stock options outstanding at February 1, 2009:

	Options Outstanding			Options Exercisable	
Range of Exercise Prices	Number Outstanding	Weighted Average Remaining Contractual Life	Weighted Average Exercise Price	Number of Shares Exercisable	Weighted Average Exercise Price
$7.70 - $15.98	769	1.80	$13.01	718	$13.33
$16.00 - $23.00	926	3.55	$17.57	456	$18.07
	1,695	2.76	$15.56	1,174	$15.17

The Company issues director stock units ("DSU"), restricted stock units ("RSU") and performance stock units ("PSU") from time to time. These units are accounted for as liability-classified awards and are measured at their intrinsic value on the date of issuance, and re-measured at each reporting period, until settlement.

During the year, 166,865 (2008 – 168,390) PSUs were issued and an expense of $1,710,000 (2008 – $2,428,000) was charged to compensation expense.

During the year, 46,622 (2008 – 49,520) RSUs were issued and an expense of $580,000 (2008 - $137,000) was charged to compensation expense.

During the year, 20,327 (2008 – 16,049) DSUs were issued and $630,000 (2008 - $154,000 expense) was credited to compensation expense due to a reduction in the fair value of units.

As at February 1, 2009, the Company has recorded a total amount payable for all units outstanding of $2,149,000 (2008 - $2,172,000) of which $1,346,000 (2008 - $1,976,000) relates to DSUs, paid when a director leaves the Board of Directors.

(e) Normal Course Issuer Bid

For the year ended February 1, 2009, 2,694,376 (2008 – 1,802,900) Class A shares were repurchased pursuant to the Company's Normal Course Issuer Bid for a total expenditure of $44,027,000 (2008 - $33,331,000) or $16.34 (2008 - $18.49) per share. The consideration in excess of the stated value of $31,063,000 (2008 – $24,898,000) was changed to retained earnings.

(f) Dividends

On April 7, 2009 the Company declared a dividend of $0.075 per Class A common share, payable on May 4, 2009 to shareholders of record on April 20, 2009. The Company's stated intention is to declare annual dividends of $0.30 per share, payable quarterly, subject to the Board of Directors discretion.

The Company has declared quarterly dividends of $0.075 per Class A common share, payable to shareholders of record as follows:

Date Declared	For Shareholders of Record Dated
December 7, 2007	January 21, 2008
April 9, 2008	April 21, 2008
June 10, 2008	July 21, 2008
September 2, 2008	October 20, 2008
December 12, 2008	January 19, 2008
April 7, 2009	April 20, 2009

All dividends paid by the Company are, pursuant to subsection 89 (14) of the Income Tax Act (Canada), designated as eligible dividends. An eligible dividend paid to a Canadian resident is entitled to the enhanced dividend tax credit.

12. Income Taxes

The components of the future income tax asset amounts as at February 1, 2009 and February 3, 2008 are as follows:

	2009	2008
Current assets	$ (1,286)	$ (2,401)
Capital and other assets	(10,885)	(14,957)
Tax benefit of share issuance and financing costs	87	167
Deferred lease inducements	14,198	16,863
Non-capital loss carry forward	3,156	13,345
Accruals and deferred liabilities	4,411	3,192
Future income tax asset	$ 9,681	$ 16,209

A reconciliation of income taxes, at the combined statutory federal and provincial tax rate to the actual income tax rate, is as follows:

	2009		2008	
Federal and provincial income taxes	$ 13,471	30.4%	$ 24,354	33.9%
Increase (decrease) resulting from:				
Non deductible expenses	615	1.4%	1,796	2.5%
Effect of substantively enacted tax rate changes	-	-	(2,155)	(3.0%)
Other, net	903	2.0%	395	0.5%
Provision for income taxes	$ 14,989	33.8%	$ 24,390	33.9%

The Company has non-capital losses available to be carried forward of $9,804,000 expiring in 2028.

For the period ending February 1,2009, the Company has recorded a tax receivable balance of $11,125,000 (2008 - ($3,944,000)) which is included within accounts receivable.

13. Commitments

(a) The Company is committed, at February 1, 2009, to minimum payments under long-term real property and data processing hardware and software equipment leases, for future years, as follows:

Year	Gross
2010	$ 87,523
2011	$ 77,283
2012	$ 65,083
2013	$ 52,753
2014	$ 40,403
Thereafter	$ 86,471

In addition, the Company may be obligated to pay percentage rent under certain of the leases.

(b) As at February 1, 2009, the Company has open letters of credit for purchases of inventory of approximately $1,961,000 (2008 - $1,890,000).

14. Employee Benefit Plans

The Company has a defined contribution plan and an employee profit sharing plan (replaces the previous deferred profit sharing plan). Defined contributions are paid to employee retirement savings plans and are expensed when incurred.

Under the employee profit sharing plan, the Company creates a pool of funds to distribute to participating employees on a predetermined basis. Distributions are tied to the value of the Company's common shares and the employees' achievement of individual financial and operational targets. Payouts under the employee profit sharing plan are made annually. The deferred profit sharing plan contributions were previously paid to a Trustee for the purchase of shares of the Company and then distributed to participating employees on a predetermined basis, upon retirement from the Company. Contributions to both the employee profit sharing plan and previously to the deferred profit sharing plan are recognized as an expense when incurred.

For the period ended February 1, 2009, the Company has expensed $1,090,000 (2008 - $1,095,000) to the defined contribution plan and has accrued $504,000 for the employee profit sharing plan (2008 - $150,000).

15. Contingencies and Guarantees

In the normal course of business, the Company enters into numerous agreements that may contain features that meet the Accounting Guideline ("AcG") 14 definition of a guarantee. AcG-14 defines a guarantee to be a contract (including an indemnity) that contingently requires the Company to make payments to the guaranteed party based on (i) failure of another party to perform under an obligating agreement or (ii) failure of a third party to pay its indebtedness when due.

The Company has provided the following guarantees to third parties:

(a) The Company has provided guarantees to franchisees' banks pursuant to which it has agreed to buy back inventory from the franchisee in the event that the bank realizes on the related security. The Company has provided securitization guarantees for certain franchisees to repay equity loans in the event of franchisee default. The terms of the guarantees range from less than a year to the lifetime of the particular underlying franchise agreement, with an average guarantee term of 4 years. Should a franchisee default on its bank loan, the Company would be required to purchase between 50% – 100%, with a weighted average of 65%, of the franchisee's inventory up to the value of the franchisee's bank indebtedness. As at February 1, 2009, the Company's maximum exposure is $43,707,000 (2008 - $37,174,000). Should the Company be required to purchase the inventory of a specific franchisee, it is expected that the full value of the inventory would be recovered. Historically, the Company has not had to repurchase significant inventory from franchisees pursuant to these guarantees. The Company has not recognized the guarantee in its consolidated financial statements.

(b) In the ordinary course of business, the Company has agreed to indemnify its lenders under its credit facilities against certain costs or losses resulting from changes in laws and regulations and from any legal action brought against the lenders related to the use, by the Company, of the loan proceeds, or to the lenders having extended credit thereunder. These indemnifications extend for the term of the credit facilities and do not provide any limit on the maximum potential liability. Historically, the Company has not made any indemnification payments under such agreements and no amount has been accrued in the consolidated financial statements with respect to these indemnification agreements.

(c) In the ordinary course of business, the Company has provided indemnification commitments to certain counterparties in matters such as real estate leasing transactions, securitization agreements, director and officer indemnification agreements and certain purchases of assets (not inventory in the normal course). These indemnification agreements generally require the Company to compensate the counterparties for costs or losses resulting from any legal action brought against the counterparties related to the actions of the Company or any of the obligors under any of the aforementioned matters or failure of the obligors under any of the aforementioned matters to fulfill contractual obligations thereunder. The terms of these indemnification agreements will vary based on the contract and generally do not provide any limit on the maximum potential liability. Historically, the Company has not made any payments under such indemnifications and no amount has been accrued in the consolidated financial statements with respect to these indemnification commitments.

(d) Claims and suits have been brought against the Company in the ordinary course of business. In the opinion of management, all such claims and suits are adequately covered by insurance, or if not so covered, the results are not expected to materially affect the Company's financial position.

16. Financial Instruments and Hedges

(a) Fair Value of Financial Assets and Liabilities

The following table details carrying values and fair values of financial assets and liabilities by financial instrument classification:

	As at February 1, 2009	
	Carrying Value	Fair Value
Loans and Receivables:		
Trade and accrued receivables	$ 84,455	$ 84,455
Long-term receivables	$ 2,900	$ 2,900
Other Financial Liabilities:		
Revolving credit facility	$ 17,130	$ 17,130
Trade payables and accrued liabilities	$ 277,820	$ 277,820
Current and long-term debt	$ 7,627	$ 8,288

The fair value of a financial instrument is the estimated amount that the Company would receive or pay to settle the financial assets and financial liabilities as at the reporting date. The fair values of cash, trade and accrued receivables, revolving credit facilities, trade payables and accrued liabilities, approximate their carrying values given their short-term maturities. The fair values of long-term receivables and long-term debt approximate their carrying values given the current market rates associated with these instruments. The fair value of the interest rates is determined based on current market rates and on information received from the Company's counterparties to these agreements.

b) **Interest Income and Expense, and Gains or Losses by Class of Financial Asset and Financial Liability**

All interest income and expense, regardless of the class of financial asset or financial liability, is recorded in the consolidated statement of operations as interest.

All foreign exchange gains and losses, regardless of the class of financial asset or financial liability, are recorded in the consolidated statement of operations in cost of sales (realized) or general and administrative expense (unrealized).

c) **Risks**

Exposure to credit risk and interest rate risk arises in the normal course of the Company's business. The Company does not currently enter into derivative financial instruments to reduce exposure to fluctuations in any credit or interest risks impacting the operations of the Company.

i. Credit risk

The Company is exposed to credit risk on its accounts receivable from franchisees. The accounts receivable are net of applicable allowances for doubtful accounts, which are established based on the specific credit risks associated with individual franchisees and other relevant information. Concentration of credit risk with respect to receivables is limited, due to the large number of franchisees.

As at February 1, 2009, the aging of the Accounts receivable is as follows:

Current	$ 74,924
Past due 0 - 60 days	4,190
Past due over 61 days	6,102
Accounts receivable	85,216
Less: allowance for doubtful accounts	(761)
	$ 84,455

ii. Interest rate risk

The Company is exposed to interest rate risk on the credit facility as the rate is based on an index rate and on the Company's financial performance as determined by its interest coverage ratio. As at February 1, 2009, the interest rate paid was bank prime less 0.45%.

On February 1, 2009, a 25 basis point increase or decrease in interest rates, assuming that all other variables are constant, would have resulted in a $157,000 decrease or increase in the Company's net earnings for the period ended February 1, 2009.

The Company is not exposed to interest rate risk on long-term receivables, mortgages and vendor take-back loans as the rates are fixed.

iii. Asset-backed exposures
The Company has no exposure to asset-backed securities.

iv. Exchange risk
The Company currently uses forward currency contracts and options to hedge anticipated transactions whose terms do not exceed one year.

The Company has recorded an unrealized gain in the consolidated statement of comprehensive earnings for the fiscal year ended February 1, 2009 of $1,340,000 (net of tax - $871,000) (2008 - ($138,000), net of tax -($87,000)) relating to forward foreign currency contracts that qualify for hedge accounting.

The outstanding forward foreign exchange contracts to which hedge accounting was applied at February 1, 2009 have notional amounts of $3,629,000 (2008 - $6,208,000) and terms ranging from February 6, 2009 to August 21, 2009 at forward rates ranging from $1.021 to $1.2695.

Items currently reported in AOCE will be reclassified to net earnings when the hedged item is settled and the related non-financial asset is expensed or when a hedge is deemed ineffective and the hedged item has settled.

On February 1, 2009, a 1% increase or decrease in the exchange rate of the Canadian dollar compared to the U.S dollar, assuming that all other variables are constant, would have resulted in a $85,000 decrease or increase in the Company's net earnings for the period ended February 1, 2009.

v. Liquidity Risk
Liquidity risk is the risk the Company will encounter difficulties in meeting it's financial liability obligations. The Company manages its liquidity risk through cash and debt management. See Note 10 for a more detailed discussion.

17. Acquisitions

(a) Effective September 9, 2007, the Company acquired select net assets of Al DiMarco's Custom Golf Shop Ltd. and various other related entities ("DiMarco"). The acquisition was accounted for using the purchase method as net assets acquired encompass the necessary inputs, processes and outputs to sustain the business, thereby meeting the definition of a business and accordingly the consolidated financial statements include the results of operations since the date of the acquisition.

The consideration for the transaction was $1,039,000 in cash and the settlement of an outstanding account receivable by the Company from DiMarco of $3,095,000.

The assigned fair values of the underlying assets and liabilities acquired by the Company as at September 9, 2007 are summarized as follows:

Cash	$	3
Inventory		3,755
Prepaid expenses		39
Capital assets		425
Total assets acquired		4,222
Less: amounts due to others		(88)
Net assets acquired	$	4,134

(b) Effective November 26, 2007, the Company acquired 100% of the outstanding shares of Athletes World Limited ("AWL") which was operating under Companies' Creditors Arrangement Act ("CCAA") protection. While under CCAA protection, FGL maintained its usual role in the management of the day-to-day operation of Athletes World under the supervision of a court-appointed monitor who was responsible for reviewing Athletes World's ongoing operations, assisting with the development and filing of the Court documents, liaising with creditors and other stakeholders and reporting to the Court. On June 30, 2008 AWL successfully exited from CCAA protection.

The acquisition was accounted for using the purchase method and accordingly the consolidated financial statements include the results of operations since the date of acquisition.

The assigned fair values of the underlying assets and liabilities acquired by the Company as at November 26, 2007, are summarized as follows:

Inventory	$	26,171
Capital assets		2,626
Intangible asset - trademark		2,212
Future income tax asset		13,215
Total assets acquired		44,224
Bank indebtedness		108
Accounts payable		17,254
Long-term debt		18,196
Total liabilities acquired		35,558
Net assets acquired	$	8,666
Consideration given:		
Cash	$	1,500
Acquisition costs		7,166
Total Consideration	$	8,666

18. Segmented Financial Information

The Company operates principally in two business segments: corporately-owned and operated retail stores and as a wholesale business selling to franchisees and others. Amortization and interest expense are not disclosed by segment as they are substantially retail in nature.

In determining the reportable segments, the Company considered the distinct business models of the retail and wholesale operations, the division of responsibilities, and the reporting to the CEO and Board of Directors.

	For the 52 weeks ended February 1, 2009	For the 53 weeks ended February 3, 2008
Revenues:		
Retail	$ 994,043	$ 969,256
Wholesale	352,715	361,753
	1,346,758	1,331,009
Operating Profit:		
Retail	115,431	143,517
Wholesale	37,229	35,296
	152,660	178,813
Non-segment specific administrative expenses	55,558	55,843
Operating profit before under noted items	97,102	122,970
Amortization of capital assets	47,613	44,468
Interest expense	5,175	5,797
Loss on sale of investment	-	864
	52,788	51,129
Earnings before income taxes	44,314	71,841
Income tax expense	14,989	24,390
Net earnings	$ 29,325	$ 47,451

As at	February 1, 2009	February 3, 2008
Accounts receivable		
Retail	$ 617	$ 2,796
Wholesale	74,031	71,036
Non-segment specific	9,807	1,674
	$ 84,455	$ 75,506
Capital assets		
Retail	$ 172,146	$ 164,740
Wholesale	21,262	20,596
Non-segment specific	3,357	3,285
	$ 196,765	$ 188,621
Goodwill and other intangibles/Other assets		
Retail	$ 73,162	$ 63,291
Wholesale	23,263	20,336
Non-segment specific	4,336	9,571
	$ 100,761	$ 93,198
Total assets		
Retail	$ 476,711	$ 515,739
Wholesale	169,915	164,541
Non-segment specific	42,834	74,684
	$ 689,460	$ 754,964

19. Related Party Transaction

An officer of the Company holds an interest in franchise store operations. During the year, the franchise operations transacted business, in the normal course and at fair market value, with the Company, purchasing product in the amount of $11,438,000 (2008 - $7,660,000). At the year end, accounts receivable from the franchise operation were $4,404,000 (2008 – $1,821,000).

20. Variable Interest Entities

At February 1, 2009, the Company had a long-term receivable due from an entity which is considered a variable interest entity VIE under CICA AcG 15. The entity operates several franchise stores. The Company has received guarantees for the full amount of the receivable from the shareholders of the entity. The Company has concluded that it is not the primary beneficiary of the VIE and that it is not required to consolidate this VIE in its consolidated financial statements. The Company has no exposure to loss related to the long-term receivable.

21. Sale of Investment

During fiscal 2008, the Company sold its investment in a trademark licensing company. The investment had a cost of $3,088,000 and was sold for $2,224,000 with a one-time loss of $864,000 recognized during the period ended February 3, 2008.

22. Subsequent Events

Effective February 18, 2009, the Company completed an asset purchase from Access Distribution Inc., for total expected consideration of $4,000,000, payable over 5 years on the completion of certain performance measures.

23. Comparative Figures

Certain comparative figures have been reclassified to conform to the presentation adopted for the current period.

APPENDIX B ▸ SALES TAXES

All businesses operating in Canada need to understand how sales taxes apply to their particular business in their particular province or territory. Sales taxes may take the form of the Goods and Services Tax (GST), Provincial Sales Tax (PST), or Harmonized Sales Tax (HST). GST is levied by the federal government. PST is levied by the provinces and territories, with the exception of Alberta, the Northwest Territories, Nunavut, and Yukon, where no Provincial Sales Tax is charged. Nova Scotia, New Brunswick, and Newfoundland and Labrador, and recently British Columbia and Ontario (effective July 1, 2010) have combined the GST and PST into one Harmonized Sales Tax.

A business is considered an agent of the federal and provincial governments and is therefore required to collect sales taxes on the sale of certain goods and services. In addition, businesses pay sales taxes on most disbursements. We will discuss the collection, payment, recording, and remittance of each of these types of sales taxes in the following sections.

Types of Sales Taxes

Goods and Services Tax

The GST is a federal sales tax on most goods and services provided in Canada. A business must register for the GST if it provides taxable goods or services in Canada and if it has revenues of more than $30,000 in any year. Businesses that have to or decide to voluntarily register for the GST are called registrants. Registrants can claim a credit—called an input tax credit (ITC)—for the amount of GST they pay or owe on purchases of goods or services against the GST they collect or are owed. GST returns are submitted quarterly for most registrants (monthly for large registrants) to the Canada Revenue Agency. The taxes are payable to the Receiver General, who is the collection agent for the federal government.

For those provinces that have adopted the Harmonized Sales Tax, where the PST and GST have been combined into one tax, the Receiver General is the collection agent for both the federal and provincial governments.

The GST applies at a rate of 5% on most transactions (13% in the case of HST). Transactions subject to GST/HST are called taxable supplies. There are two other categories of goods and services with respect to the GST/HST:

- zero-rated supplies, such as basic groceries and prescription drugs
- exempt supplies, such as educational services, health-care services, and financial services

No GST/HST applies to zero-rated or exempt supplies. However, zero-rated suppliers can claim input tax credits.

Illustration B-1 provides the GST/HST status of some typical goods and services.

Taxable Supplies	Zero-Rated Supplies	Exempt Supplies
Building materials	Prescription drugs	Used house
Ready-to-eat pizza	Uncooked pizza	Dental services
Two doughnuts	Six or more doughnuts	Insurance policy

Illustration B-1
Examples of GST/HST status

The reason ready-to-eat pizza and two doughnuts have GST/HST added to the purchase price is because they are considered convenience items, which are taxable, and not basic groceries, which are not taxable.

Provincial Sales Tax

Provincial sales taxes are charged on retail sales of certain goods and services. As of July 1, 2010, there are only four provinces that charge a separate Provincial Sales Tax: Saskatchewan, Manitoba, Quebec, and Prince Edward Island. In Saskatchewan and Manitoba, this tax is applied to the selling price of the item before GST is applied. Similarly, GST is charged on the selling price of the item before PST is applied, thus avoiding GST being charged on PST. In Quebec and Prince Edward Island, however, the Provincial Sales Tax is cascaded; that is, it is applied to the total of the selling price plus GST. Quebec's sales tax is also known as the QST (Quebec Sales Tax).

The following example shows the calculation of cascaded sales tax, using a taxable item sold in Quebec for $100 (at the rate applicable in 2011):

Selling price	$100.00
GST ($100 × 5%)	5.00
QST [($100 + $5) × 8.5%]	8.93
Total	$ 113.93

Provincial sales taxes are remitted periodically to the Minister of Finance or Provincial Treasurer in each province.

PST rates vary by province and can change with each provincial budget. Certain goods are exempt, such as children's clothing, textbooks, and residential rent, and may be purchased with no PST. Examples of exempt services that are not taxable include personal services such as dental and medical services. Because rates and exemptions vary by province, it is important, when starting a business, to check with provincial officials for details on how to calculate the provincial tax that must be applied to sales.

Harmonized Sales Tax

The provinces of Newfoundland and Labrador, Nova Scotia, New Brunswick, and most recently British Columbia and Ontario charge Harmonized Sales Tax, or HST. Instead of charging GST and PST separately, only the HST is charged at a combined rate of 13%, or 12% in British Columbia. Similar to GST, HST returns are submitted quarterly for most registrants (monthly for large registrants) to the Receiver General for Canada. The federal government then gives the provincial portion of the tax to the province.

To summarize, two provinces—Manitoba and Saskatchewan—apply PST and GST to the selling price of a taxable good or service. Two provinces—Prince Edward Island and Quebec—apply PST to the total of the purchase price and the GST. Five provinces—New Brunswick, Newfoundland and Labrador, Nova Scotia, British Columbia, and Ontario—charge a combined GST and PST (harmonized) rate of 13% (12% in British Columbia) on the selling price. Four provinces and territories do not charge PST: Alberta, the Northwest Territories, Nunavut, and Yukon. In addition to the different ways of applying sales taxes, the rates of sales tax differ in each province and territory, as shown in Illustration B-2.

Province/Territory	GST (HST) Rate	PST Rate	Combined Rate[1]
Alberta	5.0%	0.0%	5.0%
British Columbia	12.0%	N/A	12.0%
Manitoba	5.0%	7.0%	12.0%
New Brunswick	13.0%	N/A	13.0%
Newfoundland and Labrador	13.0%	N/A	13.0%
Northwest Territories	5.0%	0.0%	5.0%
Nova Scotia	13.0%	N/A	13.0%
Nunavut	5.0%	0.0%	5.0%
Ontario	13.0%	N/A	13.0%
Prince Edward Island	5.0%	10.0%	15.5%[2]
Quebec	5.0%	8.5%	13.925%[2]
Saskatchewan	5.0%	5.0%	10.0%
Yukon	5.0%	0.0%	5.0%

[1] These rates are in effect as of August 31, 2009, and are subject to change. Quebec rates are effective January 1, 2011, and Ontario and British Columbia rates are effective July 1, 2010.
[2] In Prince Edward Island and Quebec only, the GST is included in the Provincial Sales Tax base.

Illustration B-2
Sales tax rates

Sales Taxes Collected on Receipts

Sales taxes are collected by businesses from consumers on taxable goods and services. It is important to understand that sales taxes are not a source of revenue for a company. They are collected by a company on behalf of the federal and provincial governments. Consequently, collected sales tax is a current liability to the company until remitted to the respective government at regular intervals.

Services

Now let's look at how service companies record sales taxes on the services they provide.

Services with PST

Assume that $250 of cleaning services were provided by a company in Manitoba for cash on July 24. These services are subject to both PST (7%) and GST (5%), and would be recorded as follows:

July 24	Cash	280.00	
	Cleaning Service Revenue		250.00
	PST Payable ($250 × 7%)		17.50
	GST Payable ($250 × 5%)		12.50
	To record cleaning service revenue.		

A	=	L	+	OE
+280.00		+17.50 +12.50		+250.00

↑ Cash flows: +280.00

Note that the revenue recorded is $250, and not $280. The cleaning service revenue is exclusive of the GST and PST amount collected, which are recorded as current liabilities.

Services with HST

Assume now that these same services were provided by a company in New Brunswick, where HST is 13%. The entry would be as follows:

July 24	Cash	282.50	
	Cleaning Service Revenue		250.00
	HST Payable ($250 × 13%)		32.50
	To record cleaning service revenue.		

A	=	L	+	OE
+282.50		+32.50		+250.00

↑ Cash flows: +282.50

Merchandise

Entries are needed to record the sales taxes owed when merchandise inventory (goods) is sold, or to reduce sales taxes payable when merchandise inventory is returned.

Sales with PST

Assume that Staples sells $1,000 of office furniture, on account, in the province of Manitoba, where PST is 7%. GST is 5%. Staples uses a perpetual inventory system and the cost of the furniture to Staples was $800. Staples will make the following two entries to record the sale and the cost of the sale on May 20:

A	=	L	+	OE
+1,120		+50 +70		+1,000

Cash flows: no effect

A	=	L	+	OE
−800				−800

Cash flows: no effect

May 20	Accounts Receivable	1,120	
	Sales		1,000
	GST Payable ($1,000 × 5%)		50
	PST Payable ($1,000 × 7%)		70
	To record sale of merchandise on account.		
20	Cost of Goods Sold	800	
	Merchandise Inventory		800
	To record cost of merchandise sold.		

The merchandise inventory does not include any sales taxes that may have been paid when the company purchased the merchandise. We will learn more about that in the next section of this appendix.

Under a periodic inventory system, the second entry would not be recorded.

Sales Returns and Allowances with PST

If a $300 sales return and allowance were granted by Staples on May 25 for returned merchandise from the above sale, Staples' entries to record the sales return would appear as follows:

A	=	L	+	OE
−336		−15 −21		−300

Cash flows: no effect

A	=	L	+	OE
+240				+240

Cash flows: no effect

May 25	Sales Returns and Allowances	300	
	GST Payable ($300 × 5%)	15	
	PST Payable ($300 × 7%)	21	
	Accounts Receivable		336
	To record credit for returned merchandise.		
25	Merchandise Inventory ($300 ÷ $1,000 × $800)	240	
	Cost of Goods Sold		240
	To record cost of merchandise returned.		

Note that the GST and PST payable accounts, rather than a receivable account, are debited, to indicate that this is a return of previously collected sales tax. This entry assumes that the merchandise was in good condition and returned to inventory. Note also that, as GST and PST are not included in the original cost of the merchandise, they are therefore not considered in restoring the cost of the merchandise to the inventory account.

Under a periodic inventory system, the second entry would not be recorded.

Sales with HST

Assume now that Staples sells the same $1,000 of office furniture, on account, in the province of Nova Scotia, where there is no PST and where HST is 13%. Staples uses a perpetual inventory system and the cost of the furniture to Staples was $800. Staples will record the following two entries to record the sale and the cost of the sale on May 20:

A	=	L	+	OE
+1,130		+130		+1,000

Cash flows: no effect

A	=	L	+	OE
−800				−800

Cash flows: no effect

May 20	Accounts Receivable	1,130	
	Sales		1,000
	HST Payable ($1,000 × 13%)		130
	To record sale of merchandise on account.		
20	Cost of Goods Sold	800	
	Merchandise Inventory		800
	To record cost of merchandise sold.		

Under a periodic inventory system, the second entry would not be recorded.

Sales Returns and Allowances with HST

Assume the same $300 sales return and allowance were granted by Staples on May 25 for returned merchandise from the above sale. Staples' entries to record the sales return would appear as follows:

May 25	Sales Returns and Allowances	300	
	HST Payable ($300 × 13%)	39	
	Accounts Receivable		339
	To record credit for returned merchandise.		
25	Merchandise Inventory ($300 ÷ $1,000 × $800)	240	
	Cost of Goods Sold		240
	To record cost of merchandise returned.		

A	=	L	+	OE
−339		−39		−300

Cash flows: no effect

A	=	L	+	OE
+240				+240

Cash flows: no effect

Under a periodic inventory system, the second entry would not be recorded.

Sales Taxes Paid on Disbursements

As a consumer of goods and services, a business must pay the applicable PST and GST or HST charged by its suppliers on taxable goods and services.

Purchase of Merchandise for Resale

When purchasing merchandise for resale, the treatment of the PST is different than that of the GST. PST is a single-stage tax collected from the final consumers of taxable goods and services. Consequently, wholesalers do not charge the tax to the retailer, who will in turn resell the merchandise, at a higher price, to the final consumer. By presenting a vendor registration number, retailers are able to buy merchandise for resale, exempt of the PST.

Businesses must pay GST/HST on the purchase of merchandise but can then offset the GST/HST paid against any GST/HST collected. Consequently, when merchandise is purchased, the GST/HST paid by a business is *not* part of the inventory cost. The GST/HST paid on purchases is debited to an account called GST or HST Recoverable and is called an input tax credit.

In Quebec, the QST works somewhat like the GST. Businesses can offset QST paid against any QST collected. The QST paid on purchases is debited to an account called QST Recoverable and is called an input tax refund. Other differences also exist in the treatment of QST. This appendix will focus on PST and does not discuss the QST in any detail.

Purchases with GST

The following is an entry to record the purchase of merchandise, for resale in the province of Manitoba, on May 4 at a price of $4,000, on account, using a perpetual inventory system:

May 4	Merchandise Inventory	4,000	
	GST Recoverable ($4,000 × 5%)	200	
	Accounts Payable		4,200
	To record merchandise purchased on account.		

A	=	L	+	OE
+4,000 +200		+4,200		

Cash flows: no effect

As previously discussed, the cost of the merchandise, $4,000, is not affected by the GST, which is recorded as a receivable.

Under a periodic inventory system, the $4,000 debit would have been recorded to the Purchases account.

Purchase Returns and Allowances with GST

The entry to record a $300 return of merchandise on May 8 is as follows:

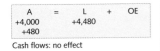

A	=	L	+	OE
−15		−315		
−300				

Cash flows: no effect

May 8	Accounts Payable	315	
	GST Recoverable ($300 × 5%)		15
	Merchandise Inventory		300
	To record the return of merchandise.		

Note that the GST Recoverable account is credited instead of the GST Payable account because this is a return of previously recorded GST.

Under a periodic inventory system, the credit of $300 would have been recorded to the Purchase Returns and Allowances account.

To summarize, PST is not paid on purchases of merchandise for resale. GST paid on purchases is recoverable and recorded as a current asset in the GST Recoverable account. Purchase returns and allowances require an adjustment of GST only, since PST was not paid on the original purchase.

Purchases with HST

The following is an entry to record the purchase of merchandise for resale in the province of British Columbia, where the HST rate is 12%, on May 4 at a price of $4,000, on account, using a perpetual inventory system:

A	=	L	+	OE
+4,000		+4,480		
+480				

Cash flows: no effect

May 4	Merchandise Inventory	4,000	
	HST Recoverable ($4,000 × 12%)	480	
	Accounts Payable		4,480
	To record merchandise purchased on account.		

The cost of the merchandise, $4,000, is not affected by the HST, which is recorded as a receivable.

Under a periodic inventory system, the $4,000 debit would have been recorded to the Purchases account.

Purchase Returns and Allowances with GST

The entry to record a $300 return of merchandise in the province of British Columbia, where the HST rate is 12%, on May 8 is as follows:

A	=	L	+	OE
−36		−336		
−300				

Cash flows: no effect

May 8	Accounts Payable	336	
	HST Recoverable ($300 × 12%)		36
	Merchandise Inventory		300
	To record the return of merchandise.		

Note that the HST Recoverable account is credited instead of the HST Payable account because this is a return of previously recorded HST.

Under a periodic inventory system, the credit of $300 would have been recorded to the Purchase Returns and Allowances account.

To summarize, HST paid on purchases is recoverable and recorded as a current asset in the HST Recoverable account.

Operating Expenses

The accounting treatment of sales taxes incurred on operating expenses depends on the type of sales taxes that the company is charged.

Operating Expenses with PST

Although PST is not charged on goods purchased for resale, it is charged to businesses that use taxable goods and services in their operations. For example, a business must pay GST and PST when it buys office supplies. As with all purchases made by a registered business, the GST is recoverable (can be offset as an input tax credit against GST collected). Because the PST is not recoverable, the PST forms part of the cost of the asset or expense that is being acquired.

The following is the entry for a cash purchase of office supplies on May 18 in the amount of $200 in the province of Saskatchewan, where PST is 5% and GST is 5%:

May 18	Office Supplies ($200 + $10* PST)	210	
	GST Recoverable ($200 × 5%)	10	
	Cash		220
	To record purchase of office supplies.		

*$200 × 5% = $10

A	=	L	+	OE
+210				
+10				
−220				

Cash flows: −220

In this situation, the cost of the supplies includes both the supplies and the PST. Because GST is recoverable, it does not form part of the asset cost.

This same purchase would be recorded as follows if it occurred in the province of Prince Edward Island, where GST is 5% and PST is charged on GST at 10%:

May 18	Office Supplies ($200 + $21* PST)	221	
	GST Recoverable ($200 × 5%)	10	
	Cash		231
	To record purchase of office supplies.		

*$200 + $10 = $210 × 10% = $21

A	=	L	+	OE
+221				
+10				
−231				

Cash flows: −231

Remember that in Prince Edward Island, the Provincial Sales Tax base includes both the cost of the item and the GST. That is, the PST of $21 is determined by multiplying 10% by $210 ($200 + $10).

Operating Expenses with HST

When HST is applied, it is treated in the same manner as GST. HST is recoverable and does not form part of the cost of the item purchased. The purchase of office supplies would be recorded as follows if it had occurred in the province of Ontario, where HST is 13%:

May 18	Office Supplies	200	
	HST Recoverable ($200 × 13%)	26	
	Cash		226
	To record purchase of office supplies.		

A	=	L	+	OE
+200				
+26				
−226				

Cash flows: −226

Note that the type and amount of sales tax paid changes the amount recorded as the cost of office supplies in each province: $210 in Saskatchewan, $221 in Prince Edward Island, and $200 in Ontario.

Property, Plant, and Equipment

Businesses incur costs other than those for merchandise and operating expenses, such as for the purchase of property, plant, and equipment. The PST and GST or HST apply to these purchases in the same manner as described in the operating expenses section above. All GST (or HST) paid is recoverable and is not part of the cost of the asset. The PST, however, is part of the cost of the asset being purchased as it is not recoverable.

Property, Plant, and Equipment with PST

The following is the entry for the purchase of office furniture on May 20 from Staples, on account, for $1,000 plus applicable sales taxes in Manitoba, where PST is 7% and GST is 5%.

A	=	L	+	OE
+1,070		+1,120		
+50				

Cash flows: no effect

May 20	Office Furniture ($1,000 + $70* PST)	1,070	
	GST Recoverable ($1,000 × 5%)	50	
	Accounts Payable		1,120
	To record purchase of office furniture.		

*$1,000 × 7% = $70

Because the PST is not recoverable, the cost of the furniture is $1,070, inclusive of the PST.

Compare this entry made by the buyer to record the purchase with the entry made by the seller (Staples) to record the sale on page B4. Both companies record accounts payable and accounts receivable in the same amount, $1,120. However, the seller records both GST and PST payable while the buyer records only GST recoverable. The PST paid by the buyer is not recoverable, so it becomes part of the cost of the office furniture, $1,070.

In Prince Edward Island, where GST is 5% and PST is charged on GST at 10%, the same entry would be recorded as follows:

A	=	L	+	OE
+1,105		+1,155		
+50				

Cash flows: no effect

May 20	Office Furniture ($1,000 + $105* PST)	1,105	
	GST Recoverable ($1,000 × 5%)	50	
	Accounts Payable		1,155
	To record purchase of office furniture.		

*$1,000 + $50 = $1,050 × 10% = $105

In P.E.I., PST is calculated on a cost base that includes the GST. Therefore, the PST of $105 is calculated on $1,050 ($1,000 + $50). Because PST is not recoverable, the cost of the furniture is $1,105.

Property, Plant, and Equipment with HST

In Nova Scotia, where HST is 13%, the entry would be recorded as follows:

A	=	L	+	OE
+1,000		+1,130		
+130				

Cash flows: no effect

May 20	Office Furniture	1,000	
	HST Recoverable ($1,000 × 13%)	130	
	Accounts Payable		1,130
	To record purchase of office furniture.		

As we have noted before, the type and amount of sales taxes paid changes the amount recorded as the cost of the office furniture in each province: $1,070 in Manitoba, $1,105 in Prince Edward Island, and $1,000 in Nova Scotia.

Remittance of Sales Taxes

As mentioned in the introduction, businesses act as agents of the federal and provincial governments in charging and later remitting taxes charged on sales and services. For example, Staples, the seller of office furniture illustrated on page B4, must remit GST or HST to the Receiver General for Canada and PST to the Minister of Revenue, where applicable. Notice that even if Staples has not received payment from a customer buying on account before the due date for the remittance, the tax must still be paid to the government authorities. As a registrant, however, Staples will also benefit from claiming input tax credits and recording a reduction in amounts payable from applying GST/HST on sales.

GST (HST)

When remitting the amount owed to the federal government at the end of a reporting period for GST (or HST), the amount of GST (or HST) payable is reduced by any amount in the GST/HST Recoverable account. Any difference is remitted, as shown in the following journal entry, using assumed amounts payable and recoverable:

June 30	GST (or HST) Payable	6,250	
	GST (or HST) Recoverable		2,500
	Cash		3,750
	To record remittance of GST (or HST).		

A	=	L	+	OE
−2,500		−6,250		
−3,750				

↓ Cash flows: −3,750

The GST (HST) remittance form requires the registrant to report at specified dates, depending on the business's volume of sales. The amount of the sales and other revenue as well as the amount of GST/HST charged on these sales, whether collected or not, is reported on the remittance form. The amount of the input tax credits claimed is also entered on the form to reduce the amount owing to the Receiver General. If the GST/HST recoverable exceeds the GST/HST payable, the remittance form should be sent as soon as possible in order to ask for a refund. The entry to record the cash receipt from a GST/HST refund will be similar to the entry shown above, except that there will be a debit to Cash, instead of a credit.

The above discussion of the remittance of GST/HST explains why all registrants need two general ledger accounts. One account, GST Payable or HST Payable, is used to keep track of all GST or HST charged on sales and revenues. The second account, GST Recoverable or HST Recoverable, is used to keep track of the GST/HST input tax credits that have been paid on all of the business's purchases. Failure by a business to capture the proper amounts of input tax credits has a significant impact on income and on cash flows.

PST

The remittance of PST to the Treasurer or Minister of Finance of the applicable province is similar to that of GST/HST except that, since no credit can be claimed, the amount paid at the end of each reporting period is the amount of the balance in the PST Payable account.

Consequently, the entry to record a remittance of PST, using an assumed amount payable, would appear as follows:

June 30	PST Payable	7,400	
	Cash		7,400
	To record remittance of PST.		

A	=	L	+	OE
−7,400		−7,400		

↓ Cash flows: −7,400

Conclusion

Be careful when you record the amounts of taxes charged or claimed in the business accounts. Numbers must be rounded carefully. If the amount of the tax calculated is less than half a cent, the amount should be rounded down. If the amount of the tax as calculated comes to more than half a cent, the amount should be rounded up. For example, applying 13% HST on an amount of $49.20 would give you $6.396. The tax amount to be recorded can be rounded up to $6.40. Rounding might seem insignificant, but when a business has many transactions, the amounts can add up and the registrant is responsible to the government authorities for any shortfall created in error.

Sales tax law is intricate. It has added a lot of complexity to the accounting for most transactions flowing through today's businesses. Fortunately, computers that are programmed to automatically determine and record the correct sales tax rate for each good or service provided have simplified matters somewhat. Before recording sales tax transactions, however, it is important to understand all of the relevant sales tax regulations. Check the federal and provincial laws in your jurisdiction.

Brief Exercises

Record inventory purchase—perpetual inventory system.

BEB–1 Record the purchase on account of $4,500 of merchandise for resale in the province of Manitoba. The company uses a perpetual inventory system and the purchase is PST exempt.

Record purchase return—perpetual inventory system.

BEB–2 Record the return of $1,000 of the merchandise purchased in BEB–1.

Record inventory purchase—perpetual inventory system.

BEB–3 Record the purchase on account of $4,500 of merchandise for resale in the province of Ontario, where HST is 13%. The company uses a perpetual inventory system.

Record purchase return—perpetual inventory system.

BEB–4 Record the return of $1,000 of the merchandise purchased in BEB–3.

Record purchase of supplies.

BEB–5 Record the cash purchase of $600 of office supplies in the province of Saskatchewan, where PST is 5%.

Record purchase of supplies.

BEB–6 Record the cash purchase of $600 of office supplies in the province of British Columbia, where HST is 12%.

Record purchase of capital item.

BEB–7 Record the purchase on account of a $25,000 delivery truck in the province of Ontario, where HST is 13%.

Record purchase of capital item.

BEB–8 Record the purchase on account of a $25,000 delivery truck in the province of Saskatchewan, where the PST is 5% and the GST is 5%.

Record purchase of supplies and inventory—perpetual inventory system.

BEB–9 Record the purchase on account of $200 of office supplies and $4,000 of merchandise for resale in the province of Manitoba. The company uses a perpetual inventory system and the purchase of merchandise is PST exempt. The PST rate is 7%.

Record sales—perpetual inventory system.

BEB–10 Record the sale on account, for $1,800, of merchandise costing $1,100 in the province of Quebec. Assume the company uses a perpetual inventory system. The QST is 8.5% and the GST is included in the Quebec Sales Tax base.

Record sales return—perpetual inventory system.

BEB–11 Half of the shipment described in BEB–10 is returned as the incorrect sizes have been shipped. Record the return of merchandise on the seller's books.

Record sales and sales return—periodic inventory system.

BEB–12 Record the sale in BEB–10 and the sales return in BEB–11 assuming the business uses a periodic inventory system.

Record exempt services.

BEB–13 Record the billing for $250 of services by D. R. Wong, dentist, in the province of British Columbia. Dental services are exempt from GST and PST.

Record fees.

BEB–14 Record the billing of accounting fee revenue of $400 for the preparation of personal income tax returns in the province of Alberta. GST is applicable on this service. Alberta does not charge PST.

Record remittance of GST and PST.

BEB–15 Record two payments: one cheque to the Receiver General for GST and one to the Minister of Finance of Saskatchewan for PST. The balances in the accounts are as follows: GST Payable $4,450, GST Recoverable $900, and PST Payable $4,870.

Record HST refund.

BEB–16 Record the deposit of a cheque from the Receiver General for a refund of $1,690 following the filing of an HST return. The balances in the accounts are as follows: HST Payable $2,920 and HST Recoverable $4,610.

Exercises

EB–1 Stratton Company is a merchant operating in the province of Manitoba, where the PST rate is 7%. Stratton uses a perpetual inventory system. Transactions for the business are shown below:

Record sales transactions—perpetual inventory system.

Mar. 1 Paid March rent to the landlord for the rental of a warehouse. The lease calls for monthly payments of $5,500 plus 5% GST.
3 Sold merchandise on account and shipped merchandise to Marvin Ltd. for $20,000, terms n/30, FOB shipping point. This merchandise cost Stratton $10,600.
5 Granted Marvin a sales allowance of $700 for defective merchandise purchased on March 3. No merchandise was returned.
7 Purchased on account from Xu Ltd. merchandise for resale at a list price of $14,000, plus applicable tax.
12 Made a cash purchase at Home Depot of a desk for the shipping clerk. The price of the desk was $600 before applicable taxes.
31 Paid the quarterly remittance of GST to the Receiver General. The balances in the accounts were as follows: GST Payable $5,280 and GST Recoverable $1,917.

Instructions

(a) Prepare the journal entries to record these transactions on the books of Stratton Company.
(b) Assume instead that Stratton operates in the province of Alberta, where PST is not applicable. Prepare the journal entries to record these transactions on the books of Stratton.
(c) Assume instead that Stratton operates in the province of Prince Edward Island, where PST is charged on GST at 10%. Prepare the journal entries to record these transactions on the books of Stratton.
(d) Assume instead that Stratton operates in the province of Ontario, where HST is 13%. Prepare the journal entries to record these transactions on the books of Stratton. Assume that the GST balances on March 31 are the balances in the HST accounts.

EB–2 Using the information for the transactions of Stratton Company in EB–1, assume now that Stratton uses a periodic inventory system.

Record sales transactions—periodic inventory system.

Instructions

(a) Prepare the journal entries to record these transactions on the books of Stratton Company.
(b) Assume now that Stratton operates in the province of Alberta, where PST is not applicable. Prepare the journal entries to record these transactions on the books of Stratton.
(c) Assume now that Stratton operates in the province of Prince Edward Island, where PST is charged on GST at 10%. Prepare the journal entries to record these transactions on the books of Stratton.
(d) Assume now that Stratton operates in the province of Ontario, where HST is 13%. Prepare the journal entries to record these transactions on the books of Stratton. Assume that the GST balances on March 31 provided in EB–1 are the balances in the HST accounts.

EB–3 Otto Cheng is a sole proprietor providing accounting services in the province of Manitoba, where PST is charged at the rate of 7% and GST is at the rate of 5%. Transactions for the business are shown below:

Record service transactions.

June 8 Purchased a printer on account at a cost of $1,500. The appropriate sales taxes were added to this purchase price.
10 Purchased toner for the printer for $50 cash from a local stationery store. The store added the appropriate sales taxes to the purchase price.
12 Billed a client for accounting services provided. The fee charged was $950 and the appropriate sales taxes were added to the fee billed.

15 Collected $112 on account. The original fee was $100, the GST charged was $5 and the PST charged was $7.
30 Paid the quarterly remittance of GST to the Receiver General. The balances in the accounts were as follows: GST Payable $1,520.60 and GST Recoverable $820.45.
30 Paid the quarterly remittance of PST to the Minister of Revenue for the province of Manitoba. The balance in the PST Payable account was $2,128.84.

Instructions

Prepare the journal entries to record these transactions on the books of Otto Cheng's accounting business.

Record service transactions.

EB–4 Baole Chen is a sole proprietor providing legal services in the province of Ontario, where the HST rate is 13%. Transactions for the business are shown below:

June 8 Purchased a printer on account at a cost of $1,500. The appropriate taxes were added to this purchase price.
10 Purchased toner for the printer for $50 cash from a local stationery store. The store added the appropriate taxes to the purchase price.
12 Billed a client for accounting services provided. The fee charged was $950 plus appropriate taxes.
15 Collected $113 on account. The original fee was $100; the HST charged was $13.
30 Paid the quarterly remittance of HST to the Receiver General. The balances in the accounts were as follows: HST Payable $1,520.60 and HST Recoverable $820.45.

Instructions

Prepare the journal entries to record these transactions on the books of Baole Chen's legal practice.

Problems

Record purchase and sales transactions—perpetual inventory system.

PB–1 Mark's Music is a store that buys and sells musical instruments in Ontario, where the HST rate is 13%. Mark's Music uses a perpetual inventory system. Transactions for the business are shown below:

Nov. 2 Purchased two electric guitars from Fender Supply Limited, on account, at a cost of $700 each.
4 Made a cash sale of two keyboards for a total invoice price of $2,200, plus applicable taxes. The cost of each keyboard was $950.
5 Received a credit memorandum from Western Acoustic Inc. for the return of an acoustic guitar that was defective. The original invoice price before taxes was $400 and the guitar had been purchased on account.
7 One of the keyboards from the cash sale of November 4 was returned to the store for a full cash refund because the customer was not satisfied with the instrument.
8 Purchased store supplies from a stationery store. The price of the supplies is $100 before all applicable taxes.
10 Sold one Omega trumpet to the Toronto Regional Band, on account, for an invoice price of $2,700 before applicable taxes. The trumpet had cost Mark's Music $1,420.
13 Purchased two saxophones from Yamaha Canada Inc. on account. The invoice price was $2,100 for each saxophone, excluding applicable taxes.
14 Collected $3,990 on account. The payment included all applicable taxes.
16 Returned to Yamaha Canada Inc. one of the saxophones purchased on November 13, as it was the wrong model. Received a credit memorandum from Yamaha for the full purchase price.
20 Made a payment on account for the amount owing to Fender Supply Limited for the purchase of November 2.

Instructions

(a) Prepare the journal entries to record the Mark's Music transactions.
(b) Assume now that Mark's Music operates in the province of Manitoba, where the PST rate is 7% and the GST rate is 5%. Prepare the journal entries to record these transactions on the books of Mark's Music.

PB–2 Transaction data for Mark's Music are available in PB–1. Assume Mark's Music uses a periodic inventory system instead of a perpetual inventory system.

Record purchase and sales transactions—periodic inventory system.

Instructions

(a) Prepare the journal entries to record the Mark's Music transactions.
(b) Assume now that Mark's Music operates in the province of Manitoba, where the PST rate is 7% and the GST rate is 5%. Prepare the journal entries to record these transactions on the books of Mark's Music.

PB–3 David Simmons, L.L.B., is a lawyer operating as a sole proprietor in Nunavut. Nunavut does not charge provincial sales taxes and the GST rate is 5%. Transactions for the business are shown below:

Record service transactions.

May 1 Signed a two-year lease for the office space and immediately paid the first and last months' rent. The lease calls for the monthly rent of $1,800 plus applicable taxes.
4 Purchased an office suite of furniture, on account, from George's Furniture at a cost of $3,100. The appropriate sales taxes were added to this purchase price.
5 Returned one chair to George's due to a defect. The cost of the chair before taxes was $400.
6 Billed a client for the preparation of a will. The client was very pleased with the product and immediately paid David's invoice for fees of $1,000 plus taxes.
10 Purchased paper for the photocopier for $300 cash from a local stationery store. The store added the appropriate sales taxes to the purchase price.
13 Billed Manson Ltd. for legal services rendered connected with the purchase of land. The fee charged is $900 plus applicable taxes.
18 Paid George's for the furniture purchase of May 4, net of returned items.
19 Paid $15 cash to a local grocery store for coffee for the office coffee machine. Groceries are GST exempt.
21 In accordance with the lease agreement with the landlord, David must pay for water supplied by the municipality. The water invoice was received and the services amounted to $100. No GST is charged for municipal water.
25 Collected a full payment from Manson Ltd. for the May 13 bill.
27 Completed the preparation of a purchase and sale agreement for Edwards Inc. and billed fees of $1,200.

Instructions

(a) Prepare the journal entries to record these transactions on the books of David Simmons' law practice.
(b) Determine the balances GST Payable and GST Recoverable accounts. Determine if the company must make a payment to the Receiver General or if it will apply for a refund. Record the appropriate journal entry.
(c) Assume now that David Simmons operates in the province of Ontario, where the HST rate is 13%. Prepare the journal entries to record these transactions on the books of David Simmons' law practice.
(d) Determine the balances HST Payable and HST Recoverable accounts. Determine if the company must make a payment to the Receiver General or if it will apply for a refund. Record the appropriate journal entry.

APPENDIX C ▸ SUBSIDIARY LEDGERS AND SPECIAL JOURNALS

In the textbook, we learned how to record accounting transactions in a general journal. Each journal entry was then individually posted to its respective general ledger account. However, such a practice is only useful in a company where the volume of transactions is low. In most companies, it is necessary to use additional journals (called special journals) and ledgers (called subsidiary ledgers) to record transaction data.

We will look at subsidiary ledgers and special journals in the next sections. Both subsidiary ledgers and special journals can be used in either a manual accounting system or a computerized accounting system.

Subsidiary Ledgers

Imagine a business that has several thousand customers who purchase merchandise from it on account. It records the transactions with these customers in only one general ledger account—Accounts Receivable. It would be virtually impossible to determine the balance owed by an individual customer at any specific time. Similarly, the amount payable to one creditor would be difficult to locate quickly from a single accounts payable account in the general ledger.

Instead, companies use subsidiary ledgers to keep track of individual balances. A subsidiary ledger is a group of accounts that share a common characteristic (for example, all accounts receivable). The subsidiary ledger frees the general ledger from the details of individual balances. A subsidiary ledger is an addition to, and an expansion of, the general ledger.

Two common subsidiary ledgers are:

1. The accounts receivable (or customers') ledger, which collects transaction data for individual customers
2. The accounts payable (or creditors') ledger, which collects transaction data for individual creditors

Other subsidiary ledgers include an inventory ledger, which collects transaction data for each inventory item purchased and sold, as was described in Chapter 5. Some companies also use a payroll ledger, detailing individual employee pay records. In each of these subsidiary ledgers, individual accounts are arranged in alphabetical, numerical, or alphanumerical order.

The detailed data from a subsidiary ledger are summarized in a general ledger account. For exaple, the detailed data from the accounts receivable subsidiary ledger are summarized in Accounts Receivable in the general ledger. The general ledger account that summarizes subsidiary ledger data is called a control account.

Each general ledger control account balance must equal the total balance of the individual accounts in the related subsidiary ledger. This is an important internal control function.

Example

An example of an accounts receivable control account and subsidiary ledger is shown in Illustration C-1 for Mercier Enterprises.

Illustration C-1

Accounts receivable general ledger control account and subsidiary ledger

GENERAL LEDGER

Accounts Receivable — No. 112

Date	Explanation	Ref.	Debit	Credit	Balance
2011					
Jan. 31			12,000		12,000
31				8,000	4,000

ACCOUNTS RECEIVABLE SUBSIDIARY LEDGER

Aaron Co. — No. 112-172

Date	Explanation	Ref.	Debit	Credit	Balance
2011					
Jan. 11	Invoice 336		6,000		6,000
19	Payment			4,000	2,000

Branden Inc. — No. 112-173

Date	Explanation	Ref.	Debit	Credit	Balance
2011					
Jan. 12	Invoice 337		3,000		3,000
21	Payment			3,000	0

Caron Co. — No. 112-174

Date	Explanation	Ref.	Debit	Credit	Balance
2011					
Jan. 20	Invoice 339		3,000		3,000
29	Payment			1,000	2,000

The example is based on the following transactions:

Credit Sales			Collections on Account		
Jan. 11	Aaron Co.	$ 6,000	Jan. 19	Aaron Co.	$4,000
12	Branden Inc.	3,000	21	Branden Inc.	3,000
20	Caron Co.	3,000	29	Caron Co.	1,000
		$12,000			$8,000

The total debits ($12,000) and credits ($8,000) in Accounts Receivable in the general ledger match the detailed debits and credits in the subsidiary accounts. The balance of $4,000 in the control account agrees with the total of the balances in the individual accounts receivable accounts (Aaron $2,000 + Branden $0 + Caron $2,000) in the subsidiary ledger.

Rather than relying on customer or creditor names in a subsidiary ledger, a computer system expands the account number of the control account. For example, if the general ledger control account Accounts Receivable was numbered 112, the first customer account in the accounts receivable subsidiary ledger might be numbered 112-001, the second 112-002, and so on. Most systems allow inquiries about specific customer accounts in the subsidiary ledger (by account number) or about the control account.

As shown, postings are made monthly to the control account in the general ledger. We will learn, in the next section, how special journals facilitate monthly postings. We will also learn how to fill in the posting references (in the Ref. column) in both the general ledger and subsidiary ledger accounts. Postings to the individual accounts in the subsidiary ledger are made daily. The rationale for posting daily is to ensure that account information is current. This enables Mercier Enterprises to monitor credit limits, send statements to customers, and answer inquiries from customers about their account balances. In a computerized accounting system, transactions are simultaneously recorded in journals and posted to both the general and subsidiary ledgers.

Advantages of Subsidiary Ledgers

Subsidiary ledgers have several advantages:

1. They show transactions that affect one customer or one creditor in a single account. They provide up-to-date information on specific account balances.
2. They free the general ledger of excessive details. A trial balance of the general ledger does not contain vast numbers of individual customer account balances.
3. They help locate errors in individual accounts. The potential for errors is minimized by reducing the number of accounts in one ledger and by using control accounts.
4. They make possible a division of labour in posting. One employee can post to the general ledger while different employees post to the subsidiary ledgers. This strengthens internal control, since one employee verifies the work of the other.

In a computerized accounting system, the last advantage doesn't apply. Computerized accounting systems do not make errors such as calculation errors and posting errors. Other errors, such as entry errors, can and do still occur. Internal control must be done using different means in computerized systems since account transactions are posted automatically.

Special Journals

As mentioned earlier, journalizing transactions in a two-column (debit and credit) general journal is satisfactory only when there are few transactions. To help with the journalizing and posting of multiple transactions, most companies use special journals in addition to the general journal.

If a company has large numbers of similar transactions, it is useful to create a special journal for only those transactions. Examples of similar transactions that occur frequently include all sales of merchandise on account, or all cash receipts. The types of special journals a company will use depend largely on the types of transactions that occur frequently for that company.

While the form, type, and number of special journals used will vary among organizations, many merchandising companies use the journals shown in Illustration C-2 to record daily transactions. The letters that appear in parentheses following the journal name represent the posting reference used for each journal.

Sales Journal (S)	Cash Receipts Journal (CR)	Purchases Journal (P)	Cash Payments Journal (CP)	General Journal (J)
All sales of merchandise on account	All cash received (including cash sales)	All purchases of merchandise on account	All cash paid (including cash purchases of merchandise)	Transactions that cannot be entered in a special journal, including correcting, adjusting, and closing entries

Illustration C-2

Use of special journals and the general journal

If a transaction cannot be recorded in a special journal, it is recorded in the general journal. For example, if you have four special journals, as listed in Illustration C-2, sales returns and allowances are recorded in the general journal. Similarly, correcting, adjusting, and closing entries are recorded in the general journal. Other types of special journals may sometimes be used in certain situations. For example, when sales returns and allowances are frequent, an additional special journal may be used to record these transactions. A payroll journal is another example of a special journal. It organizes and summarizes payroll details for companies with many employees.

The use of special journals reduces the time needed for the recording and posting process. In addition, special journals permit a greater division of labour. For example, one employee may journalize all cash receipts. Another may journalize credit sales. The division of responsibilities ensures that one person does not have control over all aspects of a transaction. In this instance, recording the sale has been separated from recording the collection of cash from that sale. This may reduce the opportunity for intentional or unintentional error, and is one aspect of good internal control.

For a merchandising company, the same special journals are used whether a company uses the periodic or perpetual system to account for its inventory. The only distinction is the number of, and title for, the columns each journal uses. We will use Karns Wholesale Supply to show the use of special journals in the following sections. Karns uses a perpetual inventory system. The variations between the periodic and perpetual inventory systems are highlighted in helpful hints for your information. In addition, special journals under a periodic inventory system are shown more fully at the end of this appendix.

Sales Journal

The sales journal is used to record sales of merchandise on account. Cash sales of merchandise are entered in the cash receipts journal. Credit sales of assets other than merchandise are entered in the general journal.

Journalizing Credit Sales

Under the perpetual inventory system, each entry in the sales journal results in one entry at selling price and another entry at cost. The entry at selling price is a debit to Accounts Receivable (a control account supported by a subsidiary ledger) and a credit of an equal amount to Sales. The entry at cost is a debit to Cost of Goods Sold and a credit of an equal amount to Merchandise Inventory. Some companies also set up Merchandise Inventory as a control account supported by a subsidiary ledger.

A sales journal with two amount columns can show a sales transaction recognized at both selling price and cost on only one line. The two-column sales journal of Karns Wholesale Supply is shown in Illustration C-3, using assumed credit sales transactions.

Illustration C-3

Sales journal—perpetual inventory system

KARNS WHOLESALE SUPPLY
Sales Journal S1

Date	Account Debited	Invoice No.	Ref.	Accounts Receivable Dr. Sales Cr.	Cost of Goods Sold Dr. Merchandise Inventory Cr.
2011					
May 3	Abbot Sisters	101		10,600	6,360
7	Babson Co.	102		11,350	7,370
14	Carson Bros.	103		7,800	5,070
19	Deli Co.	104		9,300	6,510
21	Abbot Sisters	105		15,400	10,780
24	Deli Co.	106		21,210	15,900
27	Babson Co.	107		14,570	10,200
				90,230	62,190

Helpful hint In a periodic inventory system, the sales journal would have only one column to record the sale at selling price (Accounts Receivable Dr., Sales Cr.). The cost of goods sold is not recorded. It is calculated at the end of the period.

The reference (Ref.) column is not used in journalizing. It is used in posting the sales journal, as explained in the next section. Also, note that, unlike in the general journal, an explanation is not required for each entry in a special journal. Finally, note that each invoice is prenumbered to ensure that all invoices are journalized.

If management wishes to record its sales by department, additional columns may be provided in the sales journal. For example, a department store may have columns for home furnishings, sporting goods, shoes, etc. In addition, the federal government, and practically all provinces, require that sales taxes be charged on items sold. If sales taxes are collected, it is necessary to add more credit columns to the sales journal for GST Payable and PST Payable (or HST Payable).

Posting the Sales Journal

Postings from the sales journal are made daily to the individual accounts receivable accounts in the subsidiary ledger. Posting to the general ledger is done monthly. Illustration C-4 shows both the daily postings to the accounts receivable subsidiary ledger and the monthly postings to the general ledger accounts. We have assumed that Karns Wholesale Supply does not maintain an inventory subsidiary ledger. However, if it did, the procedure is similar to that illustrated for the accounts receivable subsidiary ledger.

A check mark (√) is inserted in the reference posting column to indicate that the daily posting to the customer's account has been made. A check mark is used when the subsidiary ledger accounts are not individually numbered. If the subsidiary ledger accounts are numbered, the account number is used instead of the check mark in the reference posting column. At the end of the month, the column totals of the sales journal are posted to the general ledger. Here, the column totals are posted as a debit of $90,230 to Accounts Receivable (account no. 112), a credit of $90,230 to Sales (account no. 401), a debit of $62,190 to Cost of Goods Sold (account no. 505), and a credit of $62,190 to Merchandise Inventory (account no. 120). Inserting the account numbers below the column totals indicates that the postings have been made. In both the general ledger and subsidiary ledger accounts, the reference S1 indicates that the posting came from page 1 of the sales journal.

Illustration C-4

Sales journal—perpetual inventory system

KARNS WHOLESALE SUPPLY
Sales Journal S1

Date	Account Debited	Invoice No.	Ref.	Accts. Receivable Dr. Sales Cr.	Cost of Goods Sold Dr. Merchandise Inventory Cr.
2011					
May 3	Abbot Sisters	101	√	10,600	6,360
7	Babson Co.	102	√	11,350	7,370
14	Carson Bros.	103	√	7,800	5,070
19	Deli Co.	104	√	9,300	6,510
21	Abbot Sisters	105	√	15,400	10,780
24	Deli Co.	106	√	21,210	15,900
27	Babson Co.	107	√	14,570	10,200
				90,230	62,190
				(112)/(401)	(505)/(120)

Individual amounts are posted daily to the subsidiary ledger.

Totals are posted at the end of the accounting period to the general ledger.

ACCOUNTS RECEIVABLE SUBSIDIARY LEDGER

Abbot Sisters

Date	Ref.	Debit	Credit	Balance
2011				
May 3	S1	10,600		10,600
21	S1	15,400		26,000

Babson Co.

Date	Ref.	Debit	Credit	Balance
2011				
May 7	S1	11,350		11,350
27	S1	14,570		25,920

Carson Bros.

Date	Ref.	Debit	Credit	Balance
2011				
May 14	S1	7,800		7,800

Deli Co.

Date	Ref.	Debit	Credit	Balance
2011				
May 19	S1	9,300		9,300
24	S1	21,210		30,510

The subsidiary ledger is separate from the general ledger.

GENERAL LEDGER

Accounts Receivable No. 112

Date	Ref.	Debit	Credit	Balance
2011				
May 31	S1	90,230		90,230

Merchandise Inventory No. 120

Date	Ref.	Debit	Credit	Balance
2011				
May 31	S1		62,190	62,190cr[1]

Sales No. 401

Date	Ref.	Debit	Credit	Balance
2011				
May 31	S1		90,230	90,230

Cost of Goods Sold No. 505

Date	Ref.	Debit	Credit	Balance
2011				
May 31	S1	62,190		62,190

Accounts Receivable is a control account.

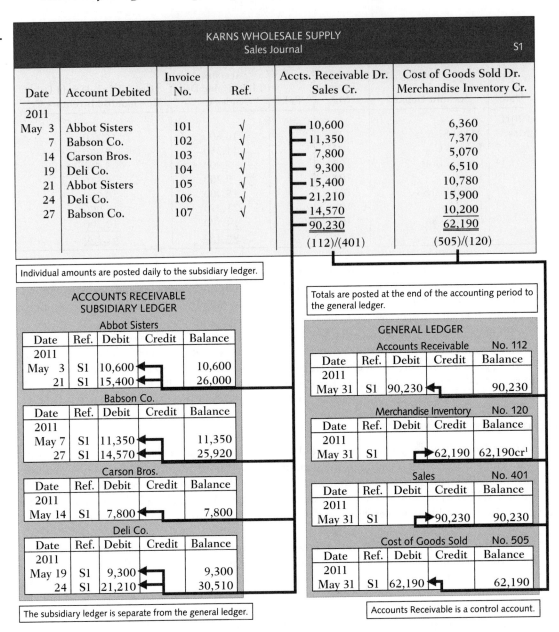

[1] The normal balance for Merchandise Inventory is a debit. But, because of the sequence in which we have posted the special journals, with the sales journal first, the credits to Merchandise Inventory are posted before the debits. This posting sequence explains the credit balance in Merchandise Inventory, which exists only until the other journals are posted.

Proving the Ledgers

The next step is to "prove" the ledgers. To do so, we must determine two things: (1) The sum of the subsidiary ledger balances must equal the balance in the control account. (2) The total of the general ledger debit balances must equal the total of the general ledger credit balances. The proof of the postings from the sales journal to the general and subsidiary ledgers follows:

Accounts Receivable Subsidiary Ledger	
Abbot Sisters	$26,000
Babson Co.	25,920
Carson Bros.	7,800
Deli Co.	30,510
	$90,230

General Ledger	
Debits	
Accounts Receivable	$ 90,230
Cost of Goods Sold	62,190
	$152,420
Credits	
Merchandise Inventory	$ 62,190
Sales	90,230
	$152,420

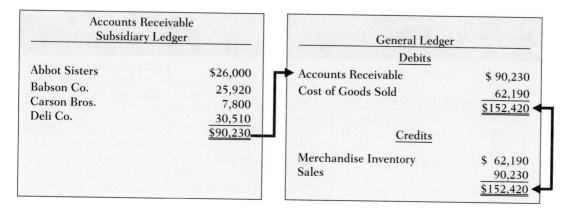

Advantages of the Sales Journal

The use of a special journal to record sales on account has a number of advantages. First, the one-line–two-column entry for each sales transaction saves time. In the sales journal, it is not necessary to write out the four account titles for the two transactions. Second, only totals, rather than individual entries, are posted to the general ledger. This saves posting time and reduces the possibility of errors in posting. Third, the prenumbering of sales invoices helps to ensure that all sales are recorded and that no sale is recorded more than once. Finally, a division of labour results, because the individual responsible for the sales journal does not have to take responsibility for other journals, such as cash receipts. These last two advantages help internal control.

Cash Receipts Journal

All receipts of cash are recorded in the cash receipts journal. The most common types of cash receipts are cash sales of merchandise and collections of accounts receivable. Many other possibilities exist, such as a receipt of money from a bank loan and cash proceeds from disposals of equipment. A one- or two-column cash receipts journal would not have enough space for all possible cash receipt transactions. A multiple-column cash receipts journal is therefore used.

Generally, a cash receipts journal includes the following columns: a debit column for cash, and credit columns for accounts receivable, sales, and other accounts. The Other Accounts column is used when the cash receipt does not involve a cash sale or a collection of accounts receivable. Under a perpetual inventory system, each sales entry is accompanied by another entry that debits Cost of Goods Sold and credits Merchandise Inventory. A separate column is added for this purpose. A five-column cash receipts journal is shown in Illustration C-5.

Additional credit columns may be used if they significantly reduce postings to a specific account. For example, cash receipts from cash sales normally include the collection of sales taxes, which are later remitted to the federal and provincial governments. Most cash receipts journals have a separate credit column for sales tax collections. Other examples include the cash receipts of a loan company, such as Household Financial Centre, which cover thousands of collections from customers. These collections are credited to Loans Receivable and Interest Revenue. A significant saving in posting time would result from using separate credit columns for Loans Receivable and Interest Revenue, rather than using the Other Accounts credit column. In contrast, a retailer that has only one interest collection a month would not find it useful to have a separate column for Interest Revenue.

Illustration C-5 ➔

Cash receipts journal—perpetual inventory system

Helpful hint In a periodic inventory system, the Cash Receipts journal would have one column fewer. The Cost of Goods Sold Dr. and Merchandise Inventory Cr. would not be recorded.

KARNS WHOLESALE SUPPLY
Cash Receipts Journal

CR1

Date	Account Credited	Ref.	Cash Dr.	Accounts Receivable Cr.	Sales Cr.	Cost of Goods Sold Dr. Mdse. Inv. Cr.	Other Accounts Cr.
2011							
May 1	D. Karns, Capital	301	5,000				5,000
7			1,900		1,900	1,240	
10	Abbot Sisters	√	10,600	10,600			
12			2,600		2,600	1,690	
17	Babson Co.	√	11,350	11,350			
22	Notes Payable	200	6,000				6,000
23	Carson Bros.	√	7,800	7,800			
28	Deli Co.	√	9,300	9,300			
			54,550	39,050	4,500	2,930	11,000
			(101)	(112)	(401)	(505)/(120)	(X)

Individual amounts are posted daily to the subsidiary ledger.

Totals are posted at the end of the accounting period to the general ledger.

ACCOUNTS RECEIVABLE
SUBSIDIARY LEDGER

Abbot Sisters

Date	Ref.	Debit	Credit	Balance
2011				
May 3	S1	10,600		10,600
10	CR1		10,600	0
21	S1	15,400		15,400

Babson Co.

Date	Ref.	Debit	Credit	Balance
2011				
May 7	S1	11,350		11,350
17	CR1		11,350	0
27	S1	14,570		14,570

Carson Bros.

Date	Ref.	Debit	Credit	Balance
2011				
May 14	S1	7,800		7,800
23	CR1		7,800	0

Deli Co.

Date	Ref.	Debit	Credit	Balance
2011				
May 19	S1	9,300		9,300
24	S1	21,210		30,510
28	CR1		9,300	21,210

The subsidiary ledger is separate from the general ledger.

Accounts Receivable is a control account.

GENERAL LEDGER

Cash — No. 101

Date	Ref.	Debit	Credit	Balance
2011				
May 31	CR1	54,550		54,550

Accounts Receivable — No. 112

Date	Ref.	Debit	Credit	Balance
2011				
May 31	S1	90,230		90,230
31	CR1		39,050	51,180

Merchandise Inventory — No. 120

Date	Ref.	Debit	Credit	Balance
2011				
May 31	S1		62,190	62,190Cr.
31	CR1		2,930	65,120Cr.

Notes Payable — No. 200

Date	Ref.	Debit	Credit	Balance
2011				
May 22	CR1		6,000	6,000

D. Karns, Capital — No. 301

Date	Ref.	Debit	Credit	Balance
2011				
May 1	CR1		5,000	5,000

Sales — No. 401

Date	Ref.	Debit	Credit	Balance
2011				
May 31	S1		90,230	90,230
31	CR1		4,500	94,730

Cost of Goods Sold — No. 505

Date	Ref.	Debit	Credit	Balance
2011				
May 31	S1	62,190		62,190
31	CR1	2,930		65,120

Journalizing Cash Receipt Transactions

To illustrate the journalizing of cash receipts transactions, we will continue with the May transactions of Karns Wholesale Supply. Collections from customers are for the entries recorded in the sales journal in Illustration C-3. The entries in the cash receipts journal are based on the following cash receipts:

May	1	D. Karns makes an investment of $5,000 in the business.
	7	Cash receipts for merchandise sales total $1,900. The cost of goods sold is $1,240.
	10	A cheque for $10,600 is received from Abbot Sisters in full payment of invoice No. 101.
	12	Cash receipts for merchandise sales total $2,600. The cost of goods sold is $1,690.
	17	A cheque for $11,350 is received from Babson Co. in full payment of invoice No. 102.
	22	Cash is received by signing a 4% note for $6,000, payable September 22 to the National Bank.
	23	A cheque for $7,800 is received from Carson Bros. in full payment of invoice No. 103.
	28	A cheque for $9,300 is received from Deli Co. in full payment of invoice No. 104.

Further information about the columns in the cash receipts journal follows:

Debit Columns:

1. Cash. The amount of cash actually received in each transaction is entered in this column. The column total indicates the total cash receipts for the month. The total of this column is posted to the cash account in the general ledger.
2. Cost of Goods Sold. The Cost of Goods Sold Dr./Merchandise Inventory Cr. column is used to record the cost of the merchandise sold. (The sales column records the selling price of the merchandise.) The cost of goods sold column is similar to the one found in the sales journal. The amount debited to Cost of Goods Sold is the same amount credited to Merchandise Inventory. One column total is posted to both accounts at the end of the month.

Credit Columns:

3. Accounts Receivable. The Accounts Receivable column is used to record cash collections on account. The amount entered here is the amount to be credited to the individual customer's account.
4. Sales. The Sales column is used to record all cash sales of merchandise. Cash sales of other assets (property, plant, and equipment, for example) are not reported in this column. The total of this column is posted to the account Sales.
5. Merchandise Inventory. As noted above, the Cost of Goods Sold Dr./Merchandise Inventory Cr. column is used to record the reduction in the merchandise available for future sale. The amount credited to Merchandise Inventory is the same amount debited to Cost of Goods Sold. One column total is posted to both accounts at the end of the month.
6. Other Accounts. The Other Accounts column is used whenever the credit is not to Accounts Receivable, Sales, or Merchandise Inventory. For example, in the first entry, $5,000 is entered as a credit to D. Karns, Capital. This column is often referred to as the sundry accounts column.

In a multi-column journal, only one line is generally needed for each entry. In some cases, it is useful to add explanatory information, such as the details of the note payable, or to reference supporting documentation, such as invoice numbers if cash sales are invoiced. Note also that the Account Credited column is used to identify both general ledger and subsidiary ledger account titles. The former is shown in the May 1 entry for Karns' investment. The latter is shown in the May 10 entry for the collection from Abbot Sisters.

Debit and credit amounts for each line must be equal. When the journalizing has been completed, the amount columns are totalled. The totals are then compared to prove the equality of debits and credits in the cash receipts journal. Don't forget that the Cost of Goods Sold Dr./Merchandise Inventory Cr. column total represents both a debit and a credit amount. Totalling the columns of a journal and proving the equality of the totals is called footing (adding down) and cross-footing (adding across) a journal.

The proof of the equality of Karns' cash receipts journal is on the following page:

Debit		Credits	
Cash	$54,550	Accounts Receivable	$39,050
Cost of Goods Sold	2,930	Merchandise Inventory	2,930
	$57,480	Sales	4,500
		Other Accounts	11,000
			$57,480

Posting the Cash Receipts Journal

Posting a multi-column journal involves the following steps:

1. All column totals, except for the Other Accounts total, are posted once at the end of the month to the account title specified in the column heading, such as Cash, Accounts Receivable, Sales, Cost of Goods Sold, and Merchandise Inventory. Account numbers are entered below the column totals to show that the amounts have been posted.
2. The total of the Other Accounts column is not posted. Individual amounts that make up the Other Accounts total are posted separately to the general ledger accounts specified in the Account Credited column. See, for example, the credit posting to D. Karns, Capital. The symbol X is inserted below the total for this column to indicate that the amount has not been posted.
3. The individual amounts in a column (Accounts Receivable, in this case) are posted daily to the subsidiary ledger account name specified in the Account Credited column. See, for example, the credit posting of $10,600 to Abbot Sisters.

The abbreviation CR is used in both the subsidiary and general ledgers to identify postings from the cash receipts journal.

Proving the Ledgers

After the posting of the cash receipts journal is completed, it is necessary to prove the ledgers. As shown below, the sum of the subsidiary ledger account balances equals the control account balance. The general ledger totals are also in agreement.

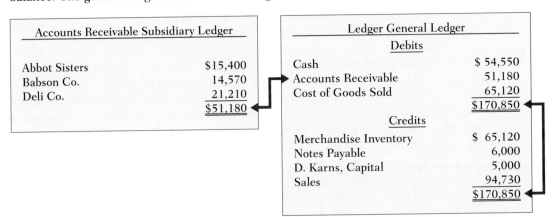

Accounts Receivable Subsidiary Ledger	
Abbot Sisters	$15,400
Babson Co.	14,570
Deli Co.	21,210
	$51,180

Ledger General Ledger	
Debits	
Cash	$ 54,550
Accounts Receivable	51,180
Cost of Goods Sold	65,120
	$170,850
Credits	
Merchandise Inventory	$ 65,120
Notes Payable	6,000
D. Karns, Capital	5,000
Sales	94,730
	$170,850

Purchases Journal

All purchases of merchandise on account are recorded in the purchases journal. Each entry in this journal results in a debit to Merchandise Inventory and a credit to Accounts Payable. When a one-column purchases journal is used, other types of purchases on account and cash purchases cannot be journalized in it. For example, credit purchases of equipment or supplies must be recorded in the general journal. Likewise, all cash purchases are entered in the cash payments journal. If there are many credit purchases for items other than merchandise, the purchases journal can be expanded to a multi-column format.

The purchases journal for Karns Wholesale Supply is shown in Illustration C-6, with assumed credit purchases.

Illustration C-6
Purchases journal— perpetual inventory system

KARNS WHOLESALE SUPPLY
Purchases Journal P1

Date	Account Credited	Terms	Ref.	Merchandise Inventory Dr. Accounts Payable Cr.
2011				
May 6	Jasper Manufacturing Inc.	n/20	√	11,000
10	Eaton and Howe, Inc.	n/20	√	7,200
14	Fabor and Son	n/20	√	6,900
19	Jasper Manufacturing Inc.	n/20	√	17,500
26	Fabor and Son	n/20	√	8,700
28	Eaton and Howe, Inc.	n/20	√	12,600
				63,900
				(120)/(201)

Individual amounts are posted daily to the subsidiary ledger.

Totals are posted at the end of the accounting period to the general ledger.

ACCOUNTS PAYABLE SUBSIDIARY LEDGER

Eaton and Howe, Inc.

Date	Ref.	Debit	Credit	Balance
2011				
May 10	P1		7,200	7,200
28	P1		12,600	19,800

Fabor and Son

Date	Ref.	Debit	Credit	Balance
2011				
May 14	P1		6,900	6,900
26	P1		8,700	15,600

Jasper Manufacturing Inc.

Date	Ref.	Debit	Credit	Balance
2011				
May 6	P1		11,000	11,000
19	P1		17,500	28,500

GENERAL LEDGER

Merchandise Inventory No. 120

Date	Ref.	Debit	Credit	Balance
2011				
May 31	S1		62,190	62,190Cr.
31	CR1		2,930	65,120Cr.
31	P1	63,900		1,220Cr.

Accounts Payable No. 201

Date	Ref.	Debit	Credit	Balance
2011				
May 30	P1		63,900	63,900

Accounts Payable is a control account.

The subsidiary ledger is separate from the general ledger.

Helpful hint When a periodic inventory system is used, this journal is still known as a purchases journal. The debit to the Merchandise Inventory account is replaced by a debit to the Purchases account.

Journalizing Credit Purchases of Merchandise

Entries in the purchases journal are made from purchase invoices. The journalizing procedure for the purchases journal is similar to that for the sales journal. In contrast to the sales journal, the purchases journal may not have an invoice number column, because invoices received from different suppliers would not be in numerical sequence.

Posting the Purchases Journal

The procedures for posting the purchases journal are similar to those for the sales journal. In this case, postings are made daily to the accounts payable subsidiary ledger accounts and monthly to the Merchandise Inventory and Accounts Payable accounts in the general ledger. In both ledgers, P1 is used in the reference column to show that the postings are from page 1 of the purchases journal.

Proof of the equality of the postings from the purchases journal to both ledgers is shown by the following:

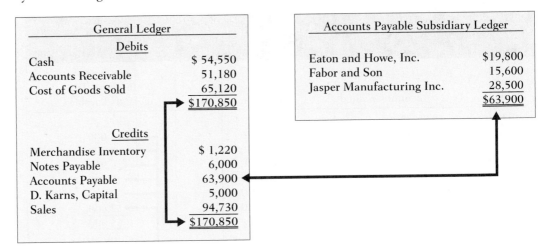

General Ledger	
Debits	
Cash	$ 54,550
Accounts Receivable	51,180
Cost of Goods Sold	65,120
	$170,850
Credits	
Merchandise Inventory	$ 1,220
Notes Payable	6,000
Accounts Payable	63,900
D. Karns, Capital	5,000
Sales	94,730
	$170,850

Accounts Payable Subsidiary Ledger	
Eaton and Howe, Inc.	$19,800
Fabor and Son	15,600
Jasper Manufacturing Inc.	28,500
	$63,900

Note that not all the general ledger accounts listed above have been included in Illustration C-6. You will have to refer to Illustration C-5 to determine the balances for the accounts Cash, Accounts Receivable, Cost of Goods Sold, Notes Payable, Capital, and Sales.

Cash Payments Journal

Alternative terminology The cash payments journal is also called the *cash disbursements journal*.

All disbursements of cash are entered in a cash payments journal. Entries are made from pre-numbered cheques. Because cash payments are made for various purposes, the cash payments journal has multiple columns. A four-column journal is shown in Illustration C-7.

Journalizing Cash Payments Transactions

The procedures for journalizing transactions in this journal are similar to those described earlier for the cash receipts journal. Each transaction is entered on one line, and for each line there must be equal debit and credit amounts. It is common practice in the cash payments journal to record the name of the company or individual receiving the cheque (the payee), so that later reference to the cheque is possible by name in addition to cheque number. The entries in the cash payments journal shown in Illustration C-7 are based on the following transactions for Karns Wholesale Supply:

May 3	Cheque No. 101 for $1,200 issued for the annual premium on a fire insurance policy from Corporate General Insurance.
3	Cheque No. 102 for $100 issued to CANPAR in payment of freight charges on goods purchased.
7	Cheque No. 103 for $4,400 issued for the cash purchase of merchandise from Zwicker Corp.
10	Cheque No. 104 for $11,000 sent to Jasper Manufacturing Inc. in full payment of the May 6 invoice.
19	Cheque No. 105 for $7,200 mailed to Eaton and Howe, Inc., in full payment of the May 10 invoice.
24	Cheque No. 106 for $6,900 sent to Fabor and Son in full payment of the May 14 invoice.
28	Cheque No. 107 for $17,500 sent to Jasper Manufacturing Inc. in full payment of the May 19 invoice.
31	Cheque No. 108 for $500 issued to D. Karns as a cash withdrawal for personal use.

KARNS WHOLESALE SUPPLY
Cash Payments Journal CP1

Date	Cheque No.	Account Credited	Cash Cr.	Mdse. Inventory Dr.	Accounts Payable Dr.	Account Debited	Ref.	Other Accounts Dr.
2011								
May 3	101	Corporate General Ins.	1,200			Prepaid insurance	130	1,200
3	102	CANPAR	100	100				
7	103	Zwicker Corp.	4,400	4,400				
10	104	Jasper Manufacturing Inc.	11,000		11,000	Jasper Manuf. Inc.	√	
19	105	Eaton & Howe, Inc.	7,200		7,200	Eaton & Howe, Inc.	√	
24	106	Fabor & Son	6,900		6,900	Fabor and Son	√	
28	107	Jasper Manufacturing Inc.	17,500		17,500	Jasper Manuf. Inc.	√	
31	108	D. Karns	500			D. Karns, Drawings	310	500
			48,800	4,500	42,600			1,700
			(101)	(120)	(201)			(X)

Individual amounts are posted daily to the subsidiary ledger.

Totals are posted at the end of the accounting period to the general ledger.

ACCOUNTS PAYABLE SUBSIDIARY LEDGER

Eaton and Howe, Inc.

Date	Ref.	Debit	Credit	Balance
2011				
May 10	P1		7,200	7,200
19	CP1	7,200		0
28	P1		12,600	12,600

Fabor and Son

Date	Ref.	Debit	Credit	Balance
2011				
May 14	P1		6,900	6,900
24	CP1	6,900		0
26	P1		8,700	8,700

Jasper Manufacturing Inc.

Date	Ref.	Debit	Credit	Balance
2011				
May 6	P1		11,000	11,000
10	CP1	11,000		0
19	P1		17,500	17,500
28	CP1	17,500		0

The subsidiary ledger is separate from the general ledger.

GENERAL LEDGER

Cash No. 101

Date	Ref.	Debit	Credit	Balance
2011				
May 31	CR1	54,550		54,550
31	CP1		48,800	5,750

Merchandise Inventory No. 120

Date	Ref.	Debit	Credit	Balance
2011				
May 31	S1		62,190	62,190Cr.
31	CR1		2,930	65,120Cr.
31	P1	63,900		1,220Cr.
31	CP1	4,500		3,280

Prepaid Insurance No. 130

Date	Ref.	Debit	Credit	Balance
2011				
May 31	P1	1,200		1,200

Accounts Payable No. 201

Date	Ref.	Debit	Credit	Balance
2011				
May 31	C1		63,900	63,900
31	CP1	42,600		21,300

D. Karns, Drawings No. 310

Date	Ref.	Debit	Credit	Balance
2011				
May 31	CP1	500		500

Accounts Payable is a control account.

Illustration C-7
Cash payments journal—perpetual inventory system

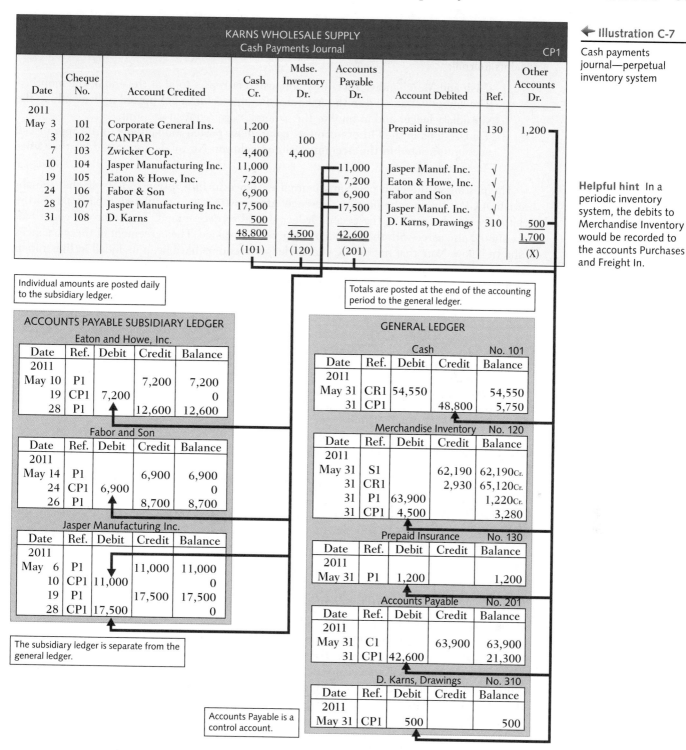

Helpful hint In a periodic inventory system, the debits to Merchandise Inventory would be recorded to the accounts Purchases and Freight In.

Note that whenever an amount is entered in the Other Accounts column, a specific general ledger account must be identified in the Account Debited column. The entries for cheque numbers 101 and 108 show this situation. Similarly, a subsidiary account must be identified in the Account Debited column whenever an amount is entered in the Accounts Payable column (as, for example, the entry for cheque no. 104).

After the cash payments journal has been journalized, the columns are totalled. The totals are then balanced to prove the equality of debits and credits. Debits ($4,500 + $42,600 + $1,700 = $48,800) do equal credits ($48,800) in this case.

Posting the Cash Payments Journal

Helpful hint If a company has a subsidiary ledger for merchandise inventory, amounts in the merchandise inventory column would be posted daily in the cash payments journal, as well as in the sales, cash receipts, and purchases journals.

The procedures for posting the cash payments journal are similar to those for the cash receipts journal:

1. Cash and Merchandise Inventory are posted only as a total at the end of the month.
2. The amounts recorded in the Accounts Payable column are posted individually to the subsidiary ledger and in total to the general ledger control account.
3. Transactions in the Other Accounts column are posted individually to the appropriate account(s) noted in the Account Debited column. No totals are posted for the Other Accounts column.

The posting of the cash payments journal is shown in Illustration C-7. Note that the abbreviation CP is used as the posting reference. After postings are completed, the equality of the debit and credit balances in the general ledger should be determined. The control account balance should also agree with the subsidiary ledger total balance. The agreement of these balances is shown below. Note that not all the general ledger accounts have been included in Illustration C-7. You will also have to refer to Illustration C-5 to determine the balances for the Accounts Receivable, Cost of Goods Sold, Notes Payable, Capital, and Sales accounts.

General Ledger	
Debits	
Cash	$ 5,750
Accounts Receivable	51,180
Merchandise Inventory	3,280
Prepaid Insurance	1,200
D. Karns, Drawings	500
Cost of Goods Sold	65,120
	$127,030
Credits	
Accounts Payable	$21,300
Notes Payable	6,000
D. Karns, Capital	5,000
Sales	94,730
	$127,030

Accounts Payable Subsidiary Ledger	
Eaton and Howe, Inc.	$12,600
Fabor and Son	8,700
	$21,300

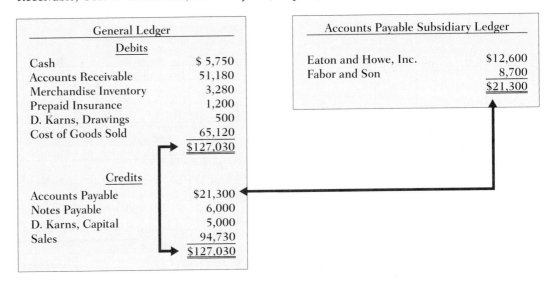

Effects of Special Journals on the General Journal

Special journals for sales, purchases, and cash greatly reduce the number of entries that are made in the general journal. Only transactions that cannot be entered in a special journal are recorded in the general journal. For example, the general journal may be used to record a transaction granting credit to a customer for a sales return or allowance. It may also be used to record the receipt of a credit from a supplier for purchases returned, the acceptance of a note receivable from a customer, and the purchase of equipment by issuing a note payable. Correcting, adjusting, and closing entries are also made in the general journal.

When control and subsidiary accounts are not used, the procedures for journalizing and posting transactions in the general journal are the same as those described in earlier chapters. When control and subsidiary accounts are used, two modifications of earlier procedures are required:

1. In journalizing, both the control and the subsidiary account must be identified.
2. In posting, there must be a dual posting: once to the control account and once to the subsidiary account.

To illustrate, assume that on May 31 Karns Wholesale Supply returns $500 of merchandise for credit to Fabor and Son. The entry in the general journal and the posting of the entry are shown in Illustration C-8. Note that if cash had been received instead of the credit granted on this return, then the transaction would have been recorded in the cash receipts journal.

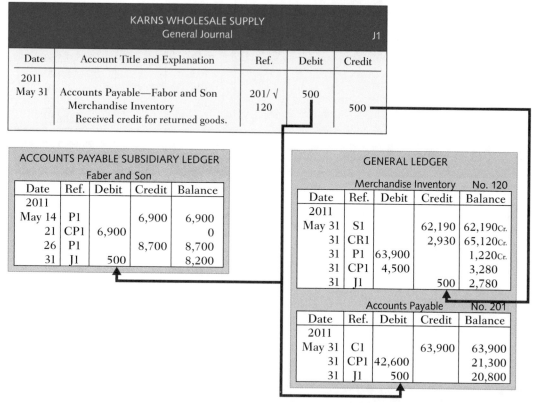

Illustration C-8
General journal

KARNS WHOLESALE SUPPLY
General Journal
J1

Date	Account Title and Explanation	Ref.	Debit	Credit
2011				
May 31	Accounts Payable—Fabor and Son	201/ √	500	
	Merchandise Inventory	120		500
	Received credit for returned goods.			

ACCOUNTS PAYABLE SUBSIDIARY LEDGER

Faber and Son

Date	Ref.	Debit	Credit	Balance
2011				
May 14	P1		6,900	6,900
21	CP1	6,900		0
26	P1		8,700	8,700
31	J1	500		8,200

GENERAL LEDGER

Merchandise Inventory No. 120

Date	Ref.	Debit	Credit	Balance
2011				
May 31	S1		62,190	62,190Cr.
31	CR1		2,930	65,120Cr.
31	P1	63,900		1,220Cr.
31	CP1	4,500		3,280
31	J1		500	2,780

Accounts Payable No. 201

Date	Ref.	Debit	Credit	Balance
2011				
May 31	C1		63,900	63,900
31	CP1	42,600		21,300
31	J1	500		20,800

Helpful hint In a periodic inventory system, the credit would be to the Purchase Returns and Allowances account rather than to Merchandise Inventory.

Notice that in the general journal two accounts are indicated for the debit (the Accounts Payable control account and the Fabor and Son subsidiary account). Two postings (201/√) are indicated in the reference column. One amount is posted to the control account in the general ledger (no. 201) and the other to the creditor's account in the subsidiary ledger (Fabor and Son).

Special Journals in a Periodic Inventory System

Recording and posting transactions in special journals is essentially the same whether a perpetual or a periodic inventory system is used. But there are two differences. The first difference relates to the accounts Merchandise Inventory and Cost of Goods Sold in a perpetual inventory system. In this system, an additional column is required to record the cost of each sale in the sales and cash receipts journals, something which is not required in a periodic inventory system.

The second difference concerns the account titles used. In a perpetual inventory system, Merchandise Inventory and Cost of Goods Sold are used to record purchases and the cost of the merchandise sold. In a periodic inventory system, the accounts Purchases and Freight In accumulate the cost of the merchandise purchased until the end of the period. No cost of goods sold is recorded during the period. Cost of goods sold is calculated at the end of the period in a periodic inventory system.

Each of the special journals illustrated in this appendix is shown again here. Using the same transactions, we assume that Karns Wholesale Supply uses a periodic inventory system instead of a perpetual inventory system.

Illustration C-9

Sales journal—periodic inventory system

Helpful hint Compare this sales journal to the one presented in Illustration C-4.

KARNS WHOLESALE SUPPLY
Sales Journal S1

Date	Account Debited	Invoice No.	Ref.	Accts Receivable Dr. Sales Cr.
2011				
May 3	Abbot Sisters	101	√	10,600
7	Babson Co.	102	√	11,350
14	Carson Bros.	103	√	7,800
19	Deli Co.	104	√	9,300
21	Abbot Sisters	105	√	15,400
24	Deli Co.	106	√	21,210
27	Babson Co.	107	√	14,570
				90,230

Illustration C-10

Cash receipts journal—periodic inventory system

Helpful hint Compare this cash receipts journal to the one presented in Illustration C-5.

KARNS WHOLESALE SUPPLY
Cash Receipts Journal CR1

Date	Account Credited	Ref.	Cash Dr.	Accounts Receivable Cr.	Sales Cr.	Other Accounts Cr.
2011						
May 1	D. Karns, Capital	301	5,000			5,000
7			1,900		1,900	
10	Abbot Sisters	√	10,600	10,600		
12			2,600		2,600	
17	Babson Co.	√	11,350	11,350		
22	Notes Payable	200	6,000			6,000
23	Carson Bros.	√	7,800	7,800		
28	Deli Co.	√	9,300	9,300		
			54,550	39,050	4,500	11,000

Illustration C-11

Purchases journal—periodic inventory system

Helpful hint Compare this purchases journal to the one presented in Illustration C-6.

KARNS WHOLESALE SUPPLY
Purchases Journal P1

Date	Account Credited	Terms	Ref.	Purchases Dr. Accounts Payable Cr.
2011				
May 6	Jasper Manufacturing Inc.	n/20	√	11,000
10	Eaton and Howe, Inc.	n/20	√	7,200
14	Fabor and Son	n/20	√	6,900
19	Jasper Manufacturing Inc.	n/20	√	17,500
26	Fabor and Son	n/20	√	8,700
28	Eaton and Howe, Inc.	n/20	√	12,600
				63,900

Illustration C-12

Cash payments journal—periodic inventory system

Helpful hint Compare this cash payments journal to the one presented in Illustration C-7.

KARNS WHOLESALE SUPPLY
Cash Payments Journal CP1

Date	Cheque No.	Payee	Cash Cr.	Accounts Payable Dr.	Account Debited	Ref.	Other Accounts Dr.
2011							
May 3	101	Corporate General Ins.	1,200		Prepaid Insurance	130	1,200
3	102	CANPAR	100		Freight In	516	100
7	103	Zwicker Corp.	4,400		Purchases	510	4,400
10	104	Jasper Manufacturing Inc.	11,000	11,000	Jasper Manuf. Inc.	√	
19	105	Eaton & Howe, Inc.	7,200	7,200	Eaton & Howe, Inc.	√	
24	106	Fabor and Son	6.900	6,900	Fabor and Son	√	
28	107	Jasper Manufacturing Inc.	17,500	17,500	Jasper Manuf. Inc.	√	
31	108	D. Karns	500		D. Karns, Drawings	310	500
			48,800	42,600			6,200

Brief Exercises

BEC–1 Information related to Bryan Company is presented below for its first month of operations. Calculate (a) the balances that appear in the accounts receivable subsidiary ledger for each customer, and (b) the accounts receivable balance that appears in the general ledger at the end of January.

Calculate subsidiary ledger and control account balances.

Credit Sales			Cash Collections		
Jan. 7	McNeil Co.	$800	Jan. 17	McNeil Co.	$700
15	Hanson Inc.	6,000	24	Hanson Inc.	5,000
23	Lewis Co.	9,500	29	Lewis Co.	9,500

BEC–2 Identify in which ledger (general or subsidiary) each of the following accounts is shown:

Identify general and subsidiary ledger accounts.

1. Rent Expense
2. Accounts Receivable—Chen
3. Notes Payable
4. Service Revenue
5. Wages Payable
6. Accounts Payable—Kerns
7. Merchandise Inventory
8. Sales

BEC–3 Chiasson Co. uses special journals and a general journal. Identify the journal in which each of the following transactions is recorded:

Identify special journals.

1. Paid cash for equipment purchased on account.
2. Purchased merchandise on credit.
3. Paid utility expense in cash.
4. Sold merchandise on account.
5. Granted a cash refund for a sales return.
6. Received a credit on account for a purchase return.
7. Sold merchandise for cash.
8. Purchased merchandise for cash.
9. Received a collection on account.
10. Recorded depreciation on vehicles

BEC–4 Swirsky Company uses the cash receipts and cash payments journals illustrated in this appendix for a perpetual inventory system. In October, the following selected cash transactions occurred:

Identify special journals—perpetual inventory system.

1. Made a refund to a customer for the return of damaged goods that had been purchased on credit.
2. Received payment from a customer.
3. Purchased merchandise for cash.
4. Paid a creditor.
5. Paid freight on merchandise purchased.
6. Paid cash for office equipment.
7. Received a cash refund from a supplier for merchandise returned.
8. Withdrew cash for personal use of owner.
9. Made cash sales.

Instructions

Indicate (a) the journal, and (b) the columns in the journal that should be used in recording each transaction.

BEC–5 Identify the journal and the specific column title(s) in which each of the following transactions is recorded. Assume the company uses a periodic inventory system.

Identify special journals—periodic inventory system.

1. Cash sale
2. Credit sale
3. Sales return on account
4. Cash purchase of merchandise

5. Credit purchase of merchandise
6. Payment of freight on merchandise purchased from a supplier
7. Return of merchandise purchased for cash refund
8. Payment of freight on merchandise delivered to a customer

Use general journal for closing entries.

BEC–6 Willis Company has the following year-end account balances on September 30, 2011: Service Revenue $53,800; Salaries Expense $15,400; Rent Expense $12,000; Supplies Expense $3,500; B. Willis, Capital $67,000; and B. Willis, Drawings $22,000.

Instructions

Prepare the closing entries for Willis Company.

Use general journal for adjusting entry.

BEC–7 As part of the year-end procedures, depreciation for furniture was recorded in the amount of $2,500 for Leelantna Company. Prepare the adjusting entry dated October 31, 2011, using the appropriate journal.

Exercises

Identify special journals.

EC–1 Below are some transactions for Dartmouth Company:

1. Credit received for merchandise returned to a supplier
2. Payment of employee wages
3. Revenues and expenses closed to income summary
4. Depreciation on building
5. Purchase of office supplies for cash
6. Purchase of merchandise on account
7. Purchase of equipment for cash
8. Payment on account
9. Return of merchandise sold for credit
10. Collection on account from customers
11. Sale of land for cash
12. Sale of merchandise on account
13. Sale of merchandise for cash

Instructions

For each transaction, indicate whether it would normally be recorded in a cash receipts journal, cash payments journal, sales journal, purchases journal, or general journal.

Record transactions in sales and purchases journals—perpetual inventory system.

EC–2 Sing Tao Company uses special journals and a general journal. The company uses a perpetual inventory system and had the following transactions:

Sept. 2 Sold merchandise on account to T. Lu, $1,520, invoice #101, terms n/30. The cost of the merchandise sold was $960.
3 Purchased office supplies on account from Berko Co., $350.
10 Purchased merchandise on account from Lavigne Co., $800, FOB shipping point, terms n/30. Paid freight of $50 to Apex Shippers.
11 Returned unsatisfactory merchandise to Lavigne Co., $200, for credit on account.
12 Purchased office equipment on account from Wells Co., $8,000.
16 Sold merchandise for cash to L. Maille, for $800. The cost of the merchandise sold was $480.
18 Purchased merchandise for cash from Lavigne Co., $450, FOB destination.
20 Accepted returned merchandise from customer L. Maille, $800 (see Sept. 16 transaction). Gave full cash refund. Restored the merchandise to inventory.

Sept. 24 Paid the correct amount owing for the merchandise purchased from Lavigne earlier in the month.
25 Received payment from T. Lu for Sept. 2 sale.
26 Sold merchandise on account to M. Christie, $890, invoice #102, terms n/30, FOB destination. The cost of the merchandise was $520. The appropriate party paid $75 to Freight Co. for shipping charges.
30 Paid September salaries, $2,800.
30 Withdrew cash for owner's personal use, $800.
30 Paid for office supplies purchased on September 3.

Instructions

(a) Draw a sales journal and a purchases journal (see Illustrations C-3 and C-6). Use page 1 for each journal.
(b) Record the transaction(s) for September that should be recorded in the sales journal.
(c) Record the transaction(s) for September that should be recorded in the purchases journal.

EC–3 Refer to the information provided for Sing Tao Company in EC–2.

Record transactions in cash receipts, cash payments, and general journals—perpetual inventory system.

Instructions

(a) Draw cash receipts and cash payments journals (see Illustrations C-5 and C-7) and a general journal. Use page 1 for each journal.
(b) Record the transaction(s) provided in EC–2 that should be recorded in the cash receipts journal.
(c) Record the transaction(s) provided in EC–2 that should be recorded in the cash payments journal.
(d) Record the transaction(s) provided in EC–2 that should be recorded in the general journal.

EC–4 Narang Company has the following selected transactions during March:

Record transactions in general journal and explain posting.

Mar. 2 Purchased equipment on account, costing $7,400, from Lifetime Inc.
5 Received credit memorandum for $300 from Lyden Company for merchandise returned that had been damaged in shipment to Narang.
7 Issued a credit memorandum for $400 to Marco Presti for merchandise the customer returned. The returned merchandise has a cost of $275 and was restored to inventory.

Narang Company uses a purchases journal, a sales journal, two cash journals (receipts and payments), and a general journal. Narang also uses a perpetual inventory system.

Instructions

(a) Record the appropriate transactions in the general journal.
(b) In a brief memo to the president of Narang Company, explain the postings to the control and subsidiary accounts.

EC–5 Maureen Company uses both special journals and a general journal. On April 30, after all monthly postings had been completed, the Accounts Receivable control account in the general ledger had a debit balance of $320,000, and the Accounts Payable control account had a credit balance of $87,000.

Determine control account balances and explain posting.

The May transactions recorded in the special journals are summarized below. Maureen Company maintains a perpetual inventory system. No entries that affected accounts receivable and accounts payable were recorded in the general journal for May.

Sales journal: total sales, $161,400; cost of goods sold, $112,800
Purchases journal: total purchases, $56,400
Cash receipts journal: accounts receivable column total, $141,000
Cash payments journal: accounts payable column total, $47,500

Instructions

(a) What is the balance of the Accounts Receivable control account after the monthly postings on May 31?
(b) What is the balance of the Accounts Payable control account after the monthly postings on May 31?
(c) To what accounts are the column totals for total sales of $161,400 and cost of goods sold of $112,800 in the sales journal posted?
(d) To what account(s) is the accounts receivable column total of $141,000 in the cash receipts journal posted?

Record transactions in sales and purchases journals—periodic inventory system.

EC–6 Refer to the information provided for Sing Tao Company in EC–2. Complete instructions (a), (b), and (c), assuming that the company uses a periodic inventory system instead of a perpetual inventory system.

Post journals to control and subsidiary accounts.

EC–7 On September 1, the balance of the Accounts Receivable control account in the general ledger of Pirie Company was $10,960. The customers' subsidiary ledger contained account balances as follows: Jana, $2,440; Kingston, $2,640; Cavanaugh, $2,060; Zhang, $3,820. At the end of September, the various journals contained the following information:

Sales journal: Sales to Zhang, $800; to Jana, $1,260; to Iman, $1,030; to Cavanaugh, $1,100. The cost of each sale, respectively, was $480, $810, $620, and $660.
Cash receipts journal: Cash received from Cavanaugh, $1,310; from Zhang, $2,300; from Iman, $380; from Kingston, $1,800; from Jana, $1,240.
General journal: A $190 sales allowance is granted to Zhang, on September 30.

Instructions

(a) Set up control and subsidiary accounts, and enter the beginning balances.
(b) Post the various journals to the control and subsidiary accounts. Post the items as individual items or as totals, whichever would be the appropriate procedure. Use page 1 for each journal.
(c) Prepare a list of customers and prove the agreement of the control account with the subsidiary ledger at September 30.

Record transactions in cash receipts, cash payments, and general journals—periodic inventory system.

EC–8 Refer to the information provided for Sing Tao Company in EC–3. Complete instructions (a) to (d), assuming that the company uses a periodic inventory system instead of a perpetual inventory system.

Problems

Record transactions in special and general journals—perpetual inventory system.

PC–1 Selected accounts from the chart of accounts of Genstar Company are shown below:

101 Cash	201 Accounts payable
112 Accounts receivable	401 Sales
120 Merchandise inventory	412 Sales returns and allowances
126 Supplies	505 Cost of goods sold
157 Equipment	726 Salaries expense

The company uses a perpetual inventory system. The cost of all merchandise sold is 60% of the sales price. During January, Genstar completed the following transactions:

Jan. 3 Purchased merchandise on account from Sun Distributors, $9,800.
4 Purchased supplies for cash, $280.
4 Sold merchandise on account to R. Hu, $6,500, invoice no. 371.
5 Returned $450 of damaged goods to Sun Distributors.
6 Made cash sales for the week totalling $4,650.
8 Purchased merchandise on account from Irvine Co., $5,400.

Jan. 9 Sold merchandise on account to Mays Corp., $5,600, invoice no. 372.
11 Purchased merchandise on account from Chaparal Co., $4,300.
13 Paid Sun Distributors account in full.
13 Made cash sales for the week totalling $5,290.
15 Received payment from Mays Corp. for invoice no. 372.
15 Paid semi-monthly salaries of $14,300 to employees.
17 Received payment from R. Hu for invoice no. 371.
17 Sold merchandise on account to AMB Co., $1,500, invoice no. 373.
19 Purchased equipment on account from Johnson Corp., $4,800.
20 Cash sales for the week totalled $3,400.
20 Paid Irvine Co. account in full.
23 Purchased merchandise on account from Sun Distributors, $7,800.
24 Purchased merchandise on account from Levine Corp., $4,690.
27 Made cash sales for the week totalling $3,370.
30 Received payment from AMB Co. for invoice no. 373.
31 Paid semi-monthly salaries of $13,200 to employees.
31 Sold merchandise on account to R. Hu, $9,330, invoice no. 374.

Genstar Company uses a sales journal, a purchases journal, a cash receipts journal, a cash payments journal, and a general journal.

Instructions

(a) Record the January transactions in the appropriate journal.
(b) Foot and cross-foot all special journals.
(c) Show how postings would be made by placing ledger account numbers and check marks as needed in the journals. (Actual posting to ledger accounts is not required.)

PC–2 Selected accounts from the chart of accounts of Tigau Company are shown below:

Record transactions in special and general journals—perpetual inventory system.

101	Cash	145	Buildings
112	Accounts receivable	201	Accounts payable
120	Merchandise inventory	401	Sales
126	Supplies	505	Cost of goods sold
140	Land	610	Advertising expense

The company uses a perpetual inventory system. The cost of all merchandise sold was 65% of the sales price. During October, Tigau Company completed the following transactions:

Oct. 2 Purchased merchandise on account from Madison Co., $5,800.
4 Sold merchandise on account to Petro Corp., $8,600, invoice no. 204.
5 Purchased supplies for cash, $315.
7 Made cash sales for the week that totalled $9,610.
9 Paid the Madison Co. account in full.
10 Purchased merchandise on account from Quinn Corp., $4,900.
12 Received payment from Petro Corp. for invoice no. 204.
13 Issued a debit memorandum to Quinn Corp. and returned $260 of damaged goods.
14 Made cash sales for the week that totalled $8,810.
16 Sold a parcel of land for $45,000 cash, the land's book value.
17 Sold merchandise on account to Martin Co., $5,530, invoice no. 205.
18 Purchased merchandise for cash, $2,215.
21 Made cash sales for the week that totalled $8,640.
23 Paid in full the Quinn Corp. account for the goods kept.
25 Purchased supplies on account from Frey Co., $260.
25 Sold merchandise on account to Golden Corp., $5,520, invoice no. 206.
25 Received payment from Martin Co. for invoice no. 205.
26 Purchased for cash a small parcel of land and a building on the land to use as a storage facility. The total cost of $45,000 was allocated $26,000 to the land and $19,000 to the building.

Oct. 27 Purchased merchandise on account from Schmid Co., $9,000.
28 Made cash sales for the week that totalled $9,320.
30 Purchased merchandise on account from Madison Co., $16,200.
30 Paid advertising bill for the month from The Gazette, $600.
30 Sold merchandise on account to Martin Co., $5,200, invoice no. 207.

Tigau Company uses a sales journal, purchases journal, cash receipts journal, cash payments journal, and general journal.

Instructions

(a) Record the October transactions in the appropriate journals.
(b) Foot and cross-foot all special journals.
(c) Show how postings would be made by placing ledger account numbers and check marks as needed in the journals. (Actual posting to ledger accounts is not required.)

Record transactions in special and general journals—perpetual inventory system.

PC–3 The post-closing trial balance for Gibbs Music Co. follows:

GIBBS MUSIC CO.
Post-Closing Trial Balance
December 31, 2010

	Debit	Credit
101 Cash	$ 49,500	
112 Accounts receivable	15,000	
115 Notes receivable	45,000	
120 Merchandise inventory	22,000	
140 Land	25,000	
145 Building	75,000	
146 Accumulated depreciation—building		$ 18,000
157 Equipment	6,450	
158 Accumulated depreciation—equipment		1,500
200 Notes payable		–
201 Accounts payable		42,000
275 Mortgage payable		82,000
301 M. Gibbs, capital		94,450
310 M. Gibbs, drawings	–	
401 Sales	–	
410 Sales returns and allowances	–	
505 Cost of goods sold	–	
725 Salaries expense	–	
920 Loss—damaged inventory	–	
	$237,950	$237,950

The subsidiary ledgers contain the following information:

1. Accounts Receivable—R. Goge, $3,000; B. Zerrs, $7,500; S. Armstrong, $4,500
2. Accounts Payable—Fieldstone Corp., $9,000; Watson & Co., $17,000; Harms Distributors, $16,000

Gibbs Music Co. uses a perpetual inventory system. The transactions for January 2011 are as follows:

Jan. 3 Sold merchandise to B. Rohl, $1,000. The cost of goods sold was $550.
5 Purchased merchandise from Warren Parts, $2,400.
7 Received a cheque from S. Armstrong, $3,000, in partial payment of its account.
11 Paid freight on merchandise purchased, $350.
13 Received payment of account in full from B. Rohl.
14 Issued a credit memo to acknowledge receipt of $600 of damaged merchandise returned by R. Goge. The cost of the returned merchandise was $250. (*Hint*: Debit Loss—Damaged Inventory instead of Merchandise Inventory.)

Jan. 15 Sent Harms Distributors a cheque in full payment of account.
17 Purchased merchandise from Lapeska Co., $1,900.
18 Paid salaries of $3,700.
20 Gave Watson & Co. a 60-day note for $17,000 in full payment of account payable.
23 Total cash sales amounted to $8,200. The cost of goods sold was $3,840.
24 Sold merchandise on account to B. Zerrs, $7,800. The cost of goods sold was $3,300.
27 Sent Warren Parts a cheque for $950 in partial payment of the account.
29 Received payment on a note of $35,000 from S. Lava.
30 Returned merchandise costing $600 to Lapeska Co. for credit.
31 Withdrew $1,800 cash for personal use.

Instructions

(a) Open general and subsidiary ledger accounts and record December 31, 2010, balances.
(b) Record the January transactions in a sales journal, a purchases journal, a cash receipts journal, a cash payments journal, and a general journal, as illustrated in this appendix.
(c) Post the appropriate amounts to the subsidiary and general ledger accounts.
(d) Prepare a trial balance at January 31, 2011.
(e) Determine whether the subsidiary ledgers agree with control accounts in the general ledger.

PC–4 The post-closing trial balance for Lee Co. follows:

Record transactions in special and general journals, post, and prepare trial balance—perpetual inventory system.

LEE CO.
Post-Closing Trial Balance
April 30, 2011

	Debit	Credit
101 Cash	$ 36,700	
112 Accounts receivable	15,400	
115 Notes receivable—Cole Company	48,000	
120 Merchandise inventory	22,000	
157 Equipment	8,200	
158 Accumulated depreciation—equipment		$ 1,800
200 Notes payable	–	
201 Accounts payable		43,400
301 C. Lee, capital		85,100
310 C. Lee, drawings	–	
401 Sales		–
410 Sales returns and allowances	–	
505 Cost of goods sold	–	
725 Salaries expense	–	
730 Rent expense	–	
	$130,300	$130,300

The subsidiary ledgers contain the following information:

1. Accounts Receivable—W. Karasch, $3,250; L. Cellars, $7,400; G. Parrish, $4,750
2. Accounts Payable—Winterware Corp., $10,500; Cobalt Sports, $15,500; Buttercup Distributors, $17,400

Lee uses a perpetual inventory system. The transactions for May 2011 are as follows:

May 3 Sold merchandise to B. Simone, $2,400. The cost of the goods sold was $1,050.
5 Purchased merchandise from WN Widgit, $2,600, on account.
7 Received a cheque from G. Parrish, $2,800, in partial payment of account.
11 Paid freight on merchandise purchased, $318.
12 Paid rent of $1,500 for May.
13 Received payment in full from B. Simone.
14 Issued a credit memo to acknowledge $750 of merchandise returned by W. Karasch. The merchandise (original cost, $325) was restored to inventory.

May 15 Sent Buttercup Distributors a cheque in full payment of account.
17 Purchased merchandise from Lancio Co., $2,100, on account.
18 Paid salaries of $4,700.
20 Gave Cobalt Sports a two-month, 10% note for $15,500 in full payment of account payable.
20 Returned merchandise costing $510 to Lancio for credit.
23 Total cash sales amounted to $9,500. The cost of goods sold was $4,450.
27 Sent WN Widgit a cheque for $1,000, in partial payment of account.
29 Received payment on a note of $40,000 from Cole Company.
31 C. Lee withdrew $1,000 cash for personal use.

Instructions

(a) Open general and subsidiary ledger accounts and record April 30, 2011, balances.
(b) Record the May transactions in a sales journal, a purchases journal, a cash receipts journal, a cash payments journal, and a general journal, as illustrated in this chapter.
(c) Post the appropriate amounts to the subsidiary and general ledger accounts.
(d) Prepare a trial balance at May 31, 2011.
(e) Determine whether the subsidiary ledgers agree with the control accounts in the general ledger.

Record transactions in special and general journals—periodic inventory system.

PC–5 Selected accounts from the chart of accounts on Weir Company are shown below:

101	Cash	401	Sales
112	Accounts receivable	412	Sales returns and allowances
126	Supplies	510	Purchases
157	Equipment	512	Purchase returns and allowances
201	Accounts payable	726	Salaries expense

During February, Weir completed the following transactions:

Feb. 3 Purchased merchandise on account from Zears Co., $9,200.
4 Purchased supplies for cash, $290.
4 Sold merchandise on account to Gilles Co., $7,220, invoice no. 371.
5 Issued a debit memorandum to Zears Co. and returned $450 worth of goods.
6 Made cash sales for the week totalling $3,950.
8 Purchased merchandise on account from Fell Electronics, $5,200,
9 Sold merchandise on account to Mawani Corp., $7,050, invoice no. 372.
11 Purchased merchandise on account from Thomas Co., $3,100.
13 Paid Zears Co. account in full.
13 Made cash sales for the week totalling $4,850.
15 Received payment from Mawani Corp. for invoice no. 372.
15 Paid semi-monthly salaries of $14,700 to employees.
17 Received payment from Gilles Co. for invoice no. 371.
17 Sold merchandise on account to Lumber Co., $1,600, invoice no. 373.
19 Purchased equipment on account from Brown Corp., $6,400.
20 Cash sales for the week totalled $4,900.
20 Paid Fell Electronics account in full.
23 Purchased merchandise on account from Zears Co., $8,800.
24 Purchased merchandise on account from Lewis Co., $5,130.
27 Made cash sales for the week totalling $3,560.
28 Received payment from Lumber Co. for invoice no. 373.
28 Paid semi-monthly salaries of $14,900 to employees.
28 Sold merchandise on account to Gilles Co., $9,810, invoice no. 374.

Weir Company uses a sales journal, purchases journal, cash receipts journal, cash payments journal, and general journal. Weir uses a periodic inventory system.

Instructions

(a) Record the February transactions in the appropriate journal.
(b) Foot and cross-foot all special journals.
(c) Show how postings would be made by placing ledger account numbers and check marks as needed in the journals. (Actual posting to ledger accounts is not required.)

Cumulative Coverage—Chapters 2 to 6 and Appendix C

LeBrun Company has the following opening account balances in its general and subsidiary ledgers on January 1. All accounts have normal debit and credit balances. LeBrun uses a perpetual inventory system. The cost of all merchandise sold was 40% of the sales price.

GENERAL LEDGER

Account No.	Account Title	January 1 Opening Balance
101	Cash	$ 35,050
112	Accounts receivable	14,000
115	Notes receivable	39,000
120	Merchandise inventory	20,000
125	Office supplies	1,000
130	Prepaid insurance	2,000
140	Land	50,000
145	Building	100,000
146	Accumulated depreciation—building	25,000
157	Equipment	6,450
158	Accumulated depreciation—equipment	1,500
201	Accounts payable	36,000
275	Mortgage payable	125,000
301	A. LeBrun, capital	80,000

Accounts Receivable Subsidiary Ledger

Customer	January 1 Opening Balance
R. Draves	$1,500
B. Jacovetti	7,500
S. Kysely	5,000

Accounts Payable Subsidiary Ledger

Creditor	January 1 Opening Balance
Liazuk Co.	$10,000
Mikush Bros.	15,000
Nguyen & Son	11,000

LeBrun's January transactions follow:

Jan. 3 Sold merchandise on credit to B. Sota $3,100, invoice no. 510, and J. Ebel $1,800, invoice no. 511.
5 Purchased merchandise on account from Welz Wares for $3,000 and Laux Supplies for $2,700.
7 Received cheques for $5,000 from S. Kysely and $2,000 from B. Jacovetti on accounts.
8 Paid freight on merchandise purchased, $180.
9 Sent cheques to Liazuk Co. for $10,000 and Nguyen & Son for $11,000 in full payment of accounts.
9 Issued credit memo for $400 to J. Ebel for merchandise returned. The merchandise was restored to inventory.
10 Summary cash sales totalled $16,500.

Jan. 11 Sold merchandise on credit to R. Draves for $1,900, invoice no. 512, and to S. Kysely for $900, invoice no. 513.

15 Withdrew $2,000 cash for A. LeBrun's personal use.

16 Purchased merchandise on account from Nguyen & Son for $15,000, from Liazuk Co. for $13,900, and from Welz Wares for $1,500.

17 Paid $400 cash for office supplies.

18 Returned $500 of merchandise to Liazuk and received credit.

20 Summary cash sales totalled $17,500.

21 Issued $15,000 note to Mikush Bros. in payment of balance due. The note bears an interest rate of 10% and is due in three months.

21 Received payment in full from S. Kysely.

22 Sold merchandise on credit to B. Soto for $1,700, invoice no. 514, and to R. Draves for $800, invoice no. 515.

23 Sent cheques to Nguyen & Son and Liazuk Co. in full payment of accounts.

25 Sold merchandise on credit to B. Jacovetti for $3,500, invoice no. 516, and to J. Ebel for $6,100, invoice no. 517.

27 Purchased merchandise on account from Nguyen & Son for $14,500, from Laux Supplies for $1,200, and from Welz Wares for $2,800.

28 Paid $800 cash for office supplies.

31 Summary cash sales totalled $19,920.

31 Paid sales salaries of $4,300 and office salaries of $2,600.

31 Received payment in full from B. Soto and J. Ebel on account.

In addition to the accounts identified in the trial balance, the chart of accounts shows the following: No. 200 Notes Payable, No. 230 Interest Payable, No. 300 Income Summary, No. 310 A. LeBrun, Drawings, No. 401 Sales, No. 410 Sales Returns and Allowances, No. 505 Cost of Goods Sold, No. 711 Depreciation Expense, No. 718 Interest Expense, No. 722 Insurance Expense, No. 725 Salaries Expense, and No. 728 Office Supplies Expense.

Instructions

(a) Record the January transactions in the appropriate journal—sales, purchases, cash receipts, cash payments, and general.

(b) Post the journals to the general and subsidiary ledgers. New accounts should be added and numbered in an orderly fashion as needed.

(c) Prepare an unadjusted trial balance at January 31, 2011. Determine whether the subsidiary ledgers agree with the control accounts in the general ledger.

(d) Prepare adjusting journal entries. Prepare an adjusted trial balance, using the following additional information:

1. Office supplies at January 31 total $700.
2. Insurance coverage expires on September 30, 2011.
3. Annual depreciation on the building is $6,000 and on the equipment is $1,500.
4. Interest of $45 has accrued on the note payable.
5. A physical count of merchandise inventory has found $44,850 of goods on hand.

(e) Prepare a multiple-step income statement and a statement of owner's equity for January, and a classified balance sheet at the end of January.

(f) Prepare and post the closing entries.

(g) Prepare a post-closing trial balance.

Company Index

A cumulative index appears at the end of each Part.

Subject Index

A cumulative index appears at the end of each Part.